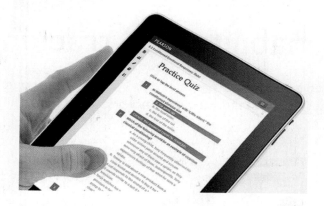

Located throughout REVEL, **quizzing** affords students opportunities to check their understanding at regular intervals before moving on.

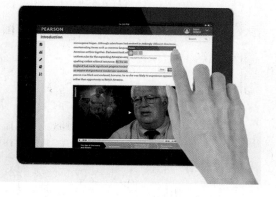

REVEL enables students to read and interact with course material on the devices they use, **anywhere** and **anytime**. Responsive design allows students to access REVEL on their tablet devices, with content displayed clearly in both portrait and landscape view.

Highlighting, **note taking**, and a **glossary** personalize the learning experience. Educators can add **notes** for students, too, including reminders or study tips.

REVEL's variety of **writing** activities and assignments develop and assess concept **mastery** and **critical thinking**.

Superior assignability and tracking

REVEL's assignability and tracking tools help educators make sure students are completing their reading and understanding core concepts.

REVEL allows educators to indicate precisely which readings must be completed on which dates. This clear, detailed schedule helps students stay on task and keeps them motivated throughout the course.

REVEL lets educators monitor class assignment completion and individual student achievement. It offers actionable information that helps educators intersect with their students in meaningful ways, such as points earned on quizzes and time on task.

How the World Works

A Brief Survey of International Relations

THIRD EDITION

Russell Bova
Dickinson College

PEARSON

Boston   Columbus   Indianapolis   New York   San Francisco   Amsterdam
Cape Town   Dubai   London   Madrid   Milan   Munich   Paris   Montréal   Toronto   Delhi
Mexico City   São Paulo   Sydney   Hong Kong   Seoul   Singapore   Taipei   Tokyo

Editorial Director: Dickson Musslewhite
Publisher: Charlyce Jones Owen
Editorial Assistant: Laura Hernandez
Program Manager: Rob DeGeorge
Project Manager: Carol O'Rourke
Field Marketer: Brittany Pogue-Mohammed
Product Marketer: Tricia Murphy
Operations Specialist: Mary Ann Gloriande
Media Project Manager: Tina Gagliostro
Permissions Project Manager: Peggy Davis
Full Service Project Management: Integra Software Services Pvt. Ltd.
Full Service Project Manager: George Jacob
Cover Design Manager: Maria Lange
Cover Image: Rawpixel/Fotolia
Printer and Binder: RRD-Crawfordsville
Cover Printer: Lehigh-Phoenix Color/Hagerstown

Credits and acknowledgments for material borrowed from other sources and reproduced, with permission, in this textbook appear on page 315.

Library of Congress Cataloging-in-Publication Data
Names: Bova, Russell
   Title: How the world works: a brief survey of international relations/Russell Bova.
   Description: Third edition. | Boston: Pearson, 2016. | Includes bibliographical references and index.
   Identifiers: LCCN 2015026636 | ISBN 9780134378848 | ISBN 0134378849
   Subjects: LCSH: International relations—Textbooks.
   Classification: LCC JZ1242 .B68 2016 | DDC 327—dc23 LC record available at http://lccn.loc.gov/2015026636

Instructor's Review Copy:
ISBN-10: 0-13-438160-2
ISBN-13: 978-0-13-438160-2

Brief Contents

Contents

Preface

As I wrote in the prefaces to the first two editions of this text, teachers of international relations are fortunate to have the media do such a good job of marketing their courses. The constant swirl of news about global events provides a steady stream of students eager to make sense of world politics and the implications for their own lives. Since the publication of the second edition, that swirl of events has continued unabated. The Arab Spring, the Russian invasion of Crimea, the rise of ISIS, and the West African Ebola epidemic are just a few of the noteworthy developments to take place subsequent to the completion of the second edition. Part of the goal in writing this third edition was to incorporate those events into the analysis of the book.

Even more important, this third edition provides an opportunity to make more general improvements to the book. In revising the text, however, the central goal of the first two editions has remained unchanged. That goal is to tap into and maintain the interest in global events that leads students to enroll in international relations classes and to translate that interest into a conceptual and theoretical sophistication that will remain useful long after today's current events become the stuff of history and long after the course in which this book is assigned is completed.

To that end, *How the World Works* provides the detailed micro-level knowledge and information that is necessary to understand world politics. Students will read about such things as the structure of the United Nations, trends in international conflict, the sources of international law, and the role of the World Trade Organization. They will simultaneously pick up a new vocabulary, which will include such terms as "deterrence," "hegemony," "collective security," and "comparative advantage." But facts and concepts are not enough. In acquiring a new vocabulary and in learning about the details of institutions and events, it is important that students not become lost in the thicket of world politics to the extent that they lose sight of the forest for the trees. Thus, they also need a larger framework that provides context and meaning for the data, trends, and terminology to which they are exposed.

In teaching over the years, I have found that most beginning students of international relations and world politics come to the first class already in possession of predispositions regarding how the world works. Some are inclined to accept conflict and violence in international life as inescapable, and this leads such students to endorse approaches to foreign policy that entail a reliance on military power and a suspicion of global institutions. These students are "instinctive realists," even though they may never have encountered the "realist" perspective on international relations as a formal theory. Others come to the first class more optimistic about the prospects for global cooperation and are thereby more inclined to eschew power-oriented approaches to foreign policy and to favor working through institutions such as international law and the United Nations. These students are "instinctive critics of realism" even though they too have never formally encountered "realism" as a concept in international relations theory and could not tell a "liberal" from a "constructivist" from a "feminist" approach to world politics.

How the World Works helps students examine their natural inclinations, question their assumptions, and subject their conclusions to the fire of classroom debate and discussion. The most general goal of the book is to get students to think about how the world works. To this end, the book is organized around the story of realism and its critics, conveying the message that scholars disagree among themselves about the world's political and economic interactions and trends. While some scholars, in recent years, have questioned the utility of examining international relations through the lenses of the various paradigms, the TRIP surveys of international relations scholars continue to show that the majority of scholars continue to work within one or more of those paradigms and that many of the most influential scholars in the field (e.g., Alexander Wendt, Robert Keohane, Kenneth Waltz, John Mearsheimer) are strongly associated with paradigmatic analysis.

That said, it is important to note that this is not a "realist" book, and it does not attempt to profess the merits of any single paradigm. On the contrary, the goal is to expose students to contending perspectives and to provide the empirical and conceptual foundation upon which they can begin to develop their own assessment of how the world works. This book does not take sides.

New to This Edition
Revel™

Educational technology designed for the way today's students read, think, and learn

When students are engaged deeply, they learn more effectively and perform better in their courses. This simple fact inspired the creation of REVEL: an immersive learning experi-ence designed for the way today's students read, think, and learn. Built in collaboration with educators and students nationwide, REVEL is the newest, fully digital way to deliver respected Pearson content.

REVEL enlivens course content with media interactives and assessments—integrated directly within the authors' narrative—that provide opportunities for students to read about and practice course material in tandem. This immersive educational technology boosts student engagement, which leads to better understanding of concepts and improved performance throughout the course.

Learn more about REVEL at http://www.pearsonhighered.com/revel/.

The third edition of *How the World Works* features a number of substantive revisions, including the following:

CHAPTER 1

- New section on non-paradigmatic research
- New Theory in Practice box on Obama and constructivism in his labeling of terrorists

CHAPTER 2

- Takes account of recent scholarship on "the myth of 1648"
- Updated with discussion of Ukraine crisis and Arab Spring

CHAPTER 3

- Chapter reorganized around two themes: the levels of analysis and the assumption of rationality in foreign policy decision-making
- More extended discussion of the cognitive model of decision-making
- New Theory in Practice box which applies rational actor, cognitive, and poliheuristic decision-making approaches to student selection of colleges

CHAPTER 4

- New breakout section on the causes of war
- New Theory in Practice box on "The Drone Revolution"

CHAPTER 5

- General updating of all sections

CHAPTER 6

- Clarified the role of the Human Rights Council
- Added discussion of Libya to section on humanitarian intervention
- Expanded discussion and assessment of the record of R2P
- New Theory in Practice box on Palestine and the International Criminal Court

CHAPTER 7

- Updated EU discussion to take account of post-2008 trends and Greek crisis
- Updated discussion of the global financial crisis and its aftermath

CHAPTER 8

- Clearer discussion of concepts of (global) public goods and common pool resources
- Discussion of the fracking revolution and its impact on both the environment and global energy politics
- Updated discussion of global climate governance post-Kyoto
- Discussion of the 2014 Ebola scare
- New Theory in Practice box on Ebola vs. the Flu: The Risks of a Pandemic
- Discussion of role of social media in the Arab Spring

CHAPTER 9

- Retained the seven competing visions of the global future approach, but changed the hypothetical future histories style to a more straightforward presentation and critique of the seven global futures

In addition to the key revisions noted above, many smaller substantive revisions are found in every chapter. They include updating of data including that found in many of the tables and figures, expanded or improved discussion of some key concepts to reflect the latest literature, and use of new examples from recent events to illustrate larger points.

Features

How the World Works begins by laying out the central assumptions of the realist paradigm in Chapter 1 and then discussing the challenges posed to the realist worldview by the paradigms that have emerged as alternatives to realism. Each subsequent chapter then examines a specific issue in the real world of international politics—such as war, human rights, and economic globalization—to shed light on the differences between the realist approach and the alternative paradigms. In different chapters of the book, the essential subject matter may seem to privilege one theoretical perspective or another, but there will be enough competing evidence and perspectives provided so that students will be encouraged to think about and question the various worldviews.

Chapter 2 of the text examines the history of international relations and the related rise and fall of the theoretical paradigms over time. Chapter 3 looks at foreign policy-making and the several levels of analysis that are involved in shaping state behavior, including the domestic sources of state behavior that realists traditionally have tended to downplay. Given the centrality of war to the realist perspective, the discussion of war and violence in Chapter 4 takes place on realism's turf, though there is plenty in the chapter to provide ammunition for critics of realism. Chapter 5 then moves to the turf of liberal institutionalism as the focus shifts to international law and organization. Constructivism gets the home-field advantage in Chapter 6, with its focus on international human rights. Chapters 7 and 8 examine economic globalization and transnational issues, spotlighting the liberal commercialist and neo-Marxist perspectives and discussing in some detail the tension between globalization and many of the core realist assumptions.

Chapter 9 concludes the book with a discussion of seven alternative global futures. Each of these seven different visions of the future extends the logic of a different theoretical perspective on world politics. And each vision is then subjected to a short critique. The goal of this chapter is to bring the reader full circle to the theoretical perspectives presented in Chapter 1. On the basis of this discussion of possible global futures, and in light of the data and analysis absorbed from Chapters 2 through 8, the reader should be in a good position to articulate and defend, in a reasonably sophisticated manner, his or her own theoretical preferences for understanding world politics.

Each chapter in *How the World Works* is structured not only to address the central question of that chapter but also to contribute to an understanding of the book's larger themes and goals. The result is a book that hangs together and that is more than just a collection of useful concepts and pieces of information examined in isolation. The approach to each chapter reflects an assumption that, for beginning students, theoretical sophistication must be based on an understanding of the real world of international relations and world politics. For example, if students are going to be in a position to decide whether liberal institutionalists best explain how the world works, they have to examine the record of liberal institutions such as international law and organizations in practice. Similarly, if students are to be in a position to judge the constructivist notion that norms and ideas can shape world politics, then it is useful and necessary to examine in detail the emergence and impact of the idea of human rights in the conduct of world politics since World War II. To help students keep larger goals in mind, each chapter begins and ends with a reminder of the larger theoretical debate, but the bulk of each chapter focuses on the empirical record of the topic at hand.

You will find pedagogical features that support the goals in each chapter and throughout the book:

- **Theory in Practice.** Each chapter includes two or three "Theory in Practice" boxes, in which students will find a key chapter concept applied to a recent world event. The goal is to reinforce the idea, stressed throughout the book, that international relations concepts and theories have direct relevance to the world in which students are living. Critical thinking questions at the end of each box encourage students to start doing their own analysis using international relations concepts.

- **Photos and Figures.** Each chapter includes an opening photo and two interior photos related to the substance of the chapter. Where appropriate, figures are included to help visualize key ideas or put them into quantitative context.

- **Key Terms and Glossary.** In each chapter, key terms are highlighted and then listed again at the end of the chapter. A marginal glossary provides brief definitions of those terms for quick reference in the context of the chapter. Through the key terms and glossary, students have a comprehensive list of the key ideas and concepts necessary to understand world politics.

- **Review Questions.** At the end of each chapter, students are given three review questions that focus on the big issues raised in the chapter. While the list of key terms helps students ascertain whether they understand the details and specifics of a chapter (whether they see the "trees"), the review questions help students test their knowledge of the larger significance of those details (to determine if they see the "forest").

- **Map Insert.** A four-color insert with maps of the world, North America, South America, Africa, Europe, the Middle East, East and South Asia, and Australia and Oceania is included following page xix of this book. Basic geographical knowledge is essential in the study of international relations, and the insert is intended to put this knowledge within students' immediate reach.

How the World Works strives for a conversational style that keeps its student readers in mind. This approach does not require dumbing down the content. On the contrary, the clearer the writing, the better the organization, and the more accessible the style, the more one can succeed in conveying sophisticated content to the reader. Especially in a field as intrinsically interesting and compelling as world politics, and at a time in world history when so much is in flux, there is no reason that a text on the topic cannot be intellectually sophisticated and, at the same time, readable, engaging, and even fun. This text introduces students to the concepts and developments at the core of the discipline of world politics but in a way that makes sense to them.

While *How the World Works* is perhaps half the length of many introductory textbooks, it has the advantage of focusing attention on the most salient issues and concepts that often get buried in longer texts. Brevity also provides greater opportunity for instructors to assign supplementary readings that reinforce and develop concepts and issues discussed in this text. There is such an array of good writing, accessible at the undergraduate level, on issues of world politics and international relations that it would be an omission not to be able to incorporate as much of it as possible into the introductory course. Students will be armed with the basic concepts and issues from reading this text. Thus, instructors can assign additional readings by proponents or critics of a particular theory to extend the discussion beyond the text.

Supplements

Pearson is pleased to offer several resources to qualified adopters of *How the World Works* and their students that will make teaching and learning from this book even more effective and enjoyable. Several of the supplements for this book are available at the Instructor Resource Center (IRC), an online hub that allows instructors to quickly download book-specific supplements. Please visit the IRC welcome page at http://www.pearsonhighered.com/irc to register for access.

Instructor's Manual/Test Bank This resource includes learning objectives, lecture outlines, multiple-choice questions, true/false questions, and essay questions for each chapter. Available for download from the IRC.

Pearson MyTest This powerful assessment generation program includes all of the items in the instructor's manual/test bank. Questions and tests can be easily created, customized, saved online, and then printed, allowing flexibility to manage assessments anytime and anywhere. To learn more, please visit http://www.mypearsontest.com or contact your Pearson representative.

PowerPoint Presentation Organized around a lecture outline, these multimedia presentations also include photos, figures, and tables from each chapter. Available for download from the IRC.

Longman Atlas of World Issues (0-205-78020-2) From population and political systems to energy use and women's rights, the *Longman Atlas of World Issues* features full-color thematic maps that examine the forces shaping the world. Featuring maps from the latest edition of *The Penguin State of the World Atlas*, this excerpt includes critical thinking exercises to promote a deeper understanding of how geography affects many global issues. Available at no additional charge when packaged with this book.

Goode's World Atlas (0-321-65200-2) First published by Rand McNally in 1923, *Goode's World Atlas* has set the standard for college reference atlases. It features hundreds of physical, political, and thematic maps as well as graphs, tables, and a pronouncing index. Available at a discount when packaged with this book.

Research and Writing in International Relations (0-205-06065-X) With current and detailed coverage on how to start research in the discipline's major subfields, this brief and affordable guide offers the step-by-step guidance and essential resources needed to compose political science papers that go beyond description and into systematic and sophisticated inquiry. This text focuses on areas where students often need help—finding a topic, developing a question, reviewing the literature, designing research, and finally, writing the paper. Available at a discount when packaged with this book.

Acknowledgments

In writing this book, I received valuable assistance from a number of people who reviewed various editions of the text and offered their advice:

Nozar Alaolmolki, Hiram College; Kristian Alexander, University of Utah; Stephanie Anderson, University of Wyoming; Vincent Auger, Western Illinois

University; William Batkay, Montclair State University; Eric Cox, Texas Christian University; Richard Chadwick, University of Hawaii, Manoa; John Dietrich, Bryant University; Gregory C. Dixon, University of West Georgia; Vittorio Nicholas Galasso, University of Delaware; Stephanie Hallock, Harford Community College; Maia Hallward, Kennesaw State University; James Hentz, Virginia Military Institute; Nathan Jensen, Washington University in St. Louis; Michael Koch, Texas A&M University; William Lahneman, Towson University; Howard Lehman, University of Utah; Keith Lepak, Youngstown State University; Kristina Mani, Oberlin College; Scott Nelson, Virginia Tech; Laura Neack, Miami University; Mark Schroeder, University of Kentucky; Johanes Sulaiman, Ohio State University; Eugene Tadie, George Mason University; James Toole, Indiana University-Purdue; Ivani Vassoler, SUNY-Fredonia; Julie Webber, Illinois State University; and Andrew Yeo, Catholic University.

I would also like to thank Charlyce Jones Owen, Rob DeGeorge, Carol O'Rourke, and the rest of the team at Pearson for shepherding this third edition through to completion. I also appreciate the efficient work done by George Jacob at Integra Software Services in overseeing the production of the print book from manuscript to final printer files. Lastly, Susan Messer did a superb job as development editor in helping to polish the writing of the very first edition of the book. Though I have not worked with her on subsequent editions, her impact on the book and on my approach to writing it are still very much in evidence in the third edition.

In many ways, this book reflects a career spent teaching and writing at Dickinson College, where I have been surrounded by first-class colleagues, excellent students, and an administration committed to fostering an environment where both good scholarship and good teaching can thrive. In particular, I would like to thank my colleagues Douglas Stuart, for his thoughtful comments on Chapters 1 and 3, and David Strand, for his useful suggestions on Chapter 6. Students in numerous sections of my Political Science 170 International Relations class who have used the earlier editions of this book also helped improve this new edition in various ways.

I have been sustained in the long process of writing and revising this book by the memory and thoughts of those people (Rosemary, Serf, Sam, Tina, Shelly, Angie, Elmer) whom I have cared most about in this world. Most important of all, this edition, like the first two, is dedicated to my three daughters—Laura, Samantha, and Alex—who give meaning and purpose to everything I do, and to Candace L. Bova—my wife, my best friend, and my partner-in-life.

—Russell Bova

Maps

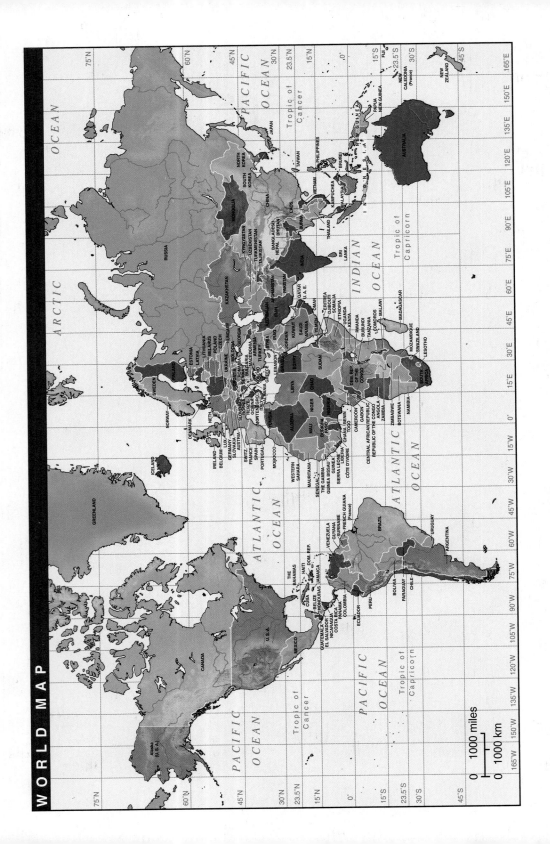

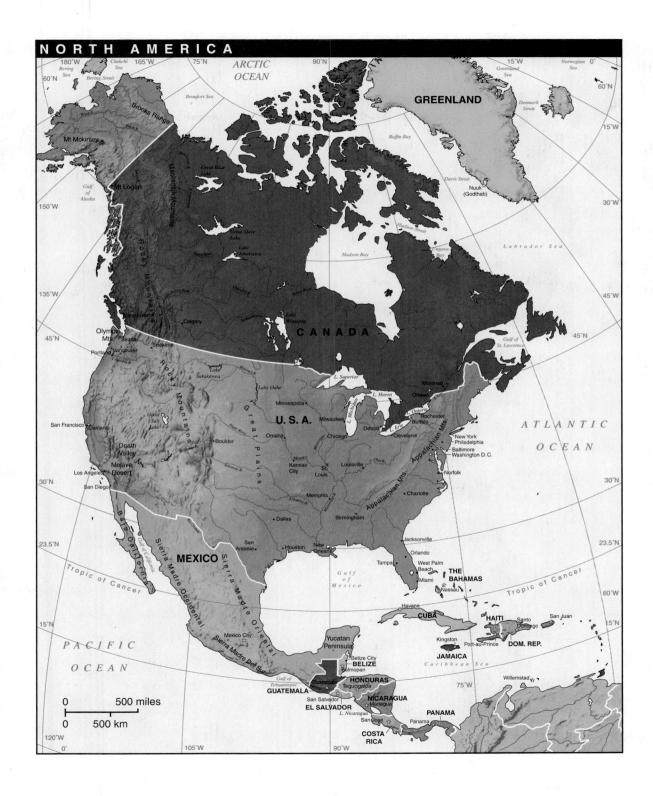

NORTH AMERICA

ARCTIC OCEAN

180°W 165°W 75°N 90°N 15°W 0°

60°N
Bering Sea
Chukchi Sea
Bering Strait
Beaufort Sea

Norwegian Sea
Greenland Sea
60°N

GREENLAND

Brooks Range
Mt Mckinley
Great Bear Lake
Baffin Bay
Denmark Strait

150°W
Gulf of Alaska
Mt Logan
Mackenzie Mountains
15°W

Davis Strait
Nuuk (Godthab)
30°W

135°W
Great Slave Lake
Lake Athabasca
Hudson Strait
Ungava Bay

Peace River
Churchill R.
Hudson Bay
Labrador Sea
45°W

Vancouver Island
Calgary
Lake Winnipeg
CANADA
Nelson River
Gulf of St. Lawrence
45°N

45°N
Olympic Mts.
Seattle
Spokane
Rocky Mountains
Lake Sakakawea
Lake Oahe
Montreal
Ottawa

Portland
Vancouver
Columbia River
L. Superior
L. Huron
L. Michigan
Minneapolis
Milwaukee
Detroit
L. Ontario
L. Erie
Rochester
Buffalo

San Francisco
Oakland
Great Salt Lake
U.S.A.
Platte River
Omaha
Chicago
Cleveland
New York
Philadelphia
ATLANTIC OCEAN

Death Valley
Boulder
Missouri R.
Kansas City
St. Louis
Louisville
Baltimore
Washington D.C.

30°N
Mojave Desert
Los Angeles
San Diego
Arkansas R.
Memphis
Appalachian Mts.
Norfolk

Charlotte
30°N

23.5°N
Baja California
Gulf of California
MEXICO
Sierra Madre Occidental
San Antonio
Dallas
Houston
New Orleans
Birmingham
Jacksonville
Orlando
Tampa
West Palm Beach
Miami
THE BAHAMAS
Nassau
23.5°N

Tropic of Cancer
Sierra Madre Oriental
Gulf of Mexico
Havana
CUBA
HAITI
Santo Domingo
San Juan
Tropic of Cancer
60°W

15°N
Mexico City
Sierra Madre Del Sur
Yucatan Peninsula
Kingston
Port-au-Prince
JAMAICA
DOM. REP.

PACIFIC OCEAN
Gulf of Tehuantepec
Belize City
Belmopan
BELIZE
Caribbean Sea
Willemstad
75°W

0 500 miles
Guatemala
HONDURAS
Tegucigalpa

0 500 km
GUATEMALA
San Salvador
NICARAGUA
Managua

EL SALVADOR
L. Nicaragua
San Jose
PANAMA
Panama

120°W
0°
105°W
90°W
COSTA RICA

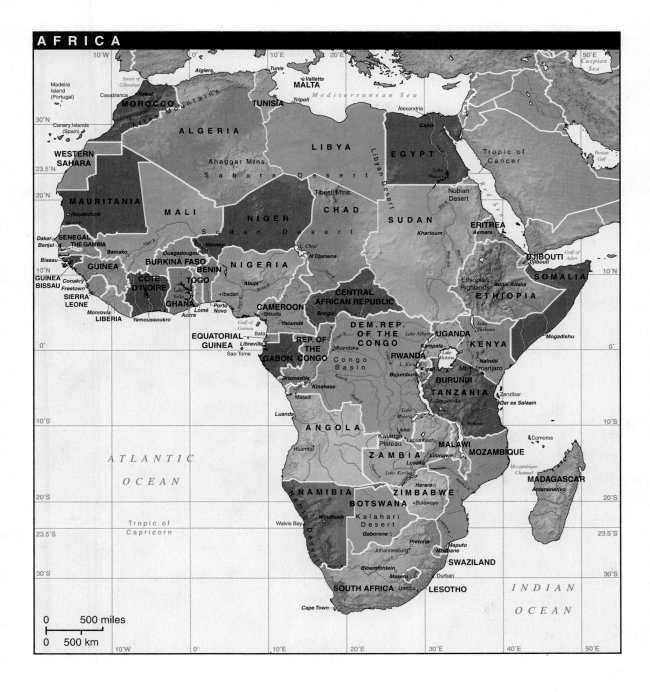

AFRICA

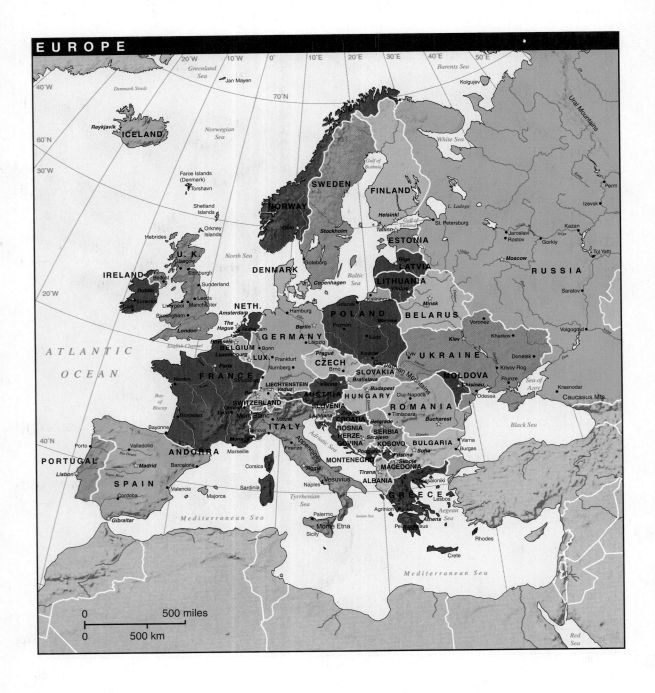

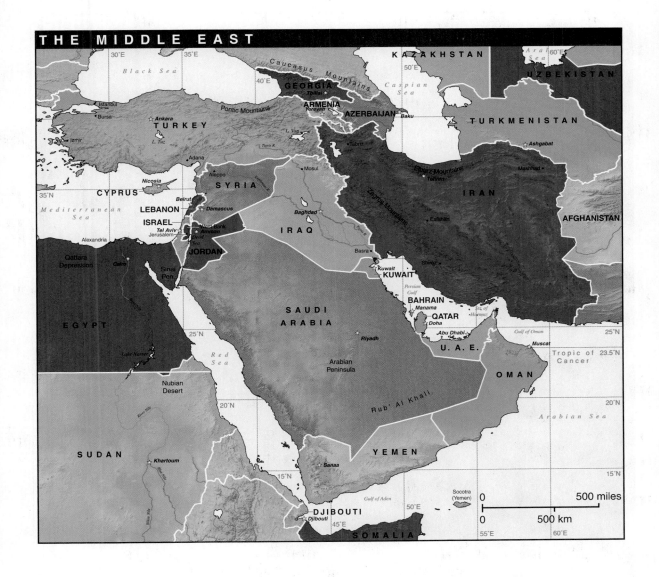

THE MIDDLE EAST

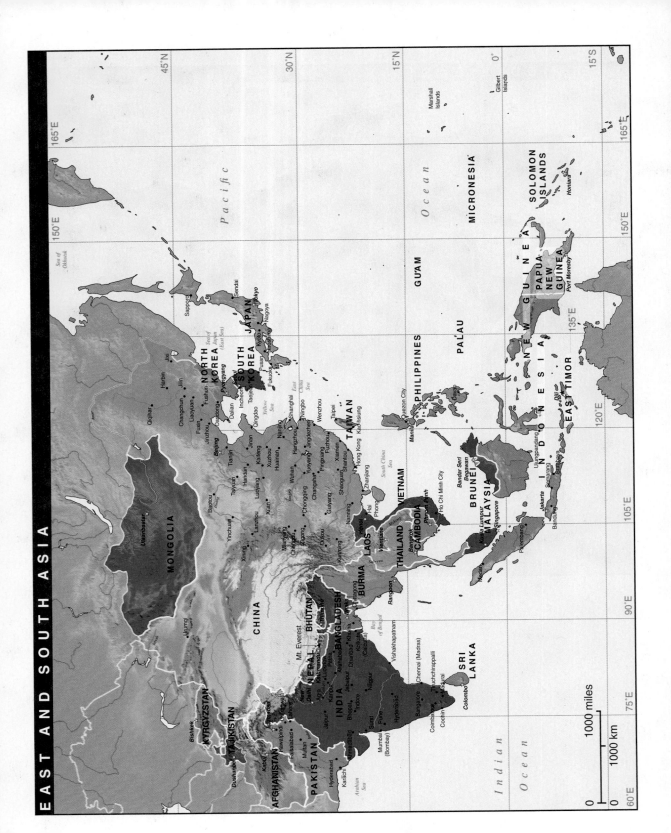

EAST AND SOUTH ASIA

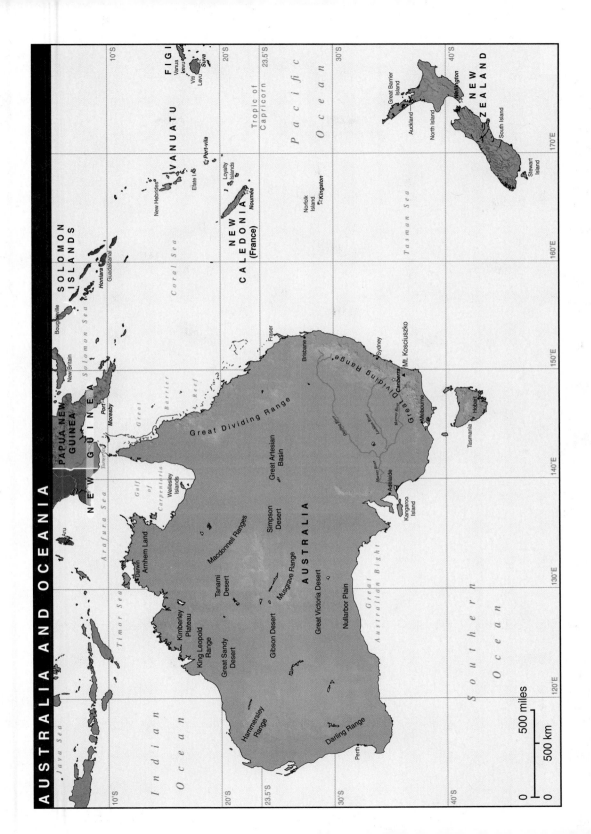

AUSTRALIA AND OCEANIA

Indian Ocean

Java Sea

Aru

Timor Sea

Arafura Sea

PAPUA NEW GUINEA

NEW GUINEA

New Britain

Moresby
Port

Gulf of Carpentaria

Darwin

Arnhem Land

Wellesley Islands

Great

Barrier

Reef

SOLOMON ISLANDS

Bougainville

Honiara

Guadalcanal

Solomon Sea

Coral Sea

Kimberley Plateau

King Leopold Range

Great Sandy Desert

Tanami Desert

Macdonnell Ranges

Simpson Desert

Great Artesian Basin

Great Dividing Range

Fraser I.

Brisbane

VANUATU

New Hebrides

Efate I.

Port-vila

Loyalty Islands

NEW CALEDONIA (France)

Nouméa

FIJI

Vanua Levu

Viti Levu

Suva

Tropic of Capricorn

23.5°S

Pacific Ocean

Hammersley Range

Gibson Desert

Musgrave Range

Great Victoria Desert

Nullarbor Plain

AUSTRALIA

Murray River

Darling River

Lachlan River

Murray River

Sydney

Canberra

Mt. Kosciuszko

Great Dividing Range

Norfolk Island

Kingston

Darling Range

Perth

Great Australian Bight

Adelaide

Kangaroo Island

Melbourne

Tasmania

Hobart

Tasman Sea

Great Barrier Island

Auckland

NORTH ISLAND

Wellington

NEW ZEALAND

SOUTH ISLAND

Stewart Island

Southern Ocean

0   500 miles

0   500 km

10°S

20°S

23.5°S

30°S

40°S

120°E   130°E   140°E   150°E   160°E   170°E

Chapter 1
How to Think About World Politics

Realism and Its Critics

World Trade Center, September 11, 2001. After 9/11 a common response was that "everything has changed." Is that the case? How would realists respond to that observation?

 ## Learning Objectives

1-1 Explain the three grand debates over how scholars should study international relations.

1-2 Identify and explain the key assumptions and arguments of the realist paradigm.

1-3 Compare and contrast the liberal, constructivist, feminist, and neo-Marxist paradigms.

All politics is global. Whether you live in New York or Shanghai, in a small town in Kansas or a village in rural India, in the heart of a prosperous European city or on an impoverished subsistence farm in sub-Saharan Africa, your life is affected in countless ways by developments in world politics. Of course, during times of war, global politics becomes a matter of life and death for individuals and, sometimes, for entire societies. However, even during more "normal" times, global events continually reverberate through our lives. For example, how much it costs you to travel to school could be affected by political instability in an oil-producing country located far from where you live and study. Whether you will be able to afford to study abroad during your college career can be affected by the value of your country's currency in global currency markets. Getting the job of your choice when you graduate might depend on the evolving patterns of global trade.

The impact of global trends on your life is not merely economic. The quality of the air you breathe can be a direct consequence of pollutants poured into the atmosphere by factories located halfway across the world and on the success or failure of global efforts to regulate the environment. The level of respect given to your human rights increasingly depends on emerging global human rights norms and institutions that go beyond your own government's policies. Your physical security as you go about your daily life can be affected by trends in global terrorism or the proliferation of weapons of mass destruction. Indeed, as many discovered after the terrorist attacks of September 11, 2001, you don't have to be a direct victim of global terrorism to feel its impact. Increased security at airports, tightened immigration rules, and a recalibrated balance between security and civil liberties affected Americans as well as those who wanted to visit or study in the United States.

Global events have always affected individuals' lives, particularly through war, conflict, and trade across national borders. However, in recent decades, developments in the technologies of transportation and, especially, telecommunications have shrunk the world and allowed individuals to become increasingly interconnected. Thus, more than ever before, in the twenty-first century being an informed individual requires understanding the larger world in which we live. But having such an understanding requires more than accumulating information, facts, and details about the world. It also requires a more generalized understanding of how the world works—an understanding that will allow us to make sense of the day-to-day events reported in the news. That is what formal study of international relations (IR) and world politics seeks to attain.

Studying International Relations and World Politics

1-1 **Explain the three grand debates over how scholars should study international relations.**

The phrases "international relations" and "world politics" are often used interchangeably, including in this book, to refer to the full range of political, military, and economic relations and interactions occurring among nation-states, such as the United States, Russia, and China, and nonstate actors, such as the United Nations (UN), al-Qaeda, and Amnesty International. At the same time, the two phrases do not have precisely the same meaning. "International relations" suggests a focus on relations among nation-states as the key actors. "World politics," in contrast, implies the casting of a broader net to include nonstate actors. Thus, the trend in recent years has been toward using "world politics" to label the field of study covered in this book.

Whatever label one prefers, the important point is that the scholarly study of international relations and world politics is not the same as journalism or political punditry. Journalists and many other commentators on contemporary history are usually content to describe and analyze specific, discrete events, but political scientists look for patterns and generalizations that can illuminate how the world works. For example, while a journalist might describe and explain al-Qaeda's terrorist attacks of September 11, 2001, a political scientist will try to understand more generally the causes and consequences of terrorism. While a journalist might report and describe Iranian efforts to acquire a nuclear weapons capability, the goal of international relations scholarship is to better understand both the causes and consequences of nuclear proliferation in general.

Though international relations scholars generally agree that their work is different from that of journalists, those scholars disagree among themselves on a number of fundamental questions over how best to study and understand how the world works. Indeed, the scholarly study of international relations has been marked by a series of grand debates. The three most important of those debates are: (1) the debate over whether international relations is a positivist science, (2) the debate over the appropriate methods to be employed in scholarship, and (3) the debate over the choice of paradigms from which to view the world. Each of these debates will be explained below.

The Debate over Positivist Science

For much of the twentieth century, the study of international relations was dominated by discussion and analysis of diplomatic history, international law, and international institutions. The emphasis was on description of historical events and trends combined with interpretation of those events by scholars, with an eye toward providing advice about how states and their leaders should act to achieve their goals in international relations. In this era, the most influential scholars were those whose historical narratives and institutional analyses seemed most persuasive.

By the 1960s, however, a new generation of scholars had become dissatisfied with this approach. In their view, the traditional scholarship was too descriptive and not much more than a sophisticated type of journalistic analysis. What they wanted was to transform the study of international relations into a more rigorous enterprise modeled on the natural sciences. In particular, they embraced an approach to science known as **positivism**.

positivism
An approach to knowledge based on the scientific method and the observation and analysis of empirical data.

The positivist approach seeks to apply the scientific method, common in the natural sciences, to the study of international relations. One starts with a hypothesis that specifies a relationship between two variables. Consider for example the following hypothesis: a democratic regime reduces the propensity of a country to go to war. In that example, democracy is the independent variable and war is the dependent variable. The independent variable is the one that the scholar manipulates to see what impact it has on the dependent variable. In a chemistry lab, one can manipulate the independent variable by adding or subtracting the presence of a chemical agent to see what result is produced. In international relations, one cannot do that, but what one can do is to compare the war propensity of democratic and authoritarian regimes. Thus to test the hypothesis, one looks at empirical data on the war propensity of democratic versus nondemocratic regimes, and that data will serve to either support or to falsify the hypothesis.

The goal of a positivist science of international relations is the development of scientific laws of international behavior. Those laws are not absolute but, instead, probabilistic. It is unlikely that one will ever be able to say with certainty, for example, that democracies are always peaceful or that democratic regime X necessarily will be more peaceful in its approach to international relations than authoritarian regime Y. Instead the goal would be to be able to say that the probability of a democratic regime going to war is lower.

rational choice theory
An approach to social science, borrowed from economics, that assumes individuals are rational actors who make decisions intended to maximize their interests on the basis of cost–benefit calculations.

A manifestation of this new, more scientific approach was the ascendance of **rational choice theory**. The theory of rational choice stood in sharp contrast to the historically grounded descriptions characteristic of the study of international relations in the first half of the twentieth century. Borrowing heavily from the discipline of economics, rational choice assumed that individuals were rational actors whose primary commitment was to the advancement of their own interests. On that basis, economists had long developed laws of economic behavior that were deemed to hold true regardless of historical and cultural context. Likewise, in international relations rational choice theorists sought to develop laws of international behavior with universal applicability across time and place.

Traditional scholars resisted, suggesting that the study of human behavior is fundamentally different from the study of the natural world. They argued that is difficult, if not impossible, to study the human world with the cool, intellectual detachment with which natural scientists study the laws of physics. But the positivists gained the upper hand, and for the next couple of decades they came to dominate international relations scholarship.

In the 1990s a backlash emerged against the dominance of the positivist approach in international relations theory. A new generation of "post-positivist" scholars argued that because the study of international relations is about the actions of human beings, it is a mistake to try to mimic positivist natural science. Their argument rests on a distinction between "explaining" and "understanding." Positivists seek to explain international behavior by reference to objective cause-and-effect relationships present in the external world. For example, a positivist might argue that when one country acquires nuclear weapons, its neighbors will seek to acquire them in self-defense.

For a post-positivist, that conclusion cannot be formulated into a general law. Instead, one's reaction to the arms acquisition of a neighboring state will be determined by one's own subjective understanding of one's neighbor as a friend or a foe, the history of relations between the two states, and the preconceived perceptions and ideas held by leaders about the nature of the threat posed by one's neighbor. Thus, one can come to "understand" the nature of a state's behavior but one cannot "explain" it by general laws applicable across time and place.

The Debate over Methods

A second area of debate among international relations scholars is related to method. Some, though not all, scholars committed to a positivist science of international relations argued that the search for objective laws of international relations requires one to analyze large numbers of cases using sophisticated statistical techniques. Purely qualitative methodologies—for example, case studies of a particular war or even a side-by-side comparison of two wars—might provide interesting insights into those cases but cannot allow one to formulate general laws about when wars will occur. To be able to generalize in that fashion, many scholars argue that one needs to analyze large numbers of cases via quantitative methods.

Take, once again, the question of the impact of democracy on the propensity of countries to go to war. Looking at a handful of cases may point in the direction of an answer but is unlikely to be conclusive. A more convincing answer to the question would require analysis that looks at dozens, perhaps hundreds of cases. One might start by defining terms such as democracy and authoritarianism, placing countries into one category or the other, and then looking at the relationship between regime type and frequency of involvement in wars.

Of course, any such study would quickly become more complex than that as one would have to consider how much fighting is necessary to consider an event to be a war as well as differing degrees of democracy and authoritarianism in individual countries. Then, one would have to account for other causal factors that might influence the propensity to fight wars, including such things as level of economic development, preexisting arms races, etc. Teasing out the impact of all of these factors is not easy, and the most effective way to do that might well be via sophisticated statistical analysis.

The turn to greater use of quantitative methods was accompanied by much dissent from scholars who argued that quantitative analysis sacrificed the richness of case studies and other forms of qualitative research. Those critics complained that there were many aspects of political life that could not be reduced to quantitative data analysis and that the emphasis on statistical techniques was producing scholars who knew more about the methods of data analysis than about the real substance of political history. In fact, both approaches currently coexist in the study of international relations. A recent survey of international relations scholars suggests that while the field remains dominated by those who use qualitative methods in their research, a significant percentage (about a quarter in the case of US-based scholars) specialize in quantitative methods.[1]

The Interparadigm Debate

paradigm
A conceptual or theoretical perspective or framework commonly accepted within a scholarly discipline that helps to inform and guide thinking and research.

A third debate that has raged among international relations scholars is the "interparadigm debate." A **paradigm** is a way of thinking about and approaching an area of scientific or scholarly inquiry that is widely accepted within a particular discipline and that guides the direction of scientific research. In the natural sciences, scientists typically operate within a single paradigm. If at some point the paradigm no longer explains new information or discoveries, a scientific revolution occurs in which scholars develop a new paradigm to replace the old.[2] For example, Einstein's theory of relativity overturned the existing Newtonian paradigm of physics, providing a new framework within which subsequent research would be conducted. However, in the social sciences in general, and in the study of international relations in particular, several competing paradigms typically coexist and compete with one another. To relate this to the larger theme of this book, the main competing paradigms adopted by scholars of international relations and world politics provide different ways of understanding how the world works.

The so-called paradigm wars that have characterized the field of international relations were particularly heated in the 1980s and 1990s. Since that time, many scholars have sought to move beyond those wars and to focus on what is often called "non-paradigmatic research." Still, a 2014 survey of international relations scholars found that roughly three-quarters of international relations scholars continue to see their research as rooted in one of the major paradigms.[3]

Thus, the remainder of this chapter will focus on comparison of the main competing international relations paradigms. One virtue of examining competing paradigms is that a paradigm provides a simplified map of reality; it takes the complexity of the real world and reduces it to a core set of assumptions that make the twists and turns of daily events and the relationships among them comprehensible.[4] As you think about the merits of the competing paradigms discussed in the pages that follow, keep in mind a few cautionary points:

1. To be valuable, a paradigm of world politics need not explain every event. In simplifying reality, a paradigm will miss certain things. The test of a paradigm, and your assessment of its utility, is how much of the reality of world politics it does manage to capture and how efficiently it does so. The best test is one of relative utility. The paradigm that one adopts should be the one that, in comparison to others, most comprehensively and efficiently explains how the world works.

2. The various paradigms offer different descriptions of how the world works, not how you might wish it to work. However, those competing descriptions can also give rise to prescriptive guidelines for formulating policy. Thus, the paradigm you embrace will affect the policy choices you might recommend. That is why understanding and evaluating the competing paradigms is more than an academic exercise. It has implications for your view of what constitutes wise policy-making in practice.

3. The paradigms presented below are what social scientists would call **ideal types**. That is, for purposes of analytical clarity and conceptual comparison, they are defined and stated in a pure and almost exaggerated form. The real world rarely conforms precisely to any single ideal type. Scholars working within different paradigms will often learn from one another, borrow from one another, and modify their theories on that basis. However, substantial differences among the paradigms remain. While the ultimate goal might be the emergence of a single paradigm that all scholars in the field can embrace, we are not yet at that point.

ideal type
A concept that provides an exaggerated and oversimplified version of reality as a way to promote analytical clarity and conceptual comparison.

In this chapter, we will look first at realism—the paradigm that dominated the field of international relations in the era following World War II. Following that, we will turn to a variety of competing paradigms that have arisen to challenge the realist view. In completing this chapter, you will not yet be in a position to decide whether you are more persuaded by realists or their various critics. That will require reading the rest of the book. What you will have by the end of this chapter is a sense of where and how realists and their critics think differently about how the world works.

The Realist Paradigm

1-2   Identify and explain the key assumptions and arguments of the realist paradigm.

From the end of World War II at least through the end of the Cold War, the dominant paradigm in the field of international relations was **realism**. Realist scholars see international relations as driven by the unrelenting and competitive

realism
Dominant post–World War II era paradigm; based on the assumption that international relations is a struggle for power among sovereign states.

human nature realists
Scholars (also called "classical realists") who see the struggle for power that characterizes international relations as rooted in the essential character of human nature.

structural realists
Scholars (also called "neorealists") who see the struggle for power that characterizes international relations as rooted in the structure of the international system, especially the condition of anarchy.

anarchy
The absence of an effective world government capable of enforcing rules and norms of behavior.

state of nature
Situation of anarchy in which there is no government. Thomas Hobbes posited that humans once existed in a state of nature but elected to create governments; they thereby surrendered some personal liberty in exchange for order and security.

pursuit of power by states in the effort to secure state interests. For realists, the most important source of power is military capability, and the acquisition and use of that military capability make the realists' world one prone to violence and warfare.

Human nature realists (or classical realists) see world politics driven by certain essential characteristics of human nature. For them, states seek power and use violence because human beings are essentially violent, power-seeking beings. Theirs is a particularly pessimistic worldview, as war and violence in world politics are viewed as an inherent part of the human condition. Most contemporary realists, however, are **structural realists** (also called neorealists). For them, the behavior of states has less to do with essential characteristics of the human species than with the structure of the international system within which states operate.

The ten points below summarize the structural realist perspective; the first three represent its core assumptions:

1. **Anarchy exists in world politics.** For most contemporary realists, the first and most important thing one needs to know and remember is that world politics takes place within a context of **anarchy**. In international relations, anarchy refers to the absence of any world government. This situation differs significantly from what we are accustomed to in our domestic political life, where functioning governments provide rules and laws to govern individual behavior and where institutions, such as police, courts, and prisons, exist to ensure enforcement of such rules.

   What would domestic political life be like without such governments and the order they provide? The sixteenth-century British political philosopher Thomas Hobbes imagined such a world, referring to it as a **state of nature**.[5] Such a world would, arguably, have its positive side. After all, you could do as you pleased, unhampered by the countless rules and constraints imposed by governmental law and regulation. You could drive down the street at 90 miles per hour without fear that a police officer would issue a ticket. You would not need to pay taxes out of your hard-earned income, and if you wanted something but could not afford it, well, you could just take it without fear that the police would arrest you. It would also mean you could read what you wanted, drink what you wanted, smoke what you wanted, and in general, do what you wanted without restrictions imposed by a government.

   On the other hand, would you really choose to live in the world just described? After all, though you would be free of governmental constraints, you would be subject to greater and more unpredictable threats from others. A speeding car can hit and kill *you*. A thief might steal from *you*. And your ability to do what you want might be constrained not by a government but by a powerful neighbor who decides to benefit in some way at your expense. Hobbes described the state of nature as a perpetual "war of all against all," in which life was "nasty, brutish, and short." For this reason, Hobbes suggests, people choose to live under the constraints imposed by government. The sacrifice of some liberty to that government is the price we pay for order and security.

But whereas individuals have made and accepted this trade-off in the domestic political realm, states have not yet been willing to do so in the international realm. The creation of a truly powerful and effective world government is still seen by most observers as not worth the limiting effect on the ability of states to do what they want, when they want. Of course, as in the domestic example, this leaves us all vulnerable to the bad intentions of neighboring states. Thus, unlike domestic politics, world politics still essentially operates in a "state of nature." The violence, the chaos, the death and destruction that often accompany world politics reflect the "war of all against all" that international anarchy directly implies.

2. **States are sovereign.** The term **sovereignty** is defined by Webster's dictionary as "supreme and independent political authority."[6] That is why, in the days of monarchy, the king or queen was often referred to as "the sovereign." The term reflected the fact that "supreme and independent political authority" rested in the hands of the one person who occupied the throne. In a democratic political system, in contrast, sovereignty can be said to rest collectively in the people who exercise political power through a democratically elected and constituted government. That government wields sovereign power in the name of the citizens.

> **sovereignty**
> Condition of supreme, independent political authority answerable to no higher authority. In international relations theory, and especially among realists, states are often regarded as sovereign.

At the global level, no supreme sovereign authority exercises all-encompassing political authority. As noted above, the international system is, instead, characterized by anarchy. The highest sovereign actors in the global system are the close to 200 independent states, each of which claims exclusive right to control events taking place in its territory. Those sovereign states range from large superpowers like the United States to small city-states like Singapore. Irrespective of size, wealth, or military power, international legal norms recognize that each of these duly recognized states has equal right to govern the affairs taking place within its borders. This state system dates back to 1648 and the Peace of Westphalia, which ended the Thirty Years' War (see Chapter 2).

Of course, the behavior of one state inevitably affects the well-being and interests of others, whether through trade and economic interaction; through the travel of the state's citizens; through the need of each state to have access to and consume the earth's finite resources; or through the influence that a state's culture, ideology, and values have on others. Especially given the shrinking of the world via modern advances in transportation and communications technology, the idea of 200 completely self-absorbed sovereign actors is almost absurd. We have a world of almost 200 interdependent actors, whose behaviors, values, and interests inevitably interact with and conflict with one another. And the absence of a world government means that we have no overriding sovereign authority to regulate and resolve those disputes. The 200 sovereign states must work out their differences and conflicts of interest themselves.

3. **States are unitary rational actors.** In suggesting that states are *unitary* actors, realists are saying that states have a set of core **national interests** that transcend the special interests associated with the individuals and groups they govern. At the most general level, those core state interests include, at a minimum, (1) the physical security and survival of the country in the face of potential threats of foreign aggression, and (2) the promotion of the country's general level of prosperity and economic well-being. To take a more specific example, some observers might argue that the United States has a national interest in preventing the spread of nuclear weapons in the Middle East. Think about that for a moment. The United States is a country of over 300 million people, with competing political parties and a multitude of interest groups that take varying positions on virtually every issue of foreign policy—including policy in the Middle East. Yet realists argue that there is a core set of interests characteristic of the United States that rise above the "special interests" or varying perspectives found within domestic society.

> **national interests**
> State objectives and needs that transcend the particular interests of individuals and groups that reside within a state and that drive state behavior in the international system.

In suggesting that states are also *rational* actors, realists do not mean to imply that states always act wisely in the pursuit of their interests. Nor are they making any kind of moral commentary on either the ends or means of a state's foreign policy. Instead, realists are simply saying that an ends–means relationship exists between state interests (the ends) and the foreign policy choices that states make (the means) to reach those ends. States, in other words, engage in policies intended to advance their interests. Given interest X, states will engage in polices intended to achieve X at least cost. Both the assumption that states are unitary actors and that they behave rationally can be illuminated further by a comparison with domestic politics.

The essence of domestic politics, especially in democratic states, is a constant pulling and hauling in different directions of various individuals, interest groups, political parties, and government institutions attempting to shape public policy. The essence of politics, from this view, is a struggle between competing interests. The policy outcomes thus generated are often compromises. If we worked backward, trying to reconstruct the interests that the US tax code was created to serve, we would have a difficult time. The US tax code is a complex and often contradictory set of rules that can be fully understood only in terms of the struggles among various interested parties over the decades. It would be hard to detect a consistent and rational ends–means relationship between the tax policies adopted and a single, unified concept of the national interest.

Most realists would concede that some of this political tug of war plays itself out in the shaping of a country's foreign policy as well. Actors within a state can differ regarding how best to secure those core interests as well as how much those interests might be under threat at any given time. The debate over the US decision to go to war in Iraq in 2003 illustrates just how contentious foreign policy can be. Politicians and pundits disagreed over whether Iraq had weapons of mass destruction, whether it could be deterred from using them, whether economic sanctions or the UN could sufficiently contain Saddam Hussein's international ambitions, and whether there was a pattern of cooperation between Saddam and al-Qaeda terrorists. But even in the Iraq debate, realists would argue that there remained a set of truly "national interests"—preventing another 9/11, maintaining access to Persian Gulf oil, limiting the spread of weapons of mass destruction—which transcend the particular interests of subnational groups. The debate was less over whether these interests mattered than over how much they were in jeopardy and how best to defend them.

Given acceptance of the three essential assumptions of anarchy, state sovereignty, and unitary rational state actors, the next four points examine the implications for understanding the behavior of states.

4. **National security requires self-help.**   In domestic society, where effective institutions of law and order exist, individuals can rely on those institutions to protect their legitimate interests and security. If someone is breaking into your house, you dial 911, and hopefully a police car quickly arrives. As long as citizens maintain confidence in the efficacy and fairness of the central authority, most of them refrain from arming themselves for self-defense. However, when confidence in central authority breaks down, attitudes and behaviors change. If crime in your neighborhood increases dramatically, and you become increasingly uncertain about the willingness or ability of the police to come to your aid, you might indeed decide that you need to act to protect yourself.

In the world of anarchy and state sovereignty, there is no higher authority to impose order, and there is no international 911 number for states to call when their interests are threatened. States must therefore provide for their own defense and protection. Realists refer to this effort by states to defend their own interests as **self-help**. A state can engage in self-help in two ways.

self-help
State efforts to protect their interests through the accumulation of military power or the forging of alliances.

First, it can accumulate military assets—troops, tanks, warships, and even nuclear, chemical, and biological weapons. But relatively small, poor, or sparsely populated states will have a hard time acquiring the military wherewithal to match that of larger, richer, and more densely populated neighbors. Thus, alliance with other states is a second form of self-help, insofar as alliance formation does not rely on a central authority that stands above that of independent sovereign states. An analogy might be the neighborhood watch group. If you rely on your neighbors for protection during a crime wave, that is fundamentally different from relying on the police. The neighbors in the watch group are legal equals who voluntarily come together to achieve a common purpose. The police, in contrast, have authority above all neighbors, and adherence to police directives is not voluntary.

5. **One nation's security can mean another nation's insecurity.** An unfortunate consequence of the simultaneous pursuit of national interests by sovereign states via self-help is what has been termed the **security dilemma**: what one country does for reasons of self-defense can be viewed by other countries as threatening to their interests and national security. Why? The military hardware and alliances that one country accumulates for defensive purposes may be seen by another country as useful for offensive purposes. This is one reason arms races and the tensions they produce can be so hard to regulate. Country A builds up arms because it fears Country B, then Country B responds in kind because of its escalating fear of Country A. In this way, two countries with no offensive intentions toward one another can end up in an expensive arms race that neither wants but that neither is able to effectively control.

This security dilemma is an application to international relations of the more general concept of "the prisoner's dilemma." Suppose two suspected bank robbers are picked up by the police. The police suspect that the two are guilty but have no hard evidence; thus, they need a confession from at least one suspect. They bring them to the police headquarters, place them in separate rooms where they cannot communicate with one another, and begin the interrogation.

Depending on whether the prisoners confess or remain silent, assume the results of the interrogation will eventually lead to the possible outcomes illustrated in Table 1.1. Clearly, both suspects will be better off if neither confesses (outcome 4 in the table). Without a confession, there cannot be a conviction, and each prisoner goes free. Yet in simulations of this situation, both sides typically end up confessing, leading each to receive a five-year jail term (outcome 1), which could have been avoided if they had just kept quiet. Why then do they confess? The answer is clear. Both suspects are trying to avoid outcome 2 or outcome 3. In those cases, where one confesses but the other remains silent, the former receives a reduced sentence as a reward for helping the police close the case; meanwhile, the one who remains silent

security dilemma
The notion that what one state does for purely defensive purposes might appear to other states as threatening to their security and interests.

Table 1.1 The Prisoner's Dilemma

	Suspect A Confesses	Suspect A Silent
Suspect B Confesses	(1) Both get 5 years	(2) A gets 10 years, B gets 1 year
Suspect B Silent	(3) B gets 10 years, A gets 1 year	(4) Both go free

gets a 10-year sentence for failing to cooperate. Because each prisoner cannot be sure what the other is doing, the safe strategy (the one that avoids the 10-year sentence) is often seen as confessing.

Now, return to the world of international relations and substitute India and Pakistan, two countries with nuclear weapons, for the two prisoners. One might argue that India and Pakistan would both be better off without those nuclear weapons. For one thing, nuclear weapons are very costly, and the money used to develop, produce, and maintain them might be better spent on education, health care, road construction, or other pressing domestic needs. Military leaders might also view the diversion of scarce resources from more usable conventional weapons to nuclear programs as a poor use of those resources. Perhaps most important, ending the nuclear arms race in South Asia would reduce and perhaps eliminate the prospect of nuclear war between India and Pakistan, an outcome that both countries presumably want.

So why can't they cooperate and disarm (outcome 4 in Table 1.2)? The reason is that neither country can be sure the other country will disarm. If only one country disarms, it would be vulnerable to nuclear blackmail by the other in some future crisis. As in the prisoner's dilemma, we end up with outcome 1 because of the fear of outcomes 2 and 3. While outcome 1 is arguably inferior to outcome 4, it does assure equality between the countries, and it avoids the possibility that one can be subject to nuclear blackmail.

Of course, if the two countries (India and Pakistan in our example) had some higher authority to prevent them from cheating and secretly maintaining a nuclear arsenal, and if that authority could punish the cheater and protect the potential victim, then the possibility of solving this dilemma would be greater. But because we have no effective higher power in this world of international anarchy, cooperation is more difficult and risky.

6. **War is inevitable.**   The points discussed above lead, unfortunately, to the conclusion among realists that war is an unavoidable and natural part of world affairs. In a world with no higher power to impose order and resolve disputes, with almost 200 sovereign actors looking to defend their interests via self-help, and where efforts at self-help and self-defense can threaten other actors in the system, states sometimes need to use force to resolve disputes with other states.

Table 1.2 The Security Dilemma

	India Arms	India Disarms
Pakistan Arms	(1) Military equality, but high cost, tension	(2) India vulnerable, Pakistan superior
Pakistan Disarms	(3) Pakistan vulnerable, India superior	(4) Low costs, no nuclear war

This conclusion does not imply that every state is in a shooting war all the time. Nonetheless, virtually all states continue to view war as a viable option to resolve disputes when the interests at stake seem sufficient and are deemed unachievable by other means. As the nineteenth-century Prussian military strategist Carl von Clausewitz stated in his famous book *On War* (a book that is still read and studied by military strategists today), "War is the continuation of policy by other means."[7] In other words, Clausewitz understood war to be neither a senseless and random act of violence nor a strange and unusual occurrence. On the contrary, for Clausewitz, war was simply one more instrument on the shelf that could be taken down and dusted off, so to speak, when needed to achieve some important foreign policy goal.

In effect, then, according to the realist perspective, if countries are not always in a state of shooting war, they are always in a state of potential war. This is what Hobbes meant when he suggested that life in a state of nature, with no higher authority to impose order, is a perpetual state of "war of all against all." That is not to say that Clausewitz or Hobbes or anyone else "likes" this fact of international life. The point is that realists see this as how the world works, as long as international anarchy and state sovereignty continue to prevail.

7. **Peace and order are a function of the distribution of power.**   Although realists assert the inevitability of war as a general characteristic of international relations, they accept that the distribution of power among states can affect the prospects for peace and order in the short term. Realists themselves are divided as to what type of distribution of power is most conducive to order. **Defensive realists** argue that states will feel secure, and that the odds of peace and order will be maximized, when there exists a **balance of power** among the great powers. The logic behind the balance of power idea is very simple. Assuming states are rational actors, they would only choose to initiate a war in which they had a reasonable chance of victory. Rational actors do not pick fights they are clearly destined to lose. Thus, assuming that the power of any one state or any one alliance of states can be roughly balanced by the power of another state or alliance of states, neither side could be guaranteed victory, and the incentive to begin a war is reduced.

According to the classical model of balance of power, balancing in the international system will occur more or less automatically. Sovereign states, sensing the balance of power shifting in the direction of another state (or alliance of states), will increase their own power or forge coalitions with other potentially threatened states to restore the balance. Note that this is a dynamic process; it never reaches a state of final equilibrium. The power of individual states is always ebbing and flowing in comparison to that of others, and alliances are flexible and shifting. Countries choose alliance partners not because of political or ideological affinity but on the basis of what needs to be done to maintain the power balance. An old rule of thumb in balance of power politics is that in international relations there are no permanent allies,

defensive realists
Subcategory of realists who suggest that to feel secure, great powers seek, and are satisfied by, a balance of power.

balance of power
Approach to order that assumes a rough equilibrium among the great powers helps to maintain stability, since no state can initiate war and be confident of victory.

only permanent interests. Your adversary today can be your ally tomorrow (or vice versa). In the final analysis, according to the classical balance of power model, states act in ways that, on average, maintain a systemwide equilibrium. If that is the case, then the chances of war, though never totally eliminated, are minimized.

In contrast to defensive realists, **offensive realists** suggest that in a world of anarchy, balance of power is not enough to makes states feel fully secure.[8] Instead they argue that great powers seek not balance but hegemony, that is, dominant power and influence in the international system. Whereas balance implies a relatively orderly world of multiple states or alliance systems of roughly equivalent power, hegemony implies a single top dog able to dominate the international system by virtue of its capabilities and will to establish and enforce the rules of world politics. Related to this offensive realist view is **hegemonic stability theory**, which suggests that the world will be most orderly and peaceful not when there is a balance of power but when a great power establishes such dominant power as to make others reluctant to challenge its position.

Note that while defensive and offensive realists disagree about how much power states need to feel secure and what kind of a distribution of power is most conducive to order (a balance among the great powers vs. hegemony by one dominant state), both subgroups are clearly identifiable as realists for two different reasons. First, both see the key to order as rooted in the distribution of power among sovereign states; neither sees and order as resulting from things like the United Nations or international law. Second, while both suggest that a particular distribution of power can minimize the chances of war in the short run, they both maintain that, in the long run, the possibility of war can never be completely erased. Balancing efforts may be inadequate, a hegemon might show signs of weakness and face a challenge, or leaders may miscalculate. In fact, small wars might sometimes be necessary to maintain either the balance of power or a hegemon's dominance if tested. At best, according to realists of both types, the distribution of power can produce relative peace and order in the short run, but it can never make war obsolete indefinitely. (For an application of balance of power and other key realist concepts to domestic society, see Theory in Practice 1.1.)

Note that the discussion of realist assumptions and their behavioral implications to this point has ignored normative considerations of ethics and morality in international relations. However, as the next two points indicate, the realist paradigm does address such matters.

8. **Power trumps justice.**   In his classic account of the Peloponnesian Wars fought between the ancient Greek city-states of Athens and Sparta in 431–404 BCE, Thucydides recounts the famous Melian dialogue between representatives of powerful Athens and the largely powerless little island of Melos. The situation was that Melos, once a dependency of Sparta, saw an opportunity for independence, as Sparta had lost interest in Melos. But the

offensive realists
Subcategory of realists who suggest that to feel secure great powers seek, and are only satisfied by, hegemony.

hegemonic stability theory
Idea that peace and stability in the international system increase when a powerful state or "hegemon" has the ability and will to dominate and to establish and enforce the rules of the international order.

Theory in Practice 1.1

Youth Gangs: An Analogy to International Relations

Many American cities have been plagued by the problem of youth gangs and their violence. Insofar as most victims of gang violence are gang members themselves, the question of why one creates or joins such organizations might seem puzzling. This is not the place to attempt a full explanation of this phenomenon. But inner-city gangs might be viewed as simply a more violent equivalent of the suburban neighborhood watch organization, and both are related to the alliances that states form in international politics.

All three—gangs, neighborhood watch groups, and international alliances—are responses to a context of insecurity in which institutions of law and order do not seem sufficient for one's protection. The anarchy of some city neighborhoods, in which law and order appear to have broken down, might lead some youths to join gangs (form alliances) for the security they provide (self-help) and to provide a counterweight to other gangs that have formed and that appear potentially threatening (balance of power). Of course, what one person does for reasons of defense and security can appear to others as potentially offensive and threatening to *their* security (the "security dilemma"). Thus, the tensions and wars that ensue become the inevitable, paradoxical result of efforts to achieve security via self-help in an environment of anarchy.

- In what ways are the motives to create gangs, watch groups, and alliances similar?
- Why are gangs, watch groups, and alliances characterized as efforts at "self-help" when all three seem to rely on others to increase one's security?
- What would it take to make gangs, watch groups, and alliances unnecessary for their members' security?

Athenians sought to take the island as their own. In the excerpts from the dialogue below, the Melians appeal to the justice of their position and the honor found in seeking to protect their independence. The Athenians, in contrast, consider justice and honor irrelevant in a world where power prevails.[9]

ATHENIANS: … We both alike know that into the discussion of human affairs the question of justice only enters where the pressure of necessity is equal, and that the powerful exact what they can, and the weak grant what they must.

MELIANS: It may be in your interests to be our masters, but how can it be ours to be your slaves?

ATHENIANS: To you the gain will be that by submission you will avert the worst; and we all shall be the richer for your preservation.

MELIANS: … How base and cowardly would it be in us, who retain our freedom, not to do and suffer anything rather than be your slaves.

ATHENIANS: Not so, if you calmly reflect: for you are not fighting against equals to whom you cannot yield without disgrace, but you are taking counsel whether or not you shall resist an overwhelming force. The question is not one of honour but of prudence.

MELIANS: Nevertheless we do not despair of fortune; for we hope to stand as high as you in the honour of heaven, because we are righteous, and you against whom we contend are unrighteous.

After some further back and forth, the Athenians dismiss all such talk of honor, justice, and righteousness and make clear the nature of the choice the Melians must make.

ATHENIANS: For surely you cannot dream of flying to that false sense of honour which has been the ruin of so many when danger and dishonour were staring them in the face.... You ought to see that there can be no disgrace in yielding to a great city which invites you to become her ally on reasonable terms, keeping your own land, and merely paying tribute; and that you will certainly gain no honour if, having to choose between the two alternatives, safety and war, you obstinately prefer the worse. To maintain our rights against equals, to be politic with superiors, and to be moderate toward inferiors is the path of safety. Reflect once more when we have withdrawn, and say to yourselves over and over again that you are deliberating about your one and only country, which may be saved or destroyed by a single decision.

The Melians stood by the justice of their cause and refused to capitulate to the Athenians. The Athenians immediately surrounded the town of Melos with a wall to serve as a blockade, and they eventually put to death all Melians of military age and made slaves of all the women and children. As Thucydides makes clear, the high-minded rhetoric of the Melians did not save them, and, as the Athenians might have told them, it was the very weakness of the Melian position that caused them, foolishly, to seek refuge behind the walls of justice and righteousness. Two thousand years later, Thomas Hobbes made essentially the same point when he argued that in a condition where there is no "common power" (what contemporary realists call "anarchy"), "The notions of right and wrong, justice and injustice, have no place. Where there is no common power there is no law; where no law, no injustice."[10] For better or worse, realists embrace the view of Thucydides and Hobbes: that independence and survival depend on the accumulation of sufficient power and that appeals to justice provide scant protection from those, like the Athenians, able and willing to use power to serve their interests.

9. **World politics is not primarily about good and evil.**   The realist notion that power trumps justice in world politics sometimes leads to the conclusion that realists are completely amoral. But that is a caricature of the realist position. As Hans Morgenthau, the preeminent proponent of twentieth-century realist thinking, wrote, "Political realism is aware of the moral significance of political action."[11] Indeed, most realists

subscribe to some version of a personal moral code that would allow them to condemn certain actions as immoral. To take an obvious example, most realists would have little hesitation in condemning the Nazi Holocaust as evil.

At the same time, realists perceive a line between personal morality and state policy. As Morgenthau argued, states must be guided in their behavior by what he called the principle of prudence: they must temper their application of abstract moral principles by considering the consequences of political action (or inaction). While an individual might sacrifice him- or herself in pursuit of some higher moral cause, states cannot let moral considerations interfere with their survival. While individuals might choose to be guided by an absolute ethical code, states must be guided also by the pursuit of the national interest.

Morgenthau cautions us to avoid identifying any state's interests with a larger moral purpose. All peoples and their leaders tend to use the language of good and evil in the conduct of their foreign policy—for example, your war is fought for a noble cause, theirs for aggressive purposes; you seek to defend human rights, but they engage in ethnic cleansing; you seek peaceful resolution of disputes, but they choose war and violence. However, realists suggest that such characterizations—that justify one's own policies and demonize those of one's opponents—be viewed with some skepticism. Many conflicts and wars are about claims to land, resources, or security in which both sides can make legitimate claims, and no state or people has a clear monopoly on either vice or virtue when it comes to how such claims are pursued.

The point is that the nature of the international system often leads to highly destructive actions and behaviors by states and their leaders. As individuals, leaders might find such actions morally reprehensible; as leaders, however, they may find them necessary. In fact, according to realists, a view of world politics as a struggle between good and evil can lead to at least two kinds of problematic results: (1) an overly simplistic, knee-jerk defense of one's own country's actions as inherently good and one's enemy's as inherently evil, or (2) an equally simplistic and naive condemnation of one's own country's policies when they, inevitably, fail to live up to the kind of high and consistent moral standards one might apply to individuals.

Finally, realists arrive at the following conclusion about the possibility of cooperation and change.

10. **The possibility of cooperation and change is limited.**   Virtually everything discussed above about the realist paradigm rests on the very first assumption of international anarchy. The need to accumulate and balance power, the inevitability of war, the minimal role assigned to justice and morality in world politics all flow from the assumption that there is no higher power to maintain order, to stifle aggression, or to enforce global standards of justice and morality. Eliminate anarchy and it's a whole new global order in which

all the other realist assumptions begin to unravel. Realists would say as much, but they would also suggest that the elimination of anarchy to the degree sufficient to render realism obsolete is highly unlikely.

As realists recognize, we can offer plenty of examples of international cooperation among nations, in areas ranging from trade to human rights to international peacekeeping. But short of eliminating the sovereign state's near monopoly on the legitimate use of violence in world politics and transferring that monopoly to some global entity, the essential anarchy of the international system will remain unchanged. Realists contend that such a transfer of power is not only highly unlikely; it might not even be particularly desirable. Such a global entity, charged with maintaining stability over the planet, is unlikely to be a paragon of democracy. On the contrary, maintaining order in a conflict-ridden world would likely require a highly oppressive and dictatorial central authority that, in turn, would likely engender all kinds of violent resistance. In its own way, such a world would be as unappealing as the current world as understood by realists.

Thus, realists perceive a big difference between domestic politics and international politics. Cooperation in the former is possible due to the existence of laws and institutions with power above that of individual actors. But the absence of such a higher power in international affairs means that cooperation and the possibility of fundamental change in the world will always be limited. Whether we like it or not (and realists, one must emphasize, do not necessarily like the world they describe), this is how the world works. Leaders and states, like Melos, that do not understand and operate according to this understanding will, in the view of realists, run the risk of conquest, subjugation, and even elimination as sovereign entities.

Alternatives to Realism

1-3   Compare and contrast the liberal, constructivist, feminist, and neo-Marxist paradigms.

Although realism was the dominant paradigm of the post–World War II era, not everyone accepted its assumptions as essential truths. Realism has always had its critics, and that criticism has become especially loud and sustained in the post–Cold War era. The dramatic events of the last quarter century—including the end of the Cold War, the global spread of democracy, economic globalization, and the 9/11 terrorist attacks on the United States—have led many to question whether realism is equipped to explain the twenty-first-century world. Given the degree of flux in the contemporary global landscape, it is not surprising that a once-dominant paradigm would come under challenge. In a recent survey, scholars estimated that roughly one-third of the international relations literature is rooted in the realist paradigm.[12] That's a healthy plurality, but not even close to a majority.

At this point, however, no single paradigmatic challenger to realism has emerged. What one finds is an array of competing perspectives that all reject realism even if they disagree about what should replace it. In the following sections, we will examine four of these alternative paradigms: liberalism, constructivism, feminism, and neo-Marxism. We will highlight their differences from realism as well as their differences and similarities in relation to one another. We will conclude the chapter with a brief examination of the argument for non-paradigmatic research.

Liberalism

idealism
Post–World War I perspective on world politics; assumes that ideas about reform of the international system could move us beyond the world of power politics emphasized by realism.

The period after World War I is often associated with a perspective on world politics that is called **idealism**. Idealists questioned many of the lessons about how the world works handed down by Thucydides and Hobbes and subsequently adopted by twentieth-century realists. Instead, idealists believed that it would be possible to transform the world of power-seeking and war into one in which peace and cooperation among states might prevail. Calling adherents of this view idealists, however, seemed to give an advantage to "realists," insofar as the latter term suggested a perspective well grounded in the "realities" of the world. Idealism, in contrast, suggested a well-intentioned but utopian perspective that was out of touch with how the world really operated. Although some scholars continue to employ the idealist label, today the descendants of the idealist perspective are found in two distinct paradigms: liberalism (discussed in this section) and constructivism (discussed in the following section).

liberalism
Paradigm that suggests global cooperation is possible and that challenges the realist assumption that the competitive, power-oriented, violent character of world politics is inevitable.

Liberalism has long been the most well-established paradigmatic challenger to realism. Liberals accept, *more or less*, some of the key assumptions of realism. In particular, liberals accept that states remain the key actors in world politics and that the absence of a world government means that anarchy remains a largely accurate characterization of the international system. However, liberals do not accept those assumptions without qualification. States may remain key actors, but they are not the only significant actors in world politics. Anarchy may still exist, but it can be mitigated to some degree. As a result, unlike realists, liberals accept the following:

- There are alternatives for survival beyond self-help.
- There is a possibility of escaping the security dilemma.
- There is a role for justice and morality in world politics.
- There is a possibility that war will no longer be inevitable.
- There is a possibility of significant cooperation among states.

In short, unlike realists, who assert that the competitive, power-oriented, and violent character of world politics is an unchangeable fact of life in the anarchic international system, liberals believe that significant global cooperation is possible and that we can move beyond the power politics at the heart of the realist paradigm.

For liberals, the key assumption is that cooperation among states can produce **absolute gains** for all. As long as your state is better off as a result of cooperating with others, the gains of others should not matter. For realists, in contrast, the issue is **relative gains**. Because realists are concerned with the balance of power among states, what matters most is not whether your state benefits in absolute terms but, rather, how much it benefits in comparison to other states. So from that realist perspective, even if international trade, for example, allows a state to grow in wealth and prosperity, that state should be wary if other states become wealthier and more prosperous. That is because economic wealth can be translated into military power that could put the first state at risk. The liberal focus on absolute gains is clearly more conducive to international cooperation than is the realist focus on relative gains.

This liberal emphasis on absolute gains and the possibilities of global cooperation among states can be illustrated by returning to the discussion of the prisoner's dilemma (recall point 5 in the discussion of realism). Absolute gains for the prisoners would be maximized when each of them remains silent and refuses to confess to the police. In that case, as we saw, each would go free. However, each prisoner fears that if he or she remains silent, the other will confess and maximize his or her relative gains at the silent prisoner's expense. For realists, it is hard to escape this dilemma. Even if the prisoners would like to cooperate with one another, and even if they had a prior agreement with one another to do so, there is no higher authority to enforce that agreement. Mistrust and defection from the agreement prevail.

Liberals disagree. In a famous study of prisoner's dilemma strategies based on computer simulations, political scientist Robert Axelrod found that cooperation is possible.[13] The key is to think in terms of what he calls an "iterated prisoner's dilemma" in which the game is not a one-time event but one in which the same players repeatedly play the game. What he found is that one can elicit a good deal of cooperation in the game by following a "tit for tat" strategy. One starts out with a cooperative strategy, and from there one mimics whatever the other player does. If the other player selects the cooperative option, you do the same. If the other player defects and fails to cooperate, you do likewise. Eventually, the other player learns that cooperation breeds cooperation and that defection breeds defection. The title of Axelrod's book, *The Evolution of Cooperation*, aptly summarizes the lesson that cooperation can emerge even when not present at the outset.

Because interactions between states are not one-time events but a series of "iterated" interactions across a range of issues, liberals argue that cooperation can evolve in international relations as well. Indeed, liberals would argue that that are countless examples of cooperative relations among states in the international system that defy realist expectations of mistrust and defection. In some cases, that cooperation is among countries that have had friendly relations for long periods of time (e.g., the United States and Canada). In other cases, more limited cooperative agreements can emerge from countries that have been

absolute gains
The total benefits that accrue to a state as a consequence of its interactions with other states without regard to the benefits that accrue to others.

relative gains
Benefits that accrue to a state from its international interactions assessed in comparison to the benefits that accrue to other states.

long-term adversaries (e.g., the various arms control agreements negotiated between the United States and the USSR during the Cold War). One of the strategies for getting adversaries to "learn" to cooperate is to start with more limited **confidence-building measures** such as notification of troop movements or minor limits on armaments designed, as in the iterated prisoner's dilemma, for countries gradually to build trust in one another.

confidence-building measures
Small-scale agreements and forms of cooperation between states that serve to develop the trust and confidence necessary for resolution of larger conflicts.

While liberals are clearly more optimistic than realists about the possibility for cooperation in the international system, they share with realists the assumption that the structure of that international system will have a large impact on the extent and depth of that cooperation. The origin of much contemporary liberal thinking about international relations along these lines can be traced back to the German philosopher Immanuel Kant. In his 1795 essay *To Perpetual Peace*, Kant argued that, "The state of peace among men living side by side is not the natural state *(status naturalis);* the natural state is one of war. This does not always mean open hostilities, but at least an unceasing threat of war." To that extent he sounds much like Thomas Hobbes and contemporary realists. However, unlike Hobbes and contemporary realists, he also suggested that a state of perpetual peace can be established. For Kant, that peace would be the result of several factors, including (1) the creation of a loose "federation of free states" whose members were committed to maintaining international order and security; (2) the "spirit of commerce," which in Kant's view "is incompatible with war" and which "sooner or later gains the upper hand in every state"; and (3) the creation of republican governments in which executive power is checked by an independent legislature.[14]

Contemporary liberals differ among themselves in which elements of Kant's approach to perpetual peace they stress. Political scientist Michael Doyle divides liberalism into three subgroups: liberal institutionalism, liberal commercialism, and liberal internationalism.[15]

liberal institutionalism
Subtype of the liberal paradigm; suggests that international institutions such as law, regimes, and international organizations mitigate anarchy and facilitate international cooperation.

LIBERAL INSTITUTIONALISM   Proponents of **liberal institutionalism** look to international institutions to reduce the anarchy of the international system. By *institutions*, they mean "the rules that govern elements of world politics and the organizations that help implement those rules."[16] Central to this institutionalist perspective is a formal system of international law that regulates and constrains the behavior of states and that thereby limits their sovereign ability to act as they wish in some areas. To be maximally effective, those legal rules require the establishment of international organizations (IOs) that can adjudicate, monitor, and enforce the rules.

The ultimate fulfillment of the liberal institutionalist road to peace would be something along the lines of Kant's "federation of free states," in which members agree to avoid the use of violence in resolving their differences and to work cooperatively to maintain peace and security in the international system. This Kantian ideal was at least imperfectly reflected in the creation of both the United Nations and its predecessor, the League of Nations. In the twenty-first century there also exists an extensive body of international law along with hundreds of international organizations intended to regulate state behavior and promote cooperation on issues ranging from trade to human rights to weapons proliferation.

The goal in all this institution-building is to provide an opportunity for actors in the global system to transcend the Hobbesian state of nature that realists take as a given. In particular, effective institutions increase the possibility of escaping the security dilemma. For example, as we saw in our earlier discussion of Indian-Pakistani nuclear arms competition, cooperation to limit that competition is difficult because of mutual mistrust. However, in a world in which institutions exist to monitor agreements, to publicize violations, and perhaps even to punish those who commit such violations, the risks involved in cooperation are reduced.

Note that realists and liberal institutionalists share a common assumption: that as long as anarchy exists, world politics will retain its power-oriented and often violent character. Where they differ, as will be discussed in detail in Chapter 5, is in how they assess (1) the effectiveness of existing institutions, such as international law and the UN, in limiting international anarchy, and (2) the possibility of improving on the record of institutions either via reform of those existing institutions or the creation of new ones.

LIBERAL COMMERCIALISM   Like their institutionalist cousins, the proponents of **liberal commercialism** share a belief that a state of more or less permanent peace among nations can replace the Hobbesian permanent state of war. But the emphasis here is less on institution-building and more on "the spirit of commerce." The assumption is that war is bad for business in a capitalist, market economy; it disrupts profitable trade and investment opportunities, and it denies entire societies the economic gains that free trade and commerce produce. Thus, governments as well as the private sector have a significant stake in global peace.

liberal commercialism
Subtype of the liberal paradigm; suggests that commerce among states leads to a mutual economic interdependence that raises the cost and reduces the likelihood of wars.

The economic globalization that has characterized the late twentieth and early twenty-first century has reinforced the position of liberal commercialists. This expansion of global trade, production, and investment has, in their view, raised the costs of disruption to such a level that major war has become almost unthinkable. To the extent that some nations resist the trend toward interdependence and choose to remain outside the global economy (e.g., North Korea), they remain a problem whose solution in the long term is their integration into the globalization system.

Journalist and author Thomas Friedman has articulated a popularized version of this liberal commercialist view in his *New York Times* commentaries and in his books on globalization. In both his "Golden Arches Theory" and "Dell Theory" of conflict prevention, he suggested that globalization was rendering war, geopolitics, and, in effect, the realist view of how the world works, obsolete.[17] In arguing that two countries with McDonald's restaurants or two countries that are a part of the Dell computer supply chain are unlikely to fight wars with one another, Friedman makes two related points: (1) countries at a level of economic development high enough to support a McDonald's restaurant will have achieved a level of prosperity that gives them a lot to lose in war, and (2) their level of prosperity is directly and inextricably tied to the fate of other countries that are a part of their supply chains for Dell computers (or iPhones or automobiles or countless other goods and services).

Liberals and realists disagree on the extent to which economic interdependence and globalization do, in fact, change the nature of world politics, with realists suggesting that more economic interaction, rather than reducing the likelihood of war, can actually produce more points of interstate friction. We will return to this debate in Chapter 7.

liberal internationalism

Subtype of the liberal paradigm; suggests that domestic regime type has an impact on a state's foreign behavior. In particular, it is associated with the theory of democratic peace.

LIBERAL INTERNATIONALISM   According to Doyle, proponents of **liberal internationalism** draw their inspiration primarily from Kant's notion that republican government is an important source of "perpetual peace." Kant argued that in places where government is based on consent of the citizenry, there will be a reluctance to go to war because of the hardships that war invariably imposes on those citizens. In fact, Kant's federation of free states was premised on the assumption that its members would be republics with this domestic political disincentive to go to war.

Thus, the key to peace from the liberal internationalist perspective is expanding the number of republics. Kant was wary of democracy in which citizens made decisions directly, but in the modern world, states characterized as liberal democracies generally equate with what Kant meant by republican government. And trends in the late twentieth century provided contemporary Kantians with reason for optimism, as democracy has spread to a number of new locations in Latin America, Eastern and Central Europe, and many countries in Asia and Africa. In arguing that democracies have historically tended not to fight wars with one another, an argument that will be further examined in Chapters 3 and 4, some proponents of this **democratic peace theory** have argued that the Kantian vision is becoming more and more a reality.

democratic peace theory

Idea that democracies tend not to fight wars against one another and that the spread of democratic government can be the antidote to war in the international system.

A unique twist on this democratic peace idea came from thinkers and policy-makers associated with the administration of US President George W. Bush. A central argument offered by Bush administration members and advisors in favor of the 2003 US-led invasion of Iraq was that it would allow for democracy to emerge. The assumption was that the Iraqi people wanted democracy and would be able to achieve that goal if only Saddam Hussein, the major obstacle to democracy, was removed from power with US assistance. The hope (subsequently left unfulfilled) was that Iraq could serve as a model for Arab and Islamic democracy that would spread to the rest of the region. Before long, the democratization of the region would provide, as liberal adherents to the democratic peace idea suggest, the long-elusive solution to the problem of war and conflict in the region. This policy of promoting democracy through the use of military power is a tenet of **neoconservatism**; it is sometimes characterized as using realist means (military power) to achieve liberal ends (a democratic peace).

THE KANTIAN TRIANGLE   The strongest statement of the liberal perspective emerges when we combine the essential assumptions of all three liberal subgroups discussed above. In what political scientists Bruce Russett and John Oneal refer to as the **Kantian triangle**, international institutions, economic interdependence, and democracy mutually reinforce the global propensity toward international cooperation and peace (see Figure 1.1).[18] Thus, even if any one of those three factors by itself cannot induce international peace and cooperation, their combined impact produces a three-pronged assault on the nature of international relations as traditionally understood by realists.

Furthermore, institutions, economic interdependence, and democracy not only favor peace independently and directly, but they also do so indirectly by mutually reinforcing one another. Thus, democracies are more likely to trade with other democracies than with nondemocracies, which tightens their economic interdependence. That trade, in turn, increases the prosperity that political scientists argue is strongly associated with democracy. Similarly, economic interdependence increases the need for institutions and international organizations to regulate economic relations, and once established, those institutions further ensure that economic interdependence proceeds without interruption or crisis. Thus, Russett and Oneal conclude, the vicious circle of fear, mistrust, and conflict that characterizes the realist "security dilemma" can be replaced by a "virtuous circle" of mutual interests and cooperation produced by the mutually reinforcing impact of all three points of this Kantian triangle.[19]

neoconservatism
View, associated with intellectuals close to the administration of George W. Bush and used to justify the war in Iraq, that suggests the diffusion of democracy sometimes has to be jump-started through military means.

Kantian triangle
Idea that international institutions, economic interdependence, and the diffusion of democratic government are mutually reinforcing and together support liberal notions of a trend toward peace and cooperation among states.

Figure 1.1 The Kantian Triangle

SOURCE: Adapted from Bruce Russett and John Oneal, "International Systems: Vicious Circles and Virtuous Circles," in Russett and Oneal, *Triangulating Peace* (Norton, 2001), 35.

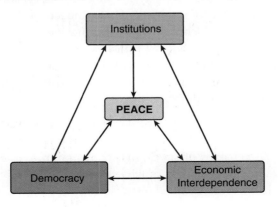

Constructivism

A more recent challenge to realist orthodoxy comes from a perspective known as **constructivism**. The "constructivist turn" in international relations theory dates to the end of the US–Soviet Cold War in the late 1980s and early 1990s. Critics argued that the realist understanding of how the world works neither led us to anticipate nor provided an explanation of the sudden and peaceful end of that Cold War and the dramatic improvement in US–Russian relations. Constructivists believe that realism not only failed to explain that improvement in the deeply adversarial US–Soviet relationship, but it also was unable to explain how those two countries escaped the "security dilemma" in which they had been trapped for almost half a century. After all, both sides still had massive conventional and nuclear forces built expressly to counter one another, and realists would predict that those forces should have continued to fuel mutual insecurity.

Liberalism, according to constructivists, also fails to explain the end of the Cold War. Due to different economic systems and to security considerations, international trade and financial interactions between the United States and the USSR were, at the time, modest in scope; there was little of the economic interdependence that characterized relations between the United States and western Europe or Japan. Moreover, although the Soviet Union under Mikhail Gorbachev did hesitantly experiment with more democratic forms of government in the late 1980s, the USSR could still not be described as a democracy at the point when the Cold War ended. Finally, though the United States and USSR were both party to many international treaties and were members of many international organizations, none of these were new developments that could explain the change of relations beginning in the late 1980s. In short, none of the points of the Kantian triangle seem sufficient, individually or together, to explain the most significant geopolitical change in world politics of the second half of the twentieth century.

Despite their critique of realism, constructivists do not necessarily dispute the realist description of how international relations currently are conducted. In fact, they acknowledge in many cases that power-seeking, self-help, and war are contemporary facts of international life. Indeed, pick up any daily newspaper, and one can see evidence of all those things on the front page. However, what constructivists do question are realist assumptions and explanations about how and why we have arrived at the current state of affairs. Three points in particular summarize the essence of the constructivist perspective and its differences from both realism and liberalism:

1. *Material structure is not all determining.* Constructivists dispute the core realist assumption that anarchy has an unavoidable, deterministic impact on the behavior of states. Instead, as political scientist Alexander Wendt has argued, "Anarchy is what states make of it."[20] According to Wendt, while anarchy *permits* the realist world of power politics and self-help to

emerge, it does not by itself *necessitate* such a response. To the extent that we respond to anarchy by engaging in realist forms of self-help, that is a socially constructed response shaped by our collective experiences, understandings, and ideas about how the world works. Rather than passively responding to the impersonal logic of the international system, constructivists see a greater role of for human agency, than do realists, in shaping and constructing (hence, the label *constructivism*) the kind of system in which we operate.

To make the point, Wendt suggests that we consider the possible range of human responses if we were contacted by an alien civilization. One response might be to assume the worst and launch an immediate attack on the first alien spacecraft to arrive. But such a response would probably depend on how the aliens approached us. As Wendt argues, we would have one kind of response if they arrived with a fleet of spacecrafts and destroyed New York, and another if they peacefully landed one craft, preceded by reassurances that they had no hostile intentions. Of course, even in the latter case, we would likely be cautious. Still, you can see how those early interactions might shape emerging relations.

To return to the real world, contrast the relations between (1) the United States and the Soviet Union during the Cold War with (2) the relations between the United States and Canada. Both those relationships exist in the same system of international anarchy, but they differ considerably. In the Cold War, US efforts at self-help—for example, the buildup of the US nuclear deterrent—arguably contributed to the kind of security dilemma that realists discuss, as did Soviet efforts to respond in kind. But those same US nuclear weapons, which could theoretically devastate Ottawa and Toronto as easily as they could Moscow and Leningrad, never produced the same security dilemma with Canada. Why the difference? Constructivists would argue that past patterns of interaction, expectations regarding the motives and behaviors of others that emanate from that prior experience, and the subjective identities we assign to others as friend or enemy led the Soviet Union and Canada to interpret the "threat" posed by US nuclear weapons very differently. Anarchy alone, they conclude, neither predetermines nor allows us to predict the nature of either relationship.

Some realists at least partially concede this point. In a modification of the traditional realist notion of balance of power, realist scholar Stephen Walt has suggested that what really drives states is the **balance of threat**.[21] Traditional balance of power theory suggests that states will fear other states based purely on their capabilities and geographical proximity. In other words, one will most fear militarily powerful states that are located nearby. Those objective factors alone will cause states to balance the power of the more powerful neighbor, and security dilemmas will ensue. But the balance of threat idea suggests that there is a third factor, aside from capabilities and geography, that must be considered and that is the perception of the

balance of threat
Modification of the notion of balance of power; it is the idea that what drives state behavior is the subjective assessment of the threat that others pose to the national interest.

intentions of one's more powerful neighbor. Canada shares a long border with the world's greatest military power, the United States, but neither fears nor attempts to balance US power. That is because Canadians generally do not believe that the United States has aggressive intentions toward them. In integrating objective material conditions and considerations of intentions and identities, the balance of threat idea thereby combines realist and constructivist assumptions. In the process, it provides a good illustration of how scholars working in different paradigms can influence one another.

2. *Norms and ideas are important.* Material structure alone is not destiny, constructivists explain, because ideas and norms of behavior are also powerful in shaping human action. Consider the case of a fire in a crowded theater with only one available exit.[22] The structure of the situation might seem to allow for only one behavioral response—a panicked and chaotic scramble for the exit. Yet before one assumes that outcome, one might need to know more. Is the theater located in a place where the cultural norm is women and children first? Are all the people in the theater strangers? Is the audience made up mainly of schoolchildren on a field trip with adult chaperones? Depending on the answers, the response to the fire might be quite different. The material structure of the situation (i.e., the fire and the one exit) provides at best only a partial source of human behavior in this case. You also need to know something about how the people relate to larger cultural norms and how they see their own identities in relation to those norms.

   For constructivists, the power of changing ideas and understandings of the world provides the key to understanding the end of the Cold War. Absent any changes in the structure of the international system, Soviet leader Mikhail Gorbachev began to question traditional assumptions and ideas about how the world works. What he called his "new thinking" on foreign affairs included the following elements, each of which directly challenged traditional realist thinking:

   - National security requires international security; you cannot be secure if others are insecure.
   - Economic power is more important than military power as a source of national security.
   - Threats, such as environmental degradation and nuclear war, are global problems that imperil the world and require global solutions. Self-help alone is not sufficient for national survival.[23]

   To be sure, as realists might suggest, some of this "new thinking" was a response to the internal weaknesses plaguing the USSR in the mid-1980s and to its worsening position compared to the United States in the high-tech arms race. However, a regime facing such challenges might have chosen to go out with a bang rather than a whimper. Why did Gorbachev choose the more peaceful path? In the constructivist view, Gorbachev's "new thinking" provided an

US President Ronald Reagan and Soviet General Secretary Mikhail Gorbachev signing a treaty limiting intermediate range nuclear weapons. The treaty (1987) was a step in the reduction of Cold War tensions. How would realists, liberals, and constructivists each explain the end of the Cold War?

alternative to traditional realist ideas. Indeed, a constructivist might argue that realism is a self-fulfilling prophecy. If we understand the world in realist terms, we will act as realists describe. But if we change our assessment of how the world works, as Gorbachev did, then we can change that world as well.

3. *Individuals and nonstate actors are key to the promotion of ideas.* Gorbachev's "new thinking" was not literally new; the ideas did not simply come to him in a flash of inspiration. Instead, the kinds of ideas he articulated had been in circulation for some time among academics, among human rights and peace activists, and within various international organizations and nongovernmental organizations (NGOs). In particular, constructivist scholars have pointed to the emergence of **transnational advocacy networks** composed of individuals and nonstate actors with shared values who exchange information and resources to promote such values globally. Thus, Gorbachev had a repertoire of ideas to draw on in formulating his response to Soviet decline. It is precisely this power of ideas and norms—along with the role played by individuals, international organizations, and nongovernmental organizations in diffusing those ideas and norms—that constructivists suggest is missing from realist and liberal views of the world.

transnational advocacy networks Mixes of individuals and organizations with transnational representation who interact, exchange information, and share and promote common values.

While Gorbachev's ideas arguably offered new, welcome ways of thinking about security, constructivism can also explain the emergence, diffusion, and influence of less positive ideas. For example, political scientist Marc Lynch has argued that Osama bin Laden and al-Qaeda were, in effect, natural constructivists who understood that the outcome of their war with the West would be determined not just by military power and other material capabilities. Instead, the al-Qaeda strategy seems to be based on the assumption that victory would go to whichever side can prevail in developing and promoting a narrative that describes and explains the nature of the relationship between Islam and the West. Thus, Lynch argued that al-Qaeda "seeks to promote an Islamic identity," to define Muslim interests "as necessarily in confrontation with the West," to emphasize "the salience of religion in all aspects of political life," and "to frame world politics as a clash of civilizations."[24] This is not, of course, to imply that constructivists support al-Qaeda. Constructivism is neither an ideology nor a political viewpoint. It is, like the other paradigms of world politics, merely a framework within which one tries to understand the world. Like all the other paradigms, sometimes it might lead us to a better understanding of things we do not like (see Theory in Practice 1.2).

In their critique of realism, constructivists share with liberals a greater openness to the possibility of change in the character of world politics and, with that, a degree of optimism that such change could be (though, as the al-Qaeda example illustrates, not necessarily) in the direction of a more peaceful

Theory in Practice 1.2

Obama the Constructivist?

Barack Obama's characterization of groups like al-Qaeda and ISIS (or ISIL) as "violent extremists" rather than "Islamic extremists" generated a lot of criticism from those who saw it as example of misplaced political correctness and a failure to understand the nature of the threat posed to the West by such groups. One can debate whether the critics have a point, but Obama supporters would argue that Obama's choice of words reflected neither naïveté about the threat faced nor knee-jerk political correctness. Instead it was an attempt to avoid buying into the al-Qaeda/ISIS narrative of a clash of civilizations between Islam and the West. Consider Obama's words:

Al-Qaeda and ISIL and groups like it are desperate for legitimacy. They try to portray themselves as religious leaders—holy warriors in defense of Islam. That's why ISIL presumes to declare itself the "Islamic State." And they propagate the notion that America—and the West, generally—is at war with Islam. That's how they recruit. That's how they try to radicalize young people. We must never accept the premise that they put forward, because it is a lie. Nor should we grant these terrorists the religious legitimacy that they seek. They are not religious leaders—they're terrorists. And we are not at war

with Islam. We are at war with people who have perverted Islam.

Obama's words suggested that he believed that victory against groups like ISIS is as much about winning the narrative about Muslim identity as it is about a clash of military capabilities. It is also about supporting norms against terrorism and the other atrocities committed by ISIS in the name of Islam. In emphasizing competing *narratives*, questions of subjective *identity*, and moral and political *norms*, Obama sounds very much like a constructivist.

- In your view, was Obama right to eschew the phrase "Islamic extremists" in favor of "violent extremists"?
- Who is winning the battle of competing narratives between ISIS and other such groups and the West?
- Taken as a whole, was Obama's foreign policy more realist, liberal, or constructivist? Can you find reflections of each in his approach to international affairs?

SOURCE: "Remarks by the President in Closing of the Summit on Countering Violent Extremism," February 18, 2015, http://www.whitehouse.gov/the-press-office/2015/02/18/remarks-president-closing-summit-countering-violent-extremism.

and cooperative world. But where constructivists part company with liberals is over the assumption that change in the actions of states can only emerge from a prior change in the basic institutions and structures of the international system. Liberal optimism requires the elimination of anarchy via an effectively adjudicated system of international law, an increase in the level of economic interdependence, or the spread of democratic states. Change, in the constructivist view, can come if and when a state redefines its interests and its concept of the motives and interests of other states independently of such structural change.

Feminism

Politically, feminism in the United States and elsewhere has been largely, though not exclusively, concerned with the acquisition of equal rights for women and men. Although the status of women varies greatly around the world, and although much work remains to be done before success can be proclaimed even in the most progressive societies, women's access to education, jobs, and positions of power throughout society has improved markedly in many countries. With some notable exceptions, however, the conduct of foreign affairs and international relations has remained a heavily male-dominated preserve.

As a *political movement*, therefore, one goal of feminism might be to increase the access of women to positions of power and authority in the realm of foreign affairs. On this point, most women and men who think of themselves as feminists would likely agree. Once in such positions of power, however, women may behave much as men do. Realists would argue that any American president, male or female, will confront the same international system, the same balance of power considerations, and the same need to protect the national interest, so that gender differences will be largely inconsequential. In this sense, realists claim, one could simultaneously be a woman, a feminist, and a realist.

But as a *theoretical movement* in the scholarly discipline of international relations, what is important about **feminism** are two further assertions: (1) that our traditional scholarship on international relations reflects a predominantly male perspective on the world, and (2) that the inclusion of more women in positions of authority in international relations could change the way world politics is conducted.

Feminist scholarship has come later (late 1980s, early 1990s) to the field of international relations than to many other fields of study. Some international relations scholars still hesitate to call it a fully developed paradigm; for example, some see it as a subcategory of constructivism. Others, including some feminist scholars, see it less as a separate paradigm than a perspective that sheds new light on work in all of the other paradigms. [25] However, in recent years, feminist critiques of the received wisdom in international relations, and especially of the realist perspective, have begun to multiply and develop, and many scholars (feminists and nonfeminists alike) suggest that those critiques do provide a distinct paradigmatic framework for understanding how the world works.[26] In

feminism
Paradigm that suggests (1) the inclusion of more women in positions of authority could change the way world politics is conducted, and (2) traditional scholarship, especially realism, reflects a gendered perspective on the conduct of international relations.

support of this view, a recent and widely cited survey of scholars working in the field of international relations cited feminism (along with realism, liberalism, constructivism, and Marxism) as one of the key paradigms embraced by scholars.[27]

Like the adherents of all of the other IR paradigms, feminists disagree among themselves on many issues. However, what all IR feminists share in common is a commitment to inserting considerations of gender into the study of international relations. As opposed to "sex" which is a biological concept, "gender" refers to socially constructed roles and ways of understanding and interacting with the world. According to feminist scholars, in neglecting consideration of gender, mainstream IR theory has tended to universalize assumptions about international behavior that are actually based on a particular gendered perspective. At the same time, that gendered perspective has led scholars to focus their attention on particular sets of issues to the neglect of others. This critique of mainstream IR theory is perhaps clearest in the feminist critique of realism.

REALISM AS A GENDERED PERSPECTIVE   Feminist scholarship asserts that realism is an essentially male perspective on how the world of international relations works—in other words, a "gendered perspective." Realism's core assumptions such as anarchy, the dominant role of sovereign states, and the need for self-help, according to feminist scholar J. Ann Tickner, make "claims to be universal and objective" when they are "in reality based on knowledge primarily from men's lives." [28] For example, Tickner argues that certain "foundational myths" of the realist paradigm, such as Hobbes' understanding of how people must behave in the state of nature, leap to conclusions about human behavior based only on the presumed behavior of males.[29]

Moreover, feminists assert that the neglect of considerations of gender and, specifically, gender-based inequalities and disparities of power, lead realists to ignore the relationship of world politics to women's domestic and private lives. In the realist world where everything revolves around the acquisition of power and security by unitary, sovereign states, the impact of world politics on women and children, issues of inequality and poverty, and considerations of power relations among groups in domestic society, are inevitably ignored. Noting the relationship between the personal, the political, and the international, feminist theorists like Cynthia Enloe argue that world politics is not just about high-level security relations among states, but also about how interstate relations affect the everyday lives of individuals.[30]

The dominance of realism throughout much of the latter half of the twentieth century may, according to feminist scholars, be at least partially a reflection of the fact that the field of international relations has been dominated by men. In a 2012 survey, close to 3,500 international relations scholars from twenty countries identified their choices of the four scholars who had the greatest influence on the field over the past 20 years. The 20 top vote-getters are listed in Table 1.3. With only two exceptions, this list is overwhelmingly male. Moreover, the two women on the list (#15, Finnemore; #19, Strange) did not appear on the initial

---

Table 1.3 The Most Influential International Relations
Scholars: A Man's World?

1. Alexander Wendt
2. Robert Keohane
3. Kenneth Waltz
4. Joseph Nye
5. John Mearsheimer
6. James Fearon
7. Samuel Huntington
8. Robert Cox
9. Barry Buzan
10. Peter Katzenstein
11. Bruce Bueno de Mesquita
12. Robert Jervis
13. Stephen Walt
14. Stephen Krasner
15. Martha Finnemore
16. John Ikenberry
17. Bruce Russett
18. John Ruggie
19. Susan Strange
20. James Rosenau

SOURCE: Daniel Maliniak, Susan Peterson, and Michael J. Tierney, "TRIP around the
World: Teaching, Research, and Policy Views of International Relations Faculty in 20
Countries," May 2012, Institute for the Theory and Practice of International Relations,
The College of William and Mary, 34, https://www.wm.edu/offices/itpir/_documents/
trip/trip_around_the_world_2011.pdf.

2004 version of this survey, nor did any other women. The dominance of males
should not be surprising, as the field has been disproportionately male in composition. Thus, the pool of established scholars from which to choose and the
pool of survey respondents were both disproportionately male. In recent years,
more women have received PhDs in international relations, so a similar survey
done 20 years down the road might look very different.

Not every scholar on this list is a realist. Of the top three vote-getters, Wendt
is a constructivist, Keohane is a liberal, and Waltz is a realist. Likewise, women
in this field also run the gamut of paradigmatic approaches. Nevertheless,
feminists argue that the traditional lack of gender diversity did, to some extent,
shape the field of international relations in the twentieth century.

FOREIGN POLICY-MAKING AS A MALE PRESERVE   Perhaps even more central to feminist scholarship than its view that males dominate the *study* of international relations is its view that males dominate the *conduct* of international relations. As of January 2015, only 10 women served as Head of State and 15 as Head
of Government—very low numbers in a world where there are close to 200 sovereign states.[31] Moreover, only 17 percent of government ministers worldwide

were women with most serving as ministers or cabinet heads in social welfare areas (e.g., education, health) and very few as Ministers or Secretaries of Defense or Foreign Affairs.[32]

An important question that feminists thus ask is "whether it makes a difference that most foreign policy leaders in the world are men."[33] Do state behaviors that realists attribute to the structure of the international system have more to do with the gender of those who make foreign policy within that system? Is it possible, for example, that women would tend to be more inclined toward nonviolent, cooperative solutions to global issues than their more aggressive, war-prone male counterparts?

For some, these differences are a function of biology. Political scientist Francis Fukuyama has argued that the greater propensity to violence that we see manifested in many facets of male behavior—from crime to violent sports to, presumably, the conduct of foreign affairs—is biologically hard-wired from birth.[34] In focusing on biology (sex) as opposed to gender, Fukuyama is really not an IR feminist. Recall that for feminists it is gender roles and norms rather than biology and sex that are key. Still feminist scholars might agree that the practice of international relations has been shaped and defined by a predominantly male outlook, and having more women in power would result in a more peaceful world.

Feminists thus share with liberals a view of the world in which the scope for cooperation among states is much greater than realists will concede. In fact, Fukuyama sees a direct connection between the liberal theory of the "democratic peace" and aspects of feminist theory. He argues that the main reason democracies tend not to fight wars with one another is because women tend to have a greater voice in politics (if not through leadership positions, then through the ballot box) in democracies than they do in authoritarian regimes. It is, in his words, the "feminization of politics" in democratic societies that makes those societies more peaceful.

Other feminists argue that the advancement of the liberal institutionalist approach to peace would be aided by including more women in both the policy-making process and in the conduct of negotiations and diplomacy. Scholar/activists Swanee Hunt and Cristina Posa have argued in support of that claim by pointing to numerous cases—including Northern Ireland, the Indian subcontinent, the Middle East, the Balkans—where the involvement of women has helped resolve long-standing national and ethnic conflict.[35] Former US President Bill Clinton is reported to have noted, following failed peace talks between Israelis and Palestinians in 2000, "If we'd had women at Camp David, we'd have an agreement."

Feminists also share certain positions with constructivists. In the constructivist view, you will recall, human actors shape and reshape the world in accordance with the ideas they hold and the identities they assign to themselves and others. Assuming constructivists are right in the role they assign to norms and ideas, and assuming feminists are right that women have different ideas and ways of thinking about the world than do men, it follows that having more women in power could change the way the world of international relations works. Specifically, as feminists argue, because women have a less "realist" view of the world, the process of reconstructing international relations along more cooperative lines will increase with more involvement of women.

Critics of feminism often point to examples of women in power who have seemed to be as inclined and willing to use force and violence in the pursuit of state interests as any man. Feminist scholar Cynthia Enloe notes three cases that critics of feminism most frequently cite in this regard:[36]

- Indira Gandhi: the first woman to be prime minister of India (1966–1977 and 1980–1984). On her watch, India waged a successful war against Pakistan in 1971, which led to the creation of the country of Bangladesh, and in 1974, India exploded its first nuclear warhead.
- Golda Meir: the first woman to be prime minister of Israel (1969–1974). Meir led the country through the 1973 Yom Kippur War that began with a surprise attack on Israel by Egyptian and Syrian forces. Following some initial setbacks, Israel, backed by US assistance, won the war.
- Margaret Thatcher: the first woman to be prime minister of the United Kingdom (1979–1990). Nicknamed "the Iron Lady," she led her nation to war in response to Argentina's 1982 invasion of the Falklands Islands, which the British had claimed for over 150 years.

However, Enloe and other feminists would counter with two observations: first, women remain a distinct minority at such high levels of foreign policy-making authority, and in order to both rise to power and maintain that power, they have to operate within the rules of the game of politics and foreign policy as it is designed and played by men. Second, the background of the women in power makes a difference. Women who emerge through the feminist movement will approach foreign policy differently than those who emerge through the traditional male-dominated foreign policy apparatus. Thus, the key is to have a critical mass of women in power who do not emerge directly out of that male world (see Theory in Practice 1.3).

Margaret Thatcher, Britain's first female Prime Minister (1979-1990), was known as the "iron lady" for her steely resolve as manifested, for example, in her decision to go to war with Argentina in 1982 over the Falkland Islands. Does gender make a difference in the way leaders conduct foreign policy?

Neo-Marxism

The twentieth century witnessed the rise of Communist regimes beginning in Russia in 1917 and then spreading in the post–World War II era to China, Eastern Europe, Southeast Asia, the Korean Peninsula, and Cuba. The Cold War confrontation between the United States and the Soviet Union, which lasted from 1945 until the collapse of the

Theory in Practice 1.3
Women in Power: A New Generation?

Although women with foreign policy-making authority continue to be a distinct minority around the world, the twenty-first century has witnessed a new generation of women rise to power in several countries. In 2005, Angela Merkel became the first female Chancellor of Germany, and in 2014, Forbes magazine ranked her as the fifth most powerful individual in the world. In 2012, Park Geun-hye broke another barrier in becoming the first female President of South Korea and the first female leader in all of Northeast Asia.

While Merkel and Park emerged from within the political establishment (Park is the daughter of a former South Korean president) other women who came to power after 2000 emerged from backgrounds outside the political establishment. In Liberia in 2005, Ellen Johnson-Sirleaf became Africa's first elected female head of state. She had been prosecuted and imprisoned during the tenure of her predecessors. In Chile, Michele Bachelet was elected president in 2006. Bachelet's father had been tortured by the Chilean military regime of Augusto Pinochet, while she and her mother were both detained. In 2010, Dilma Rousseff was elected President of Brazil. In the 1960s, Rousseff joined an armed guerrilla group to fight against Brazil's military dictatorship and spent time in jail as a result. This trend has raised the hope of many feminists that a larger critical mass of female leaders is emerging and

that their approaches to world politics will distinguish them from their predecessors.

Among the countries where a woman has not yet risen to the pinnacle of political power is the United States. In recent years, women have been elevated to key political positions with foreign policy authority. From 1997–2001 Madeleine Albright was the first woman to serve as Secretary of State, and since that time two other women, Condoleezza Rice (2005–2009) and Hillary Clinton (2009–2013) also served in that same position. However, there has never been a female US Secretary of Defense and, most importantly, no woman has ever been elected President of the United States. The first serious female contender for the presidency of the United States was Hillary Clinton (2008), and it is possible that by the time you read these words, she (or another woman) might have broken through the gender barrier to the White House.

- Why has it taken so long for a woman to be elected President of the United States?

- Do you think you will see in your lifetime a world in which a majority of world leaders are women? Why or why not?

- Would a world in which the majority of world leaders were women be a more peaceful world? Why or why not?

Soviet Union in late 1991, was not just a confrontation between two superpowers; it was also a clash of two ideological systems: Western democratic capitalism versus Communism.

Recent decades, however, have not been kind to Communist regimes. The USSR and its Communist system collapsed; much of formerly Communist Eastern and Central Europe has adopted Western-style economic and political systems; and the Chinese Communist Party, though still in power, has spent the past quarter century replacing, with much economic success to show for it, its centrally planned Communist economic system with a market economy. Except as the subject of historical curiosity, there would seem to be little remaining relevance for a perspective on world politics rooted in the thought of Karl Marx, the nineteenth-century German philosopher who provided much of the intellectual inspiration for the Communist parties and Communist regimes that have now largely been swept into the dustbin of history. In fact, it is the case that the proportion of international relations scholars who work within the neo-Marxist paradigm has declined over the past quarter century.

But stripped of both its expectations for the victory of the Communist cause and its role as the philosophical foundation of real-world Communist regimes, **neo-Marxism** is still seen by some scholars as a relevant alternative view of how world politics operates. Like the other paradigms discussed, the neo-Marxist paradigm is marked by internal variation, but at its core, it has some fundamental assumptions to which all neo-Marxist analysis would subscribe.

In certain very important respects, the neo-Marxist perspective shares some assumptions with realism. Both agree that world politics is inherently conflictual. Moreover, both neo-Marxists and realists see that conflict is rooted in certain structural characteristics of the international and world system. These characteristics largely predetermine the behavior of the human actors who make national policy. Thus, both perspectives share the realist's skepticism toward liberal, constructivist, and feminist optimism that cooperation, under certain conditions, can replace conflict as the central feature of world politics.

At the same time, realists and neo-Marxists diverge on the nature of the conflict driving world politics. For realists, the competitive pursuit of the national interest is at the core of world affairs. International relations, in their view, is about the struggle for power among sovereign states. For neo-Marxists, however, the competitive pursuit of class interests is key to understanding the world. For them, what drives world politics are the competing interests of workers and capitalists in the global economy.

Moreover, neo-Marxists define those class interests in economic terms. Thus, in their view, economic interests drive politics. For realists, in contrast, national interests are defined primarily in terms of military security, and the pursuit of national security drives economics. So, for example, while a neo-Marxist might see US military intervention in the Persian Gulf as driven by the desire to protect the economic interests of big multinational oil companies, realists would see that same intervention as a means to ensure that the United States as a country retains access to oil resources vital to both economic and military security.

These differences can be further illustrated by returning to the case of the US–Soviet Cold War. For realists, it was Soviet military power that doomed the United States to treat the USSR as a threat. The fact that a Communist regime ruled the USSR may have added to American hostility and suspicion, but at its root lay the fact that the Soviet Union was for a long time the only

neo-Marxism
Paradigm that accepts the realist notion that conflict is inherent in world politics, but sees that conflict as driven more by the economic interest of socioeconomic classes than by the geopolitical interests of sovereign states.

country capable of posing a serious military threat to US security (and vice versa). The Cold War was, in other words, a classic case of a security dilemma.

Neo-Marxists view the threat very differently. In their eyes, the clash between economic systems—a Communist economy as opposed to a capitalist one—posed the main threat, as the Soviet regime took a big chunk of the world's people and territory out of economic play. Because of the differences in economic systems, American capitalists could no longer freely invest in, trade with, or exploit the natural resources of the Soviet Union. Thus, neo-Marxists argue, the fact that the USSR had significant military capability may have added to American hostility and suspicion, but the Cold War was determined at its root by the threat to the interests of American business.

Neo-Marxists apply this same type of class-based, economic analysis to a wide range of global events. At the risk of great oversimplification of what are often detailed and nuanced analyses, one might suggest two divergent views of World War I. While realists might see a geopolitical struggle over the military/political balance of power in Europe, neo-Marxists might describe it as an intracapitalist struggle among the ruling classes of Europe over who would economically dominate the less developed world. Likewise, realists might see US intervention in the Third World during the Cold War as efforts to maintain the global balance of power in favor of the United States by keeping friendly, anti-Soviet regimes in power. In contrast, neo-Marxists would view that intervention as the US government acting to support the interests of US business concerned about yet a further loss of markets, investment opportunities, and access to resources.

Non-Paradigmatic Research

non-paradigmatic research

Research conducted outside of the boundaries of the grand IR paradigms.

Amidst the debate among realists, liberals, constructivists, feminists, and neo-Marxists over which of the paradigms is most helpful in understanding the world of international relations, a growing number of scholars have argued for moving beyond the paradigms altogether in favor of **non-paradigmatic research**. In an article that is tellingly called, "Why 'isms' Are Evil," David Lake argues that the interparadigm debate has done more to retard than to advance our understanding of how the world works.[37] According to Lake and others, the paradigms divide scholars into quasi-religious "sects" rooted in competing, and often unsubstantiated, assumptions that lead scholars to talk past one another. Moreover, the search for an overriding grand theory of international relations rooted in one paradigm or the other is viewed by the critics as something akin to the search for the Holy Grail: overly ambitious, doomed to fail, and producing an endless repetition of old debates that does little to advance our cumulative knowledge.

Instead of the search for grand theories that try to explain everything, supporters of non-paradigmatic research argue in favor of "middle-level theories" that address more specific and limited phenomena in international relations. Take the issue of international terrorism for example. Proponents of middle-level theorizing would caution that instead of spending time writing and talking about whether the recent surge in terrorist activity is or is not consistent with realism, the focus should be on less ambitious but arguably more productive studies of the causes of terrorism. Is terrorism associated with poverty, with failed states, with a particular type of political regime, and so forth? Research of this sort often takes the form of hypothesis testing—that is., one looks to see if there is a relationship between an independent variable (e.g., poverty) and a dependent variable (e.g., suicide terrorism) and, by collecting data on suicide terrorism and, in many cases, applying statistical methods, one tests to see whether there is a demonstrable correlation with poverty.

Supporters of the paradigms and grand theory counter that non-paradigmatic research does not advance our knowledge as much as its supporters claim. The challenges of selecting cases to study, measuring variables, choosing the right statistical techniques, or accounting for third variables that might be shaping the outcomes one is observing all inject elements of uncertainty into the seemingly precise findings such research produces. Moreover, the grand theorists argue that even at its best, non-paradigmatic research and the research challenges noted above lead scholars to focus on ever more narrow questions that fail to provide a broader understanding of how the world works.

Who is winning this argument? At the moment there is evidence for both sides. On the one hand, it is indeed the case that non-paradigmatic research has accounted for a growing slice of the international relations scholarship produced since the 1990s. In 2014, a global survey found that 27 percent of IR scholars characterized their work as non-paradigmatic, up from 22 percent just two years earlier.[38] Moreover, the scholarship published in the most prestigious journals contains an even higher percentage of non-paradigmatic work, to the extent that some leading proponents of the paradigms have lamented the fact that the field is more and more abandoning grand theory in favor of simple hypothesis testing.[39]

On the other hand, almost three-quarters of international relations scholars still assert that their research remains rooted in one of the paradigms. Moreover, a closer look at the survey data suggests that even among those who say their work is non-paradigmatic, many have not entirely abandoned the paradigms. When asked their reason for indicating that they do not use paradigmatic analysis, almost half of the 27 percent noted above said it is because their research is based on more than one paradigm.[40] Thus, rather than abandoning the paradigms entirely, they are simply more eclectic in their use of them. If you subtract that group from the 27 percent, you end up with roughly 85 percent of scholars who still see their approach to the study of IR as rooted in one or more of the major paradigms. At the same time, IR scholars continue to see colleagues whose work is strongly associated with the major paradigms as the most influential in the discipline. Asked which scholars have been most influential in the past 20 years (see Table 1.3), the top three vote-getters were Alexander Wendt (a constructivist), Robert Keohane (a liberal), and Kenneth Waltz (a realist).

Conclusion

As noted in the introduction to this chapter, the scholarly study of international relations and world politics aims to develop generalized understandings of how the world works. The goal is not just to understand the cause of a particular war, but of wars in general; it is not merely an attempt to understand how an organization like the UN might successfully resolve a particular conflict, but also what circumstances and strategies are most likely to promote peace in general. As a student, acquiring a general understanding of how the world works is crucial both because it will help you make sense of the mass of information about world events that is reported daily and because it will provide you with a set of concepts, tools, and ways of thinking that you can apply to the global developments you will read about throughout your life.

As also stressed in this chapter, however, scholars of world politics approach their understanding of how the world works through different paradigmatic lenses. The paradigms make different assumptions about how the world works, and these assumptions lead scholars to different conclusions about such key issues as the cause of war, the possibilities for peace, or the potential for institutions like the UN to regulate state behavior (see Table 1.4).

For structural realists, understanding how the world works must begin with the fact of interna-

Table 1.4 Summary of the Major Paradigms

	Realism	Liberalism	Constructivism	Feminism	Neo-Marxism
Nature of World Politics	Unavoidably conflictual	Potentially cooperative	Potentially cooperative	Potentially cooperative	Unavoidably conflictual
Key Actors	States	States and international organizations (IOs)	Individuals, NGOs, transnational advocacy networks	Individuals, gender-based NGOs, and advocacy groups	Socioeconomic classes
Central Idea (Bumper-Sticker Version)	Anarchy breeds insecurity and conflict	Institutions facilitate cooperation	Anarchy is what states make of it	Gender makes a difference	Classes will conflict
Policy Prescriptions	Acquire power (especially military power)	Create IOs, promote democracy, promote economic interdependence	Develop and diffuse norms of cooperation and other valued ideas	Have more women in power	Acquire wealth
Trend-Line in the Discipline[*]	Once dominant paradigm under increasing challenge	Holding steady	Rising fast; the "growth stock" of the discipline	Slow to make inroads, but rising in importance	Steep decline after the Cold War

[*]The trend-line is not necessarily a reflection of the inherent value of each paradigm, but rather, of their trends in popularity among international relations scholars since the 1980s.

tional anarchy. Everything else we see in world politics—in particular, the war and violence that characterize the world—flows from that fundamental assumption. In different ways, all the other paradigms take issue with this realist view. Liberals suggest that international institutions, economic interdependence, and the spread of democratic government can mitigate the negative effects of anarchy. Constructivists argue that the emergence and diffusion of new norms and understandings of how the world works can themselves change the behavior of states and other actors. Feminists argue that to understand how the world works requires accounting for the influence of gender. And neo-Marxists, though sharing much of the realist pessimism about the inherently conflictual nature of world politics, see conflict as driven more by considerations of economic wealth than geopolitical power.

Despite the proliferation of alternative perspectives, the realist paradigm still has its supporters. In fact, although realism's near monopoly on thinking about world politics has been increasingly challenged in recent years, it retains its status as one of the most important paradigms, and it is the paradigm that most often serves as the primary foil for those alternative conceptions. The staying power of realism is in large part rooted in its elegance and efficiency. From a few simple assumptions about the structure of the international system, most notably, the assumption of international anarchy, realism purports to tell us much about how the world works.

However, critics suggest that this very elegance and simplicity lead to an oversimplification of the modern world. Especially in light of recent trends in world politics, the critics charge that realism is not particularly *realistic*, and each of the alternative paradigms suggests different shortcomings of the realist view of the world. Having read this chapter, you are not yet in a position to determine who you think is right. What you now have at your disposal are several frameworks for beginning to understand how the world works.

In the chapters that follow, you will examine in more depth the place of war and violence in world politics, the role of nonstate actors, the patterns of international economic relations, and much more. In examining those issues, we will not in every case explicitly apply all five paradigms discussed in Chapter 1. Instead, the approach in each of the chapters will be to look at the issue through the lens of realism and whatever competing paradigm or paradigms have the most to say about the limits of the realist approach with respect to the topic of that chapter. By the end of each chapter, and even more so at the end of the book, you will be in a position to decide which paradigmatic perspective on world politics you think is most useful in understanding how the world works.

Review Questions

- What, for realists, are the key differences between domestic politics and international politics? What is the significance of those differences?
- What similarities, if any, can you find in the liberal, constructivist, feminist, and neo-Marxist perspectives? How do those perspectives differ from one another?

- The end of the Cold War put realists on the defensive in the 1990s. However, developments in world politics over the past decade or so have led some to argue that rumors of the demise of realism were premature. Do they have a point?

Key Terms

positivism
rational choice theory
paradigm
ideal type
realism
human nature realists
structural realists
anarchy
state of nature
sovereignty
national interests
self-help

security dilemma
defensive realists
balance of power
offensive realists
hegemonic stability theory
idealism
liberalism
absolute gains
relative gains
confidence-building measures
liberal institutionalism
liberal commercialism

liberal internationalism
democratic peace theory
neoconservatism
Kantian triangle
constructivism
balance of threat
transnational advocacy
networks
feminism
neo-Marxism
non-paradigmatic
research

Endnotes

1. Daniel Maliniak, Susan Peterson, Ryan Powers, and Michael J. Tierney, "TRIP 2014 Faculty Survey Report," https://trip.wm.edu/reports/2014/rp_2014/.

2. Thomas S. Kuhn, *The Structure of Scientific Revolutions*, 3rd ed. (University of Chicago Press, 1996).

3. Maliniak et al., "TRIP 2014 Faculty Survey Report."

4. Samuel P. Huntington, *The Clash of Civilizations and the Remaking of World Order* (Simon & Schuster, 1996), 29–30.

5. See the brief selection from Thomas Hobbes's classic work, *Leviathan*, in Phil Williams, Donald M. Goldstein, and Jay M. Shafritz, *Classic Readings of International Relations* (Wadsworth, 1994), 28–30.

6. Webster's *Deluxe Unabridged Dictionary*, 2nd ed., 1983.

7. Carl von Clausewitz, *On War* (Penguin, 1982).

8. John J. Mearsheimer, *The Tragedy of Great Power Politics* (Norton, 2001) is the classic statement of the offensive realist view.

9. The excerpts that follow come from Benjamin Jowett, *Thucydides* (Lothrop, 1883), Book 5. Available online at http://www.shsu.edu.

10. Thomas Hobbes, *Leviathan*, ch. 13.

11. Hans J. Morgenthau, *Politics Among Nations: The Struggle for Power and Peace*, 5th ed. (Knopf, 1978), 10.

12. Daniel Maliniak, Susan Peterson, and Michael J. Tierney, "TRIP Around the World: Teaching, Research, and Policy Views of International Relations Faculty in 20 Countries," May 2012, Institute for the Theory and Practice of International Relations, The College of William and Mary, 34, https://www.wm.edu/offices/itpir/_documents/trip/trip_around_the_world_2011.pdf.

13. Robert Axelrod, *The Evolution of Cooperation* (Basic Books, 1984).

14. Kant, *Perpetual Peace: A Philosophical Sketch* (1795), available online at http://www.constitution.org/kant/perpeace.htm.

15. Michael W. Doyle, *Ways of War and Peace* (Norton, 1997).

16. Robert O. Keohane, "International Institutions: Can Interdependence Work?" *Foreign Policy* (Spring 1998): 82.

17. Thomas Friedman, *The Lexus and the Olive Tree* (Knopf, 2000); Thomas Friedman, *The World Is Flat* (Farrar, Straus and Giroux, 2005).

18. Bruce Russett and John Oneal, *Triangulating Peace: Democracy, Interdependence, and International Organizations* (Norton, 2001).

19. Russett and Oneal, *Triangulating Peace*, ch. 1.
20. Alexander Wendt, "Anarchy Is What States Make of It: The Social Construction of Power Politics," *International Organization* 46:2 (1992): 391–425.
21. Stephen Walt, "Alliance Formation and the Balance of Power," *International Security* 9:4 (1985): 3–43.
22. This scenario is a summary of that developed in Ted Hopf, "The Promise of Constructivism in International Relations Theory," *International Security* 23:1 (1998): 173.
23. For an extended treatment of his "new thinking," see Mikhail Gorbachev, *Perestroika: New Thinking for Our Country and the World* (Perennial Library, Harper and Row, 1988).
24. Marc Lynch, "Al-Qaeda's Constructivist Turn," Praeger Security International, May 5, 2006, online at http://psi.praeger.com.
25. Laura Sjoberg, "Feminist IR 101, Post #4: Common Myths About Feminist IR (and the 'truth')," *Duck of Minerva*, December 13, 2010, online at duckofminerva.com.
26. See, for example, Joyce McCarl Nielsen, ed., *Feminist Research Methods: Exemplary Readings in the Social Sciences* (Westview, 1990). Also see J. Ann Tickner, "What Is Your Research Program? Feminist Answers to IR's Methodological Questions," *International Studies Quarterly* 49 (2005): 1–21.
27. Maliniak et al., "TRIP 2014 Faculty Survey Report."
28. J. Ann Tickner, "Gendering a Discipline: Some Feminist Methodological Contributions to International Relations," *Journal of Women in Culture and Society* 30:4 (2005): 2177.
29. J. Ann Tickner, "Searching for the Princess? Feminist Perspectives in International Relations," *Harvard International Review* (Fall 1999): 47.
30. Cynthia Enloe, *Bananas, Beaches and Bases: Making Feminist Sense of International Politics* (University of California Press, 2001).
31. "Facts and Figures: Leadership and Political Participation," *UN Women*, January 2015, http://www.unwomen.org/en/what-we-do/leadership-and-political-participation/facts-and-figures.
32. "Facts and Figures"
33. Tickner, "Gendering a Discipline," 2177.
34. Francis Fukuyama, "Women and the Evolution of World Politics," *Foreign Affairs*, (September/October 1998): 24–40.
35. Swanee Hunt and Cristina Posa, "Women Waging Peace," *Foreign Policy* (May/June 2001): 38–48.
36. Cynthia Enloe, "Women and Men in the Iraq War: What Can a Feminist Curiosity Reveal?" lecture at Dickinson College, Carlisle, Pennsylvania, March 24, 2008.
37. David Lake, "Why 'isms' Are Evil: Theory, Epistemology, and Academic Sects as Impediments to Understanding and Progress," *International Studies Quarterly* 55 (2011): 465–480.
38. Maliniak et al., "TRIP 2014 Faculty Survey Report," and Maliniak et al., "TRIP around the World," 27.
39. John J. Mearsheimer and Stephen M. Walt, "Leaving Theory Behind: Why Simplistic Hypothesis Testing Is Bad for International Relations," *European Journal of International Relations* 19:3 (2013): 427–457.
40. Maliniak et al., "TRIP 2014 Faculty Survey Report."

Chapter 2
Historical Perspectives
Continuity and Change in World Politics

The November 1989 fall of the Berlin Wall, which had divided Communist East Berlin from democratic West Berlin, symbolized the end of the Cold War. Compared to the way other eras in international relations discussed in this chapter ended, what was different about the end of the Cold War era, and how did that shape the post-Cold War world?

  Learning Objectives

2-1 Explain why 1648 is said to mark the beginning of the modern international system.

2-2 Explain the concert model and its implementation in nineteenth-century Europe.

2-3 Compare and contrast the balance of power and collective security approaches to order.

2-4 Discuss how the Cold War era combined multiple approaches to international order.

2-5 Identify the key characteristics of the post–Cold War era and explain their contribution to international order.

2-6 Compare and contrast the world of the 1990s with the trends in world politics emerging in the first decades of the twenty-first century.

The aphorism that "nothing endures but change" certainly seems applicable to international relations. Weak countries rise to become great powers, while empires that once seemed invulnerable fall. Friendly nations develop differences and become rivals, while historic adversaries mend fences and become allies. Boundaries are constantly redrawn, so maps from decades past no longer accurately represent the contemporary world.

For realists, however, a fundamental continuity remains beneath the surface of ongoing change. While the specific players and issues may change, the nature of the game remains the same. As Hans Morgenthau, the father of twentieth-century realism argued, that game is the struggle for power, and that struggle is "universal in time and space." [1] Thus, from this perspective, we can today learn little about the essence of world politics that Thucydides did not already reveal in his study of the Peloponnesian Wars (see Chapter 1).

For critics of realism, this emphasis on continuity fails to appreciate how international relations have evolved over time. In a world where everything else has evolved—from science and technology to political regime types to social and cultural values—the character of international relations must have changed as well. Surely, the critics might argue, realists cannot seriously assert that the lessons provided by relations among ancient Greek city-states remain the last word on world politics in the globalized, digitally connected world of the twenty-first century. Indeed, some critics argue that in their failure to appreciate the changing character of world politics, realists are blinded to the significant, if still incomplete, progress made in creating a better world.

This chapter will provide a brief survey of world politics from the 1648 Peace of Westphalia to the present. Space precludes in-depth examination of all the twists that world history has provided over the past four centuries. Instead, this chapter focuses on six key dates and the six broad periods in modern international history that those dates have come to symbolize:

1648—the emergence and consolidation of the state system
1815—the Concert of Europe
1919—the post–World War I experiment with collective security
1945—the post–World War II bipolar era
1989—the post–Cold War international system
2001—the world after 9/11

Note that these dates were not selected at random. With one exception (2001), they each mark the end of a major international conflict and the beginning of a new effort to reconstruct a more stable international order. Thus, as we will see, there is a recurrent pattern of conflict, followed by an attempt to redesign the international order, and, eventually, the emergence of another conflict.

In part, this survey is intended to familiarize you with key events in world history. However, more important is the use of those events to (1) compare and contrast the approach to international order represented by each era, (2) consider what these historical events say about continuity (as realists would emphasize) versus change (as critics of realism would emphasize), and (3) see how approaches to international relations theory emerged from and were influenced by specific historical events as scholars attempted to better understand how the world works.

1648: The Birth of the State System

2-1   Discuss the emergence of the modern international system.

state
A political unit able to exercise effective governance and control over a well-defined piece of territory and its population.

nation
Group of people who see themselves, due to shared historical and cultural experiences, as members of a common group.

nation-state
A state that exists to provide territory and governance for a group of people who see themselves as a single nation.

nationalism
Idea that people care about their national identity and are motivated to seek national self-determination by acquiring a state of their own.

A student of world politics in the early twenty-first century might find it hard to imagine a world organized as anything but a system of sovereign nation-states. The modern idea of the nation-state represents the combination of two other relatively recent concepts—the state and the nation. Although those terms are sometimes casually used as synonyms, they mean different things. A **state** is a political unit able to exercise effective governance and control over a well-defined piece of territory and its population. A **nation**, in contrast, refers to a group of people who see themselves, due to shared historical experiences and cultural characteristics, as members of a common group. By combining the two, one ends up with the idea of the **nation-state**—defined as a state that exists to provide territory and governance for a group of people who see themselves as a single nation.

A world that perfectly matches the nation-state ideal of one state to represent every individual nation has never been fully realized. Some nations (the Palestinians and the Kurds are the best-known contemporary examples) lack a state of their own. Some states, such as the former USSR, contain within their borders members of many nations. The modern ideology of **nationalism** is based on the belief that people care about their national identity and that they are motivated to seek national self-determination by acquiring a state of their own.[2] This ideology of nationalism did not exist before the seventeenth century, since neither the idea of the nation nor the concept of the state was very well developed. As a result, the political map of the pre-seventeenth-century world looked very different than it does today.

In Europe, one would have found a map with multiple overlapping political units invoking competing claims to power and authority over the same territory. Some of these would have been the small, localized political units that dotted the political landscape of medieval Europe. Those units included city-states such as Florence and Venice as well as a host of other tiny, by modern standards, territories over which princes, bishops, barons, and trade guilds claimed authority. Overlaying those small political units was the Holy Roman Empire, which claimed authority over all of Christian Europe. While its name conjured the memory of the Roman Empire that dominated Europe through the fifth-century CE, in fact, the Holy Roman Empire was a much less powerful and less centralized political unit. Its geographic reach through much of its history was confined to the territory of contemporary Central Europe, including what is today modern Germany, Austria, parts of northern Italy, and some immediately neighboring territories.

Not only did the size and composition of the main political units differ from the ones in which we now live, but so did the notion of sovereignty. The modern system in which states acquire international recognition as the sole governing authority over a chunk of territory had not yet emerged. The authority of the empire competed with that of the various local political units, and a clear map with sharply defined boundaries separating one duly recognized sovereign political unit from another would not have reflected the realities of the era.

Over time this combination of local and imperial claims to authority came under increasing challenge from two sources. First, advances in industry and technology were rendering the tiny political units of medieval Europe obsolete. In particular, innovations in military technology were a key source of change. The importation of gunpowder from China and its use in new weapons like the cannon made it possible for ambitious monarchs to challenge the authority of smaller political units and amalgamate them into larger political entities that could now be defended and maintained. Thus, the tiny principalities and city-states of medieval Europe were fast becoming obsolete.[3]

Second, religious changes affecting the continent were making the Holy Roman Empire seem anachronistic. The legitimacy of the empire was based largely on the authority the Roman Catholic pope granted to the monarch. However, the Protestant Reformation that occurred in Europe during the sixteenth century led to a series of schisms between Catholicism and a host of new Protestant sects for whom the pope's blessing of imperial rule carried little political or moral weight. Thus, the combination of technological and religious trends affecting Europe at the time pointed toward political units that were both larger and smaller than those that had characterized the continent for several hundred years.

Until recently, scholars argued that it took the Thirty Years' War (1618–1648) to provide a definitive reworking of the map of Europe and the gradual emergence of the medium-sized political units that were the early manifestation of modern sovereign states. The cost of that war was very high. As many as 400,000 soldiers and millions of civilians perished. One estimate is that the population of Germany fell 69 percent, from 13 million to 4 million, and of 35,000 villages in Bohemia, only 6,000 remained after the war.[4] The 1648 **Peace of Westphalia**, according to the conventional wisdom, not only marked the end of the war but also the birth of the modern international system, thusly called the Westphalian system. Three things in particular were said to characterize the post-1648 world and distinguish it from the preceding centuries of European history. First, reforms negotiated at Westphalia led to the effective dissolution of the Holy Roman Empire. Second, the eventual dissolution of the empire cleared the way for the emergence of sovereign political units within the old empire. Third, the Peace of Westphalia marked the end of the period of religious wars in Europe and the beginning of an era in which the great conflicts of the continent were primarily over secular concerns such as territory.

Peace of Westphalia
Collective term for two 1648 treaties that brought an end to the Thirty Years' War and marked the birth of the modern international system in which states are the primary actors.

To be sure, no one ever argued that all those changes occurred overnight. Some of the motion of change was set in place long before Westphalia and much of that change was still incomplete for decades afterwards. Some recent scholarship goes even further in suggesting that the whole idea of Westphalia marking the birth of modern international system is a historical myth.[5] Indeed, the post-1648 map of Europe (see Figure 2.1) would still look very foreign to a twenty-first-century European. Westphalia recognized 300 sovereign states for Germany alone. Moreover, keep in mind that this emerging idea of sovereign states and nations was largely limited to Europe itself. By 1648, Europeans were in the midst of a 500-year period of colonial expansion that lasted from the fifteenth through the twentieth centuries. Over that period, many of the rest of the world's peoples were becoming subjects of European states and thus denied the rights of sovereignty that Europeans were developing for themselves.

Figure 2.1 Political Map of Europe in 1648

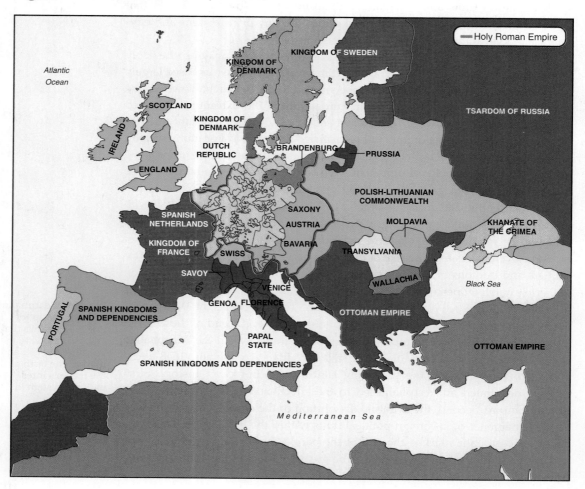

Nevertheless, over time, the emerging recognition of the right of European states to govern their territory and the consequent abolition of the right of the Holy Roman Empire or any higher power to interfere in those affairs laid the foundation of the anarchic system of sovereign states that structural realists still emphasize today. And despite the debate over 1648 itself, the concept of the "Westphalian system" is still generally recognized and utilized as a shorthand for this anarchic era of sovereign states and its consequences—self-help, security dilemmas, war—that those realists might anticipate (recall the discussion of these consequences of anarchy in Chapter 1).

Historians are also divided over the extent to which the new Westphalian order dealt with those dangerous consequences. Some suggest that out of the ideas of sovereignty and nonintervention in the internal affairs of states emerged a primitive approach to security in which the states of Europe were committed to punishing any state that violated the sovereignty of another. In particular, the post-1648 era came, in time, to be characterized by a self-regulating balance of power system (see Chapter 1) in which states would automatically check the rising power of other states by forging temporary alliances. To the extent that such a system worked, its beauty was that states, by acting individually in pursuit of their self-interest, would maintain peace in the international system as a whole.[6]

While recognizing these tendencies, other historians argue that these ideas fall far short of an organized system for ensuring order.[7] Though lasting until 1806, the Holy Roman Empire was, following the Thirty Years' War, weakened but not replaced with a comprehensive and authoritative system for resolving conflicts among the newly sovereign actors. Instead there was heavy reliance on self-restraint and on the ability of key actors, most of whom were monarchies, to see the virtue in maintaining the balance of power. What was missing was a formal system to constrain the newly acquired sovereignty of states and to prevent them from infringing on the sovereignty of others. As one historian put it, such ideas were discussed but were largely "publicists' talk, the discourse of philosophers and theorists. It was not reflected in the deliberations and activities of governments."[8]

What finally forced the Europeans to create a system for order were revolution and war—specifically the 1789 revolution in France and the Napoleonic Wars that followed. The monarchs of Europe viewed the French Revolution as a direct threat to their power and legitimacy. As a model for an alternative form of government, the new French Republic posed an ideological challenge to the European monarchies. And the French buildup of its military power in the ensuing years added a military threat to the established European order. The hostility of the monarchs raised France's fear that the Westphalian principle of state sovereignty would not be extended to their revolutionary regime, and some suspected that the monarchs were plotting to overthrow the new French order.

Napoleon's subsequent conquest of much of the European continent ended any illusion of a continentwide commitment to state sovereignty, collective security, and balance of power. On the contrary, Napoleon's march across Europe was noteworthy precisely for its rejection of those values and for its attempt at total subjugation of defeated states. Indeed, Napoleon's aim seemed to be the creation of a new European empire with France at its core.

Napoleon's reign was essentially ended by his failed campaign in Russia in 1812. Though he hung onto power until 1814, he was eventually exiled to the island of Elba. After escaping from exile in 1815, he returned to France and attempted to reestablish the empire. But after the Hundred Days of renewed Napoleonic warfare, he was defeated at Waterloo and sent into a final exile until his death in 1821. Meanwhile, prompted once again by the experience of warfare, the European powers took another stab at crafting a postwar settlement that would bring order and stability to Europe.

1815: The Concert of Europe

2-2   **Explain the concert model and its implementation in nineteenth-century Europe.**

As the Napoleonic era drew to a close, the Congress of Vienna (September 1814–June 1815) brought together the great powers of Europe, both to settle a series of specific postwar territorial issues and to establish a more general system for order in Europe that would avoid another major war. The key players at Vienna were the members of the Quadruple Alliance: Great Britain, Russia, Austria, and Prussia. In many ways, the system they established for nineteenth-century Europe resembled that of the previous century. European peace was to remain based on a system of sovereign states without a higher power to limit state sovereignty. Likewise, the key to order was still presumed to be found in maintaining a balance of power among the most important states in the system. France was eventually readmitted into the system and considered to be an important player in maintaining that balance.

However, the lesson of the Napoleonic era was that order, security, and balance of power could not be counted on to occur automatically. Individual states, whether because of miscalculation, domestic problems, or limited resources, may fail to adequately balance. In fact, rather than balancing a rising power, a state might be tempted to engage in **bandwagoning**—joining sides with the rising power—in order to be on the winning side of a future conflict.

Beginning at the Congress of Vienna and in a series of subsequent meetings, therefore, the great powers established a more managed system of balancing. This approach is known as the **concert model**. It rejected the assumption of the classical balance of power system of the eighteenth century that the balance would be preserved by self-interested states acting independently and instead relied on collective oversight and maintenance of the balance by the great powers.

bandwagoning
Joining sides with a dominant or rising power in order to be on the winning side. It is the opposite of balancing.

concert model
Balance of power system that relies on collective oversight and maintenance of the balance by the great powers.

Thus, out of Vienna in 1815 emerged a series of informal rules and norms of behavior:

- The great powers have a collective responsibility for overseeing the territorial decisions made at Vienna in 1815.
- Changes to the Vienna settlement cannot be made unilaterally but must emerge from consultation and consensus among the great powers.
- No changes can be made that advantage one power over the others or that upset the overall balance of power.[9]

Collectively, these rules—along with the series of meetings and conferences held among the great powers throughout the nineteenth century—came to be referred to as the **Concert of Europe**.

This concert did not presume to end, once and for all, the problem of war in Europe. Indeed, preserving the balance of power was assumed to require occasional wars against those whose actions posed a threat to that balance. Parts of Europe were rife with war and conflict as well as revolution and counterrevolutionary intervention throughout much of the nineteenth century. By midcentury, wars between great powers central to the concert (e.g., the Crimean War between Russia and Britain) were also taking place. However, there were no continentwide world wars, and, compared to both the eighteenth century and the twentieth century, the nineteenth century was relatively peaceful in Europe.

Two key factors contributed to the successes of the nineteenth-century concert system. First and foremost was the consensus among the great powers, especially in the first few decades after Vienna, that the status quo in Europe was worth preserving. While Britain, Austria, Russia, and Prussia differed in some of their interests, these differences were not sufficient to undermine the commitment to territorial settlements reached in 1815. Second, at various points a key state played the role of a **balancer state** with the power and interest in tending to the balance even when other key states wavered. Historically, Britain was the key balancer in Europe, as an imbalance of power in continental Europe caused by one country or alliance would, in turn, threaten Britain. It also had the means to maintain the balance, especially in light of the dominance of the seas by the British Royal Navy. It is no accident that the nineteenth century is called the era of **Pax Britannica** (the "British peace").

Although the concert system remained more or less in place throughout the nineteenth century, political and economic changes reshaping the continent by midcentury undermined its effectiveness. For one thing, the ideology of nationalism was becoming more powerful, challenging the notion of a shared common interest in stability among the great powers. At the same time, this rising tide of nationalism was linked to a growing demand for popular sovereignty—the idea that final authority and the legitimacy of a state rest on the notion that it reflects the will of the people it governs. This idea of popular sovereignty was central to both the American and French revolutions, and it was later manifested in the revolutions of 1848, during which the expanding class of urban workers created

Concert of Europe
Series of meetings and conferences, and the rules they generated, that took place among the great powers of Europe from 1815 to 1848 and that were intended to produce stability and order.

balancer state
In a balance of power system, a balancer state is one with both an interest and capability to ensure that power is kept relatively in balance.

Pax Britannica
Era of peace produced by British power and hegemony in the nineteenth century.

by the Industrial Revolution challenged the ruling monarchies of Europe. The result was that diplomacy became less about the interests of monarchs and more about the interests of nations. Thus, domestic pressures made concerts and power balances all the more difficult to maintain.

By the end of the nineteenth century, the balance of power in Europe was taking on a new form. Gone was the commitment of the great powers to work in concert to preserve order and the status quo. Gone also was the balance of power system with its flexible, shifting alliances in support of the balance. And gone was the role of Britain as the balancer state untied to any particular alliance.

Instead, two competing and rigid alliances emerged. In 1882 the Triple Alliance—composed of Austria-Hungary and the newly unified German and Italian nation-states—was formed. Subsequently, the Triple Entente of Britain, France, and Russia emerged in opposition. This rigid system ran contrary to the key assumptions of the balance of power system. Consensus and consultation among the great powers were replaced by dissention and confrontation. The days of the European concert were over.

In 1914 a small event with big consequences occurred. Archduke Ferdinand, heir to the throne of Austria-Hungary, was assassinated in Sarajevo by a Serbian nationalist. With backing from its ally Russia, Serbia rejected key elements of the ultimatum issued by Austria-Hungary in response to the assassination. Shortly thereafter, Austria-Hungary declared war against Serbia. Thus contained, such a war would not have been unlike the series of conflicts that characterized Europe during the nineteenth century. Indeed, the hope and expectation in some quarters was that if war did occur, it would be localized in the Balkans. However, the rigid alliance commitments that had evolved extended the Sarajevo incident into the most destructive war in human history. Austria's declaration of war led to Russian military mobilization in support of Serbia, and that led Germany to mobilize and declare war on Russia. In a matter of days in August 1914 France declared war against Germany, Austria-Hungary against Russia, and France and Britain against Austria-Hungary. By late August the war extended to the Far East, as Japan declared war against Germany, and Austria-Hungary declared war against Japan.

The breakdown of the concert system and the emergence of competing alliances help one understand the breakout and rapid spread of the conflict. But other forces were at work as well, and the causes of the war were varied. The rise of nationalism, as previously noted, sharpened the sense of conflicting interests among the European states. In particular, the unification of Germany and its rapid rise in power created a state in Central Europe that posed a special concern to its neighbors. Marxist scholars would add the imperial competition for colonies among the European powers as an important and perhaps primary cause of the war.

While historians are divided as to which factors best explain World War I, all agree that the result was a war unlike even the worst of the nineteenth-century conflicts. Indeed, when measured by the number of casualties produced in a compressed period, World War I was clearly the worst war in human history to that point. By the time the war ended in 1918, approximately 9 million soldiers were dead, with total military and civilian deaths somewhere in the 15 to 20 million range. Millions more were injured. The economic and psychological costs of the war are virtually incalculable.

With the war concluded, attention once again turned to the shape of the postwar international system. That included questions related to territorial settlements and how to deal with vanquished countries. At the more general level, however, leaders wondered how they might reconstruct an international system that could avoid another world war. Thus, just as the Thirty Years' War prompted the creation of the Westphalian system, and as the Napoleonic Wars led to the establishment of the Concert of Europe, World War I led to an effort to create a new system for establishing order and stability.

1919: The Experiment in Collective Security

2-3 Compare and contrast the balance of power and collective security approaches to order.

The vision for creating a new approach to international relations following World War I came from US President Woodrow Wilson. Wilson's vision was notable both for what it rejected and for what it saw as the better alternative. What Wilson clearly rejected was balance of power. As Wilson put it, "The balance of power is the great game now forever discredited. It's the old and evil order that prevailed before this war. The balance of power is a thing that we can do without in the future."[10]

In a January 1918 address to the US Congress, Wilson laid out his famous "Fourteen Points." In point 14, he called for the formation of "a general association of nations" that would provide the basis for order in the international system.[11] Later elaborating on the idea, he noted that the nations of this association would "bind themselves to use economic pressure or military force against any state which should go to war without first resorting to peaceful means.... It was the application to the society of nations of the principle in force in every state. The law breaker who violates the rights of another finds the combined force of society arrayed against him."[12] What Wilson was proposing was a system of **collective security**. As an approach to international order, collective security differs from the idea of balance of power in three important ways.

First, while balance of power assumes that international stability is most likely to be maintained when equilibrium of power exists, collective security assumes that stability results from disequilibrium of power in favor of peace-loving nations. Second, while balance of power theory assumes multiple, flexible alliances as the mechanism for maintaining equilibrium, collective security

collective security
Approach to order in which a global coalition of states agrees to act collectively to repel aggression against any other state in the international system. Also used to apply to regional alliances (such as NATO) that adopt a collective security approach among their own membership.

Table 2.1 Approaches to International Order: Balance of Power Versus Collective Security

	Balance of Power	Collective Security
Preferred Distribution of Power	Equilibrium among great powers	Disequilibrium in favor of peace-loving states
Role of Alliances	Multiple, shifting alliances	One grand alliance of peace-loving states
State Sovereignty	Retained	Transferred to a higher authority
Self-Help	Essential	No longer necessary
Main Paradigm	Realism	Liberalism

systems eschew such competitive alliances in favor of one grand alliance of peace-loving nations. Third, while balance of power remains a system based on self-help, collective security creates a collective organization of states with the right, obligation, and power to monitor and regulate the behavior of individual states in matters of war and peace. In effect, collective security moves toward creating an international sheriff ("the general association of nations") to impose order (see Table 2.1).

For Wilson, this collective security approach was related to his expectation that democratic governments based on the principle of popular sovereignty were the wave of the future. In his view, the potential for the success of collective security was "immeasurably advanced by the destruction of autocracy and the universal establishment of democracy."[13]

Wilson's vision and approach were to become the dominant perspective in the newly emerging scholarly discipline of international relations following World War I. Like Wilson, many scholars in this new field—previously the turf of historians and philosophers—were influenced by the failure of balance of power politics to prevent world war. These Wilsonian scholars were eventually labeled "idealists" (discussed in Chapter 1) by their more skeptical realist critics as a way to discredit their Wilsonian views as naive and utopian. A test of this Wilsonian idealism was the newly established League of Nations.

League of Nations
Organization established, in 1919, to create a global system of collective security in which an attack on one member would be viewed as an attack on all. Replaced after World War II by the United Nations.

The **League of Nations** was established in 1919 by the Treaty of Versailles, and it was very much the product of Wilson's vision and efforts. As noted in its founding covenant, its purpose was to promote international cooperation, peace, and security "by the firm establishment of the understandings of international law as the actual rule of conduct among Governments." As noted in Article 10, "The Members of the League undertake to respect and preserve as against external aggression the territorial integrity and existing political independence of all Members of the League."[14] In other words, aggression against any one member would be met by a collective response from all the other members.

Even in Wilson's purest conception, the League idea was not a complete break from the Westphalian system of sovereign states established in 1648. It was instead a means for sovereign states to work collectively to preserve both the general peace and the sovereign authority of all states when threatened by others. In matters affecting world peace, primary responsibility would reside in the League Council, a smaller body within the larger organization composed of the "principal allied and associate powers" along with four other League members on a rotating basis. In this regard, the League echoed the Concert of Europe's reliance on the great powers to oversee peace and order.

At the same time, the League clearly repudiated the Concert's balance of power approach in favor of the preponderant power of the League itself. Moreover, the concert system had resulted from a series of meetings and understandings among the great powers; the parties did not create a formal, global organization separate from those sovereign states to oversee order and stability in the system. With the League, in contrast, a permanent organization was established for maintaining peace, and member states could not withdraw from their formal commitment to preserve the peace without withdrawing from the organization itself.

While the League helped defuse some disputes among minor powers, it fared less well when great powers were parties to a conflict. When Japan invaded Manchuria in 1931, League action was stymied by Japan, which was a member of the League Council. When Italy invaded Ethiopia in 1934, the League responded with economic sanctions but failed to respond militarily when the sanctions did not have the desired impact on Italian behavior. As Germany threatened its neighbors, culminating in the 1939 invasion of Poland, the League stood by powerless.

Thus, only two decades following the end of World War I, the second great power war of the twentieth century began. In failing to prevent the outbreak of World War II so quickly on the heels of World War I, the League failed in its most important purpose—the preservation of peace. In fact, the League essentially ceased operations during the war. As the most destructive war in world history unfolded, the League Council—the organ of the League directly responsible for maintaining world peace—never met, and the organization shriveled to a bare-bones staff.

The failures of the League were due to numerous factors, not least of which was the absence of several key international players from its membership. As the loser of World War I and the country blamed by the victors for that war, Germany was excluded until 1926. Russia, embroiled in revolution and civil war and now led by the radical Bolshevik regime, did not become a member until the 1930s, by which time other countries (Italy, Japan, Germany) were withdrawing. In 1939, following its invasion of Finland, the Soviet Union (as Russia was then called) was expelled from the League. Perhaps most significant, the United States refused to join, despite the fact that it was US President Woodrow Wilson who advocated its creation. Ironically, the US Senate, dominated by isolationist sentiments, voted down US membership in 1919, the same year Wilson was awarded the Nobel Peace Prize for his contribution to the founding of the League.

More fundamental than the question of membership were inherent limitations of League structures and processes. Decisions in the League Council and in the larger Assembly where all League members were represented were based on the principle of unanimity. One no vote effectively stymied League action. Likewise, implementation of sanctions against those that threatened peace or engaged in other illegal behaviors was left largely to the discretion of sovereign states.

A still larger and even more fundamental criticism goes to the concept of collective security itself. Realist critics of the idea argue that it works best when the great powers are of one mind in responding to a conflict among minor powers. Yet in such circumstances, they would suggest, a formal organization like the League is unnecessary, as the great powers could address such issues on an ad hoc basis. Indeed, that is exactly what the nineteenth-century Concert of Europe was, at least in part, intended to do.

On the other hand, when one or more great powers are engaged in conflict, the collective security system faces a very different challenge. Against a great power determined to act aggressively, the costs of collective action are very high and hard to embrace and implement. When Hitler demanded at the Munich Conference in 1938 that the Sudetenland, an area of Czechoslovakia inhabited by many ethnic Germans, be incorporated into Germany, British Prime Minister Neville Chamberlain gave in. In what came to be viewed as a classic and failed case of **appeasement**—making a concession in order to avoid war—the League of Nations was largely irrelevant.

appeasement
Making of concessions in order to avoid war.

In effect, the complaint of the critics is that collective security works best when it is least needed, but it fails precisely when it is most needed. As Italian dictator Benito Mussolini reportedly put it, "The League is very well when sparrows shout, but no good at all when eagles fall out."

1945: The Postwar Bipolar System

2-4 **Discuss how the Cold War era combined multiple approaches to international order.**

As World War II wound down in 1944 and 1945, world leaders once again faced the question of the shape of the postwar world. As usual, this involved specific territorial issues, but the larger underlying issue, as was the case in 1648, 1815, and 1919, was construction of a system of world order that would help avoid another great power war. One option was to rejuvenate the League of Nations and the idea of collective security. Supporters of this idea argued that the problems of the League had less to do with the general concept of collective security than with the manner of its implementation in the 1920s and 1930s. In particular, they suggested that the absence of key countries from membership and the requirement of unanimity in decision-making had doomed the institution.

However, the leaders of the Allied countries after the war were not among those collective security optimists. Neither US President Franklin D. Roosevelt nor British Prime Minister Winston Churchill nor Soviet leader Josef Stalin harbored serious thoughts of replacing power as the prime currency of international relations or of dramatically curtailing state sovereignty in favor of an international sheriff. In general, because collective security had failed in the 1930s, the idealist approach to international relations that was popular in the interwar period was now giving way to resurgent "realist" thinking. Signifying this shift was the 1948 publication of Hans Morgenthau's classic realist text, *Politics Among Nations*.[15] In systematically articulating and defending the realist view, the book influenced scholars of international relations for generations, and it heralded a paradigm shift in the direction of realism that remained in place at least until the end of the Cold War 40 years later.

The realist approach to order is the balance of power, and according to historian Gordon Craig and political scientist Alexander George, there were at least three versions of balance of power systems from which the victorious states after World War II might choose.[16] First, they could return to the classical balance of power politics that characterized eighteenth-century Europe. Second, they could recreate the concert system of the nineteenth century. Third, they could adopt a revised approach to balance of power based on the idea of **spheres of influence**. In this scheme, key parts of the world would be placed under the influence of one of the great powers. The system would differ from the eighteenth-century model, as it rejected the notion of flexible, shifting alliances to preserve the balance. It also rejected the concert model, in which the great powers cooperatively dealt with challenges to peace and stability whenever and wherever they emerged. Instead, each of the great powers, by mutual agreement among themselves, would be given sole responsibility and free reign to handle its sphere of influence as it saw fit.

spheres of influence
Approach to international order in which key parts of the world would be designated as under the influence of one or the other of the great powers.

Though the idea was attractive to Churchill and Stalin, Roosevelt was skeptical that the spheres of influence approach would permanently stifle each great power's urge to expand outside its sphere. Moreover, even if it did work, it would deny the sovereignty and right of self-determination of smaller, weaker nations within each sphere. Roosevelt's vision was more in keeping with the concert model. As he saw it, the new concert would be based on a consortium of the four Allied powers—the "Four Policemen" as he called them (the United States, Great Britain, the Soviet Union, and China)—who would effectively and with a sense of common purpose maintain order and stability, and prevent the emergence of new powers that would upset the status quo.

In practice, the postwar order that emerged combined elements of several of these approaches. At the February 1945 Yalta Conference, the United States and Britain reluctantly accepted the reality of Soviet dominance of the eastern half of Europe, and Yalta has, in the view of its critics, become a symbol of the spheres of influence idea that Roosevelt in principle had opposed. Meanwhile, at a series of 1944 meetings held at an estate called Dumbarton Oaks in Washington, DC,

British Prime Minister Winston Churchill, U.S. President Franklin D. Roosevelt, and Soviet Communist Party leader Josef Stalin meet to discuss the shape of postwar Europe at Yalta in February 1945. What were the defining characteristics of the post-WWII international system?

the United States, Britain, the USSR, and China discussed a framework for a new postwar collective security organization. In April 1945, at a follow-up conference in San Francisco, the United Nations (UN) was born.

The purpose and structure of the UN reflected a marriage of idealism (or what we called liberal institutionalism in Chapter 1) and realism. On the one hand, the UN resurrected the lofty goal of the League to create a global organization with the authority to monitor war and peace among states. In this regard, the new UN Security Council would be the successor to the defunct League Council. As we will see in more detail in Chapter 5, the Security Council was empowered to use force to deter and respond to countries that violated international peace and security. On the other hand, the United Nations embraced realist notions of state sovereignty and power politics. The Security Council would include as permanent members all the great powers that were victorious in the war, and those permanent members (the United States, the USSR, Britain, France, and China) would have to agree unanimously before the UN could act. Indeed, idealists who were looking to create a successor to the League were disappointed in what emerged. In the words of a Colombian participant in the San Francisco conference, the United Nations "is no more than a police license by means of which a kind of big stick is placed in the hands of the great powers to maintain peace by force, according to political conventions and without any consideration of the notions of justice, fairness, good faith, and legality."[17]

In effect, the new UN resembled an institutionalized version of the 1815 Concert of Europe. It looked to the great powers as the key to peace, and it assumed that those great powers could act "in concert" based on a shared commitment to order and stability. However, instead of doing this through ad hoc meetings and congresses as in nineteenth-century Europe, it was to be done via a permanent international organization.

If the common commitment to peace and security among the victorious Allied powers held up, UN supporters expected that it could provide the basis for a new system of international order. But that hope was soon undermined by the emerging tensions between the United States and the Soviet Union. The end of the hot war in which the United States and the USSR fought as allies against Hitler soon gave way to the **Cold War**—a period of crisis and tension that lasted from the mid-1940s through the end of the 1980s. It was called a "cold war" because direct conflict between US and Soviet military forces was avoided. However, the era was marked by numerous crises, some of which brought the two rivals to the brink of a shooting war.

Cold War
Period of crisis and tension between the United States and the USSR that began shortly after World War II; it ended with the fall of the Berlin Wall in 1989 and the disintegration of the USSR in 1991.

While many of the early Cold War crises centered on tensions in Europe, post–World War II decolonization extended the geographic scope of the US–Soviet rivalry. As the former European colonies acquired independence, and at least the formal recognition of their sovereignty, the United States and USSR engaged in a global competition for influence. In some cases, they sought to buy influence via transfers of military equipment or through economic assistance and investment. In other cases, military intervention occurred. Because direct military confrontation between the United States and USSR was too dangerous, the two superpowers instead confronted one another indirectly via proxy wars.

A **proxy war** is a conflict in which one state confronts a main rival via third parties rather than confronting the main adversary directly. In both the Korean War (1950–1953) and the Vietnam War (1960–1975), the United States fought Communist forces presumed to be advancing the spread of Soviet influence in East Asia. Likewise, after the Soviet invasion of Afghanistan in 1979, the United States provided material support, including sophisticated military hardware, to the Islamic fighters known as the *mujahideen* (whose members included future al-Qaeda leader Osama bin Laden) to aid them in their struggle with the Soviet Red Army.

proxy war
A conflict in which one state confronts a main rival via third parties.

What made Cold War tensions especially dangerous was the existence of nuclear weapons. The United States first acquired the atom bomb in 1945 and used two of them on the Japanese cities of Hiroshima and Nagasaki in August 1945 to bring the war in the Pacific to an end (for more on the impact of nuclear weapons, see Chapter 4). The USSR's acquisition of nuclear weapons in 1949 and the rapid expansion of the nuclear arsenals by both countries kept the superpower relationship on the brink of nuclear disaster.

The closest call was the October 1962 **Cuban Missile Crisis**—a two-week period of extreme tension precipitated by the discovery of offensive Soviet nuclear missiles on the island of Cuba. Soviet leader Nikita Khrushchev later

Cuban Missile Crisis
Two-week period of extreme tension precipitated by the US discovery of offensive Soviet nuclear missiles on the island of Cuba in October 1962.

noted that he had placed those missiles in Cuba to deter a US attack on the Communist Cuban regime headed by Soviet ally Fidel Castro. Perhaps an even stronger motive was to offset the strategic nuclear advantage that the United States held at the time. The United States not only had numerous missiles capable of striking the Soviet Union from US bases, but it also had weapons based in Turkey. The USSR, in comparison, had a much more limited intercontinental capability and lacked any bases in the Western Hemisphere. Among the options for response considered by US President John F. Kennedy were air strikes on the Cuban missile bases and a full-scale invasion of the island. Both options were ultimately rejected as too dangerous, running the risk of inciting a nuclear World War III. Instead, Kennedy ordered a naval blockade of Cuba to prevent Soviet ships from delivering additional missiles. After hours of high tension while the United States waited to see how the Soviets would react to the blockade, the USSR backed down. In exchange for US promises not to invade Cuba and other concessions, Khrushchev ordered the nuclear weapons in Cuba to be dismantled and removed.

The early 1970s witnessed a thaw in the iciness of Cold War relations as US President Richard M. Nixon tried a new policy of **détente**—or relaxation of tensions. Increased US–Soviet trade and educational and cultural exchanges were important elements of the détente policy. But the centerpieces of détente were nuclear arms control talks and high-visibility summit meetings between US and Soviet leaders that came to symbolize the era. In 1972, Nixon and Soviet leader Leonid Brezhnev signed the first **SALT (Strategic Arms Limitation Talks)** agreement, which limited the number of offensive nuclear arms each side could possess and which sharply restricted the deployment of nuclear missile defense systems.

Several factors led to this change. In part, flirtation with nuclear holocaust during the Cuban Missile Crisis suggested to leaders on both sides that they needed to do something to de-escalate Cold War tensions. And by the 1970s, both sides faced weaknesses that increased their interest in reducing tensions. The United States was bogged down in an increasingly unpopular war in Vietnam and was looking for a way out—"peace with honor," as Nixon put it. Because the Soviet Union might be able to pressure its North Vietnamese ally to help achieve that goal, Nixon came to see improved relations with the Soviets as helpful. In general, the US Congress and public had become averse to any US intervention abroad. Thus, the United States sought to relax tensions with the USSR, hoping to restrain it from mischief-making, particularly in developing countries where the Americans and Soviets had been competing for influence. As for the USSR, it was facing economic challenges that made the prospect of increased trade with the United States—especially the import of grain and technology—highly desirable. Thus, each side had something to gain. Henry Kissinger, Nixon's national security advisor and then his secretary of state,

détente
(French for a "relaxation of tensions.") The term is used to refer specifically to the relaxation of Cold War tensions that took place between the United States and USSR in the 1970s.

SALT (Strategic Arms Limitation Talks)
Discussions and agreements signed between the United States and Soviet Union in the 1970s, intended to limit the expansion of offensive nuclear weapons.

sought to pursue a policy of **linkage** in which Soviet access to US trade would be linked to good behavior around the world.

Another important consideration was the China factor. When the Chinese Communists came to power under Mao Zedong in 1949, the assumption was that China and the Soviet Union formed a monolithic Communist bloc united by their common ideology and antagonism toward the United States. While Moscow and Beijing were allies in the early years after the Chinese Revolution, signs of a Sino-Soviet split eventually became evident. By the late 1960s, Soviet and Chinese troops were engaging in border skirmishes. Aware of this growing Sino-Soviet tension, Nixon and Kissinger sought, in improving relations with both those Communist regimes, to play them against one another and extract concessions. In 1972 Nixon became the first US president to visit China since the 1949 revolution, and that visit was followed, for the first time, by the establishment of normal diplomatic relations between the United States and the Chinese Communist regime (see Theory in Practice 2.1).

linkage
Henry Kissinger's 1970s strategy of linking Soviet access to US trade to "good behavior" on the part of the Soviet Union around the world.

realpolitik
Term for "realist politics," or policy based on practical concerns about national interests rather than ideological or moral considerations.

Theory in Practice 2.1
The Foreign Policy of Henry Kissinger

The foreign policy of US President Richard M. Nixon (1969–1974) is often considered a textbook example of the realist paradigm embraced and applied in practice. To the extent that this is the case, it is no doubt a reflection of the influence of Henry Kissinger—Nixon's national security advisor and later his secretary of state. Kissinger was a student of the history of international relations. His PhD dissertation, published in 1957 under the title *A World Restored*, was a study of the nineteenth-century Concert of Europe and of the key personalities who shaped that world. It is also an excellent introduction to political realism that finds echoes in the Nixon/Kissinger foreign policy of the 1970s. Realist elements of that policy include the following:

- **Opening to China.** Despite Nixon's long-established anti-Communist credentials, he pursued the China opening as a means to balance the power of the Soviet Union.
- **US–Soviet détente.** Ideological distaste for a Communist regime was trumped by what Nixon and Kissinger believed they needed to do to forge a relationship with the Soviet Union that would serve American interests.
- **Human rights policy.** Nixon and Kissinger were criticized in many quarters for allowing **realpolitik** (literally "realist politics," or policy based on national interests rather than ideological or moral considerations) to dominate human rights considerations. For example, when the acclaimed Russian novelist and anti-Communist dissident Aleksandr Solzhenitsyn was exiled from the Soviet Union in 1974, the Nixon administration's primary concern was that this not undercut the US–Soviet détente. Thus, the Nixon administration avoided harsh criticism of the USSR, and on Solzhenitsyn's arrival in the United States, there was no ceremony organized by the US government.

The Kissinger case illustrates the interaction of theory and practice and of the descriptive and prescriptive elements present in each paradigm. Like the other paradigms, realism is first and foremost an attempt to describe and explain how the world of international relations works. But implicit in those descriptions are prescriptions for how foreign policy should be conducted. Kissinger, a former academic turned policy-maker, provided one of the best examples of the conscious application of theory to policy of any recent world leader.

- In what sense was the policy of détente a reflection of Kissinger's realism?

- For different reasons, Kissinger is often sharply criticized by both liberals and conservatives. What do you think each side likes and dislikes about Kissinger?

- How would you have handled the Solzhenitsyn case? Why?

The election of Ronald Reagan as US president in 1980 symbolized the end of détente. Reagan famously referred to the Soviet Union as an "evil empire" in a 1983 speech, and his first term marked a shift in emphasis from bilateral arms control to unilateral arms buildup by the United States. However, critics were pointing to the failures of détente as early as 1976 when presidential candidate Gerald Ford went so far as to ban the use of the word in his reelection campaign. Critics on the right (including Reagan) argued that détente placed too much trust in Soviet leaders to live up to arms control agreements and led to the abandonment of allies like Taiwan in order to appease the Communist regime in Beijing. Critics on the left (including President Jimmy Carter) argued that the realism of Nixon and Kissinger led to a neglect of core American values such as the promotion of human rights. The 1979 Soviet invasion of Afghanistan and the Carter administration's decision to boycott the 1980 Olympics in Moscow, to end grain sales to the USSR, and to increase US defense spending effectively ended the détente era a year before Reagan's election.

bipolarity
An international system in which only two major powers are capable of seriously threatening the security and sovereignty of one another.

Despite tensions and crises, the Cold War never turned hot. Realists suggest two key explanations. First, they point to **bipolarity**—the dominance of two major powers. While a bipolar world almost guarantees hostility and suspicion between the two poles, it also, according to many realist scholars, provides a more predictable and stable balance of power in which each side has a lot to lose in going to war with the other. Second, nuclear weapons raised the stakes for both sides and transformed the bipolar balance of power into a bipolar "balance of terror" in which a great power war would obliterate both sides (see Chapter 4).

For some realists, the end of the Cold War seemed a mixed blessing.[18] While the Cold War brought its share of tensions and close calls, it also was one of the longest periods of peace between great powers in modern history. For other observers, however, we were just lucky. In their view, the end of the Cold War era provided an opportunity to create a more positive peace among nations—one based less on the threat of mutual annihilation and more on the original UN idea that peace and stability can result from cooperation and common interests.

1989: The Post–Cold War Era

2-5 **Identify the key characteristics of the post–Cold War era and explain their contribution to international order.**

On December 25, 1991, Soviet President Mikhail Gorbachev resigned and accepted the dissolution of the Soviet Union and the end of the Communist regime that had ruled the country since the revolution of 1917. While Gorbachev's Christmas announcement hammered the final nail into the coffin of Soviet Communism, the symbolic end of the Cold War era was the 1989 fall of the Berlin Wall. Following World War II, Germany had been divided into two countries. The Federal Republic of Germany (West Germany) was a democracy tied to the United States and its West European neighbors, while the German Democratic Republic (East Germany) was governed by a Communist regime and allied with the USSR. The prewar German capital of Berlin was located inside East Germany, but the city itself was divided into democratic West Berlin and Communist East Berlin. The wall was constructed by the Soviets in 1961 to keep East Germans from escaping to West Berlin.

The breaching of the wall on November 9, 1989, by hundreds of thousands of East German protesters was the culmination of a process of political change that Soviet President Gorbachev had unleashed with the reforms of the late 1980s. Faced with a stagnant economy at home and an increasingly assertive political and military challenge from the United States, Gorbachev sought to revive the Soviet system through a comprehensive program of political and economic reforms. His policy of **perestroika** (economic restructuring) introduced elements of free market economics into the Communist system, while his policy of **glasnost** (openness) allowed for a relaxing of state censorship of the media and increased access to information.

perestroika
Policies of economic restructuring in the USSR initiated by Mikhail Gorbachev in the mid-1980s to cautiously introduce elements of market economics into the Communist system.

Although they were intended to save the Soviet system, the Gorbachev reforms unleashed forces that led to the collapse of Communist rule in the USSR and Eastern Europe. The USSR dissolved into 15 separate sovereign states, of which Russia was the largest (see Figure 2.2 and Figure 2.3). Under Boris Yeltsin, the new president of post-Communist Russia, relations with the United States warmed, and the Cold War was declared over. Thus, 1989—like 1648, 1815, 1919, and 1945—was a watershed year in world history.

glasnost
Policy of "openness" initiated by Soviet leader Mikhail Gorbachev in the mid-1980s. It allowed for relaxation of state censorship of the media and increased access to information.

At the same time, 1989 differs in two significant ways from the other key dates in this chapter. First, 1648, 1815, 1919, and 1945 each marked the end of a major world war. In 1989 what ended was not a traditional war but a period of tension known as the Cold War. While one might reasonably suggest that the Soviet Union lost the Cold War, it did not lose in the traditional military fashion, and unlike in the other cases, it did not lose at the hands of a foreign army fighting on its territory or occupying it for years to come.

That first difference largely accounts for the second, which is that the great powers did not make a conscious effort to devise a new system for world order in the name of preventing another major war. The end of the Cold War did not

Figure 2.2 Cold War Eurasia

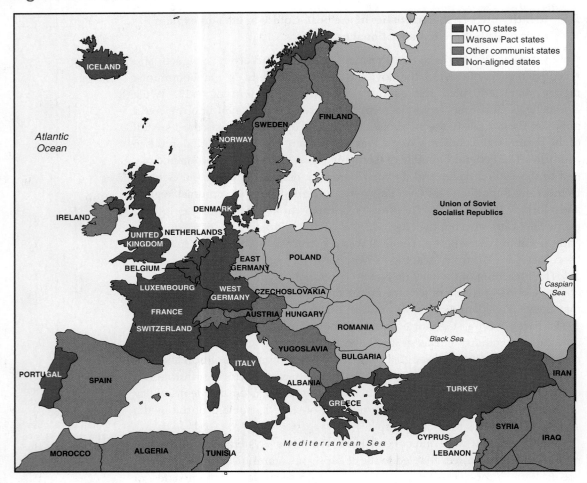

produce a Peace of Westphalia, a Congress of Vienna, a Treaty of Versailles, or a Yalta to provide the framework of a new system. Yet, changes were proceeding nonetheless, and, in the eyes of many observers, those changes were providing the basis for a new era of peace and stability. Among the most significant changes were the following:

unipolarity
International system in which one great power has military capability far greater than its nearest rival, and no other great power is in a position to threaten its security and sovereignty.

1. *The end of bipolarity.* The end of the Cold War was about more than ending a rivalry between the United States and the Soviet Union. It also brought a change in the structure and distribution of power within the international system. The immediate result of the Soviet collapse was the emergence of a period of American hegemony or what one observer called a "unipolar moment."[19] **Unipolarity** refers to a system with one dominant power.

Figure 2.3 Post–Cold War Eurasia

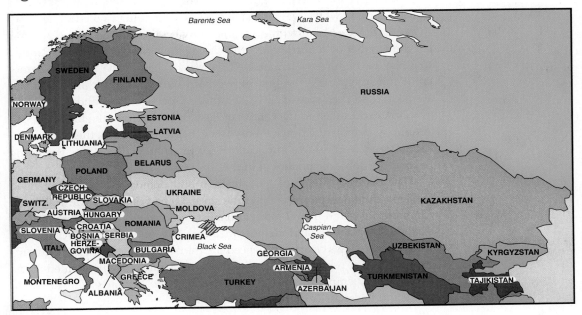

Almost by default, the collapse of the USSR left the United States as that dominant power. The combination of US military, economic, political, and cultural influence after the Cold War could not be matched by any other state. As discussed in Chapter 1, hegemonic stability theory predicts that periods of hegemony or unipolarity will tend to be more stable and peaceful insofar as the dominant power, or hegemon, has the ability to establish and defend rules of the international system. Those rules may, of course, favor the interests of the hegemon, and there is nothing to insure that the stability and order that results will be perceived as just and fair by all. Nevertheless, aggrieved states will not be in a position to challenge the hegemon, and peace will prevail for a time.

2. *Globalization.* While American hegemony provides a realist explanation of post–Cold War peace and stability, critics of realism suggest that there were other factors at work. The telecommunications revolution of the late twentieth century facilitated a dramatic growth in economic interdependence (discussed in detail in Chapter 7). The expansion of global trade and investment, and the incorporation of more and more countries into this interconnected global economic system, produced an era of unprecedented global prosperity in the 1990s. That economic interaction carries political and cultural spillover as global commerce and the technologies, such as the Internet, that facilitate it bring different cultures into ever closer contact. While some see the intersection between the forces of cultural preservation

and those of globalization as prime areas for conflict in the twenty-first century, others see the emergence of an increasingly homogenous and interconnected world in which war and violence in world politics will decline.

3. *Democratization.* Along with economic globalization, in the post–Cold War era the number of countries governed by democratic regimes has expanded to a historic high (see Chapter 4). This trend began in the 1970s, as democratic transitions occurred first in Southern Europe (specifically Spain and Portugal) and then spread to Latin America, parts of Asia and Africa, and even to the post-Communist states of Eastern Europe and the former USSR. Assuming democratic peace theory (see Chapter 1) is right, this democratization trend would have implications for international relations extending beyond the domestic politics of individual states.

The one-two punch of globalization and democratization challenged realism's dominance for the first time since the end of World War II. Liberal commercialists and liberal internationalists pointed to the pacifying impact of the globalization and democratization sweeping the post–Cold War world. Their views clearly influenced the thinking of President Bill Clinton's administration, whose 1996 National Security Strategy for the United States placed heavy emphasis on the importance of those trends both to global peace and the security of the United States:

> Free market nations with growing economies and strong and open trade ties are more likely to feel secure and to work toward freedom. And democratic states are less likely to threaten our interests and more likely to cooperate with the United States to meet security threats and promote free trade and sustainable development. These goals are supported by ensuring America remains engaged in the world and by enlarging the community of secure, free market and democratic nations.[20]

Meanwhile, liberal institutionalists argued that the end of the US–Soviet bipolar rivalry was allowing the United Nations to become a guarantor of order and security for the first time. A promising harbinger of this "new" United Nations was seen during the 1991 Persian Gulf War against Iraq. When Saddam Hussein sent Iraqi forces to invade Kuwait in the summer of 1990, the great powers represented on the UN Security Council responded with one voice in authorizing military action to remove Iraqi troops from Kuwait.

In short, liberals argued that all three points of the Kantian triangle were simultaneously converging in the direction of peace and creating a world that realists could no longer fully explain.

Just as the end of the Cold War emboldened liberals, it also encouraged the emergence of constructivism as a credible challenger both to realist orthodoxy and to liberalism's status as the primary alternative to realism. As noted in Chapter 1, constructivists argued that the end of the Cold War rivalry between the United States and the USSR preceded Soviet democratization and integration into the global economy. Moreover, they argued that these changes occurred without any significant prior reform of the UN or other international institutions. Contrary to what realists and liberals would predict, the radical improvement in US–Soviet relations in the late 1980s and 1990s did not depend on structural change in the international system or the Soviet regime. Instead, constructivists would say, it depended on the diffusion of new ways of thinking about international relations that, over time, influenced the policies of key actors.

2001: The World After 9/11

2-6   Compare and contrast the world of the 1990s with the trends in world politics emerging in the first decades of the twenty-first century.

On September 11, 2001, 19 suicide terrorists hijacked airplanes in the United States and flew two of them into the twin towers of the World Trade Center complex in lower Manhattan. They flew a third into the Pentagon, near Washington, DC. A fourth plane, presumably heading for the US Capitol or the White House, crashed into a field in rural Pennsylvania following a struggle between the hijackers and passengers. Close to 3,000 people died that day.

A common reaction in the popular media to the events of 9/11 was to declare that "everything's changed." But did it really? In the view of some observers, the events of 9/11 mark less a departure from the previous decade than just one more development in the slow unfolding of the post–Cold War international system. Indeed, from this perspective, the 1990s and the 2000s look less like two separate eras than a single post–Cold War era still in the making. That the contours of this new era have taken so long to become clear is perhaps due to the fact that the immediate post–Cold War transition did not occur as the result of a major shooting war among the great powers.

At least for Americans, however, 9/11 represented change because it brought the post–Cold War optimism about a peaceful world bound together by democracy and markets to a sudden halt. Likewise it eroded the sense of invulnerability that America had long enjoyed by virtue not only of its military power but also by the luck of its geographic position in the Western hemisphere. The world, for Americans, suddenly seemed much more dangerous, and the post-9/11 foreign policy of President George W. Bush's administration clearly reflected this change in attitude. Instead of assuming that democratization was automatically leading to global peace, American neoconservatives (see Chapter 1) now argued that democracy had to be exported—in some cases, by military means. Adding into the equation a newly elevated fear that the next terror attack on US soil might involve nuclear, chemical, or biological weapons only heightened the sense of insecurity.

Without waiting for approval from the UN Security Council, the United States initiated a **preemptive war** against Iraq in 2003, ostensibly to eliminate the

preemptive war
A war in which a country fires the first shot in the expectation of an imminent attack by an adversary that would severely compromise vital interests.

In one of the most famously symbolic images from the Iraq War, U.S. forces pull down a statue of Saddam Hussein from Baghdad's Firdos Square as Iraqis cheer them on. The Bush administration suggested that the US invasion of Iraq was a justified preemptive war. Do you agree? Why or why not?

threat of Iraqi weapons of mass destruction and to facilitate Iraqi democratization. Under international law, initiating a war does not necessarily constitute illegal aggression if: (1) it is done in anticipation of an imminent military attack on one's vital interests, and (2) waiting for the other side to strike first would put one at such a disadvantage as to place those vital interests at risk. The 2002 US National Security Strategy was notable precisely for its emphasis on the right of the United States to act unilaterally and preemptively if necessary to forestall another 9/11 type of attack on US soil.[21] The document suggested that the combination of weapons of mass destruction and international terrorism made the threat to US vital interests permanently imminent.

At the same time, the events of 9/11 can also be used to symbolize more deep-rooted changes in the international system that extend well beyond their impact on the United States; some have begun to talk about the emergence of a "post-post–Cold War era."[22] General characteristics of the emerging world order have been increasingly debated and include the following:

1. *A new multipolarity?* For most realists, the "unipolar moment" that characterized the 1990s was always assumed to be temporary as concentration of power eventually leads to balancing efforts by others. Thus, unipolar moments eventually end and are replaced by either a new bipolarity or an emergent **multipolarity** with three or more dominant powers. In the late 1990s, however, some observers argued that such balancing efforts against the United States were not yet in evidence and that realists had some explaining to do.[23] But fast forward to the world of 2015, and evidence of balancing was becoming apparent, less via a formal anti-American alliance

multipolarity
An international system in which three or more great powers have the capability to threaten the security and sovereignty of one another.

than through largely uncoordinated efforts taken in tandem by actors seeking to challenge US dominance. Significant, long-term increases in Chinese military spending, a more assertive Russian foreign policy acting contrary to US interests, Iranian efforts to acquire nuclear weapons and to assert a greater role in the Middle East, North Korea's continuing development of nuclear warheads and missiles, and the anti-American policies of former Venezuelan president Hugo Chavez and his successors can all be viewed as challenges to US dominance and unipolarity.

One of the more obvious efforts to challenge US hegemony and the US-dominated world order was represented by Russia's 2014–2015 invasion of Crimea and eastern Ukraine. In so doing, Russian President Valdimir Putin had multiple motivations, not all of which had to do with balancing against the United States. For Putin, as for many Russians, Crimea, and Ukraine were historically a part of the Russian and, later, the Soviet Empire and were lost as the Cold War ended at a moment of Russian weakness. The 2014–2015 invasions were thus intended to restore, in Putin's view, the natural order of things in Ukraine. But, at the same time, Putin's actions were a direct challenge to the United States and to the post–Cold War order established by the United States and its allies in Europe. In particular, Putin's larger game was to undercut the NATO alliance—through which the US exercised its hegemony in Europe—by raising doubts about the credibility of NATO's commitment to preserving order in Europe and about the willingness of the United States to come to the defense of countries both outside of NATO (e.g., Ukraine) and inside NATO (e.g., the Baltic states). Whether or not Putin's efforts at balancing the United States in Europe succeed, it seems clear that such balancing was his goal.

Such actions by other states—combined with the strains of America's continuing involvement in the quagmire of the Middle East, its massive budget and trade deficits, its polarized and often dysfunctional political system, and its continued vulnerability to terrorist attacks—have led its adversaries to suggest that US global dominance is in decline. Allies of the United States seem to be wondering about the same thing. By 2015, Israel, Saudi Arabia, and Egypt all seemed to have growing doubts about the will, wisdom, and capabilities of American leadership. In East Asia, many US observers have been concerned that Japan and South Korea were also beginning to question the reliability of US security guarantees. And the nature of the US response to Putin's Ukrainian policy has led even NATO members—especially new members in Central and Eastern Europe—to worry as well.

The concern is not only that American hard power—the ability to get one's way by threats or use of military or economic coercion—is on the wane but that America is also facing a decline in its soft power. **Soft power** is the ability to influence others via attraction rather than coercion. According to Joseph Nye, the political scientist most responsible for the development of the concept, the sources of a country's soft power are a country's culture

soft power
Ability to shape the preferences and influence the behavior of others via attraction rather than coercion.

("From Hollywood to Harvard"), its political values ("from democracy to freedom of speech to opportunity"), and the legitimacy of its foreign policy (as seen by others). [24] The economic crisis that began in 2008, the seeming inability of the US political system to respond effectively to the many current challenges it faces, and unpopular and unsuccessful American Middle East policies have combined to deplete US soft-power resources.

While the challenges facing the United States are real, it is important to emphasize that the United States remains the predominant global power in many respects. In particular, what continues to separate the United States from potential challengers is that its combination of economic, military, and technological prowess remains unmatched by any other country. In 2006 the United States accounted for two-thirds of great power defense expenditures, while China, America's presumed twenty-first-century rival, accounted for only 6 percent.[25] Despite expectations of a decline in US defense spending in 2015, along with expectations of Russian and Chinese increases, the gap remains large, with the United States spending more than twice as much as Russia and China combined.[26] Likewise, measured by market exchange rates, the US economy remains the world's largest, accounting for roughly one-quarter of global production.[27] Of all the Western economies affected by the global economic crisis of 2008, the United States has been among the very best in recovering. And one of the greatest long-standing weaknesses of the United States, its dependence on imported oil, has been greatly ameliorated by the oil-shale boom, which has sent US oil production soaring.

As for soft power, America's potential rivals all face limits of their own. In Europe, the Greek crisis, continuing economic stagnation, and increased political polarization both within and among nations have combined to take the luster off of the grand Eurozone experiment (for more details on these European challenges see Chapter 7). At the same time, Russia's economy continues to be burdened by corruption and inefficiency, and the Russian model has little global appeal beyond Russian-speaking separatists in neighboring countries and a handful of European fringe politicians. Even China, despite decades of spectacular growth, faces an increasingly uncertain future as its declining growth prospects, and the resulting concern about political instability, have taken some of the sheen off of its authoritarian capitalist model. Meanwhile, the election of Barack Obama as US president was viewed by some as a potential boost to American soft power, and there is evidence that despite the problems and challenges faced by the United States, the American global image has recovered a bit from the beating it took in the early 2000s. (see Theory in Practice 2.2).

2. *The end of Eurocentrism?* The history of modern international relations is often written as if Europe is the center of the universe. There is some justification, as Europe's leadership in the Industrial Revolution allowed it to dominate world politics in the post-1648 era. While other civilizations

Theory in Practice 2.2

Soft Power and the Obama Effect

In June 2008 political scientist Joseph Nye wrote, "It is difficult to think of any single act that would do more to restore America's soft power than the election of Obama to the presidency." Nye first coined the phrase "soft power" in 1990 and further developed and popularized the concept in his 2004 book, *Soft Power: The Means to Success in World Politics*. The prediction of an "Obama effect" was rooted in several factors: (1) he would be replacing a president, George W. Bush, who was very unpopular around the world; (2) Obama seemed poised to reverse some of the policies that had made Bush unpopular, including promising to end the war in Iraq and to close the detention center at Guantanamo Bay, where terrorist suspects were allegedly tortured by US personnel; and (3) Obama's status as the first African American US president.

Less than a year after the election, there was already evidence that the Obama effect was real. The July 2009 Global Attitudes Project survey conducted by the Pew Research Center showed that the US image had improved significantly in most of the world (Russia and the Middle East were the most notable exceptions). There was a subsequent dip generated by the NSA spying controversy, accelerating US drone strikes, and failure to follow through on the promise to close Guantanamo, but by 2014 Pew was reporting that the American global image had stabilized and was recovering. The question is whether that improvement in the US image really translates into a soft power boost for the United States.

Realists would be skeptical, arguing that Obama's personal popularity cannot trump the structural characteristics and conflicts of interest among states that shape international politics. Indeed, realists tend to view soft power less as an independent phenomenon than as a by-product of hard power, as the attraction that defines soft power is rooted in hard power assets such as economic and military strength. For liberals like Nye, in contrast, soft power is important in its own right. In fact, they would argue that the image and reputation of a country and its leaders could either augment or diminish its ability to use hard power. Others will have less reason to fear the accumulation and even the use of hard power if a country and its leaders are viewed positively. Likewise, constructivists might argue that a country's soft power is rooted in its relationship to global norms. To the extent that a country adheres to those norms, its soft power can increase, and its legitimacy and freedom of action accumulate.

- Was there any evidence of the translation of the "Obama effect" into international policy successes for the United States during the Obama presidency?

- Has the "Obama effect" stood the test of time? How has the global image of the United States evolved as we move into the post-Obama era?

- Some observers note an increase in Chinese soft power in recent years. What evidence of this trend exists, and how would realists, liberals, and constructivists explain it?

have long and proud histories, including periods when such civilizations were the most advanced, recent centuries have seen those once-proud civilizations colonized and dominated, sometimes very directly, by Europeans. Before 2001, and even before 1989, change in this regard was already in evidence. An era of decolonization and independence followed World War II, and by shear numbers alone, the voices of those newly independent states became heard. This challenge to Western dominance was evidenced in the radical extreme by the events of 9/11 and, more recently, by the rise of ISIS in Iraq and Syria and its spread to other parts of the Middle East. Perhaps even more significant over the long term, however, has been the contemporary economic emergence of Asia—and, in particular, the economic development of China and India—heralding a shift in the global balance of power and influence from West to East. In fact, today, one often hears references to the twenty-first century as "the Asian century."

As the center of gravity in world politics has shifted eastward from Europe, a new cultural dimension has arisen in international relations. If one thinks of the major conflicts, disputes, and wars that have occurred since 1648, one sees that they have centered on disputes among Western states. Even the Cold War can be viewed as an intra-Western dispute. Although the US–Soviet rivalry was often characterized as an East–West conflict, it is important to recall that the Communist doctrine of the Soviet regime was rooted in the thought of Karl Marx, a nineteenth-century German political philosopher. Moreover, Russia, the nations of Western Europe, and the United States all have Christianity as their dominant religion. As China, India, and other distinctly non-Western states emerge as key international actors, one finds for the first time in modern world politics that the dominant states, and the main focal points of international conflict, cross cultural and religious lines.

3. *A backlash to democratization and globalization?* The trends discussed above—the relative decline of the United States, the emergence of a new multipolarity, the end of Eurocentrism, the rise of Asia, and the general expansion of the global playing field across cultural lines—have all led to a reconsideration of the popular 1990s view that democratization and globalization are the unstoppable waves of the future. To the extent that political democracy and free market economics have been historically associated with the rise and dominance of the West over the past two centuries and with, more recently, the dominant role played by the United States in world politics, the relative decline of the United States and the West, in general, reopens the debate over the future of democracy and globalization. As we will discuss in more detail in later chapters, the global economic crisis that began in 2008 only added fuel to this debate.

For a time, things actually seemed to be moving in a different, more positive direction. When, in December 2010, Mohamed Bouazizi, a young Tunisian street vendor, set himself on fire following repeated harassment by local authorities, it proved to be the catalyst for the **Arab Spring**—the wave of protests that swept through the Middle East and North Africa. Those protests against corrupt, authoritarian regimes seemed to suggest that the wave of democratization, which had previously changed the course of politics in much of southern and eastern Europe, Latin America, and parts of Asia and Africa, was finally washing up on the shores of the Muslim world. Within two years, authoritarian regimes were overthrown in Tunisia, Egypt, Libya, and Yemen. All of a sudden, the view held by some that there was a fundamental incompatibility between either Islam, Arab culture (or both) and democracy seemed to be under challenge.

Arab Spring
The wave of anti-regime protests that swept through the Middle East and North Africa beginning in December 2010.

But fast forward a few years, and the picture turns rapidly bleak. In Egypt in June 2013, a military coup ended the country's brief flirtation with democracy; in Yemen in January 2015, Houthi militias, supported by Iran, forced the president to resign and dissolved the country's parliament; in Libya, following the 2011 uprising which, with NATO assistance, overthrew dictator Muammar Gaddafi, a brief experiment with democratic elections was followed by civil war, a failed state, and another base for ISIS inspired militants. Meanwhile, Syria and Iraq have descended into chaos and first-century brutality as a result of the advance of ISIS, while Saudi Arabia and the Gulf states have continued to resist any kind of democratic change. Only Tunisia thus far has seemed to defy the trend back toward authoritarian rule. And, of course, it is not just the Middle East. Putin's Russia has become increasingly authoritarian over time, and there is still no evidence of democratic reform in China.

In short, the optimism of the early post–Cold War era has been replaced by a new pessimism about world politics in the second decade of the twenty-first century. The sources of global order that characterized the 1990s seem to be weakening and have been replaced by evidence of global *dis*order and renewed great power competition. For the first time in decades, a few respectable scholars have begun to talk about the possibility, if not the probability, of a great power war between the United States and China or the United States and Russia. The questions as we move forward are (1) whether the great powers will once again join in a global effort to manage the challenges and strains of the twenty-first century, and (2) how successful those efforts will be. In one important respect, the challenge on both counts may be greater than it has been in the past. For the first time since 1648, the current and emerging great powers extend beyond the European world. Thus, the consensus for a concert in any form might be quite difficult to achieve.

Conclusion

Across the four centuries since the Peace of Westphalia, many dramatic events have occurred and much has changed in world politics. Economic development, technological advances, world wars, revolutions, the collapse of empires, and the emergence of new nations, new states, new ideologies, and new forms of governance—all would make the world of the early twenty-first century seem a largely foreign place to a resident of 1648 Europe. At the same time, we have seen amidst this change a familiar pattern: war and conflict followed by efforts to design a system to prevent similar conflicts, followed by the breakdown of that system with the next war (see Table 2.2). The central question is whether those multiple efforts have changed the way the world works. In particular, the question is whether those efforts have led to progress in creating a more peaceful and orderly world.

For realists, the twenty–first-century world is not essentially different from the world of 1648. The system of sovereign states that emerged from Westphalia has remained largely intact, military power is still the main currency of international

Table 2.2 Six Eras in International Relations History: A Summary*

War	Settlement	New Era in International Relations
Thirty Years' War (1618–1648)	Peace of Westphalia (1648)	Classical balance of power system (seventeenth and eighteenth centuries)
Napoleonic Wars (1803–1815)	Congress of Vienna (1814–1815)	Concert of Europe (1815–end of nineteenth century)
World War I (1914–1919)	Treaty of Versailles (1919)	Post–World War I collective security (1919–1939)
World War II (1939–1945)	Yalta Conference (1945)	Cold War bipolarity (1945–1989)
Cold War (1945–1989)	Fall of the Berlin Wall (1989)	Post–Cold War era (1989–2001)
2001 Terrorist attacks and US war on terror (2001–?)	?	Post-post–Cold War international system? (2001–?)

***NOTE**: Chart indicates the war that brought one era to an end, the settlement (treaty or other key event) that ended the war, and the new era in international relations history that ensued before being upset by the next war. Note that the 2001 terrorist attacks on the United States and the subsequent US war on terror have not yet produced a definitive settlement, and the contours of the "post-post–Cold War era" remain unclear.

influence, and balance of power has remained the only practical approach to the problem of war and disorder. Although idealist rhetoric after major wars sometimes promised a redesign of the international system in ways that would transcend power politics, the performance seldom met the promise. Indeed, such idealist rhetoric notwithstanding, realists would note that the approaches to order represented by 1648, 1815, 1919, and 1945 all shared an understanding that those states with the greatest power would be most essential to the postwar order, and they were accorded privileged status in the approaches to order thereby established.

While realists emphasize continuity, many critics of realism emphasize change. In particular, they call attention to the noticeable, if gradual and still incomplete, progress in moving from a completely unmanaged and unregulated system of self-help toward more managed approaches to international order. In moving from the classical balance of power system to the concert model and then to collective security as manifested in the League of Nations and the UN, we have moved perceptibly, if not completely, away from the Hobbesian war of all against all. The end of the bipolar Cold War confrontation between the United States and the Soviet Union provided, in the view of many critics of realism, a historic opportunity to further a four-centuries-long, gradual process of changing how the world of international relations works. Whether that process of change is real and whether it is, in fact, challenging realist understandings of how the world works is a story that will be examined across a range of issues in the remaining chapters of this book.

Review Questions

- Are you more impressed by the elements of change or continuity in world politics since 1648? Has there been forward progress in creating a system of world order, or are we continually reinventing the wheel?

- If an international conference of states was held this year to discuss world order in the twenty-first century, would you recommend that the world community embrace a balance of power or a collective security approach? Why?

- If such an international conference was held this year, who would and who should be the key players? Why?

Key Terms

state
nation
nation-state
nationalism
Peace of Westphalia
bandwagoning
concert model
Concert of Europe
balancer state
Pax Britannica

collective security
League of Nations
appeasement
spheres of influence
Cold War
proxy war
Cuban Missile Crisis
détente
SALT (Strategic Arms
   Limitation Talks)

linkage
realpolitik
bipolarity
perestroika
glasnost
unipolarity
preemptive war
multipolarity
soft power
Arab Spring

Endnotes

1. Hans J. Morgenthau and Kenneth W. Thompson, *Politics Among Nations: The Struggle for Power and Peace*, 6th ed. (Knopf, 1985), 37–38. Original edition published 1948.
2. *Stanford Encyclopedia of Philosophy*, http://plato.stanford.edu/entries/nationalism/.
3. On the relationship between military technology and state formation in modern Europe, see Bruce D. Porter, *War and the Rise of the State: The Military Foundations of Modern Politics* (Free Press, 1994).
4. Kalevi J. Holsti, *Peace and War: Armed Conflicts and International Order 1648–1989* (Cambridge University Press, 1991), 28–29.
5. Andreas Osiander, "Sovereignty, International Relations, and the Westphalian Myth," *International Organization* 55:2 (Spring 2001): 251–287.
6. Seyom Brown, *New Forces, Old Forces, and the Future of World Politics: Post-Cold War Edition* (HarperCollins, 1995), 47.
7. Holsti, *Peace and War*, 40. Also see Gordon A. Craig and Alexander L. George, *Force*

and Statecraft: Diplomatic Problems of Our Time, 3rd ed. (Oxford University Press, 1995), 21.
8. Craig and George, *Force and Statecraft*, 21.
9. Adapted from a more detailed summary in Holsti, *Peace and War*, 167.
10. Quoted in Joseph S. Nye Jr., *Understanding International Conflicts: An Introduction to Theory and Practice*, 4th ed. (Longman, 2003), 85.
11. Woodrow Wilson, speech to joint session of the US Congress, January 8, 1918, http://wwi.lib.byu.edu.
12. Woodrow Wilson, *The State* (D. C. Heath, 1918), from an excerpt in Evan Luard, *Basic Texts in International Relations* (St. Martin's, 1992), 270.
13. Woodrow Wilson, *The State*, in Luard, 270.
14. Covenant of the League of Nations, http://www.yale.edu/lawweb/avalon/leagcov.htm.
15. Morgenthau and Thompson, *Politics Among Nations*.
16. Craig and George, *Force and Statecraft*, 90–94.

17. Quoted in Alvaro T. Mejia and Carlos H. Holguin, *Colombia in the United Nations*, ch. 1, http://www.un.int/colombia/english/colombia_onu/chapter%201.htm.

18. John Mearsheimer, "Why We Will Soon Miss the Cold War," *Atlantic Monthly* (August 1990): 35–50.

19. Charles Krauthammer, "The Unipolar Moment," *Foreign Affairs* 70:1 (1990–1991): 23–33.

20. 1996 National Security Strategy of the United States, Preface, http://www.fas.org.

21. The National Security Strategy of the United States, September 2002, http://www.whitehouse.gov.

22. See, for example, Richard Haass, "Defining U.S. Foreign Policy in a Post-Post–Cold War World," 2002 Arthur Ross Lecture, Remarks to Foreign Policy Association, New York, April 22, 2002, http://www.state.gov.

23. See, for example, Jack Snyder, "One World, Rival Theories," *Foreign Policy* (November/December 2004): 56.

24. "Harvard Professor Joseph Nye on Hard and Soft Power," *Spiegel Online International* (August 2009) http://www.spiegel.de/international/world/harvard-professor-joseph-nye-on-hard-and-soft-power-it-is-pointless-to-talk-to-al-qaida-a-643189.html.

25. Stephen G. Brooks and William C. Wohlforth, *World Out of Balance: International Relations and the Challenge of American Primacy* (Princeton University Press, 2008), 29.

26. *The Economist*, May 3, 2014, http://www.economist.com/news/united-states/21601535-no-other-country-comes-close-americas-hard-power-its-lead-slipping-unrivalled.

27. Brooks and Wohlforth, *World Out of Balance*, 32. If measured by purchasing power parity (PPP), China and the US run neck and neck for the title of the world's largest economy. But by either measure, US GDP per capita is far higher than that in China.

Chapter 3
Levels of Analysis
The Sources of Foreign Policy

One of many photos of Russian President Vladimir Putin striking a macho pose, presumably intended to convey an image of strength and determination. To what extent does the personality and worldview of a leader shape a state's foreign policy? To what extent, in contrast, is foreign policy a reflection of the essential interest of states and the constraints imposed by the international system?

 Learning Objectives

3-1 Explain the relationship among the international system level of analysis, the rational actor model of decision-making, and the realist paradigm.

3-2 Explain how the state level of analysis and the bureaucratic politics model of decision-making each challenge the view of states as rational, unitary actors.

3-3 Discuss the role individuals play in the making of foreign policy and the conduct of international relations.

Why did Russia invade Crimea in 2014? In answering that question, realist scholar John Mearsheimer's basic answer is that the Crimea invasion was a Russian effort to protect its national interests given the post–Cold War expansion of the US-led NATO alliance into countries on Russia's western flank. Mearsheimer suggests that any Russian leader faced with this external threat, indeed any leader of any great power faced with a similar challenge, would react in much the same way.[1] Mearsheimer's analysis is classic realist. It assumes three things: (1) that Russia is a unitary actor with an overriding set of truly national interests that it consistently seeks to attain, (2) that Russian foreign policy is driven largely by challenges to those interests emanating from the larger international system, and (3) that Russian leaders are engaged in a rational process of finding and implementing the best means (foreign policies) to achieve their ends (the Russian national interest).

Critics question all three of those realist assumptions. First, they would question whether there is such a thing as an objective set of national interests that Russia, or any country, consistently seeks to defend. Instead they would suggest that there are multiple versions of "the national interest," shaped by the different interests of the various players involved in the making of Russian, or any state's, foreign policy.[2] Second, they would question whether all countries would respond in the same way to similar developments emanating from their external environment. Instead they would argue that differences in both the domestic characteristics of states and in the individual qualities of leaders who govern them might account for multiple possible responses to similar external challenges. Third, they might question whether foreign policy-making always reflects a rational process of linking ends and means. Instead, they would argue that human decision-making tends to be, at best, only imperfectly rational.

This chapter will look more closely at the sources of state behavior in international relations and world politics. In doing so, we will use the idea of **levels of analysis** as our organizing framework. The concept of levels of analysis owes much to Kenneth Waltz's classic 1959 book *Man, the State, and War* in which Waltz asks the big question of why war is such a frequent event in international relations.[3] He proposes three possible answers—what he terms "images" of international relations. The first image, the individual level of analysis, attempts to explain war as a result of characteristics that are inherent in human nature. The second image, the state or domestic level, focuses on characteristics of individual states. The third image, the international system level of analysis, incorporates all those explanations of war that lie in characteristics of the international system as a whole. Let's take a closer look, beginning with Waltz's third image—the international system level.

levels of analysis
The mix and location of the factors that influence the foreign policy behavior of states. The three most commonly considered are international system level, state level, and individual level.

The International System Level of Analysis

3-1 **Explain the relationship among the international system level of analysis, the rational actor model of decision-making, and the realist paradigm.**

Waltz's third image of international relations places the roots of state behavior in the overall structure and characteristics of the international system. Structural realists (neorealists), including Waltz himself who is generally regarded as the father of contemporary structural realism, emphasize the international system as the most important source of state behavior. They assume that a state's foreign policy can be largely understood without reference to the internal characteristics of that state. All one needs to know to understand state behavior is the nature of the larger international system within which individual states operate.

System Level Attributes

For a structural realist there are two primary attributes of the international system that shape state behavior. Most fundamental is international anarchy. As discussed in Chapter 1, anarchy mandates a number of state behaviors, including the acquisition of military power and other forms of self-help. However, while anarchy, for realists, is a constant, there is another important characteristic of the international system that is continually in flux, and that is the distribution of power. Depending on how power is distributed in the system as a whole, individual state behavior will vary accordingly. For example, in a bipolar system like that of the Cold War era, the two major poles will be unavoidably wary of one another and have an adversarial relationship regardless of internal regime type or leadership. But if your state is one of the three main powers in a tripolar system (three dominant states), your key objective is to make sure you are not the "odd man out" in an alliance of the other two major poles. In a multipolar system with more than three powers, states, according to balance of power logic, should and will seek to prevent the emergence of a dominant coalition. In all cases, the internal character of states is less important than the overriding systemic logic.

A good illustration of the changing impact of the international system on the behavior of states is the lessening of tensions (détente) that characterized both US–Soviet and US–Chinese relations in the early 1970s. As noted in Chapter 2, US President Richard Nixon established normal diplomatic relations with Communist China for the first time since the 1949 Communist seizure of power on the Chinese mainland, while simultaneously negotiating arms control agreements and expanding trade with Moscow. That Richard Nixon—a man who cut his political teeth preaching an uncompromising form of anti-Communism back in the 1950s—would be the man responsible for the openings to both Beijing and Moscow might be surprising unless one takes into account the evolving international system. By the 1970s, China was a nuclear power and, though still much weaker than either the United States or USSR, some sensed an emerging tripolar system. In that changing international system context, Nixon was engaged in a predictable strategy designed to play the other two poles against one another. Indeed, Moscow and Beijing were likely engaged in a similar strategy.

billiard ball model
View that international relations are shaped exclusively by the structure of the international system and the external interactions of states within that system. Domestic variables are largely irrelevant.

This attempt to understand individual state behavior as a function of characteristics of the international system as a whole is sometimes referred to as the **billiard ball model** of international relations. Think of the table on which a game of billiards is played as providing the basic structure for the game. The size of the table, the number of pockets, and the quality of the felt on the tabletop provide a common setting within which all the individual balls move. How those balls move has little to do with the inner qualities of the balls (they are all the same inside). Once someone takes a shot, what matters are the table and the interactions of the balls as they collide with one another. In international relations, the billiard ball model assumes that the structure of the international system (the common table) and the external interactions of states (the billiard balls) tell the whole story.

Implicit in international system level analysis and the billiard ball model is an assumption that states have interests that transcend the special interests of the individuals and groups that exist within the state borders. The overriding state interest is survival, which, broken down into its components would include: (1) the physical security of the country, its borders, and its people; (2) the economic security and prosperity of the country as a whole; and (3) the political sovereignty and independence of the state. Certainly, a state's leaders might disagree over the extent to which any one of these elements of the national interest might be in jeopardy or how best to respond to a challenge. Nevertheless, international system level analysis sees international relations and foreign policy as a continuing effort on the part of state leaders to protect and promote the national interest in light of the challenges posed by events and trends beyond state borders.

While the international system level of analysis tends to be most closely associated with the structural realist paradigm, scholars working within competing paradigms also sometimes stress systemic sources of state behavior. However, the specific systemic characteristics that they emphasize will differ from those stressed by realists. For liberals, the key systemic variables shaping state behavior would include the existence of international institutions or the degree of economic interdependence among states. In place of the realist billiard ball model, some scholars posit a "cobweb model."[4] Whereas the former focuses entirely on the external interactions of states, the latter sees world politics as a more multifaceted set of interactions across national borders involving states, individuals, and an assortment of subnational groups. For liberals, the thicker the web of ties that bind people in states together, the greater the disincentive to war and conflict among the actors in the international system.

Constructivist scholars also weigh in at the international system level. The difference between realists and constructivists employing systemic level analysis is, once again, related to the nature of the systemic variables that get stressed. While for realists the key attribute of the international system shaping state behavior is the distribution of power, for constructivists it is the prevailing global norms. The strong commitment to the norm of state sovereignty, for example, has for much of the history of international relations shaped and constrained state behavior. At the same time, constructivists would argue that such a norm is not a "given" or a "historical absolute." Instead, it is socially constructed. Thus, the challenge to absolute notions of sovereignty since World War II, specifically the emergence of the alternative idea that sovereignty can be overridden in the quest to protect human rights, created a new global norm that affects state behavior.

The Assumption of Rationality

Scholars, and especially realist scholars, working at the international system level of analysis, more often than not assume that states are not only unitary actors but also rational actors. This assumption of rationality does not imply endorsement of a state's goals or policies. Instead, it simply means that states engage in a conscious process of searching for the most efficient means to achieve its foreign policy ends. Consider, for purposes of illustration, the sequence of events set in motion by the August 2, 1990 Iraqi invasion of the neighboring, oil-rich kingdom Kuwait. Within a matter of days following the invasion, what little resistance the Kuwaiti military could manage was effectively crushed, and Iraq was in unchallenged control.

In response, key US foreign policy-makers, including the president, the secretaries of state and defense, the national security advisor, and a host of additional civilian, military, and intelligence officials held meetings, reviewed the intelligence, and consulted with one another and with US allies around the world. These US officials presumably shared a common commitment to a set of core national interests: maintaining access to Persian Gulf oil, maintaining the credibility of US commitments to its friends and allies, and maintaining a favorable balance of power in the Middle East. Thus, these US officials assessed how much those interests were threatened by the Iraqi action, considered what the range of possible policy responses might be, and sought to determine what response or set of responses would best meet the threat posed. After a brief attempt to force Iraq out of Kuwait through diplomatic pressure combined with economic sanctions, US officials concluded that military force was required. On January 17, 1991, a coalition of countries led by the United States initiated, with UN Security Council approval, Operation Desert Storm. Through a combination of air strikes followed by a ground invasion, Iraq was forced out of Kuwait. On February 27, President George H. W. Bush ordered a cease-fire in the Persian Gulf War and declared that Kuwait had been successfully liberated.

rational actor model
View of foreign policy decision-making that assumes policy-makers have a shared sense of the national interest, which they seek to attain via a rational process of finding the most efficient means to achieve those ends.

This very brief description of the US response to the Iraqi invasion of Kuwait is based, at least implicitly, on a **rational actor model** of foreign policy decision-making. The model sees decision-making as beginning with the perception of a challenge to one's interest (the Iraqi invasion of Kuwait) and the clarification of one's goals (expelling Iraq from Kuwait). In responding to that challenge or in seeking to achieve one's goal, one then develops a comprehensive list of possible options for action and response (UN diplomacy, economic sanctions, military force, etc.). After carefully weighing the costs and benefits of each of those options, one chooses and implements the option that allows one to achieve one's goals or meet the challenge at the lowest cost.

It should be emphasized that this rational actor model can be applied to an understanding of decision-making in any realm—from foreign policy, to domestic politics, to personal matters like the selection of the college that you attend. Moreover, it can be applied to individual decision-makers as well as to states. (See Theory in Practice 3.1.) When applied in the foreign policy arena by realist scholars, however, the model rests on three key assumptions about how foreign policy decisions are made.

1. *Policy-makers begin with a shared sense of the national interest.* At least at a general level, decision-makers share a common understanding of the national interest, and, as they formulate foreign policy, they are motivated and united primarily by the effort to protect and promote those national interests. A powerful national leader (a president or a prime minister) will often serve as the custodian of that national interest, making sure that others in the decision-making process keep it front and center.
2. *Policy-making is a rational, intellectual process.* Foreign policy-making is all about objectively linking ends and means. Key foreign policy decision-makers will collectively and systematically canvass the range of alternative policy choices from which they might choose and, ultimately, settle on the choice that will most effectively and efficiently promote national interests.
3. *Once a policy choice is made, it will be implemented more or less as decision-makers had intended.* This point assumes a unity of purpose between those who define policy and the individuals and agencies that must carry it out.

Note that the model does not assume total agreement among the participants in this process every step of the way. The rational actor model has room for participants to disagree—for example, the disagreement over how much of a threat was posed by the Kuwait invasion. In the days following the Kuwait invasion, some US officials argued that the United States could live with the loss of Kuwaiti sovereignty and that it did not matter whether the United States bought Kuwaiti oil from Saddam Hussein or from the Kuwaiti monarchy. Neither regime was exactly a paragon of democracy and liberty. The model

Theory in Practice 3.1

North Korean Nuclear Weapons and Rational Choice Theory

In a 2004 study, political scientist Bruce Bueno de Mesquita reached a conclusion about how best to get North Korean dictator Kim Jong II to cease his country's development of nuclear weapons. According to de Mesquita, "Security guarantees, especially a mix of assurances from the United States (not to attack) and from China (to defend North Korea if necessary), coupled with significant economic assistance (approaching $1 billion or so per year) to North Korea, would induce Kim to mothball his nuclear capability and allow continuous on-site inspections and securing of his nuclear facilities."

That conclusion was based on de Mesquita's application of "rational choice theory." Like the rational actor model discussed in this chapter, the theory of rational choice assumes that human beings are rational. That is, it assumes that people have interests and that they act in accordance with those interests in choosing the course of action that they take. However, for rational choice theorists the interests sought are not "national interests" but the individual interests of the key actors involved in making foreign policy decisions. Thus, in order to understand and predict how a country will act, it is crucial to know four things: (1) who the key players with an interest in influencing a policy are, (2) what their interests or preferences are, (3) how important the issue for each of the players is, and (4) how influential each player is.

In the North Korean case, Kim Jong II was the key actor with preponderant (though not exclusive)

influence over North Korean policy—so his interests and preferences were key. According to de Mesquita, Kim's main concern (like that of most political leaders) was remaining in power. So there was a possibility of stopping the North Korean nuclear program if it was linked to guarantees of Kim's political survival. Of course, whether Western countries would want to accept any deal that kept the ruthless Kim in power raises moral questions that have to be considered as well. But the larger point underlying the rational choice approach is that we can better understand the actions of states if we think of them in relation to the interests of the key players responsible for formulating policy.

SOURCE: Bruce Bueno de Mesquita, *The Predictioneer's Game* (Random House, 2009).

- What assumptions are shared in common by the "rational actor model" discussed in this chapter and "rational choice theory" as described in the discussion of the Korean case?

- What is the key distinction about the nature of the interests that policy-makers pursue in the "rational actor model" as compared to "rational choice theory"?

- In what sense can we say that a ruthless dictator like Kim Jong II is rational? Does that imply endorsement of his policies?

---

can also accommodate honest disagreements over the costs and benefits of the various policy responses considered. In the Kuwait case, the chair of the Joint Chiefs of Staff, Colin Powell, advocated the use of economic sanctions as the best response, while others, including President Bush, had already concluded that sanctions would not work and that a military response was necessary.[5] The model also does not assume that the policy ultimately chosen will prove to be the wisest and best of the available choices. Foreign policy-makers often make mistakes. After the 1991 Persian Gulf War, for example, some critics of the Bush administration argued that the cease-fire was declared too soon, and that toppling Saddam Hussein should have been the ultimate goal. Indeed, some within the administration had debated and disagreed over exactly this question.

However, while allowing for disagreements among policy-makers in all these areas, the rational actor model does assume that participants share and are motivated in their deliberations by an overriding commitment to promoting the national interest and to a good faith effort to find the policy response that will best promote it. At bottom, the model sees states as **unitary actors** that speak with one voice in defense of the national interest.

unitary actors
View, consistent with the realist paradigm and the rational actor model, that sees states as entities onto themselves speaking with one voice in the pursuit of their interests.

Put somewhat differently, the rational actor model assumes that "important events have important causes."[6] Thus, one could work backward from the foreign policy behavior of a state (a treaty signed, a war initiated, an international organization sponsored or joined) to some overriding national interests that can explain why the state engaged in that behavior. Indeed, much contemporary international relations punditry is aimed precisely at trying to figure back from particular foreign policy behaviors to the underlying and less transparent motives behind them. So, for example, efforts to explain why Iran is pursuing nuclear weapons or why China conducted a test of an antisatellite weapon often implicitly assume an overriding national interest goal and strategy.

If this entire description of the rational actor model seems little more than common sense, that reflects the fact that most lay observers intuitively interpret foreign policy in rational actor terms. So the initial Iraqi invasion of Kuwait must itself have been driven by some overriding Iraqi national interest. Presumably, in deciding to invade Kuwait, Saddam Hussein and his top advisors first discussed the costs and benefits of an invasion and of other options before deciding on a course of action. To reiterate, suggesting that Saddam Hussein was a rational actor does not mean that one shares or endorses his goals or methods; it simply suggests that Iraqi foreign policy resulted from a "rational" process defined as the systematic effort to link policy ends and means.

The State Level of Analysis

3-2 **Explain how the state level of analysis and the bureaucratic politics model of decision-making each challenge the view of states as rational, unitary actors.**

The attractions of both systemic level analysis and the rational actor model are their elegance and efficiency. From some basic characteristics of the international system as a whole, one is able to offer understanding and even prediction of the behavior of individual states without needing to know very much about the history of each state, its domestic politics, or its leaders. To understand Russian behavior in the Cold War, for example, does not require one to be a Russian expert, to have spent time in the country, or to know the language. All you need is to know something about the logic of bipolarity and to make the assumption of rationality.

However, in the view of many international relations scholars, this combination of systemic level analysis with the assumption of rationality provides an oversimplified view of how the world works. While it might be useful in identifying the larger systemic constraints within which individual states operate, they argue that there is great variation in how states respond to and operate within those systemic constraints. To understand that variation requires looking more closely at the unique characteristics of the individual states that make up the larger international system.

State Level Attributes

What separates all "second image" (state level) analysis from "third image" (international system level) analysis is the insistence of the former that characteristics of individual states and their societies do shape how states will behave in the international arena. One cannot, from this perspective, predict how a state will act simply from a description of the international setting within which it is operating. You also have to know something about individual states themselves. To return to the billiard ball metaphor, it is as if the game is now being played with different-sized balls made of a variety of materials. Thus, how a ball moves when struck will depend not only on the characteristics of the table and the position of the other balls, but also on the unique attributes of the ball itself.

To many, this seems obvious. Few analysts of the 2003 US decision to go to war in Iraq would fail to at least consider such issues as domestic electoral politics, public opinion, relations between Congress and the president, or the influence of interest groups ranging from big oil to the Israel lobby. Some might argue that the idea of "democracy promotion" that formed part of the Bush administration's case for the war has a long tradition in US foreign policy and is a unique attribute of the American approach to international relations that cannot be removed from the Iraq equation. Similarly, some suggest that the tendency of the Bush administration to see the world in terms of good versus evil is also an approach that is deeply rooted in the American foreign policy tradition.

A complete inventory of state level variables that might impact the foreign behavior of a state would be very long. Among the most significant are the five that follow:

1. *Type of government.* The state level variable that has received the most attention from scholars in recent years is type of government. Democratic peace theory (see Chapters 1 and 4) is a perfect example of state level analysis insofar as it suggests that democracies are less war-prone (at least when it comes to fighting other democracies) than authoritarian regimes. Type of government can affect not only how a state will behave but also how effectively it conducts its foreign policy. For example, French historian Alexis de Tocqueville, whose book *Democracy in America* sought to explain the American democratic experiment to nineteenth-century European readers, was pessimistic about the ability of a democracy to conduct an efficient foreign policy. As he famously wrote: "Foreign policy does not require the use of any of the good qualities peculiar to democracy, but does require

cultivation of almost all those which it lacks."[7] In contrast, political scientist James Fearon more recently argued that democracies have an advantage over authoritarian regimes in some respects such as crisis bargaining. In staking out a public position in an international crisis, leaders of democratic states cannot easily back down, because they face potential backlash from their citizens at home. He labels this backlash **audience costs**. Thus, their competitor states will understand that democratic leaders are not making hollow threats and will be forced to take the public position of democratic states more seriously.[8]

audience costs
In a democracy, the cost to a leader's domestic credibility and political standing that results when one backs down after staking out a position in an international crisis.

2. *Economic system and performance.* For some scholars of international relations, a state's economic system can have an even more significant impact on its behavior than its political system. For example, Marxist analyses of world affairs have traditionally argued that capitalist economies must seek markets abroad in order to deal with domestic crises of overproduction. That economic imperative, they suggest, requires imperialist foreign policies in which states assert their power to ensure continued access to those markets. In turn, those policies can lead to conflict with other imperialist states and, ultimately, are a major source of war. Economic performance of a state can also impact its foreign policy. Russian president Gorbachev's efforts to improve relations with the United States in the 1980s and to end the decades-long Cold War with the West was, by most accounts, driven in large part by the weakness of the Soviet economy. By the 1980s the Soviet economy could barely provide the necessities of life for its citizens, let alone continue to keep pace in the arms race with a technologically superior United States. The end of the Cold War brought with it the promise of some economic breathing space and economic aid.

3. *Political culture and national style.* Some observers argue that states have different political cultures and, thus, different national styles in their approach to international affairs. Those variations stem from differences in geography and historical experience. For example, because the geography and history of Russia differ from those of the United States, the two countries have very different approaches to international affairs. Russia is located in the Eurasian heartland, borders on multiple real and potential adversaries, and has a history of conflict across those borders. The United States, in contrast, is protected by two oceans with relatively weak neighbors to its north and south, and it has not fought an interstate war on its soil since 1812. As a result, some suggest, Russian policy reflects a more insecure, pessimistic, and "realist" view of the world compared with the more secure, optimistic, and "idealist" worldview reflected in much of US policy.

4. *Interest groups.* While variables such as regime type, economic system, and political culture describe long-term attributes of individual states that are deeply rooted in history, there are more changeable, shorter-term domestic factors that also help determine how a state will respond to a particular foreign policy challenge. An example is the relative power of domestic interest

groups with a stake in a particular foreign policy decision. Debates in the United States over the negotiation and ratification of free trade agreements with other countries, for example, cannot be fully understood without taking into account the views and relative political clout of groups ranging from the US Chamber of Commerce, to labor unions, to human rights and environmental protection organizations. Likewise, decisions on the development and production of new types of weapons systems may be partly driven by military necessity but also by the interests of arms manufacturers, of the labor unions who represent the workers employed by such industries, and of the cities and towns where those industries are located.

5. *Public opinion.* An even more changeable and, indeed, sometimes fickle domestic variable is the mood and intensity of public opinion. Especially in democratic countries, it is the rare political leader who is willing and able to act in clear defiance of a strong public mood. No analysis of the US withdrawal from Vietnam in the 1970s would be complete without taking into account the shift in public opinion against the war. Similarly, the initial decision to invade Iraq in 2003 and the later pressure to find an exit strategy both have to be analyzed against the backdrop of changes in the public mood. While authoritarian regimes whose leaders do not have to face elections can be more insulated from public opinion in the conduct of foreign policy, even in such cases public opinion is not entirely irrelevant. The surge in Russian President Vladimir Putin's domestic approval ratings following the 2014 invasion of Crimea might reasonably be considered a factor (even if not the decisive one) in the subsequent decision to extend the conflict to other regions of eastern Ukraine.

Pro-Putin rally in Russia following 2014 Russian invasion and annexation of Crimea. To what extent does public opinion shape foreign policy in an authoritarian regime like Russia?

As we saw to be the case with the international system level of analysis, so too is the state level of analysis compatible with most of the international relations paradigms. Liberals who emphasize the spread of international institutions or the degree of global economic interdependence operate in large part at the systemic level, but liberal democratic peace theorists focus on a state level variable (regime type). The liberal Kantian triangle (see Chapter 1) is a way of thinking about world politics that explicitly incorporates both state and systemic factors. Likewise, constructivists can interpret state behavior as reflective of global, systemwide norms or as something that is shaped by the socially constructed norms and identities at the individual state level.

The one paradigm that is intrinsically most resistant to state level analysis is structural realism, which at its core is an international system level perspective on how the world works. Unlike even classical realists who focused a lot of their attention on the individual state and its attributes, structural realists from Waltz forward have emphasized how the international system constrains and determines what individual states do. While Waltz did concede that "states are free to do any fool thing they choose," he notes that the international system creates strong pressures on states "to do some things and to refrain from doing others."[9] (For a recent example of structural realists applying state level analysis to a foreign policy issue, see Theory in Practice 3.2.)

Theory in Practice 3.2
The Israel Lobby: Realism and the Levels of Analysis

In March 2006 well-known political scientists John Mearsheimer and Stephen Walt published their controversial article "The Israel Lobby," which they expanded into a book published the following year. Their central thesis is that American foreign policy in the Middle East has for decades been at odds with vital American strategic interests in the region. They blame the disconnect between US policy and the US national interest on the influence of a diffuse but powerful Israel lobby that is more concerned with protecting Israel than in asserting what is best for the United States. The article was very controversial, with the criticisms ranging from accusations of anti-Semitism to charges of poor scholarship.

From the point of view of international relations theory, however, the most interesting thing about the article and book was that two prominent realist scholars wrote them. Mearsheimer's 2001 book *The Tragedy of Great Power Politics* is a classic of recent neorealist thinking, arguing that states consistently and predictably act to promote their national interests in response to the larger international context. Thus, the book focuses on the international system level and treats states as unitary actors that apply rational decision-making strategies. Domestic factors get little if any attention.

However, the Israel lobby thesis is focused on the impact of domestic politics. Of course, most realist scholars, though emphasizing the international system level, would acknowledge some role for domestic factors. However, for Mearsheimer and Walt, domestic factors are virtually the entire story of US Middle East policy. In their words, "The thrust of US policy in the region derives almost entirely from domestic politics."

If one thinks of realism as a prescription for how states *should* behave, then one might argue that Mearsheimer and Walt's criticism of US policy is realist in character. However, most realists argue that the power and appeal of the realist paradigm are that it describes and predicts how states actually *do* behave. If one thinks of realism this way, then the focus on the Israel lobby as the key driving force in US policy seems a decidedly nonrealist analysis.

SOURCES: John Mearsheimer and Stephen Walt, "The Israel Lobby," *London Review of Books*, March 23, 2006, http://www.lrb.co.uk; John Mearsheimer and Stephen Walt, *The Israel Lobby and U.S. Foreign Policy* (Farrar, Straus and Giroux, 2007); and John Mearsheimer, *The Tragedy of Great Power Politics* (Norton, 2003).

- Is realism an approach to understanding how the world *does* work, how the world *should* work, or some of both?
- Compare the Mearsheimer and Walt thesis on the Israel lobby to the billiard ball metaphor discussed earlier in the chapter. How do they differ?
- Is it fair to accuse Mearsheimer of being untrue to his realist paradigm in his analysis of the Israel lobby? How might he respond?

In general, state level analysis is more complex than, and lacks the elegance and efficiency of, system level analysis. Instead of looking to explain state behavior by virtue of the attributes of the international system as a whole, each state's actions must be examined in the context of the attributes unique to that state. Moreover, insofar as state level analysis allows a greater role for subnational groups and interests in the policy process, it also raises doubts about the view of states as rational, unitary actors.

The First Challenge to Rationality

In bringing state level attributes and actors into the foreign policy equation, state level analysis challenges the notion of a single-minded state rationally pursuing a commonly accepted understanding of the national interest. Consider the following case.

In August 1957 the Soviet Union launched *Sputnik I*, the first artificial satellite to be placed into orbit around the world. That was followed, on November 3, 1957, by *Sputnik II*. In the United States, the reaction was a combination of surprise and concern bordering on panic. The USSR already had the atomic bomb, and *Sputnik* now suggested a capacity to deliver atomic warheads from space. More generally, *Sputnik* indicated to some observers that the technological competition between the two Cold War rivals was now tilting in favor of the USSR. Even though President Dwight Eisenhower did not share this sense of panic and the United States was still far ahead in most significant civilian and military technologies, many believed that the United States was losing the space race.

In response to *Sputnik*, the United States sped up the schedule to test its own satellite via a Vanguard rocket. On December 6, 1957, as many Americans watched on live TV, the Vanguard rocket rose a few feet into the air before collapsing back down onto the launch pad and exploding in a cloud of smoke and fire. It was both a technological and a political defeat, and it added to the growing sense in the United States that the country was losing the space race. Seeking to add to the sense of national humiliation, Soviet officials at the United Nations

Test of the US Vanguard rocket fails in a fiery explosion on December 6, 1957. This was a failure for the United States in its space competition with the USSR, but not necessarily an unmitigated disaster from the point of view of the US Army. Why not? And what does the reaction of some in the US Army reveal about foreign policy making?

offered to provide the United States with aid typically reserved for developing nations.[10] (You can watch a newsreel clip of the failed Vanguard launch on YouTube, http://www.youtube.com/watch?v=JK6a6Hkp94o.)

Even the most sanguine observers recognized that the Vanguard failure was, at the very least, a public relations disaster for the United States. Thus, it would seem surprising that a US Army general who watched the Vanguard test with President Eisenhower reportedly gloated at the failure, declaring it to be a "great day for the army." How, one might wonder, could any officer in the US military see good news in what was obviously a technological and political setback in the US struggle with Communism? The answer may be found in the **interservice rivalry** between the US Army and US Navy over which branch of the service would take the lead in developing space for military purposes. The Vanguard, as one might guess, happened to be a navy rocket, and the failed test seemed to provide an opening for the army.

This story of the Vanguard rocket and the interservice rivalry that surrounded its development is but one illustration of the **bureaucratic politics model** of foreign policy decision-making. Sometimes referred to as the "governmental politics model" or the "institutional pluralism model," it sees foreign policy-making as a competitive struggle among various government institutions and actors to promote their version of the "national interest." Specifically, the bureaucratic politics model rests on four key assumptions regarding the policy-making process.

interservice rivalry
The struggle among the various branches and subgroups of a nation's military for funding, prestige, and influence.

bureaucratic politics model
Sees foreign policy-making as a struggle among government institutions, agencies, and actors to promote their version of the "national interest" as shaped by the interests and perspectives of their particular bureaucratic agency.

1. *Policy-making is a social process.* It involves a tug of war or a "pulling and hauling" among a multiplicity of individual and institutional actors who play a role in formulating foreign policy. Although certain leaders (e.g., presidents, prime ministers) might have ultimate responsibility for policy, they do not and cannot completely shape and control the decision-making process.

2. *There is no single version of the national interest.* While at a general level—especially when faced with some severe threat—all players might have a sense of shared national interest, each participant also brings to the table a set of

interests and perspectives shaped by the bureaucratic role he or she fills. As one political scientist famously put it, "Where you stand depends on where you sit."[11]

3. *Policy decisions are compromises.* If policy-making is, in fact, a social process involving competing interests and differing perspectives on the national interest, it follows that the policies adopted and the foreign policy behaviors that result are often compromises among those competing interests and perspectives. Thus, it is not necessarily the case that "important events have important causes," and one cannot always work back from policies adopted to a clear sense of unitary state motives and intentions.

4. *Politics does not stop once a decision is made.* To the extent that some players involved in formulating policy do not get all they want, they still may have opportunities to influence policy at the implementation stage. By dragging their feet, following the letter but not the spirit of the policy, or simply failing to follow through with policy implementation, the losers in the policy debate might, in part, still get their way.

The bureaucratic politics model sees foreign policy as a **two-level game**.[12] At the international level, states interact and bargain with one another as they jockey for influence and power in world politics. Simultaneously, at the domestic level, those charged with making foreign policy interact and bargain both with key societal actors and with other government agencies. Bureaucratic politics, it must be stressed, does not reject the idea that actors are rational, but what it does question is the rational actor model applied to a single, unitary state actor. Instead, foreign policy-making is seen as an intragovernmental struggle for influence and power among multiple rational actors driven by differences of interest, role and mission, and organizational process.[13] (For a summary of the rational actor and bureaucratic politics models, see Table 3.1.)

two-level game
Idea that leaders simultaneously negotiate with other states and with key domestic actors in the conduct of international relations.

INTERESTS At the crudest level, the differences in perspective apparent among the actors who formulate foreign policy derive from differences in interests. Those

Table 3.1 Rational Actor Versus Bureaucratic Politics Models

	Rational Actor Model	Bureaucratic Politics Model
Key Actors	Unitary states.	Multiple foreign policy bureaucracies.
Policy Process	Intellectual process.	Social process.
Policy Objectives	Promote national interests.	Promote national and bureaucratic interests.
Policy Outcomes	Maximizing of interests.	Compromising and satisficing of interests.
Policy Implementation	Administrative/technical process.	Political process.

interests are related to questions of institutional prestige, budgets, and power. The US Army general who wanted to grab control of the satellite program from the US Navy no doubt was motivated by a combination of all those selfish institutional considerations. A successful Vanguard rocket test would have meant more money to the navy and less for the army. Perhaps even more important, the race to space in the 1950s was a high-visibility endeavor. Whichever branch of the military service came out on top in this race would bask in considerable attention. Careers would be affected, as would political influence.

However, reducing foreign policy disputes merely to clashes over money and power can be overly simplistic and cynical, missing much of what motivates the actors involved in the process. In many cases, the actors bring genuine differences in judgment about how best to define and promote the national interest as each perceives it through the lens of his or her particular bureaucratic role and organizational mission.

bureaucratic role
Responsibilities associated with a particular job or position that shape the perspective and behavior of the individual who holds that position in foreign policymaking.

BUREAUCRATIC ROLES AND MISSIONS The concept of **bureaucratic role** refers to the responsibilities associated with a particular job or position. While each individual brings different qualities and approaches to any given job, the job itself can shape and constrain the perspective and behavior of the individual who holds that position. Likewise, the larger mission of the particular bureaucratic agency within which one works can also affect the perspective among the actors involved in formulating policy.

For example, in the early 1980s, during the Reagan administration, the Soviet Union was constructing a 3,000-mile pipeline through which natural gas would be exported to Western Europe. At the time, US Secretary of Defense Casper Weinberger and US Secretary of State Al Haig advocated different approaches toward their European allies. While each held a deeply ingrained suspicion of the Soviet Union and its motives, and although both worried about Western Europe becoming dependent on the USSR for energy, they disagreed on how to handle this issue. Weinberger advocated economic sanctions against Western Europe if it went ahead with the pipeline deal, whereas Haig advocated more subtle diplomacy, fearing the consequences of economic sanctions on the NATO alliance.[14] This difference in approach can be at least partly explained through differences in bureaucratic roles. As Secretary of State, it was Haig, not Weinberger, who had primary responsibility for maintaining good diplomatic relations with America's allies. Since economic sanctions would surely complicate those relations, Haig's perspective was bound to differ from that of his counterpart at Defense.

organizational process
Set of routine procedures and processes ("standard operating procedures" or SOPs) common to an organization that help shape the way that organization responds to threats and challenges.

ORGANIZATIONAL PROCESSES Differences in bureaucratic perspectives are also a function of differences in **organizational process**. Over time, bureaucracies, like individuals, develop differences in their routines or standard operating procedures. Those "standard operating procedures" (or SOPs) emerge in response to prior experiences in dealing with similar situations. They can be a source of comfort in responding to complex situations, and they can be efficient insofar as they avoid the need to reinvent the wheel every time a new situation develops. However, they can also be a source of rigidity in dealing with unique circumstances.

A classic example of the role played by organizational SOPs occurred during the 1962 Cuban Missile Crisis. John F. Kennedy's response to the discovery of Soviet offensive nuclear missiles in Cuba was to order a naval blockade of the island. Hoping to avoid a potential third world war with the USSR, Kennedy and Secretary of Defense Robert McNamara were concerned with precisely how the US Navy would respond should Soviet ships test the blockade. As Graham Allison notes in his study of the Cuban Missile Crisis, McNamara called on Admiral George Anderson, the chief of naval operations, and peppered him with questions about how the navy would respond if Soviet ships approached. Eventually, Anderson became frustrated by McNamara's efforts to micromanage the blockade:

> The Navy man picked up the Manual of Naval Regulations and, waving it in McNamara's face, shouted, "It's all in there." To which McNamara replied, "I don't give a damn what John Paul Jones would have done, I want to know what you are going to do now." The encounter ended on Anderson's remark: "Now Mr. Secretary, if you and your Deputy will go back to your office, the Navy will run the blockade."[15]

Note, in particular, that this exchange took place after the policy decision to respond with a naval blockade was adopted. The tension between McNamara and Anderson was over the implementation of this policy. Yet how this blockade was implemented was not merely a technical, administrative matter; it was potentially a matter of war or peace between the two great powers of the day. One can easily imagine, as McNamara obviously did, how the manner in which policy was implemented could easily undo what he and Kennedy were trying to accomplish.

Choosing between the rational actor and bureaucratic politics model is not an either/or proposition. Instead, the consensus in the literature is that both models provide insights, and that the relative utility of the two decision-making models varies with the circumstances. Here are three rules of thumb:

1. *Nature of the situation.* In a crisis situation where an immediate and severe threat to widely shared vital interests exists, the rational actor model is likely to prevail. In contrast, decision-making in more routine, noncrisis situations provides greater scope for the parochial interests and organizational perspectives of the subnational actors.
2. *Nature of the leader.* In any regime, high-level leaders (presidents, prime ministers, etc.) have broad responsibility for promoting the national interest. When those leaders have a high level of interest in foreign affairs, when they are politically adept, when they have expertise and experience related to foreign affairs, and when they have broad popular support (e.g., because they are charismatic or during the honeymoon period after coming into

office), the rational actor model will have maximum utility. That is because the leader will be in a better position to harness the centrifugal forces pulling policy in the direction of subnational bureaucratic interests. In contrast, when top leaders are unengaged, ineffective, inexperienced, and politically weak, the pull of bureaucratic interests will be maximized.

3. *Nature of the regime.* In open, democratic regimes, subnational interests and perspectives tend to have greater scope for influencing policy. In democratic regimes, bureaucratic actors are able to forge alliances with societal groups that share their interests. In closed, authoritarian regimes, in contrast, power is by definition more centralized, and the ability of bureaucratic actors to mobilize constituencies will be limited. Thus, a democracy has more room for bureaucratic politics than does an authoritarian regime.

While these rules of thumb do provide some insights and a starting point for analysis, they are not hard and fast laws.

The Individual Level of Analysis

3-3   Discuss the role that that individuals play in the making of foreign policy and the conduct of international relations.

Neither the international system nor the state levels of analysis assign much significance to the role of individuals in world politics. Yet on election days in countries around the world, voters in democratic countries take the time and expend the effort to cast ballots for individual leaders based, at least in part, on the assumption that the outcome of the election will have an impact on the country's foreign policy. In casting their ballots, those voters are implicitly accepting the **great man theory of history**, which suggests that the course of human history is determined not only by larger social, political, and economic forces but also by the beliefs and character of the individuals who rise to positions of influence.

great man theory of history
View that history is driven less by impersonal social, economic, and political forces than by the beliefs and character of the individual men and women who rise to positions of influence.

From this perspective, the history of the twentieth century would have unfolded very differently had such individuals as Stalin, Roosevelt, Hitler, Churchill, Mao, Reagan, Putin, and Obama not been born. Likewise, many might argue, the early history of the twenty-first century would not have been the same had Osama bin Laden been killed in the 1980s by the Russian forces he was fighting in Afghanistan or if a few hundred votes had shifted from Bush to Gore in the controversial Florida recount in the 2000 presidential election. For better or worse, the United States might not have invaded Iraq in 2003 had Gore been certified as the winner in 2000.

While scholars working at the individual level of analysis do appreciate that systemic and state level factors can shape and constrain what individual leaders do, they caution against a view of leaders as mechanically responding to those systemic and state level factors. Different leaders are fully capable of making different decisions in response to the same set of conditions. Leaders are human beings, and human beings have agency.

Individual Level Attributes

When Waltz articulated this "first image" analysis, he was most interested in examining the common qualities that human beings possess as a species, specifically, the question of whether humans have an innate instinct for violence and warfare. Since that time, scholarship examining world politics at the individual level has focused largely on how human variations can affect the conduct of international relations and foreign policy. Those variations can be related both to substantive beliefs and to aspects of individual personality and character.

BELIEF SYSTEMS   A belief system refers to the set of substantive values and understandings of the world that an individual holds. When we consider the qualities of leaders that have an impact on a country's foreign policy, we often think first of their substantive beliefs and ideas about the world.

   At the narrowest level, differences in belief systems may manifest themselves in positions on specific foreign policy challenges. Should we use force to prevent Iran from developing nuclear weapons? Should we sign a free trade agreement with Mexico? Should we join the International Criminal Court? At a higher level of generalization and sophistication, other sets of questions might be relevant. Is the individual a protectionist or a free trader? An interventionist or an isolationist? A supporter or critic of the UN? Inclined to military or diplomatic solutions to foreign policy challenges? Knowing where a potential leader stands on these kinds of questions can help us anticipate how a leader will act in future situations.

   At the most sophisticated and highly integrated level of belief systems is ideology. An **ideology** is an integrated set of assumptions and understandings about how the social, political, and economic world both is and should be structured and organized. A leader who subscribes to Marxist ideology will have a very different understanding of the world than will a fundamentalist Muslim theocrat. One is an atheist who sees world politics driven by conflict among economic interests, while the other is guided by the Qur'an and sees political leadership as an opportunity to act on religious values. Those ideological differences would presumably affect a state's view of whom its friends and foes are in the world, the nature of the challenges and threats it faces, and the instruments it might use in response to those threats.

ideology
An integrated set of assumptions and understandings about how the social, political, and economic world is and should be structured and organized.

   State behavior in the world can also be affected by the operational codes of those in power. **Operational code** refers to a leader's "beliefs about the nature of politics and political conflict, his views regarding the extent to which historical developments can be shaped, and his notions of correct strategy and tactics."[16] A leader's operational code transcends positions on specific issues or even specific ideologies. Instead, it has more to do with the person's general philosophical predispositions to politics. For example, leaders might differ as to whether they believe human beings are inherently good or evil, whether politics is more conflictual or cooperative, or whether the behavior of others is basically predictable and rational.

operational code
An individual's general predisposition to and understanding of the nature of politics and political strategy and tactics.

PERSONALITY ATTRIBUTES In addition to substantive beliefs, many scholars argue that personality attributes can also shape policy decisions. Whether an individual is, by temperament, pragmatic or dogmatic, authoritarian or democratic, impulsive or deliberative, cautious or risk-taking can have as great an impact on that individual's policy as his or her substantive beliefs.

One scholar who has devoted much of her career to examining the impact of leader personality attributes on foreign policy is Margaret Hermann. By studying what leaders say in their speeches and interviews, she distinguishes them across seven different personality traits: (1) belief that one can influence or control what happens, (2) need for power and influence, (3) level of conceptual complexity, (4) self-confidence, (5) tendency to focus on problem-solving and accomplishment versus maintenance of the group and dealing with others' ideas and sensitivities, (6) distrust or suspiciousness of others, and (7) degree of in-group bias.[17]

A simplified version of Hermann's analysis is presented in Table 3.2.[18] By combining some of the seven personality traits listed above, Table 3.2 distinguishes leaders across two dimensions: responsiveness to external constraints and openness to information. Responsiveness to constraints has to do with the extent to which a leader perceives external circumstances at the systemic and state levels of analysis to limit his or her freedom of action. Openness to information has to do with the extent to which a leader seeks and is receptive to information that is contrary to his or her preconceived policy views. The result is four basic leadership types: crusaders, opportunists, strategists, and pragmatists.

Crusaders are the least sensitive to the context in which they operate. They have a clear goal or purpose and do not let external constraints or contrary information deter them from meeting their objective. Depending on one's perspective, they can appear to be admirably bold or dangerously impetuous. At the other extreme, opportunists are the most sensitive to constraints and contrary information. For opportunists, Hermann notes, "Politics is the art of

Table 3.2 A Typology of Leadership Styles

	Respects Constraints	Challenges Constraints
Open to Information	**OPPORTUNISTS** • Most sensitive to context. • Inclined to bargaining and compromise. • Can appear excessively cautious.	**STRATEGISTS** • Have clear goals. • Seek information on best way to achieve goals. • Can appear unpredictable.
Closed to Information	**PRAGMATISTS** • Feel the pressure of external constraints. • Back off goals if the time and circumstances are not right. • Can appear indecisive.	**CRUSADERS** • Least sensitive to context. • Have clear goals and pursue them without hesitation. • Can appear bold and impetuous.

SOURCE: Margaret G. Hermann, Thomas Preston, Baghat Korany, and Timothy M. Shaw, "Who Leads Matters: The Effect of Powerful Individuals," *International Studies Review* 3:2 (Summer 2001).

the possible."[19] Their supporters might view them as appropriately cautious, while their critics might see them as excessively risk-averse. Strategists and pragmatists are also constrained by their environment more than crusaders, but in different ways. Strategists have clear goals that they consistently seek to promote, but they seek information about how best to attain those goals. To outsiders, they can seem unpredictable as they adjust their tactics in response to new information. Pragmatists see themselves as highly limited in what they can achieve by external constraints. They have goals, but they are willing to compromise if the context is not right. They can appear indecisive or lacking in commitment.

One study applying Hermann's typology classified George W. Bush as a crusader and his father, George H. W. Bush, as a hybrid pragmatist-opportunist.[20] Hermann herself suggested that former US President Bill Clinton showed respect for constraints and openness to information, placing him also in the opportunist camp.[21] While it remains for future analysts to classify conclusively more recent leaders like Barack Obama or Vladimir Putin, one can offer preliminary judgments. Obama's emphasis during his first presidential campaign on making his cabinet a "team of rivals" suggested openness to information of diverse types, placing him, depending on his relative level of respect for external constraints, in either the strategist or opportunist categories. As for Putin, his behavior as Russian President (e.g., in Ukraine) suggests he is a crusader, willing to challenge constraints and closed to information.

Hermann's typology is only one of many attempts by scholars to link the personality attributes of leaders with their public policy performance. Even the US Central Intelligence Agency (CIA) is reported to have assembled psychological profiles of world leaders for decades.[22] The application of any of these typologies to specific leaders is bound to be controversial and spark debate. But the larger question is the extent to which the beliefs and personality attributes of individuals make a difference in world politics, given the international system and state level factors also driving and constraining foreign policy. Structural realists, along with many liberals, are dubious, as they emphasize the constraints imposed on leaders by the international system. But Hermann and others operating at the individual level of analysis suggest that individuals do make a difference. How much of difference they make depends on the specific conditions present in a given situation. In general, the beliefs and personality of a leader tend to have greater impact in the following circumstances: (1) in crisis situations calling for swift and decisive actions, (2) in situations that are new or ambiguous such that standard operating procedures do not exist, and (3) at times when leaders have wide latitude (e.g., the honeymoon period just after an election).[23]

While Hermann and many other scholars working at the individual level focus on the impact of those who lead sovereign states, nonstate actors also need to be taken into account. Journalist and author Thomas Friedman argues that globalization has created the phenomenon of the "super-empowered individual"—someone who can arm him- or herself with the most advanced digital communications technologies of the twenty-first century and thus, as an individual, can influence the course of world events to an extent once reserved largely to states and international organizations.[24] Some of these super-empowered individuals are, as Friedman suggests, "super-empowered angry men" who also have the ability to do great harm to states and people around the world. As an indication of the significance of these individuals to world politics, Friedman notes that in response to the 1998 terrorist bombings of US embassies in Africa, the Clinton administration ordered cruise missile attacks in Afghanistan aimed at taking out a super-empowered man by the name of Osama bin Laden.[25] That the world's greatest superpower launched such an attack clearly suggests that you need not be the leader of a state to have your beliefs and personality attributes taken seriously in world politics.

The Second Challenge to Rationality

In examining state level analysis and, in particular, the bureaucratic politics model, we already encountered one important challenge to the realist view of states as unitary rational actors. Bureaucratic politics, as we saw, suggests that there is no single, overriding national interest, but, instead, numerous versions of the national interest as shaped by roles, organizational processes, and the competing subnational interests of the various actors involved in the foreign policy-making process. Yet, as we also noted, bureaucratic politics can still coexist with the assumption of rationality. It is just that such rationality is applied to the pursuit of individual or bureaucratic interests rather than to the national interest.

cognitive model
Foreign policy model that assumes human beings have a limited capacity to process information and that they resort to mental shortcuts in making decisions.

A second, and more fundamental, challenge to the assumption of rationality is found at the individual level of analysis. The **cognitive model** of foreign policy-making suggests that the rational actor model presents an oversimplified and idealized image of how decision-makers act that is rarely achieved in practice. The individual human beings involved in making foreign policy decisions cannot and do not achieve the level of comprehensive rationality implied in the rational actor model. There is a limit to how much time and capacity decision-makers have to collect and analyze all the relevant information about a situation; to consider all the alternative courses of action theoretically available to respond to that situation; and to then weigh accurately the consequences, cost, and benefits of each of those alternatives. From the perspective of the cognitive model, characteristics of real as opposed to idealized human decision-making include the following:

satisficing
Accepting policies and outcomes that minimally satisfy foreign policy objectives without necessarily maximizing outcomes achieved and interests attained.

1. *Satisficing.* Goals and interests are often vague and poorly defined, and, in many cases, people hold contradictory objectives. Similarly, the ability of human beings to canvass, evaluate, and predict the consequences of all the policy alternatives available will be limited. Information is usually endless, time is frequently short, and the intellectual capability of human beings to process all the available information is finite. Thus, rather than pushing to maximize their goals, foreign policy-makers often opt for **satisficing**—or

settling for an outcome that minimally satisfies a more limited set of objectives. A solution that is "good enough" (rather than "best") will often be selected.

2. *Use of Heuristics.* A **heuristic** is a mental shortcut that allows one to simplify complex decision-making. For example, you are in a wine store trying to decide which of dozens of options of dry red wine to buy for a dinner party. To do research on all the options would be impossible. So you employ multiple heuristics: only choose from California wines, don't buy the cheapest wines (under $10) but also skip the more expensive options (over $20). In employing those decision-making shortcuts, you cut your time in the wine shop down considerably, but you also might end up settling for something short of the optimal choice. Maybe there's an $8 wine that is better than those at twice the price, or maybe there is a $21 wine that is several times better than the $18 bottle you ultimately choose.

> **heuristic**
> A mental shortcut that allows one to simplify decision-making.

In foreign policy, leaders also employ heuristics. One common strategy is reasoning from historical analogy. As one scholar put it: "Policy makers seize on evils they have experienced and wish to avoid in order to organize their information about events that they do not have the time to analyze from scratch.... unfamiliar problems are discussed in terms of the familiar."[26] Thus since 1938, political leaders in Europe and the United States have repeatedly employed the lessons of the Munich appeasement of 1938 (see Chapter 2) to make the case for standing up to aggression by dictators. Likewise, critics of US intervention abroad have, since the 1970s, referred with similar frequency to the lessons of Vietnam.[27] While the "lessons of history" can often be useful, they can also be misleading as the context and details in two seemingly similar events will often vary widely.

3. *Misperception.* The rational actor model assumes that decision-makers have a clear understanding of their own interests as well as the interests and motives of their adversaries. It also assumes that they accurately perceive and understand the objective facts and information shaping the situation they are facing. However, foreign policy decision-making is often shaped by misperceptions of interests, motives, and circumstances. In an influential 1968 article, political scientist Robert Jervis listed more than a dozen common misperceptions that tend to color the decision-making process.[28] They include the following:

- Decision-makers tend to fit and shape new information into their preexisting theories and images of the world rather than allow new information to alter those preexisting theories and images.
- Decision-makers tend to view other states as more hostile than they are; at the same time, they find it hard to believe that others see them as a menace.
- Decision-makers tend to see the behavior of others as more centralized, disciplined, and coordinated than it actually is.

Such misperceptions reflect the limits of human rationality in the face of complex situations. Once again, misperceptions often result from the need to take cognitive shortcuts to make decision-making more efficient. Thus, fitting new information into preexisting theories and images of the world avoids the need to start analysis from square one every time a decision has to be made. Likewise, the tendency to engage in **worst-case analysis** and exaggerate the hostile intentions of one's adversary in the face of complex, incomplete, or contradictory information is often seen as both the easier and safer way to proceed.

4. *Groupthink.* One special problem that has been shown to limit the ability of decision-makers to maximize interests is the phenomenon of **groupthink**. Groupthink refers to the tendency most often found in small, cohesive groups operating under conditions of stress (a set of characteristics quite common in foreign policy decision-making) to quickly abandon critical thinking in favor of consensus perspectives and viewpoints that reflect group solidarity. Scholars have argued that groupthink often leads to faulty decisions that harm those outside the group as well as the larger interests of the group itself. It can also lead to the perpetuation of a misguided policy since criticism of the policy, even when it is going badly, challenges the wisdom and solidarity of the group. As Irving Janis, the scholar responsible for developing the concept of groupthink, noted: "Members consider loyalty to the group the highest form of morality."[29]

Note that all these cognitive shortcuts, though they can sometimes lead to serious mistakes and bad decisions, are not only predictable, but they can also be useful, necessary, and beneficial.[30] We probably all know someone who can never make a decision because he or she is always bogged down by one more option to consider or by a perceived need to review all the pros and cons of known options once again. There is a fine line between thoroughness and decision-making paralysis.

A bridge of sorts between the rational actor and cognitive models of decision-making (between thoroughness and paralysis) is provided by **poliheuristic theory**, which suggests that decision-making is a two-stage process. In the first stage, decision-makers take a quick, first cut at narrowing down options through the application of various heuristic devices, and only then do they engage in the second stage—a detailed, rational cost–benefit analysis of the remaining, more limited set of options. This two-stage process saves time and makes decision-making more manageable, but the best option might be discarded before undergoing serious analysis. (See Theory in Practice 3.3.)

According to Alex Mintz, the heuristic most frequently employed by foreign policy leaders in the first stage of decision-making is to discard immediately any option that promises to impose unacceptable domestic political costs and only then engage in the detailed cost–benefit analysis of the remaining alternatives.[31] For example, Mintz cites the March 2003 decision by

---

worst-case analysis
Strategy of decision-making that assumes one will face the worst possible situation imaginable and then makes policy based on that assumption.

groupthink
Tendency, most often found in small, cohesive groups operating under conditions of stress, to abandon critical thinking in favor of viewpoints that reflect group solidarity.

poliheuristic theory
Theory of decision-making as a two-stage process in which individuals first use cognitive shortcuts to reduce the range of options and then engage in a detailed, rational analysis of those that remain.

Theory in Practice 3.3

Deciding on a College: Rational Actor, Cognitive, and Poliheuristic Approaches

Recall the days when you were applying to college. According to the US Department of Education, there were 2,870 four-year colleges and universities in the United States in 2010–2011. A strict rational actor approach to choosing where to apply would involve identification and research on each of those institutions. In your analysis you would want to factor in the range of programs available at each school, the quality of those programs, the housing options available, sports and cultural amenities, the character and diversity of the student body, admission requirements, costs and financial aid practices, and probably a number of other items of interest to you in particular. Perhaps on several dozen legal pads, or more likely in a handy Smartphone app, you would list and weigh the pros and cons of each school until you came up with that list of the six or seven to which you would apply.

In practice, however, it is unlikely—in fact it is impossible—for you to do all of the above. The cognitive model suggests that you most likely employed multiple heuristic shortcuts: only look at schools within a 300 mile radius of your home, only look at schools with (or perhaps without) Division I sports, only look at schools in the US News top 100 (and don't even worry about the quality of individual programs at those schools), only look at state schools (or alternatively at private schools), etc. Misperceptions (maybe you

thought the University of Pennsylvania was a state school; maybe you thought liberal arts meant politically "liberal") and groupthink (your friends all seemed to believe, perhaps without much evidence in support, that one should only apply to private schools) probably also affected your decision.

Poliheuristic theory suggests that your college search probably combined heuristics with rational choice. That is, you most likely used some heuristic shortcuts to whittle down considerably the number of schools you considered, and then you employed a more detailed rational analysis to that smaller pool of options that remained. Of course, in utilizing heuristics you might never have seriously looked at the one school that would be your perfect match, but, on the other hand, it gave you a chance to eat and sleep and do other things besides compare colleges.

- What specific heuristics did you employ in your search for a college to attend?

- What are the costs and benefits of employing heuristics in decision-making?

- Applying to college is one thing, making foreign policy decisions about matters of war and peace is another? Can we afford to have leaders employing heuristic devices, and can it be avoided?

Turkey to deny basing rights to US troops for the invasion of Iraq despite the promise of significant US aid in return. According to Mintz, such a proposal was clearly unpopular among the Turkish public and would have carried high domestic political costs for Turkish leaders, so it was dismissed without much analysis. Subsequently, a more in-depth analysis of remaining alternatives followed, eventually leading Turkey to allow air passage over Turkish airspace to US planes.[32] Mintz also applies poliheuristic analysis to terrorist groups. Based on a study of twenty-three decisions made by al-Qaeda, Hamas, and Hezbollah, he suggests that the cognitive shortcut used by all terrorist leaders is to eliminate from serious consideration any decision that threatens their individual political or personal survival, and only then do they subject the remaining alternatives to more detailed rational analysis.[33]

Conclusion

As suggested in this chapter, most sophisticated analysts, whatever grand paradigm they work within, accept that no single level of analysis or decision-making model is capable of fully explaining how the world works. In some cases, scholars shift among levels and decision-making models, depending on the foreign policy behavior they are trying to explain. In other cases, they apply multiple levels of analysis and decision-making models to get the full picture of even a single foreign policy behavior of a state. As the controversy over the role of the "Israel lobby" suggests, even the most hard-core structural realists sometimes concede that international relations is about more than the structure of the international system.

However, certain differences of emphasis are inherent in the competing paradigms. In particular, what continues to separate realists from their critics is the general realist insistence that one begin any analysis of world politics and individual state behavior with the following assumptions: (1) states are rational and unitary actors with preestablished preferences or interests, and (2) states act to defend those interests and assert those preferences in response to the larger international context. Domestic and individual levels of analysis as well as bureaucratic politics and cognitive shortcuts enter the picture only as a secondary consideration. As one scholar put it, the tendency is to "synthesize theories by employing realism first...and then introducing competing theories of domestic politics...to explain residual variance."[34] In other words, one starts analysis with realist assumptions to explain the big picture and then looks to other theories to help explain the deviations from textbook realist expectations.

For many critics of realism, that emphasis needs to be altered. For a liberal internationalist, democracy is not a secondary factor explaining state behavior but is at the core of understanding a state's foreign policy. For a Marxist, the interests of domestic capital explain not merely "residual variance" but, rather, the essence of a capitalist state's foreign policy. For a constructivist, evolving conceptions of friends and enemies trump realist assumptions about the determining influence of international anarchy or balance of power. For many students of bureaucratic politics, bureaucratic interests and roles not only compete with the dominant pursuit of the national interest but are also crucial in deciding what that national interest might be in the first place.

In short, the realist view—that we begin with the international system level and the assumption of states as rational actors—has the virtues of elegance and analytical efficiency. It presumes that without peering inside the messy world of domestic and bureaucratic politics, let alone the beliefs and decision processes of individual human beings, we can understand and predict a great deal about state behavior. The question, however, is whether this analytical simplicity does more to illuminate or distort our understanding of how the world of international relations works.

Review Questions

- Think of a recent foreign policy decision taken by a state, and list the factors that might have influenced that decision at all three levels of analysis. Which, if any, of the levels seems primary in this case and why?

- What do realists mean by "the national interest"? Can you come up with a list of your country's national interests that most of your fellow citizens would accept?
- Every year the college or university that you attend will make a decision about

whether, and by how much, to raise tuition for the following year. How would the decision-making process proceed at your school in the rational actor model? How would it proceed in the bureaucratic politics model? And what would poliheurstic theory contribute to understanding this process?

Key Terms

levels of analysis	two-level game	operational code
billiard ball model	bureaucratic role	cognitive model
rational actor model	organizational	satisficing
unitary actors	process	heuristic
audience costs	great man theory	worst-case analysis
interservice rivalry	of history	groupthink
bureaucratic politics model	ideology	poliheuristic theory

Endnotes

1. John Mearsheimer, "Why the Ukraine Crisis Is the West's Fault: The Liberal Delusions that Provoked Putin," *Foreign Affairs* 93:5 (September–October 2014): 77–89.
2. Valerie M. Hudson, with Christopher S. Vore, "Foreign Policy Analysis Yesterday, Today, and Tomorrow," *Mershon International Studies Review* 39:2 (1995): 210.
3. Kenneth Waltz, *Man, The State, and War: A Theoretical Analysis,* 2nd ed. (Columbia University Press, 2001).
4. John W. Burton, *World Society* (Cambridge, 1972).
5. For a useful glimpse at some of these debates and interviews with some of the participants involved, see the video in the PBS Frontline series *The Gulf War, 1996,* http://www.pbs.org.
6. Graham Allison, *Essence of Decision: Explaining the Cuban Missile Crisis* (Little, Brown, 1971), 4.
7. Alexis de Tocqueville, *Democracy in America* (HarperCollins, 1835).
8. James Fearon, "Domestic Political Audiences and the Escalation of International Disputes," *American Political Science Review* 88:3 (1994): 577–592.
9. Kenneth N. Waltz, "Evaluating Theories," *American Political Science Review* 91:4 (December 1997): 915.
10. John F. Graham, *Space Exploration*, ch. 10, http://www.space.edu/projects/book/chapter10.html.
11. Allison, *Essence of Decision*, 176.
12. This concept is from Robert Putnam, "Diplomacy and Domestic Politics: The Logic of Two-Level Games," *International Organization* 42 (Summer 1988): 427–460.
13. The standard treatment of all these issues is Morton H. Halperin, *Bureaucratic Politics and Foreign Policy* (Brookings, 1974).
14. Andrew Knight, "The Conduct of American Foreign Policy: Ronald Reagan's Watershed Year," *Foreign Affairs: America and the World 1982*, http://www.foreignaffairs.org.
15. Allison, *Essence of Decision*, 131–132.
16. Alexander L. George, "The 'Operational Code': A Neglected Approach to the Study of Political Leaders and Decision-Making," *International Studies Quarterly* 13:2 (1969): 197.
17. Margaret G. Hermann, "Assessing Leadership Style: A Trait Analysis," *Social Science Automation*, 1999, 10, http://www.socialscience.net/Docs/LTA.pdf.

18. This simplified presentation is drawn from Margaret G. Hermann, Thomas Preston, Baghat Korany, and Timothy M. Shaw, "Who Leads Matters: The Effect of Powerful Individuals," *International Studies Review* 3:2 (Summer 2001): 90–97.

19. Hermann, Preston, Korany, and Shaw, "Who Leads Matters," 96.

20. Marc J. O'Reilly and Wesley B. Renfro, "Like Father, Like Son? A Comparison of the Foreign Policies of George H. W. Bush and George W. Bush," *Historia Actual Online* 10 (2006): 17–36, http://historia-actual.org/Publicaciones/index.php/haol/article/viewFile/148/136.

21. Margaret G. Hermann, "William Jefferson Clinton's Leadership Style," in Jerrold M. Post, ed., *The Psychological Assessment of Political Leaders* (University of Michigan, 2003), 313–323.

22. Benedict Carey, "Teasing Out Policy Insight from a Character Profile," March 28, 2011, http://www.nytimes.com/2011/03/29/science/29psych.html.

23. Margaret G. Hermann, "Effects of Personal Characteristics of Political Leaders on Foreign Policy," in *Why Nations Act*, Maurice A. East, Stephen A. Salmore, and Charles F. Hermann, eds. (SAGE, 1978), 49–68.

24. Thomas L. Friedman, *The Lexus and the Olive Tree* (Farrar, Straus and Giroux, 1999), 13.

25. Friedman, *The Lexus and the Olive Tree*, 12, 322–328.

26. A. F. Lowenthal, *The Dominican Intervention* (Harvard, 1972), 161.

27. Jeffrey Record, "The Use and Abuse of History: Munich, Vietnam, and Iraq," *Survival* 49:1 (Spring 2007).

28. Robert Jervis, "Hypotheses on Misperception," *World Politics* 20:3 (1968): 454–479.

29. Irving Janis, *Groupthink: Psychological Studies of Policy Decisions and Fiascos* (Houghton-Mifflin, 1982), 11.

30. Amos Tversky and Daniel Kahneman, "Judgment Under Uncertainty: Heuristics and Biases," Science 185:4157 (1974): 1124–1131.

31. Alex Mintz, "Applied Decision Analysis: Utilizing Poliheuristic Theory to Explain and Predict Foreign Policy and National Security Decisions," *International Studies Perspectives* 6:1 (2005): 94–98.

32. Alex Mintz, "How Do Leaders Make Decisions?: A Poliheuristic Perspective," *Journal of Conflict Resolution* 48:1 (2006): 8–9.

33. J. Tyson Chatagnier, Alex Mintz, and Yair Samban, "The Decision Calculus of Terrorist Leaders," *Perspectives on Terrorism* 6:4-5 (2012), http://www.terrorismanalysts.com/pt/index.php/pot/article/view/220/html.

34. Andrew Moravcsik, "Taking Preferences Seriously: A Liberal Theory of International Politics," *International Organization* 51.4 (1997): 542.

Chapter 4

War and Violence in World Politics

The Realist's World

Hiroshima, 1945. Given the devastation that a great power war would create in the nuclear era, is the Clausewitzian view of war as "the continuation of policy" now obsolete?

 Learning Objectives

4-1 Discuss both the causes and the moral implications of the resort to war in world politics.

4-2 Discuss the evolution of modern warfare and the impact of the development of nuclear weapons.

4-3 Evaluate both the evidence for and competing explanations of the decline in interstate war.

4-4 Identify the trends shaping the nature of future war.

Throughout human history, war and the threat of war have been a constant part of international life and central to understanding how the world works. Though all of the international relations paradigms both recognize and provide explanations for war, realism is most pessimistic about the chances of eliminating war or even substantially reducing its frequency. In a world with no effective and reliable higher authority to impose order, realists insist that states will, from time to time, need to protect their vital interests through the use of force and violence. As realist scholar John Mearsheimer has argued, war, including great power war, has not yet been "burned out of the system," and, thus, "the real world remains a realist world."[1]

However, this view of war has come under increasing challenge. The amount of interstate war has declined in recent decades, and, most important, the great powers have not warred directly against each other since World War II. As scholar John Mueller has argued, conflicts of interest among states might remain, but, especially among the great powers, war as a means of settling them "has increasingly been discredited and abandoned."[2]

This chapter will examine the evolving record of war in world politics. First, we will examine the role of war in world politics, including an examination of the frequency of war, its causes, and the moral questions posed by an activity that involves so much purposeful taking of human life. Second, we will examine the emergence and evolution of twentieth-century-style "total war." The destruction rendered by twentieth-century technologies of warfare raises questions, both moral and empirical, as to whether the Clausewitzian view of war as the "continuation of policy" (see Chapter 1) can remain relevant. Third, we examine the evidence of a decline of the frequency of war in recent decades and competing explanations of that decline offered by various international relations paradigms. Finally, the chapter concludes with a discussion of trends in twenty-first-century violence.

As you read, keep in mind Mearsheimer's assertion, noted previously, that "the real world remains a realist world," and ask yourself whether trends in the use of force and violence do, in fact, portend a fundamental change in how the world works. Do war and violence remain the ultimate currency of influence in world politics or have the evolution of military technology and moral norms combined to create a world in which war is increasingly "burned out of the system"?

War in World Politics

4-1 Discuss both the causes and the moral implications of the resort to war in world politics.

For many lay observers of world politics, war is an unfortunate interruption of the normal state of peace among countries. When wars do occur, they are often blamed on individual leaders with militaristic ambitions and inclinations. Go onto the street and ask passersby about the primary cause of World War II, and their answers will likely begin with the name Adolf Hitler. Likewise, depending on whom you ask or where you are doing the asking, the 2003 invasion of Iraq by the United States is likely to be blamed on either Saddam Hussein or George W. Bush.

When it comes to thinking about war, scholars suggest that Americans in particular tend not to be natural-born realists. The American view of war as an exceptional state of affairs is not hard to understand given US history and geography. Due to the luxury of its location in the Western Hemisphere, no war has been fought on American soil since the Civil War, and the last time foreign troops fought on American territory was the War of 1812. Americans have experienced terrorist attacks on the homeland, such as the September 11, 2001 attacks on the World Trade Center and the Pentagon, but no American alive today has ever had foreign soldiers march across his or her property, has ever had to hide in a shelter while bombs rained from above, or has ever experienced the death of a child on US soil at the hands of an enemy army. Nevertheless, the record of human history stands in sharp contrast to the view of peace as the norm.

The Prevalence of War and Violence

The United States, in its relatively brief history as a nation, has fought in a dozen major interstate wars and has been involved in countless smaller-scale military conflicts. The average number of years between American involvements in major wars has been less than two decades, and the result is that every American generation since the American Revolution has lived through years of America at war. Well over 1 million American soldiers have died in battle, and the number of wounded is many times that number (see Table 4.1).

The global record is even worse. Political scientist J. David Singer and his associates in the Correlates of War Project have been collecting and analyzing data on modern (nineteenth- and twentieth-century) war for more than four decades.[3] Despite defining war very conservatively as sustained military combat with a minimum of 1,000 battle deaths—a definition common among political scientists—the record of the past two centuries is sobering. According to the Correlates of War data, 401 wars occurred during the period 1816 to 1997. Those wars were of three types:[4]

- *Interstate wars:* those pitting two or more legally recognized sovereign states against one another. World Wars I and II and the 1991 Persian Gulf War are obvious examples. There were 79 of these wars from 1816 to 1997.
- *Extra-state wars:* those in which at least one participant is a nonstate actor. In many cases, these have been wars of independence waged by colonies against imperial powers. Examples include the Franco–Algerian War of 1954 and the Portuguese–Angolan War of 1975. There were 108 of these wars from 1816 to 1997.
- *Intrastate wars, or civil wars:* those fought among groups within the borders of a sovereign state. Examples include the 1992 fighting among Serbs, Croats, and Muslims in Bosnia as well as the conflict in Chechnya. This is the largest group, with 214 wars from 1816 to 1997.

Table 4.1   America at War

War	Duration	Deaths of US Military Personnel
American Revolution	1775–1783	4,435
War of 1812	1812–1815	2,260
Mexican War	1846–1848	13,283
Civil War	1861–1865	364,511 (Union) 198,524 (Confederate)
Spanish–American War	1898	2,446
World War I	1917–1918	116,516
World War II	1941–1945	405,399
Korean War	1950–1953	36,574
Vietnam War	1964–1973	58,220
Persian Gulf War	1990–1991	383
War on Terror*	2001–present	2,131[†]
Iraq War	2003–present	4,409[†]
Total Deaths	1775–present	1,209,091

NOTE: The table includes major wars but not smaller-scale conflicts, interventions, or peacekeeping operations. The figures are for deaths of military personnel in battle and (except for the American Revolution and War of 1812 for which reliable nonbattle deaths are not available) from other causes such as war-related accident, disease, and suicide.

*Includes deaths in Afghanistan, the Philippines, Southeast Asia, and elsewhere.

†Through October 22, 2012.

SOURCES: Anne Leland, "American War and Military Operation Casualties: Lists and Statistics," Congressional Research Service, November 15, 2012. Source for Confederate deaths in the Civil War is United States Civil War Center, "Statistical Summary: America's Major Wars," http://www.cwc.lsu.edu/cwc/other/stats/warcost.htm.

Collectively, there is an average of 2.22 new wars per year.[5] When one considers that most wars last more than one year, the average number of wars in progress around the world at any time is even higher. Indeed, it would be hard to find a day in the past two centuries when at least one war was not taking place somewhere.

The use of military power comes in forms other than war. **Coercive diplomacy** involves the threat or the small-scale demonstration of military power short of war in order to influence the behavior of others. The Correlates of War Project refers to conflicts that involve coercive diplomacy as militarized interstate disputes (MIDs). Since 1816 there have been thousands of such MIDs documented, including 296 new ones (almost 33 per year) that began in the period from 1993 to 2001 alone.[6] Such disputes can involve, among other things, such forms of coercive diplomacy as raising military alert levels, mobilizing troops, sending planes close to or inside of other states' airspace, firing warning shots, or even small-scale skirmishes between opposing forces (see Theory in Practice 4.1).

Most of those thousands of militarized disputes never escalated to war as we have defined it (a sustained conflict with 1,000-plus battle deaths), and the sum total of death and destruction wrought by them pales in comparison to

coercive diplomacy
Threats and small-scale demonstrations of military power designed to send a signal and impact the behavior of other actors in the international system.

Theory in Practice 4.1

Coercive Diplomacy in the Taiwan Strait

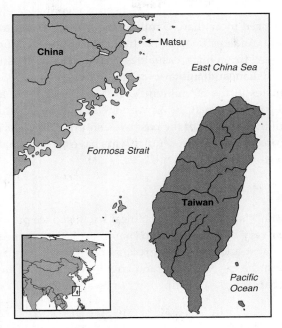

Since the Chinese Revolution of 1949, tension has prevailed in the Taiwan Strait, with China insisting that Taiwan must be reunited with the Communist mainland, Taiwan insisting on retaining its autonomy, and the United States caught between its commitment to protect Taiwan and the economic and military challenges of its relationship with Beijing. Through it all, China, Taiwan, and the United States have used coercive diplomacy as a way of signaling intentions and drawing lines in the sand. Recent examples include:

April 1, 2001: US spy plane operating off the coast of China collides with a Chinese fighter jet. China detains the US crew for 11 days and the plane for 3 months.

April 2001: Bush administration approves first US arms sales to Taiwan since 1974.

June–July 2001: Chinese war games simulate an attack on Taiwan.

January 2004: Taiwan announces referendum on acquisition of antimissile weapons unless China removes the missiles it has targeted at Taiwan.

February 2004: China begins new military exercises over coastal areas opposite Taiwan.

February 2004: United States deploys bombers to Guam.

March 8, 2005: China's People's Congress passes a law authorizing the use of force if necessary to prevent Taiwan from acquiring formal independence.

March 22, 2008: Taiwan holds presidential election and same-day referendum on whether Taiwan should be readmitted to UN. China had warned of the high risk of a military incident should the referendum pass or pro-independence party win.

2008: United States deploys three aircraft carrier strike groups to waters near Taiwan in response to Chinese election period warning.

2009–2010: Failure of referendum and defeat of pro-independence party leads to reduction of tensions, but China continued to increase the number of missiles deployed across the strait from Taiwan.

June 29, 2011: Chinese warplanes intercept a US surveillance aircraft in the strait.

August 25, 2014: Chinese surveillance planes made 4 intrusions into Taiwanese airspace within 12 hours.

What are the risks and benefits of coercive diplomacy in comparison with the use of other means to assert national interests?

Under what circumstances is coercive diplomacy likely to succeed? Explain.

In the past few years, Russia has escalated its coercive diplomacy directed at the West with bomber flights close to US and West European borders, submarine incursions in the waters off Sweden, and much more. What do you think is the purpose of this activity?

SOURCES: Map from http://archives.cnn.com. Chronology from PBS *Frontline*, "Dangerous Straits: Chronology," http://www.pbs.org; "Taiwan Confrontation: Introduction," http://www.globalsecurity.org, *Washington Times*, April 17, 2008; Ted Galen Carpenter, "Taiwan Strait," Cato Institute, January 7, 2010; *The Washington Times*, July 25, 2011; and J. Michael Cole, "Chinese Surveillance Aircraft Enter Taiwan's Airspace," *The Diplomat*, August 27, 2014, http://thediplomat.com/2014/08/chinese-surveillance-aircraft -enter-taiwans-airspace/.

full-scale warfare. But each clearly involves the use of military power and self-help, and in combination with the actual wars that break out, the prevalence of coercive diplomacy contributes to the realist characterization of world politics as a Hobbesian war of all against all.

The human cost of all this war and violence has been staggering. The 412 wars from 1816 to 1997 produced more than 53 million battle deaths.[7] Yet even that horrifying total grossly underestimates the human carnage produced by war, as it does not account for civilian casualties. In World War II alone, estimates of total deaths, civilian and military, range anywhere from 35 to 60 million, with most estimates in the 50 million range.[8] Thus, once you add in civilian deaths, the total cost in human life of World War II equaled all the military combat deaths in all the 412 wars of the past two centuries. Total deaths (military and civilian) produced by twentieth-century wars have been estimated at approximately 87 million worldwide.[9]

The Causes of War

The "central puzzle about war," as a well-known political scientist once put it, is that wars occur despite their very high costs.[10] In trying to explain that puzzle, scholars employ both rationalist and cognitive explanations of war. You will recall the distinction between the rational actor and cognitive models of decision-making discussed in Chapter 3. That distinction can be applied specifically to the issue of war.

RATIONALIST EXPLANATIONS OF WAR   Rationalist explanations of war are based on the assumption that war is a strategic activity. War is, in other words, purpose driven and based on a rational calculation of costs and benefits. Realists tend to view war in such rationalist terms.

The implicit question that any realist would ask before going to war is, "Are the interests that can be successfully protected or promoted worth it in comparison to the potential costs?" Those costs might include money expended, economic assets destroyed, political goodwill lost, and the number of one's soldiers likely to be killed. In some cases, the calculation might lead one to choose war as a necessary and prudent act. In other cases, the costs might be seen as too high. For example, John Mearsheimer, one of the most outspoken contemporary realists, and one of the theorists quoted at the beginning of this chapter, opposed the US decision to go to war in Iraq precisely because he did not believe the cost–benefit calculation added up in favor of war. In his view, continued UN sanctions, coupled with the threat of massive American military retaliation in the event that Iraq acquired and used weapons of mass destruction against the United States or its allies, were sufficient to contain Iraq at a much lower cost than going to war.[11] His opposition to the war was not simply that people would be killed but, rather, that American interests would not be served.

Given the high costs of war, some scholars ask how states can ever rationally choose to go to war. Despite Mearsheimer's opposition, the United States did indeed invade Iraq in 2003, and it has, arguably, paid a huge human and geopolitical price for that decision. Rationalist scholars argue that diplomatic solutions are always preferable to war. So why does war often win out? Two main answers are offered.[12] First, there is the problem of "credible commitment." States are often unsure if the other party is either able or willing to stick to the terms of a negotiated solution. If one is unsure of that, then it might be better to fight now before the other side's advantage increases. Second, states might intentionally misrepresent information about both their capabilities and their costs of fighting should war occur. Such misrepresentation might give them more leverage in conducting negotiations, but it could also result in the failure of those negotiations and lead to war.

A good illustration of these rationalist dilemmas was found in the discussions that took place in 2015 over Iranian nuclear weapons. The United States had an interest in preventing Iran from acquiring nuclear weapons both because of the threat posed to US interests and the fear that it would unleash a dangerous round of nuclear proliferation in the Middle East. Iran, for its part, saw nuclear weapons, at a minimum, as a deterrent against outside intervention and as support for its desire to become a regional power. Given that resolving those differences in interest through war would be extremely costly to the United States, to Iran, and to the wider Middle East, some kind of negotiated solution seemed preferable, and that is what negotiators in 2015 were seeking. But US and Israeli critics raised issues of credible commitment: Would Iran really stop its nuclear program? Would it cheat on an agreement? Would a UN inspections regime be effective? If Iran is likely to cheat, would war be better now than in 10 years after a nuclear breakout? And if both sides were also intentionally misrepresenting their capabilities and intentions, it makes the challenge of finding a negotiated settlement even more difficult. However the Iranian situation turns out (and by the time you are reading these lines we may have a clearer sense of whether war or negotiation will be the response to the Iranian nuclear issue), it is a good illustration of rationalist explanations and dilemmas.

COGNITIVE EXPLANATIONS OF WAR   In contrast to rationalist explanations of war, cognitive explanations emphasize the limits of human rationality, stressing instead the impact of cognitive biases and misperceptions in explaining the outbreak of war. Among the biases and misperceptions that can lead to war are the following:[13]

- Misjudging the other side's nature and intentions.
- Overestimating one's capabilities and chances of victory.
- Underestimating the other side's capabilities and the costs they can impose.
- Underestimating the will of the other side to fight.
- Failure to adequately anticipate the consequences of war—even a war one wins.

Examples of such misperceptions can be found in the history of every major war. In World War I, all of the major parties thought the war would be short and that they would be victorious. In World War II, Western leaders grossly underestimated Hitler's ambitions, and some thought he could be appeased. In Vietnam, the United States saw Ho Chi Minh, the North Vietnamese leader, as a tool of the USSR and Communist China, and it failed to appreciate the divisions and suspicions within world communism. In Afghanistan, the Soviet Union invaded in 1979 thinking, despite the history of failed attempts by outside powers to control the mountainous country, that it would succeed where others had failed. In a 2010 article, political scientist David Lake argued that the Bush administration's decision to invade Iraq in 2003 was based on numerous misperceptions and cognitive biases that included: overestimating the threat posed by Saddam Hussein, underestimating the costs of victory, misunderstanding Iraq's readiness to become a liberal democratic regime, and misreading the issue of Iraq's WMD intentions and capabilities.[14] In turn, Saddam Hussein misread the situation in various ways: he overestimated the ability of his military to hold out against US forces; he overestimated the degree to which world opinion, which was overwhelmingly opposed to a US invasion, might deter US military action; and he underestimated the determination of the Bush administration to act. Indeed, his unwillingness to allow greater access to UN weapons inspectors despite the fact that there was no significant Iraqi nuclear program in place by 2003, might have been based on the mistaken perception that doubts about Iraqi WMD might act as a deterrent to US intervention.

While cognitive explanations of the causes of war do not dismiss rational, strategic calculations as part of the explanation for why states fight, they suggest that rationalist explanations are at best incomplete. Decisions to go to war are made by human beings subject to intellectual and cognitive limitations that limit strict rationality in decision-making about war or, for that matter, about any substantive issue of international relations.

LEVELS OF ANALYSIS AND CAUSES OF WAR   Whether one adopts a rationalist or cognitive perspective on war, the likelihood of war breaking out will be affected by factors found at the systemic, the state, and the individual levels of analysis. Realists focus on the systemic level of analysis and always begin with the assumption of anarchy. But to say that anarchy provides a systemic context in which wars can occur does not, by itself, help us to understand why a particular war occurs at one point in time but not another. So realists point to other more specific characteristics of the international system that make the world more or less war prone at a given point in time. For example, some point to the existence of arms races as a contributing factor. Others suggest that periods of **power transition**, in which a prevailing dominant power is challenged by a rising power that is unsatisfied with the existing distribution of influence, are particularly war prone. Still other realists debate whether it is multipolar, bipolar, or unipolar systems that are most conducive to war.

Realists are not the only scholars who look at war from the systemic level of analysis. Liberals might view the level of development of international

power transition
A shift in power (especially military power) from one country or group of countries to another. Some see such transitions as periods of instability that are prone to war.

institutions or the degree of global economic interdependence as affecting the war proneness of the international system at a given point in time. Constructivists, similarly, might view the prevailing global norms about the use of force as an important factor, and Marxists sometimes place the blame for war at the foot of the global capitalist system.

Others, especially nonrealist scholars, look inside national borders, at the state level of analysis, for explanations of war. Marxist scholars look to the needs of domestic economic elites and the so called **military industrial complex** of private industries, public bureaucracies, and politicians dependent on defense spending as a spur to war. Liberal scholars sometimes focus on regime type as an important variable, with democracies seen as less war prone (at least vis-à-vis other democracies) than authoritarian regimes. At the same time, some scholars have argued that periods of democratization, when regimes are in the midst of transitions from authoritarian rule, can be especially war prone given weak regimes, rising nationalism, and the consequent efforts of elites to use war as a stimulus to national unity.[15] More generally, the diversionary theory of war suggests that political leaders sometimes resort to war to deflect attention from domestic shortcomings.

Finally, many studies of war point to the individual level of analysis as the locus of explanation. The beliefs (ideological or religious) and personality of top leaders are considered as key factors by many, as are the cognitive abilities and limitations of human beings who make decisions about matters of war and peace. At a more general level, feminist scholars might point to the gender of leaders as an important element of the war calculus. Even scholars who stress systemic and state level factors would not entirely discount the impact of individual variables. Perhaps World War II can be explained largely by the logic of multipolarity, perhaps the Russian invasion of Crimea in 2014 can be viewed in the context of security dilemmas or the influence of a Russian military industrial complex, and perhaps the prospects of a twenty-first-century war between the United States and China might be viewed in the context of the theory of power transitions. But, at the same time, no one is likely to entirely dismiss the influence of Hitler, Putin, and future American and Chinese leaders in attempting to explain and anticipate the sources of interstate war—past, present, or future. The factors affecting the propensity to war are numerous and not necessarily mutually exclusive.

military industrial complex
The interconnected web of defense industries, defense bureaucracies, and politicians dependent on military spending and the threat of war to serve their respective interests.

War and Morality

For realists, the absence of a higher authority makes it difficult to establish and enforce standards of morality in the conduct of interstate relations. Recall the quote from Hobbes in Chapter 1: "Where there is no common power, there is no law; where no law, no injustice." Thus, in the realist view, the frequency to which states resort to war to settle disputes is predictable, if not always desirable. It is, as Clausewitz suggested, the "continuation of policy."

For many, this cold, calculating, cost–benefit approach to war can be morally troubling, especially when discussing an activity in which millions of lives are at stake. But one might counter that this approach to warfare is really not so exceptional. Consider, for example, the case of the automobile. In 2003 there were 42,643 traffic deaths in the United States,[16] and since the beginning of the automobile age early in the twentieth century, close to 3 million people have been killed due to automobiles in the United States.[17] In contrast, the number of US military personnel killed in all of the major US wars of the twentieth century was approximately 624,000 (see Table 4.1), or about one-fifth the number of automobile-related deaths. Likewise, the 486 US soldiers killed in the Iraq War in 2003 represented just 1 percent of the number of people killed in US traffic deaths that year.[18]

Given such numbers, one might reasonably suggest that the human cost of the automobile rivals or even exceeds that of war. Yet while people commonly oppose war in general and individual wars in particular on moral grounds, few picket General Motors or call for governments to ban automobiles on such a basis. We need automobiles; they are essential to our modern economy and way of life, and they may even save some lives by allowing quick transport to hospitals and easy access to foods or medicines. But one can make a similar case for war as an activity sometimes needed to defend one's territory, to ensure access to vital resources, or to defeat aggressors who would do harm to one's people. In fact, one might reasonably argue that the loss of a life on a field in France fighting Nazi aggression is more noble and, in a sense, less tragic than a death in a car crash while picking up a pizza.

pacifism
View that war and other forms of violence that bring death and harm to human beings are morally unacceptable.

Critics of realism do not accept, without discussion, this view of war as a cost–benefit calculation based purely on national interests. Located at the extreme opposite end of the spectrum from realism, **pacifism** is the position that any use of violence employed with the intent to kill or do physical harm to other human beings is morally unacceptable. It is an absolutist perspective that allows for no exceptions. No good cause or vital interest can, from this perspective, ever justify the purposeful killing of another human being.

Unlike realists, who distinguish between someone's personal morality and the morality that person employs as leader of a sovereign state, a pacifist sees no such distinction. Pacifists operating within the Judeo-Christian tradition might well argue that the commandment "thou shalt not kill" contains no footnote specifying that political leaders are free to kill, or to order others to kill, if democracy, or oil supplies, or security from terrorist attacks are on the line.

Leo Tolstoy, the great Russian novelist who once served in the Russian army and who wrote about war in his novel *War and Peace*, became an ardent pacifist later in his life. At the age of 80, he stated the pacifist position on war quite clearly in his famous 1909 Address to the Swedish Peace Congress:

> War is not—as most people assume—a good and laudable affair, but … like all murder, it is a vile and criminal business…. With regard to those who voluntarily choose a military career, I would propose to state clearly and definitely that not withstanding all the pomp, glitter, and general approval with which it is surrounded, it is a criminal and shameful activity; and that the higher the position a man holds in the military profession the more criminal and shameful his occupation. In the same way with regard

to men of the people who are drawn into military service by bribes or by threats of punishments, I propose to speak clearly about the gross mistake they make— … when they consent to enter the army … they enter the ranks of murderers contrary to the Law of God.[19]

Tolstoy's words can be uncomfortable. Applied to our own times, everyone involved in the US military establishment—from the secretary of defense down to the army reservist who finds him- or herself reluctantly fighting in a place to which he or she was ordered to go—must, in Tolstoy's view, be considered a criminal and murderer.

Critics of pacifism argue that it is an unacceptable position for two reasons. First, it denies any right of self-defense in the face of violence. Realists, in particular, would suggest that any state that adopted a pacifist position in a world where anarchy prevails and where other states are willing to use or threaten violence would find its interests trampled. Second, and even more important, pacifism denies the right to use violence when needed to defend other innocent lives. Thus, critics of pacifism might ask, if someone had the opportunity to kill Hitler but refused to do so, wouldn't that person have the blood of the 6 million innocent Jews who perished in the Nazi death camps on his or her hands?

The unyielding morality of pacifism seems unacceptable to many because it does not accept the need to confront aggressors and evil-doers with force or even the threat of force. Consequently, the norm of pacifism has never diffused on a broad scope, as most observers have maintained a need to use violence in world politics from time to time (see Theory in Practice 4.2).

Theory in Practice 4.2

Are You a Pacifist?

Many people claim to be pacifists. But hard cases, like saving innocent victims of genocide in Darfur, sometimes make it difficult and put one's pacifism to the test. Take the following test to see if you might qualify as a pacifist:

- If Russia were to invade Poland, would the Poles have the moral right to take up arms in defense of their sovereignty and territory?

- Do you think it was right that the Allies went to war to stop Nazi aggression in World War II?

- Would you have endorsed a covert assassination plot against Hitler in the early 1940s if you thought it could halt the Holocaust?

- Knowing now what happened on September 11, 2001, do you wish that the Clinton administration

had launched a successful missile strike against al-Qaeda camps in Afghanistan and killed Osama bin Laden?

- Would you support use of military force to rescue victims of genocide in Darfur?

If you answered NO to all these questions, you might quality as a pacifist. But if you answered YES to even one, you cannot call yourself a pacifist.

Is pacifism a morally defensible position?

Is it possible to be a pacifist and still fight to make a better world? How so?

Is it indeed the case, as suggested in this chapter and in the test above, that pacifism must be absolute? Explain.

just war doctrine

Perspective which accepts that war can be both necessary and just, but allows that moral considerations must be part of determining when and how to fight.

Far more influential have been the norms embedded in the **just war doctrine**, a perspective on war and morality that (1) accepts, in contrast to pacifism, that war can sometimes be both necessary and just, but (2) allows, in contrast to amoral realism, that ethical and moral considerations must be part of determining when and how to fight. For a war to be considered "just," the human costs must be assessed, and those human costs extend beyond a narrow concern with the impact of war on military personnel and their fighting capabilities. Instead, in the just war perspective, human life is valuable in itself and must be factored into the equation.

Versions of the just war doctrine exist in most societies, cultures, and religious traditions. The Judeo-Christian variant makes a distinction between *jus ad bellum* ("justice of war") and *jus in bello* ("justice in war"). *Jus ad bellum* is concerned with the circumstances in which it is morally acceptable to enter into a war. There are six criteria:

jus ad bellum

(Latin for "justice of a war.") The circumstances in which it is just to enter a war.

1. *Just cause.* Going to war for reasons of legitimate self-defense or to repel and punish aggression are considered just reasons for war. The protection and promotion of human rights might also be a just cause.
2. *Right intention.* War should be fought solely to attain that just cause and not for additional, unspoken purposes of promoting self-interest.
3. *Last resort.* Before going to war, less violent means of resolving the problem must be exhausted, or a reasonable conclusion must be reached that those other means will be futile.
4. *Probability of success.* Even when fought for a just cause, war is a waste of human life if the objectives of the fighting cannot be met. Thus, there must be some reasonable expectation that the goals of the war can be successfully obtained.
5. *Limited objectives.* Fighting must cease once the just cause is obtained. Further fighting to take advantage of the weakness of one's opponent or to exact retribution for the misdeeds of one's adversary would unnecessarily threaten further human life.
6. *Legitimate authority.* The only actors with the legitimacy to use violence in world politics are sovereign states and those international organizations duly authorized by the world community to use force (e.g., the United Nations). Nonstate actors are not authorized to wage war on the grounds that chaos would result if any actor with a good cause had a green light to use violence.

jus in bello

(Latin for "justice in war.") The criteria for how a war must be fought in order to remain just.

Jus in bello is concerned with the way one conducts and fights a war once it is under way. There are two criteria of *jus in bello*:

1. *Discrimination.* Those conducting and fighting a war must take all reasonable efforts to discriminate between soldiers and civilians, and they must attempt to limit harm to the latter.

2. *Proportionality.* The degree of violence used must be proportionate to the just cause pursued. For example, dropping atomic bombs on Baghdad in 1991 to force Iraq out of Kuwait would have been a disproportionate response.

In order for a war to be considered just, all the criteria of the just war doctrine must be met. A doubt about any one of them puts the justice of that war in jeopardy.

While the just war doctrine might seem like an acceptable compromise between amoral realism and unequivocal pacifism, the doctrine has its critics. A major problem is the inherent difficulty of reaching a consensus when applying the criteria. Well-intentioned individuals might, for example, honestly disagree as to whether a particular cause is just or whether war is really a last resort in a particular case. And given that the "probability of success" criterion involves speculation about the future, how can certainty be possible? Thus, pacifists and amoral realists might well agree that the just war doctrine, with criteria loose enough to justify almost any military engagement, does little more than legitimize and give moral cover to the decision to fight. Still, just war theorists maintain the value of entering moral considerations into the calculation. War, by its very nature, is an uncertain enterprise, and virtually every calculation of war's results and impact—military, political, economic, and moral—is subject to falsification as events unfold. But that does not relieve us of attempting a good faith calculation in each area.

Moreover, constructivist and liberal critics of realism might well argue that just war doctrine has had an impact on the actual behavior of states as they contemplate both whether to fight and how to fight wars. For constructivists, just war doctrine is a good example of how powerful norms, developed and diffused over the centuries, can shape and constrain state behavior. For liberals, it is the institutionalization of those just war norms as formal laws, monitored and enforced by international institutions, that is key. For example, the Geneva Conventions of 1949 seek, among other things, to formalize the *jus in bello* principle of "discrimination" by specifying in great detail the measures that states must take to protect civilians in times of war. Though states often violate that principle in practice, it is not irrelevant to their war planning.

A good illustration was the US war in Afghanistan. Some critics argued that the US "rules of engagement" in Afghanistan (the formal rules governing when and how soldiers can use force in conducting operations) were too restrictive, giving insurgent fighters an advantage over US forces. But the concern of military planners was to avoid unnecessary civilian casualties. Those casualties could turn Afghan public opinion against the United States and, because they would violate the norm of discrimination, could also delegitimize the US war effort on a global level. That the US military felt the need to pay homage to that discrimination norm in its war planning is a good illustration of the power of such norms.

The Evolution of Modern War

4-2   **Discuss the evolution of modern warfare and the impact of the development of nuclear weapons.**

Even when constrained by just war considerations, war has always been a brutal enterprise. But as the achievements of the nineteenth-century Industrial Revolution spilled over into the military realm, the brutality of warfare increased. The result was a twentieth century that historian Niall Ferguson characterized as "the bloodiest era in history."[20] It was the era of "total war," underlined by the introduction of nuclear weapons.

The Emergence of Total War

Not only has war been a frequent element of world politics; it has also become more lethal over time. To be sure, many horrible conflicts with enormous loss of human life occurred well before the twentieth century. The Thirty Years' War (1618–1648) devastated central Europe and led to the deaths of millions of noncombatants as armies plundered and ravaged everything in their path. And the war that took the most American lives was not one of the world wars of the twentieth century but the US Civil War. However, in the twentieth century, the pace and efficiency of killing raised the destructive potential of warfare to an entirely different level.

In large part, this change is related to the evolution of technology. Prior to the twentieth century, most battle deaths resulted from close contact between soldiers. As horrible as such battles could be, the efficiency of killing with a sword, a bayonet, or a single-shot rifle cannot be compared to the efficiency of the machine gun, which was introduced in battle on a mass scale in World War I. Likewise, the twentieth-century emergence of the airplane as a tool of war that could deliver increasingly powerful explosives from high altitudes made it possible to almost instantaneously produce hundreds, even thousands of deaths.

Technology, however, is not the entire story. Thinking about warfare also evolved and, specifically, thinking about the relationship of the government and the military to the civilian population. In much of premodern Europe, wars were essentially battles among monarchs, with little emotional attachment between rulers and ruled. Insofar as they were in the path of battle, civilians often suffered greatly, but they had little of the modern notion of patriotism that would lead them to care much about which monarch ultimately won. And the soldiers were often mercenaries who worked for pay rather than love of queen or country.

By the twentieth century, the relationship among civilians, the military, and the government had all changed. All three were now bound in a common cause. Hans Morgenthau, the most influential modern realist thinker, suggested that the twentieth century was the century of **total war**, which he described as war of, by, and against total populations.[21]

total war
Wars of, by, and against total populations; characteristic of the great wars of the twentieth century.

War "of the total population" implies that the people have an emotional attachment to the war, the cause for which it is fought, and who wins and loses. This attachment stems first from the growth of the modern nation-state in post-Westphalian Europe and the sense of nationalism that accompanied it. This attachment would be strengthened even further in those states that adopted forms of democratic governance, as citizens in those states came to see an even tighter connection to their government and its wars.

War "by the total population" reflects the fact that twentieth-century wars were no longer fought by mercenaries, but by large, often conscripted, armies drawn from the nation's population. For example, in the course of World War II, more than 15 million men and women served in the US armed forces.[22] Furthermore, in the twentieth century, domestic economies were heavily militarized, with significant portions of the population, including an increasing number of women, working in factories that provided the means of fighting a war. Indeed, the American success in World War II was arguably due as much to the fighting prowess of "GI Joe" as it was to the production efficiency of "Rosie the Riveter."

Finally, if war is both "of" and "by" total populations, it follows logically that it must also be fought "against" total populations. To the extent that modern states seek the emotional support of their citizens in battle, attacks on those citizens can undermine morale and their support for the war effort. Seen in this light, the Nazi bombing of civilian targets in London in World War II was less the result of a barbaric madman than a predictable extension of the logic of modern war. If the bombing of London led British citizens to question whether the fight against Hitler was worth the cost, then Hitler's task would be made that much easier. Likewise, to the extent that the factories in Germany were churning out guns and tanks and fighter planes, then the American and British bombing raids on those factories might be considered necessary, despite the fact that many such factories were located in highly populated areas. That US factories, because of geography, were immune to attacks by the German air force was a huge advantage for the Allied forces.

The net result of war of, by, and against total populations was more than 22 million dead in World War I,[23] and, as previously noted, approximately 50 million dead in World War II. Never before had so many been killed so fast. The majority of the dead in each case were civilians.

Enter Nuclear Weapons

A new age in international relations began on August 6, 1945, when a US bomber nicknamed "Enola Gay" dropped an atomic bomb nicknamed "Little Boy" on the city of Hiroshima, Japan. In one respect, nuclear weapons represented a departure from the logic of total war. One no longer needed a mass army, or war "by" total population, to cause massive harm to one's adversary. A few planes carrying nuclear bombs and some missiles in silos tipped with nuclear warheads could do the job using only a fraction of the workforce represented by a conventional military campaign.

But in a more significant sense, nuclear weapons represented the culmination of the logic of total war. Because they were weapons of mass destruction, they were the perfect weapon for war "against total populations." According to one US estimate published in 1946, in Hiroshima, a city of 350,000 people, an estimated 70,000 to 80,000 died because of the bombing.[24] More recent data collected by the Hiroshima city government indicate that by the end of 1945, 140,000 had died as a result of the atomic bomb. From 1946 to 1951, an additional 60,000 deaths from injuries and radiation produced by the bomb are estimated, leaving a grand total of 200,000 deaths directly related to the dropping of a single, and by today's standards, relatively small atomic bomb.[25]

Despite these numbers, opinions vary as to how much of a revolution in our thinking about international relations and the role of warfare the atomic age mandated. For some, not much had changed, and atomic bombs were just the latest step in a continuing process of innovation in military technology. After all, as political scientist Thomas Schelling once noted, "Japan was defenseless by August 1945. With a combination of bombing and blockade, eventually invasion, and if necessary the deliberate spread of disease, the United States could probably have exterminated the population of the Japanese islands without nuclear weapons.... Against defenseless people, there is not much that nuclear weapons can do that cannot be done with an ice pick."[26]

Recent events have demonstrated Schelling's point all too tragically. In the East African country of Rwanda in 1994, approximately 800,000 people (many times the number killed at Hiroshima) fell victim to genocide in 100 days. While firearms, especially early in the genocide, were used in the killing, less sophisticated weapons, including knives, machetes, clubs with protruding nails, screwdrivers, hammers, and even bicycle handlebars, all eventually became a part of the technology of killing.[27] (See Figure 4.1 for a comparison of deaths produced by nuclear weapons in Japan and other conventional modes of killing.)

On the other hand, some sensed early on that nuclear weapons were more than just another step in the technology of warfare. It was the speed and the efficiency of the destruction that made nuclear weapons unique. More people may have died from knives and machetes in Rwanda than from the bombing of Hiroshima, but the Rwanda slaughter resulted from thousands of individuals engaging in sustained killings over several months. In Hiroshima, the deaths were all produced by one bomb dropped in an instant from one airplane.

As early as 1946, US military strategist and scholar Bernard Brodie observed that the nuclear age required us to rethink our approach to war and international relations in general: "Thus far the chief purpose of our military establishment has been to win wars. From now on its chief purpose must be to avert them. It can have almost no other useful purpose."[28] For Brodie, nuclear weapons had rendered obsolete Clausewitz's notion of war as the continuation of policy. Why? Because no policy benefits could outweigh the massive cost that

Figure 4.1 Deaths Produced by Various International Events

NOTE: Death figures vary by source. The figures cited here are midrange estimates of immediate deaths found in Rudolph Rummel, "Source List and Detailed Death Tolls for the Twentieth Century Hemoclysm," http://users.erols.com/mwhite28/warstat1.htm.

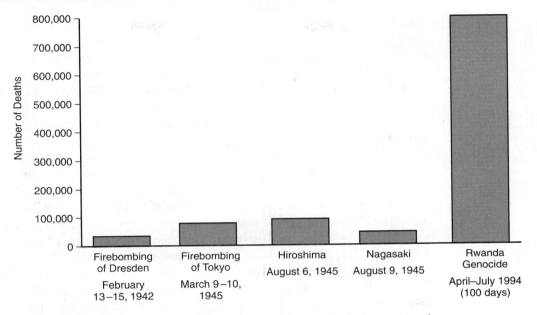

nuclear war, especially one fought between two or more similarly equipped nuclear powers, might now entail.

This view was codified in the concept of **mutual assured destruction (MAD)**. MAD was based on the assumption that as long as each side retained a **second strike capability**—that is, the ability to ride out a first strike with enough retaliatory capability intact to do unacceptable damage to one's opponent—neither side would have an incentive to strike first. MAD relied exclusively on **deterrence**. It assumed that the threat of retaliation would deter each side from launching a first strike, but it provided for no defense from the other side's nuclear attack should deterrence fail. In fact, MAD proponents argued against even trying to defend from a nuclear attack. In part, this was due to doubts about the feasibility of defensive systems. Even more important, defenders of MAD were concerned that the illusion of defense from a nuclear attack might make each side feel less vulnerable and thus more likely to use nuclear weapons. Defense, they feared, might undermine deterrence.

Thus, many came to view nuclear weapons as the basis for a somewhat perverse but stable global peace. The cost of nuclear war, the theory went, was so high that it became unthinkable. Moreover, even a conventional war between the two superpowers had to be averted for fear that once war started, it could escalate to the nuclear level. Thus, while the Cold War was filled with superpower crisis and tension, it was also the longest period of peace among the great powers in modern history.

mutual assured destruction (MAD)

A condition of mutual deterrence in which, in the event of a nuclear war, each side has the capability to inflict an unacceptable level of damage on the other.

second strike capability

Ability to ride out an initial nuclear attack with enough nuclear retaliatory capability left intact to do unacceptable damage to one's adversary.

deterrence

The ability to dissuade another state from acting against one's interests by the threat of harm one might do in response.

Clausewitz was not yet completely dead, however. During the Cold War, smaller conventional wars remained a part of the international landscape. Some of these "limited wars" were actually not so limited, often involving one of the superpowers and high casualties. The United States sacrificed close to 100,000 soldiers fighting limited wars against Communism in Korea and Vietnam, with the total casualties—soldier and civilian—on all sides in those two conflicts running in the millions. Likewise, the Soviet invasion of Afghanistan in 1979 produced 10 years of fighting in which at least 15,000 Soviet soldiers were killed along with a million Afghans.[29] Some scholars have noted the **stability/instability paradox**, in which states feel free to engage in conventional war precisely because they feel secure in the assumption that it can never escalate to nuclear war among the superpowers.

Wars completely below the level of the superpowers have also continued. To cite a few examples, India and Pakistan went to war in 1947, 1965, and 1991. And in 1999, two months of fighting erupted between the two countries over the disputed region of Kashmir, despite the fact that both sides now had nuclear capability. The Iran–Iraq War from 1980 to 1988 cost a million lives, and what has been dubbed "Africa's First World War" has raged in Central Africa since 1998, barely noticed by the world at large despite the fact that it has involved at least six countries and has claimed almost 4 million lives.[30]

Even at the nuclear level, some have attempted to resuscitate Clausewitz and restore relevance to his view of war as the continuation of policy. During the 1980s, for example, supporters and critics of MAD engaged in a heated debate over nuclear strategy. The critics were uncomfortable with MAD because it assumed that each side in the superpowers' nuclear "balance of terror" was a rational actor with the same approach to ethics and the value of human life. If that assumption was wrong and an irrational or ethically callous leader came to power in a nuclear state, those weapons might very well be used.

In light of this concern, the Reagan administration in the 1980s pursued a nuclear strategy that emphasized ways to fight, survive, and even win a nuclear war. Critics labeled the Reagan strategy NUTS—an acronym for **nuclear utilization theories**. The Reagan strategy aimed to limit the damage of nuclear war by relocating people to more rural locations in case of a nuclear confrontation and by development of more accurate offensive missiles that could destroy Soviet missiles before they were even launched. But the centerpiece of the Reagan approach was the **Strategic Defense Initiative (SDI)**. Dubbed "star wars" by its critics after a popular science fiction movie of the time, SDI was a multibillion-dollar research program intended to find ways to defend the US homeland from a nuclear attack by destroying enemy offensive missiles before they could hit their targets.

The debate is whether the NUTS approach makes the unthinkable more thinkable. Those who see MAD as a successful deterrent say "yes." The more convinced one is that nuclear war can be survived and won, the more one might tempt fate and try it. Plus, one country's preparation for limited nuclear war might frighten others to launch a preemptive strike on it. NUTS proponents say "no." Even a

stability/instability paradox
Idea that states will engage in conventional war precisely because they feel secure that it can never escalate to nuclear war among the superpowers.

nuclear utilization theories (NUTS)
Strategies for fighting, surviving, and winning a nuclear war in the event that deterrence fails.

Strategic Defense Initiative (SDI)
Reagan administration initiative designed to develop and deploy a system of nuclear defense that would render harmless enemy missiles before they could hit their targets.

limited nuclear war will be destructive enough to deter most rational leaders, and if other leaders with nuclear weapons are irrational, the need for a nuclear defense becomes even more crucial. The more prepared one country is to fight and win a nuclear war, the less someone else will be likely to start one with it.

With the disintegration of the USSR in 1991 and the end of the Cold War, the debate over nuclear strategies simmered down a bit and, to some observers, seemed increasingly irrelevant in a world where Russia and the West were enjoying more friendly relations. But by the end of the decade, the mood had changed considerably. Russian–US relations were turning cool again, concerns about the rise of China were escalating in some circles, and fears of a new round of nuclear proliferation were growing.

Nuclear proliferation is the spread of nuclear weapons to nonnuclear countries. At the beginning of the nuclear age, some anticipated the rapid spread of nuclear weapons to perhaps dozens of countries. In fact, by the 1960s only five countries (the United States, the USSR, China, Britain, and France) were members of the nuclear club. In 1968 the nuclear **Non-Proliferation Treaty (NPT)** was adopted and eventually signed and ratified by the vast majority of countries. The treaty prohibited nonnuclear countries from developing nuclear weapons and banned existing nuclear states from transferring nuclear weapons technology to nonnuclear states. The treaty further provided for inspections by the UN-related International Atomic Energy Agency to ensure that peaceful nuclear technologies were not being diverted to weapons development.

> **nuclear proliferation**
> The spread of nuclear weapons to previously nonnuclear states.

> **Non-Proliferation Treaty (NPT)**
> A 1968 treaty that sought to limit the spread of nuclear weapons to nonnuclear states.

Among the handful of countries not originally party to the NPT were Israel, Pakistan, and India. In all three cases, there was an intention to develop nuclear weapons, by the 1970s and 1980s weapons testing and development were under way, and by the 1990s it was clear that all three had nuclear weapons capability. In 1998, India and Pakistan each engaged in tit-for-tat nuclear tests designed to demonstrate their capabilities, raising a new round of concern about further proliferation. The focus of that concern in recent years has been on North Korea (which withdrew from the NPT in 2003) and Iran (which remains a party to the NPT). The challenge is not only those two countries but also the chain reaction they could produce among their neighbors. In Asia, a nuclear North Korea might provoke a rethinking of Japan's policy on nuclear weapons and also stimulate proliferation in South Korea and Taiwan. In the Middle East, International Atomic Energy Agency (IAEA) and CIA reports in 2005 noted some evidence of unreported nuclear experiments in Egypt; more recently, Saudi Arabia has indicated a willingness to go nuclear if diplomatic efforts to forestall an Iranian nuclear breakout failed.[31]

Some have suggested that this proliferation can be a stabilizing force, injecting a dose of caution into and inducing resolution of historically volatile conflicts, such as those between Israel and its Arab neighbors or between India and Pakistan. These proliferation optimists suggest that if the threat of mutual assured destruction could prevent war between the United States and USSR for half a century, it could have a similar impact elsewhere.

Others are not so confident.[32] These proliferation pessimists are concerned that as the number of nuclear states increases, the statistical probability of nuclear deterrence breaking down will increase. That breakdown can result either from a purposeful decision to use nuclear weapons or from a loss of command and control in which nuclear weapons fall into the hands of terrorists or other rogue actors.

War in Decline?: The Post–Cold War Era

4-3 **Evaluate both the evidence for and competing explanations of the decline in interstate war.**

Newspaper headlines about wars and threats of war, combined with the increasing lethality and violence associated with modern weapons of mass destruction, lead, understandably, to the popular perception of a world that has become steadily more dangerous over time. In fact, recent trends provide at least some reason for cautious optimism, as some data suggest a decline in interstate war in the post–Cold War era. Scholars working within different paradigms provide different assessments of the cause of this trend and of its long-term significance. In this section, we will begin by describing the recent decline in interstate war and then compare a few alternative explanations that have been offered.

Declining Frequency of War

The first optimistic trend to note is that, in the years since the Cold War ended, the trajectory has been an overall decline in warfare across the globe. Putting aside the years 1990 and 1991 when the Cold War was ending and intrastate, or civil, wars surged, after 1991 such wars fell back roughly to their Cold War era frequency. At the same time, interstate war declined from an average of 1.43 new wars per year during the Cold War to 0.64 new wars per year in the period from 1991 to 2013—more than a 50 percent reduction.[33] The net result, as illustrated in Figure 4.2, is that the number of states experiencing any sort of warfare rose consistently over the Cold War era, reaching a peak in 1991 of close to 30 percent of states. After 1991, however, the trend has been consistently downward, with less than 15 percent of states involved in any form of warfare in 2013.

long peace
The era from the end of World War II through the end of the Cold War and continuing into the early twenty-first century, during which there has been no great power war.

Second, the trend toward avoidance of the most destructive kinds of wars— those involving direct clashes among the great powers—has continued in the post–Cold war era. While those great powers have continued to fight wars against weaker states and to treat those wars as proxy fights against other great powers, they have not fought one another directly since the end of World War II. This is not a small accomplishment, given the lethality of wars waged by the great powers. Thus, in labeling the post–World War II era as the **long peace**,

Figure 4.2 Trends in Warfare, 1946–2013

SOURCE: Graph, "States Experiencing Warfare, 1946–2013" from Center for Systemic Peace "Global Conflict Trends" online, http://www.systemicpeace.org/CTfigures/CTfig04.htm. Used by permission of Monty G. Marshall.

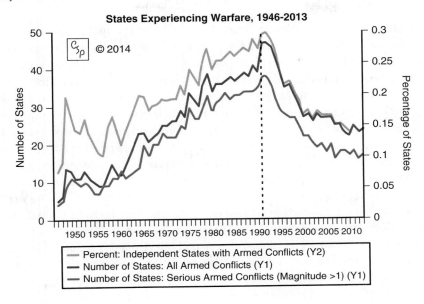

historian John Lewis Gaddis might not be literally accurate, but he does capture an important and positive characteristic of the period.[34]

Finally, some countries have essentially taken war off the table as an option in their relations with certain other countries. In particular, according to political scientist Robert Jervis, the United States, Canada, Japan, and the countries of Western Europe have created what he calls a **security community**—a group of countries that no longer threaten or fear war with one another.[35] His idea of a security community seems to trump the realist notion of the security dilemma and the feelings of mutual insecurity that it generates. No one in France, for example, fears British nuclear weapons, and no one in Canada fears the arms of the world's greatest superpower just to their south. Indeed, this security community, already in evidence during the Cold War, has since expanded. Several post-Communist states of central Europe have joined Western institutions such as the European Union and NATO, and can now be included in that group of states among whom war is virtually unthinkable.

security community
Group of states that have ruled out the use of war and violence as a means of resolving conflicts with one another.

Explanations of Peace

The evidence, discussed above, of a decline of interstate war provides cause for some to suggest both the declining utility of the realist paradigm and a cautious basis for hope that the era in which war is "the continuation of policy" may be coming to an end. Realists, however, would caution that war continues to be an instrument of policy and that the recent downturn in interstate war can be explained within the parameters of the realist paradigm.

A REALIST EXPLANATION OF PEACE Central to the realist explanation of both war and peace is the distribution of power. John Mearsheimer, for example, has argued that the "long peace" among the great powers that characterized the Cold War era was a result of the bipolar balance of power between the United States and the USSR.[36] In his view, a bipolar system is especially stable and less likely to lead to great power war than a multipolar system. Because multipolar systems have more players, they are more complex with more pairs of states with potential conflicts, more opportunity for the imbalances of power to develop, and more opportunity for miscalculation.[37] Bipolar systems, by comparison, are simpler. There is only one other state whose power must be assessed and balanced.

Reinforcing that tendency was the impact of nuclear weapons. The reality of mutual assured destruction created extra incentive for both the United States and USSR to prevent the many Cold War era crises from evolving into hot wars. Even as other countries (China, France, and the United Kingdom) acquired nuclear weapons, the gap in nuclear capabilities between the two superpowers, on the one hand, and the other smaller nuclear powers was so large that the essential bipolarity of the international system remained unaltered.

For better or worse, the distribution of power in the post–Cold War era looks very different from that of the Cold War. The collapse of the Soviet Union effectively ended the bipolar, Cold War era. However, the immediate result was not multipolarity. Bipolarity was replaced, at least temporarily, by an international system in which one superpower, the United States, seemed to be in an unchallenged position of hegemony, or dominance, in world affairs. Observers began to talk about a "unipolar moment," and well-known scholars published books on the consequences of a new period of American empire. Indeed, the American dominance not only in military power but also in economic, political, and cultural influence seemed so overwhelming in the 1990s that a French foreign minister thought it necessary to coin a new word—"hyper-puissance" or hyper-power—to fully capture the multifaceted nature of US hegemony after the Cold War.[38]

US hegemony helps explain the decline of interstate war during the 1990s. As many realists have long argued, hegemony begets peace, as other countries are wary of the power of the hegemon. At the same time, while hegemony might explain peace in the short run, it is not something that will last indefinitely. As realists would also argue, periods of hegemony eventually end, and other states do eventually attempt to balance the power of the hegemon. Such periods of challenge can be very dangerous, with great power tension and, potentially, great power war. As previously noted, the power transition theory suggests that the international system is particularly prone to great power war when the prevailing dominant power is challenged by a rising power that is unsatisfied with the existing distribution of influence.

Anticipating precisely such a challenge to the United States from the emerging power of China, some observers have suggested that we may one day look back on the 1990s as a period of calm before the storm.[39] And while the danger of a US–Chinese conflict is a long-term threat, in the wake of the tensions over Ukraine some observers have suggested that it is a US–Russian war that is the more immediate concern. Depending on how things play out, a resurgent Russia, an increasingly assertive Germany, a militarized Japan, a nuclear Iran, and a newly emergent India might all, along with the United States and China, be key players in an increasingly multipolar twenty-first century that reverses the peaceful trends of the 1990s.

Realists, in short, would argue that the post–Cold War era is barely a quarter century old, a mere blip on the radar screen of history. While the entire era of the long peace among the great powers from 1946 to the present is notable, it too is a relatively short period in the wider sweep of world history. Thus, what some see as a long-term transformation of world politics may be little more than a short-term cyclical downturn in war and violence. Indeed, in other eras, war was thought to be in decline, only to reemerge. The 1920s, for example, were an era of relative global peace, but the most destructive interstate war in the history of humanity soon followed.

A LIBERAL EXPLANATION OF PEACE   As noted in Chapter 1, the Kantian triangle suggests three potential sources of peace in world politics. The development of international institutions that reduce anarchy is one of those sources, and it will be the subject of Chapter 5. Economic interdependence is yet another explanation of peace among nations, and it will be addressed in Chapter 7. Here, the focus will be on the third point of the Kantian triangle: how change in domestic regime type affects the way the world works. Specifically, according to liberal internationalists and the democratic peace theory, the goal of eliminating, or at least substantially reducing, the use of violence to resolve differences is best served by the spread of democratic government.

The notion that democracy is the antidote to warfare is, as noted in Chapter 1, traceable to Immanuel Kant's argument that a zone of "perpetual peace" can emerge from a "pacific union" of free states (republics). Over the past quarter-century, this Kantian view has been reinvigorated and widely discussed and debated in light of two important empirical facts: (1) democratic governments tend not to fight wars with one another, and (2) the number of democratic regimes around the world is at an all-time high.

Let's take up the first point—that "democracies very rarely, if ever, make war on each other."[40] How absolutely one views that assertion is, in large part, a function of how one defines democracy and then applies that definition to

democracy
Political system characterized by (1) the right of political participation, (2) political competition and meaningful electoral choice, and (3) civil liberties.

individual states. Most contemporary discussions of **democracy** define it as a political system characterized by three essential elements:

1. *Participation.* The right of all adults to take part in the political process, including the process of electing public officials.
2. *Contestation.* Competition among political parties and individuals that allows for meaningful choice in the election of public officials.
3. *Civil liberties.* At least a minimal package of freedoms (e.g., free press, free speech, free association) essential to ensure that participation is informed and that the integrity of the democratic process is upheld.[41]

When the definition of democracy is applied most strictly, the observation that democracies do not fight wars with one another appears close to being an absolute law. One scholar, applying a strict definition of democracy, could find only one exception to the rule—the 1999 conflict between India and Pakistan.[42] But even that exception is debatable both because India and Pakistan were, at best, flawed democracies, and because the conflict itself was small-scale, barely meeting the 1,000 battle deaths minimum necessary to categorize a conflict as a war.[43]

Even if democracies tend not to fight with one another, they do frequently fight wars against nondemocratic regimes. The American experience with warfare provides ample testimony. As we saw in the 2003 US preemptive attack on Iraq, democracies are not necessarily unwilling to fire the first shot in wars against authoritarian states. Thus, if the democratic peace is to prevail on a global level, the expansion of the number of democratic states becomes the key.

The last quarter of the twentieth century witnessed an impressive wave of democratization around much of the world. It was, according to political scientist Samuel Huntington, the third such wave of democratization: the first long wave was in the nineteenth century, the second wave was in the years following World War II, and the **third wave** began in 1974 with democratization in Spain and Portugal, spreading to most of Latin America, post-Communist Europe, and parts of Asia and Africa.[44] Another political scientist, Francis Fukuyama, was so impressed by the global democratic trend that in 1989 he famously declared that we had reached the **end of history**, or the point at which the grand political debate about how best to organize ourselves politically had been resolved once and for all in favor of democratic government.[45]

third wave
Wave of democratization that began in 1974 with Spain and Portugal and then spread to other parts of the world, including Latin America, Eastern Europe, and parts of Asia and sub-Saharan Africa.

end of history
Phrase popularized by Francis Fukuyama at the end of the Cold War to describe what he thought was the end of ideological debates about how to organize economic and political affairs with the triumph of the ideas of democracy and market capitalism.

By the beginning of the twenty-first century, the number of countries democratically governed was at an all-time high. According to Freedom House, a nongovernmental organization that publishes a yearly survey of the state of democracy and political freedom around the world, the number of "free countries"—those that are more or less the equivalent of democracies—has increased significantly as the number of "not free" (or authoritarian) regimes has declined (see Table 4.2). When you marry the observation that democracies have tended not to fight one another with this reality of an expanding global community of democratic governments, the realist notion that interstate war is inevitable comes into question.

Table 4.2 Global Trends in Freedom, 1984–2014

Year	Free Countries	Partly Free Countries	Not Free Countries
1984	32%	35%	33%
1994	40%	32%	28%
2004	46%	28%	26%
2014	46%	28%	26%

NOTE: "Free countries," as defined by Freedom House, can for most intents and purposes be considered consolidated democracies; "partly free countries" are essentially equivalent to semidemocratic regimes; and "not free countries" are authoritarian regimes.

SOURCE: Freedom House, *Freedom in the World 2015*, https://freedomhouse.org/sites/default/files/01152015_FIW_2015 _final.pdf.

However, realists and other critics of democratic peace theory are not quite prepared to concede the argument. Their challenge comes on multiple levels. First, they contend, even if one accepts that democracies tend not to fight one another, the world still has a significant number of nondemocratic states. Despite the democratic gains of the "third wave" era, Table 4.2 still shows less than half of states in the "free" category. Indeed, in comparison with the impressive democratic gains of the 1970s, 1980s, and 1990s, the trend toward democracy since 2000 appears to have stalled. Among the remaining nondemocracies are some fairly important countries, including China with its population of over 1 billion, its dynamic economy, and its steady improvement in military capability. Likewise, as discussed in Chapter 2, expectations for democracy in the Middle East and North Africa raised by the Arab Spring were quickly dashed as authoritarian revival (e.g., Egypt), newly failed states (e.g., Syria, Libya), civil war and outside intervention (e.g., Yemen), and the emergence of terrorist groups that make al-Qaeda look tame by comparison (e.g., ISIS, Boko Haram) have all but eliminated near-term hopes for a democratic wave in this part of the world.

Second, realists point to the prospect of backsliding among countries currently categorized as democratic. Huntington notes that the first two waves of democratization were followed by reverse waves in which some newly democratic states reverted to authoritarian rule. The same has happened following the third wave. Perhaps most significantly, in light of political trends under Russian leader Vladimir Putin, in 2004 Freedom House downgraded Russia from "partly free" to "not free."[46] Since even one nondemocratic country with sufficient military capability can upset the democratic peace, betting on the obsolescence of war might be a losing wager.

Third, some realist critics argue that the core assumption that democracies will not fight one another, though largely true to this point in time, has not been sufficiently tested. Modern democratic government, after all, does not have a very long history. If we view the United States as the first modern democracy, then modern democracy is barely two centuries old. Even the early United States and other fledgling nineteenth-century democracies would be considered largely undemocratic by current standards, given the limitation of democratic

Famous image of a Chinese citizen attempting to block tanks from rolling into Tiananmen Square during the 1989 protests in China. With respect to the future of democracy, are you more impressed by the courage of the man in the photo or the willingness of the Chinese government to use force to crush the Tiananmen Square movement?

rights to white male property owners. In the view of realists, then, we still lack sufficient data to conclude that form of government is the key factor restraining democracies from going to war with one another. Perhaps it was the existence of a common enemy, the Soviet Union, that kept the democracies at peace with one another during the Cold War. Moreover, most democracies of the Cold War era were Western countries that shared a common European cultural identity. As the world's democracies become more culturally diverse, one cannot rule out the possibility of differences in the ways these new democracies interact with each other.

A CONSTRUCTIVIST EXPLANATION OF PEACE   While the realist explanation of peace emphasizes the distribution of power, and while the liberal democratic peace theory stresses the impact of structural changes in domestic regime type, constructivist explanations of peace would give more attention to changes in global norms. Though the prevailing norm in world politics has long held that war is an acceptable "continuation of policy," competing norms have challenged or at least sought to limit that view.

Though his work on the decline of war predates the constructivist turn of the 1990s, John Mueller provides an analysis of the long peace and the decline in the frequency of war that is consistent in many respects with the constructivist paradigm. On the one hand, Mueller rejects the realist view that the long peace of the post–World War II era was just a temporary reflection of a particular balance of power. Like liberals, Mueller sees in the long peace a more fundamental and a more permanent change in how the world works.

However, for Mueller, the recent absence of great power war and, arguably, the more general decline in the incidence of interstate wars of all types have little to do with the Kantian triangle stressed by liberals. With respect to the impact of economic interdependence and international institutions, he suggests that the traditional liberal view most likely misinterprets cause and effect. For Mueller, peace is the cause rather than the effect of expanding trade and the proliferation of institutions. As for democratic peace theory, Mueller points out that it cannot explain the central element of the long peace—the absence of a great power war between the authoritarian USSR and democratic America.[47]

Instead, for Mueller, what he calls the growing "obsolescence of major war" is a result of the fact that human beings in much of the world have concluded in ever-larger numbers that tanks and bombers are no longer acceptable means of resolving problems for civilized nations. Once viewed as an occasion for honor and glory, war is increasingly viewed as an evil to be avoided. This change in perception was facilitated by the emergence of an active peace movement beginning in the late nineteenth century and by the work of individual "idea entrepreneurs" in promoting and diffusing this presumption against war on a global basis.[48] Mueller predicts that the increasing psychological and physical costs of war, clearly demonstrated in World War I and underlined in World War II, may cause it to go out of fashion in much the same way that dueling and slavery, once viewed as acceptable institutions, would no longer be endorsed by any reasonable, modern individual.

Constructivist scholars would further add onto Mueller's explanation the role played by common identities in facilitating peace in the post–Cold War world. Thus, for constructivists, the important thing about the spread of democracy in the 1990s was less the structure of democratic institutions than the fact that democratic states see themselves as part of a common community. To the extent that shared sense of a common identity breaks down (e.g., between two democracies for whom the salient source of identity is less their common political order than their different religious traditions), constructivists would no longer expect democratic institutions by themselves to be the guarantor of peace.

The Future of War

4-4   Identify the trends shaping the nature of future war.

Let's assume, for the moment, that the "long peace," and the absence of the great power war to which it refers, continue for the indefinite future. Let's also assume the decline in interstate wars characteristic of the post–Cold War era also persists. Those assumptions seem to imply a more peaceful future. Or do they? Not according to the military historian Martin van Creveld. Van Creveld agrees that the era of interstate war is over because in the era of nuclear weapons states cannot fight one another without risking mutual suicide. War itself, however, will continue in a different form fought not by the armies of states "but by groups we today call terrorists, guerrillas, bandits, and robbers."[49] According to van Creveld,

> War will become a much more direct experience for most civilians, even to the point where the term itself might be abolished, or its meaning altered. War will affect people of all ages and both sexes. They will be affected not just accidentally or incidentally or anonymously from afar, as in the case of strategic bombing, but as immediate participants, targets, and victims. Practices that for three centuries have been considered uncivilized, such as capturing civilians and even entire communities for ransom, are almost certain to make a comeback.[50]

Welcome to the era of asymmetric war.

Asymmetric Warfare

asymmetric war
War in which there is a fundamental difference (or asymmetry) in the nature of the participants, and in their goals, capabilities, and tactics.

An **asymmetric war** is a war in which there is a fundamental difference (or asymmetry) in the nature of the participants, and in their goals, capabilities, and tactics. In a conventional (or symmetric) war, the participants are all sovereign states and their goals are to defend their national interests. While one side may be stronger than the other (have greater capabilities) and while there is often some variation in their military tactics, they are basically playing the same game with varying amounts of what are essentially the same kinds of weapons. They also tend to be fighting (though with varying degrees of concern) under the same international rules governing the ethics of warfare. To use a sports analogy, two basketball teams may have different levels of talent and may adopt different offensive and defensive schemes, but both play the same game with the same ball on the same court governed by a common set of rules.

In asymmetric war, some or all of those symmetries disappear. The participants are not all sovereign states but a mix of states and nonstate actors. The goals, therefore, are not simply national interests as defined by sovereign states, but also tribal interests, promotion of religious beliefs, or, perhaps, private financial gain. The capabilities of the participants can also vary widely not only in the number but in the type of weapons. One side may use highly sophisticated technologies, while the other uses primitive weapons from centuries past. And those differences in capabilities give rise to varying tactics guided by very different moral rules. To return to the basketball analogy, it is as if one side, unable to match the talent level of the other, begins to play a different game with tactics that violate the traditional rules of the game in order to compensate for its weaknesses.

Three examples will illustrate the concept of asymmetric war: the Kosovo War of 1999, the Gaza Wars of the winter of 2008–2009 and 2014, and the war over Crimea and Ukraine that began in 2014.

KOSOVO On March 24, 1999, President Bill Clinton addressed the American people and announced that NATO airstrikes against the former Yugoslav republic of Serbia were under way.[51] In making the case for war, Clinton pointed to the brutal treatment of Kosovar Albanians by Serbian leader Slobodan Milošević. Given NATO's primary emphasis on human rights as the reason for war, Kosovo was a new kind of war (and we will return to this aspect of the war in Chapter 6). It was also a new kind of war with respect to the manner in which it was fought.

In one respect, Kosovo was very much a conventional conflict, given that it was a war fought between sovereign states. But in other respects notable asymmetries were in evidence. Most significant was the asymmetry in capabilities. At least for one side (NATO), it was a high-tech war fought largely with the use of "smart weapons." Smart weapons or, more precisely, **precision-guided munitions (PGMs)** are missiles, bombs, or artillery shells equipped with sophisticated electronic guidance systems that direct the explosive toward a predetermined target. Whereas it required 108 bombers dropping 648 bombs to destroy a specified target at the end of World War II, that same target can now be destroyed with just a few PGMs.[52]

precision-guided munitions (PGMs) Also called "smart weapons." Missiles, bombs, or artillery shells with sophisticated guidance systems that direct the explosive toward a target with great accuracy.

For NATO forces, the result was what one observer has called a "virtual war" in which pilots spent their time looking at video screens in cockpits well out of range of enemy fire and for whom death was largely removed from the experience of battle.[53] In fact, for the United States and its NATO allies, the result was remarkable: not a single life was lost in combat.[54] Civilian casualties produced by NATO air raids were also, due to the accuracy of PGMs, relatively low. According to Human Rights Watch, during approximately 10,000 strike missions in a 78-day bombing campaign conducted by NATO against targets in Serbia, about 500 civilians were killed.[55]

For Serbia, the result was different. Unlike their NATO counterparts, Serbian forces did not escape the experience of battle. Hundreds of Serbian forces were killed and the infrastructure of the Serbian state and economy was decimated. Because they could not retaliate in kind, the asymmetrical response of Serbian forces and their associated paramilitary units was to seek revenge against Kosovar civilians, killing many and driving hundreds of thousands more into exile.

GAZA The Gaza Strip is a small, densely populated territory between Egypt and Israel that is home to approximately 1.5 million Palestinians. After changing hands several times in the Arab–Israeli wars of 1948, 1956, and 1967, control of Gaza was formally ceded to Israel after the 1967 war. As a result of the intifada of the late 1980s (the Palestinian uprising against Israeli control of Gaza and the West Bank), Israel ceded control of Gaza to the Palestinian Authority in the Oslo Accords of 1993. Despite Oslo, Israel retained a military presence in Gaza until 2005 when it evacuated in order to ease tensions with the Palestinian Authority. In 2007, fighting between the two primary Palestinian factions in Gaza, Fatah and Hamas, resulted in the victory of Hamas. The more radical of the two factions, Hamas has called for the elimination of the state of Israel and is officially labeled by the US State Department as a terrorist organization.

The prelude to the winter 2008–2009 war was a series of skirmishes in which Hamas would launch missiles into Israel, and Israel would respond with air attacks on Hamas forces and infrastructure. When a cease-fire brokered by Egypt in June 2008 broke down six months later, Israel commenced an air, naval, and ground assault on Gaza on December 27, 2008. Likewise, in July 2014 Israel once again commenced military actions in response to Hamas rocket attacks.

The ensuing conflicts were classic examples of asymmetric war. The fighting pitted a state (Israel) against a nonstate actor (Hamas). Though Hamas had access to rockets and other weapons smuggled into Gaza from the outside, its military capabilities were no match for those of Israel's high-tech military. The result was a wide asymmetry in casualties. The 2008–2009 conflict resulted in approximately 1,400 Palestinians killed (the vast majority of them civilians) and only 13 Israelis (military and civilian combined) dead.[56] The 2014 war produced more than 2,000 Palestinian deaths and the destruction of 20,000 Palestinian homes, while only 71 Israelis (including 64 soldiers) were killed.[57]

Israelis and Palestinians debate the responsibility for that wide disparity in casualties. The Israeli military blamed Hamas for violating the rules of war by hiding its fighters among the civilian population and by the absence of uniforms that would allow the distinction between civilians and fighters to be clear. Hamas blames Israel for indiscriminate attacks on densely populated urban locations. Indeed, a highly controversial UN report on Gaza (the "Goldstone Report") assigned blame to both parties and was criticized by commentators on each side of this debate. Questions of moral culpability aside, scholars of asymmetric war might argue that the results were predictable. In an asymmetric war the side with technological superiority will be able to shield its forces from harm. The weaker side thus will respond with tactics like those employed by Hamas, placing the onus of the decision to engage in attacks that will inevitably kill civilians back in the hands of the stronger party.

UKRAINE   While the Gaza wars saw a relatively weak (in conventional military terms) nonstate actor utilizing asymmetric warfare techniques, in the Ukraine crisis it was Russia, one of the world's great military powers, engaging in asymmetric warfare. The Ukrainian Socialist Republic was once one of the 15 constituent parts of what was then the Soviet Union, and indeed Ukraine had been a part of a larger Russian empire for much of its history. When the Soviet Union collapsed in 1991, Ukraine, which since 1954 has also included the Crimean peninsula, became an independent country.

Russian President Vladimir Putin was never happy about the loss of Ukraine, and in late 2013–early 2014—following debate in Ukraine over signing an association agreement with the EU, protests in Kiev, and the departure of pro-Russian Ukrainian President Viktor Yanukovich—Russia began to act. In early 2014, armed men without uniforms or insignia began seizing government buildings in Crimea. They were supported, at least indirectly, by Russian troops already located in Crimea. Later, in the other largely Russian-speaking Eastern provinces of Ukraine, a similar pattern would be repeated. While Western reports suggested that there were clandestine movements of military personnel, weapons, and supplies across the border from Russia into Ukraine, Russia has largely denied these reports, preferring to portray the events in both Crimea and eastern Ukraine as clashes between the Ukrainian government and local, largely Russian-speaking, residents of those regions. Unlike in conventional invasions, there never was an open, large-scale cross-border invasion of military personnel in uniforms.

Russian military analysts have been quite open in discussing asymmetric warfare techniques including cyber attacks, proxy attacks by armed civilians in target states, and disinformation campaigns, and Western governments and their military and intelligence organs have taken note.[58] The Russian adoption of techniques of asymmetric warfare is an attempt to give plausible denial to charges of a Russian invasion and to make it more difficult for NATO to develop a quick and unified response. Indeed, the relative success of the Russia's asymmetric war in Crimea raises fears that it can be repeated elsewhere in Eastern Europe and in the Baltic states (the latter being NATO members).

Terrorism

If the high-tech military campaigns waged by NATO in Kosovo and Israel in Gaza paint one image of how twenty-first-century warfare will be waged, the September 11, 2001 terrorist attacks on the United States paint a radically different picture. On the one hand, you have combatants largely protected from harm as they fight from 15,000 feet in the air; on the other, you have suicide attackers whose death is assured and accepted in advance. On the one hand, you have highly accurate, if imperfect, weapons designed in large part to minimize civilian casualties; on the other, the very purpose of the mission is to maximize civilian deaths. On the one hand, you use high-tech, multimillion-dollar weapons systems; on the other, the weapon of choice is a one-dollar box cutter.

WHAT IS TERRORISM? "Terrorism" is a politically loaded word, used often to characterize the actions of one's adversary while generally avoided in describing one's own behavior or that of one's allies. As the often repeated cliché suggests, "one man's terrorist is another man's freedom fighter." For purposes of analysis, therefore, we need a definition of terrorism that we can apply regardless of how we assess any particular cause. A useful starting point is the US State Department's official definition of **terrorism** as "premeditated, politically motivated violence perpetrated against noncombatant targets by subnational groups or clandestine agents, usually intended to influence an audience."[59]

terrorism
Politically motivated violence aimed at civilian targets in order to spread fear and alarm.

Much of the State Department definition is uncontroversial. Most observers would agree that terrorism involves premeditated violence distinguishable in its political goals from ordinary crime. Likewise, most observers would agree that in its purposeful targeting of noncombatants to influence its audience by spreading fear and alarm (i.e., terror), terrorism is also distinguishable from ordinary

Theory in Practice 4.3

Terrorism or Warfare?

Suicide airplane crashes were not invented by al-Qaeda on September 11, 2001. In World War II Japanese suicide pilots, or "kamikazes," purposely flew their planes into American ships, sinking or damaging more than 30 US ships and producing more than 15,000 US casualties. Thousands of other kamikaze planes were held in reserve to respond to a US naval attack on the Japanese islands, but they were never used, due to President Harry S Truman's decision to end the war by using the atomic bomb.

Those Japanese kamikaze attacks would not fit the definition of terrorism because their targets were military ships, not civilians. But suppose Japan had adopted a different tactic. Suppose the Japanese leaders had had the will and capability to fly a thousand planes into office buildings and other civilian targets in the United States, producing 100,000 or more civilian deaths.

- Would you label such a tactic terrorism? Explain.
- Would you see a difference between such a tactic and the US bombing of Hiroshima and Nagasaki? Explain.
- Would such a tactic differ from the one al-Qaeda used on September 11, 2001? Why or why not?

---

warfare, where noncombatant deaths are usually (though not always) the unfortunate by-product more than the purposeful intent. More contentious is the part of the State Department definition that associates terrorism with "subnational groups or clandestine agents" like **al-Qaeda**, but that thereby exempts such purposeful World War II attacks on civilians as the Nazi blitz of London, the Allied firebombing of Dresden, and the atomic bombing of Hiroshima and Nagasaki. Many would argue that based on those events, terrorism is a tactic that states use as well (see Theory in Practice 4.3).

al-Qaeda
(Arabic for "the base.") Radical Sunni terrorist organization composed of a loose grouping of semiautonomous terrorist cells located around the world.

WHY TERRORISM? Among Westerners, the popular view is that terrorism is an irrational activity engaged in by mentally unbalanced zealots with a fanatical devotion to their cause. It is difficult for most people to come to terms with the fact that someone would strap explosives to his or her waist and detonate them in a crowded restaurant, or crash a fully loaded plane into an office building with both the terrorist and many innocent passengers on board. Indeed, it may well be the case that some individual terrorists are, in fact, irrational and mentally unbalanced.

However, the overall record of terror suggests that it is, in fact, a rational, purposeful activity. To call it rational does not imply endorsement or justification of terror. Instead, it merely suggests that terror is utilized as a means to a larger strategic end. It is a form of asymmetric warfare employed by weaker parties in a struggle with a stronger adversary.

Take the terror attacks of 9/11 as an example. Over the years, former al-Qaeda leader Osama bin Laden, who was eventually tracked down and killed by US Special Forces in May 2011, had articulated a long list of grievances against the United States. A Saudi by birth and a self-described devout Muslim,

President Obama and his national security team watch in real time as US Navy Seals conduct the 2011 raid that killed Osama bin Laden. Does the military conflict between the US and international terrorists like bin Laden do more to support or undermine the realist view of how the world works? Why?

he was particularly enraged by the continued presence of American troops in the holy land of Saudi Arabia long after the 1991 Gulf War. Added to the list were complaints about US support of Israel, neglect of Palestinian rights, and economic sanctions against Iraq in the 1990s that caused many deaths of Iraqi civilians. His strategic calculation was fairly simple. Since he could not expel the US army from Saudi Arabia or change US policy in the Middle East by conventional military means, he would pressure the US government indirectly. By attacking the World Trade Center and other US targets, he would raise the price of US policy for Americans in the hope that they would pressure the US government to change course. If Americans had to worry about going to work, shopping in a mall, or sending their children to school, they might decide that it was not worth the price to maintain the current policies in a place far from US shores.

Indeed, in a larger study of the motivations behind suicide terrorism, political scientist Robert Pape found that the common thread was an effort by militarily weaker groups to use terror to expel foreign troops from their territory by raising the price for the civilians of the occupying country.[60] Such tactics are not guaranteed to work—indeed, they can backfire and provoke even greater intervention by one's adversary. However, Pape's study suggests that the terror strategy works more often than not and is, at the very least, a calculated risk that many terrorists think worth taking.

THE IMPACT OF TERROR   As suggested above, the goal of terror is to spread fear and alarm in an effort to pressure one's adversary to change course and policy. The spectacular nature of many terror attacks and the amount of television coverage they receive help to fuel the sense of fear that terrorists seek. Almost

3,000 people died on 9/11. A 2004 train bombing in Madrid killed 191 commuters; a 2002 hostage-taking in a Moscow theater by Chechen rebels left close to 200 dead; and the 2004 tragedy in Beslan, Russia, where Chechen rebels took over a school, left 300 people, including many schoolchildren, dead in a botched rescue attempt. More recently, the January 2015 attack on *Charlie Hebdo* headquarters in Paris left 12 dead and provoked world outrage for its purposeful assault on the idea of a free press. In April of that same year, a brutal terror attack on a Kenyan university resulted in 147 dead. These incidents are just a few of many; one think tank has catalogued over 40,000 terror incidents between 1968 and 2009.[61]

However, the number of casualties produced by terrorism remains, in comparison with ordinary warfare, relatively low. One study counted 3,299 deaths from international terrorism in the 39 most developed countries from 1994 to 2003, most of which occurred on 9/11.[62] Since then, some reports suggest that the number of terrorist casualties has increased. For example, a report produced for the US Department of Homeland Security counted 6,771 worldwide terrorist incidents producing 11,098 deaths in 2012.[63] However, half of those deaths were in Iraq and Afghanistan—active war zones—where the definitional boundary between acts of terror and acts of war is often blurry. For those living outside of such war zones, most informed observers agree that the risk of any one of us being killed in a terrorist attack is far lower than our risk of drowning in a swimming pool, being killed in a car crash, or getting struck by lightening on a soccer field or baseball diamond. We tend to exaggerate the risk entailed in dramatic events that receive a lot of television coverage and to underestimate the risk of common everyday activities.[64] Terrorists count precisely on this exaggerated reaction to produce that echo of fear and alarm that can cause their grievances to be taken seriously and addressed.

Nonetheless, our post-9/11 preoccupation with the threat of terrorism is not entirely unreasonable. In particular, two aspects of twenty-first-century terrorism combine to make it especially worrisome. First is the increasingly explicit willingness by some individuals, groups, or even states to embrace the technique of terror in pursuit of a cause and to treat anyone as a potential target. This was not always the case. Political philosopher Michael Walzer notes that the "terrorists" of the late nineteenth and early twentieth century were often guided by a "political code" that caused them to focus their bombing and assassinations on political leaders and government targets rather than random civilians.[65] Compare that with Osama bin Laden's argument that the taxes US citizens pay to their government make them complicit in their government's actions and, thus, legitimate targets. In 1998 bin Laden declared, "To kill the Americans and their allies—civilians and military—is an individual duty for every Muslim who can do it in any country in which it is possible to do it."[66] And given the kinds of brutal terrorist attacks unleashed by groups like ISIS and Boko Haram, bin Laden seems almost restrained by comparison. In short, the political morality of modern terrorism explicitly rejects both the "just war" principle of discrimination between combatants and noncombatants and the parallel "political code" of an earlier generation of political assassins.

The second worrisome aspect of contemporary terrorism is the potential for terrorists to access weapons of mass destruction. A terrorist with a conventional bomb can certainly bring grief to the lives of victims and their families, but for the nation as a whole, that threat is usually much less significant than one posed by the conventional armies of enemy countries. In fact, for a superpower like the United States, that kind of terrorism might be viewed as a mere nuisance—one of the costs of a superpower doing business in the world. Even a tragedy as significant and dramatic as that of September 11, 2001, need not, as long as one does not overreact, threaten the sovereignty, political order, or economic prosperity of a superpower like the United States. The Soviet threat during the Cold War was a threat on a completely different order of magnitude in comparison to what happened on 9/11.

However, add into the mix a terrorist cell with even a small nuclear device, a dirty bomb, a vial of anthrax, or chemical weapons, and the threat calculation grows exponentially. If one wants to worry even more, consider how the proliferation of drone technology might ease the ability of terrorists to deliver both conventional and nonconventional weapons to a target without the need to sacrifice him- or herself in a suicide attack (see Theory in Practice 4.4). The likelihood of the worst-case scenarios—detonation of an atomic device, willful spreading of infectious diseases such as smallpox, mass mailings of anthrax powder—is debated. But whatever the odds, the potential for mass casualties and serious disruption of our way of life is great enough that even unlikely scenarios have to be taken seriously.

Moreover, unlike the situation during the Cold War, deterrence is unlikely to prevent nuclear terrorism. Mutual assured destruction can only work when the first strike is launched with a return address label attached. A nuclear bomb unloaded and detonated in a container in the port of Los Angeles will not be easily traced to a specific terrorist group abroad. And even if such a trace can be developed, retaliation would be problematic if those responsible are hiding among the population of a country whose citizens do not condone the terror and may even be friendly toward the United States.

Thus, new technologies combined with terrorism pose a very dangerous twenty-first-century threat. At one time, only the greatest of the major powers could produce mass casualties on a global scale. Now we live in a world where that threat can come from any number of sources wielding weapons ranging from anthrax powder to a nuclear device. For the most pessimistic observers, it is only a matter of time.

Implications for Realism

The proliferation of asymmetric wars and, in particular, the post-9/11 fears of an escalated terror threat pose some larger theoretical questions related to the debate between realists and their critics. First, critics of realism argue that terrorism and other forms of asymmetric war challenge the realists' assumption that

Theory in Practice 4.4

The Drone Revolution

A technology with the potential to revolutionize the future of warfare is the drone. Drones are Unmanned Aerial Vehicles (UAVs) controlled from afar by "soldiers" in control rooms on the ground or even by unmanned computer programs. Originally used primarily for surveillance, they have become the attack weapon of choice by the United States (first under Bush and even more so under Obama) in the war against terrorism. They range in size from small airplanes to small birds. In the aftermath of the January 2015 terror attack on the *Charlie Hebdo* office in Paris, concerns were raised when numerous small drones were seen hovering over major tourist sites including the Eiffel Tower and the Louvre. Drones have the potential to be a transformative technology of future warfare. Consider the following:

While the United States has been the world leader in the development of military drones, dozens of other countries are believed to possess them or to be developing them.

The cost of small drones is relatively low, and thus they are accessible to even the poorest of states, to terrorist groups, or even to lone-wolf terrorists.

Drones are becoming increasingly commonplace, used not only by militaries but by private businesses. Amazon, for example, sees them as the future of their delivery model.

Drones raise interesting questions related to just war. On the one hand, their defenders suggest that they are precise weapons that can limit civilian casualties. But critics counter that they are only as accurate as their targeting instructions. Perhaps even more importantly, because they lower the risk to soldiers, they potentially make resort to the use of force easier to contemplate.

- Did the Obama administration's extensive use of drones to target suspected terrorists in Pakistan meet the criteria of just war?

- Given their potential use as an instrument of terror, should the use of drones by private companies and individuals be regulated or even prohibited?

- Is the specter of future wars fought increasingly by drones, and less directly by human beings, a source of worry or comfort? Why?

states exercise a monopoly on the use of violence in world politics. In fact, more and more of the violence we see in world politics seems to be taking the form of asymmetric war pitting states against various nonstate actors with a variety of political, cultural, and economic grievances.

Second, critics of realism suggest that the very status of states as the key actors is threatened by the changing nature of warfare. While powerful states are well equipped to fight off symmetrical threats from other similarly armed states, their conventional weapons are a lot less useful when it comes to fighting off hijackers armed with box cutters or terrorists with weapons of mass destruction with no return address that can be threatened in kind. Thus, if it is the case that the major states cannot fight one another because the cost of war in the nuclear age is too high and if they are also not particularly effective in fighting the kinds of asymmetrical threats that they now face, then the main reason for loyalty to states—their ability to provide security for their citizens—is potentially undermined.[67]

The realist response is twofold. First, they would argue that the presumed decline in the utility of states' military assets is exaggerated. The high-tech military of NATO produced a victory in Kosovo. Though a more ambiguous case, some might also argue that the Israeli military was effective, notwithstanding the human cost of the war, against an asymmetric foe in the Gaza conflict. Moreover, despite post-2001 fears of follow-on terror attacks in both the United States and the world at large, and despite the fact that many horrific terrorist attacks have indeed taken place, those attacks have neither involved WMD nor posed the kind of existential threat to developed states that worst-case scenarios imagined.

Second, and perhaps even more fundamental, realists respond that the key issues are the persistence of anarchy and war. The nature of the actors in the system and the kinds of wars they fight are less important. Thus, the realist paradigm could survive the decline of the state system. As John Mearsheimer notes, Thucydides and Machievelli—two of the key intellectual ancestors of modern realism—wrote long before the 1648 emergence of the Westphalian state system. Mearsheimer adds: "Realism merely requires anarchy; it does not matter what kinds of political units make up the system. They could be states, city-states, cults, empires, tribes, gangs, feudal principalities, or whatever."[68] In short, for realists the image of future war described by van Creveld is entirely consistent with the world as understood by realism.

Conclusion

Despite the declining incidence of interstate war in recent decades, few scholars are prepared to argue that war is likely to disappear completely from the landscape of world politics anytime soon. Although some groups of countries seem to have taken war off the table as a means to settle their disputes with one another, in the international system as a whole, war and the threat of war as a means to defend national interests remain central to how the world works.

However, once one gets past the general observation that the threat of war remains, scholars are divided as to what the degree and trajectory of violence in the twenty-first century will look like. Some suggest that the idea of war is becoming unfashionable, and they place their hope in an evolving moral consciousness that can render war less frequent. Others suggest that political change, specifically, the spread of democratic government, is our best bet for the emergence of a new, less violent world order. Still others, as will be discussed in more detail in Chapters 5 and 7, argue that international institutions and economic interdependence increasingly mitigate against violent solutions to international conflicts. At the very least, the optimists suggest, the combination of these trends might allow us to avoid the great power wars whose impact on the world is, especially in the nuclear era, most threatening.

Realists would argue, however, that in many fundamental respects, not much has changed in international relations since the days of Thucydides and the Peloponnesian Wars. In a world of anarchy, war and violence remain the ultimate recourse for states and other actors to protect their interests and to seek redress of their grievances. In their view, short-term cyclical downturns in the number of wars should not be mistaken for a permanent change in how the world works. The longer view of history suggests that despite changes in actors, the emergence of new forms of government, and the development of new and ever more lethal weapons of destruction, the one constant is that those weapons eventually are used.

This chapter examined high-stakes issues, potentially involving the lives and deaths of millions of people—even the fate of civilization as we know it. In all probability, however, the twenty-first century will not likely produce either the end of war or a global apocalypse. The difference between realists and their critics is not so much whether war or peace will prevail, but instead, how many wars will be fought, what kinds of war they will be, and where the explanations for both the amount and nature of twenty-first-century war can be found.

Review Questions

- Which explanation of the recent decline in interstate war do you find most persuasive? Why? Is the decline likely to be permanent?
- How has technological innovation changed the character of warfare? To what extent has that technological innovation either challenged or reinforced Clausewitz's view of war as the continuation of policy?
- Is a great power war a real possibility in the twenty-first century? What might be the scenario for such a war?

Key Terms

coercive diplomacy
power transition
military industrial complex
pacifism
just war doctrine
jus ad bellum
jus in bello
total war
mutual assured destruction
   (MAD)

second strike capability
deterrence
stability/instability paradox
nuclear utilization theories
   (NUTS)
Strategic Defense Initiative
   (SDI)
nuclear proliferation
Non-Proliferation
   Treaty (NPT)

long peace
security community
democracy
third wave
end of history
asymmetric war
precision-guided munitions
   (PGMs)
terrorism
al-Qaeda

Endnotes

1. John Mearsheimer, *The Tragedy of Great Power Politics* (Norton, 2001), 361.
2. John Mueller, *Retreat from Doomsday: The Obsolescence of Major War* (Basic Books, 1989), ix.
3. Much of the data collected by Singer and his associates is available online at the Cor-relates of War homepage, http://www.correlatesofwar.org.
4. The terminology and counts are adopted from Meredith Sarkees, Frank Wayman, and J. David Singer, "Inter-State, Intra-State, and Extra-State Wars: A Comprehensive Look at Their Distribution over Time, 1816–1997,"

International Studies Quarterly 47 (2003): 49–70.

5. A useful recent summary of some of the Correlates of War data on the frequency of war may be found in Sarkees, Wayman, and Singer, "Inter-State, Intra-State, and Extra-State Wars," 49–70.

6. See Faten Ghosn, Glenn Palmer, and Stuart A. Bremer, "The MID3 Data Set: Procedures, Coding Rules, and Description," *Conflict Management and Peace Science* 21 (2004): 133–154.

7. Sarkees, Wayman, and Singer, "Inter-State, Intra-State, and Extra-State Wars," 65.

8. "World War II," *Encyclopedia Britannica*, http://search.eb.com.

9. Zbigniew Brzezinski, *Out of Control* (Touchstone, 1995), 10.

10. James Fearon, "Rationalist Explanations for War," *International Organization* 49:3 (Summer 1995): 379.

11. John Mearsheimer and Stephen Walt, "An Unnecessary War," *Foreign Policy*, January/February 2003, 50–59.

12. For more detail on both explanations, see Fearon, "Rationalist Explanations for War," 379–414.

13. Robert Jervis, "War and Misperception," *Journal of Interdisciplinary History*, 18:4 (Spring 1988): 675–700.

14. David A. Lake, "Two Cheers for Bargaining Theory: Assessing Rationalist Explanations of the Iraq War," *International Security* 35:3 (Winter 2010/11): 7–52.

15. Edward Mansfield and Jack Snyder, *Foreign Affairs* 74:3 (May/June 1995): 79–97.

16. National Highway Traffic Safety Information, "Traffic Safety Facts 2003: 2003 National Statistics," http://www-nrd.nhtsa.dot.gov.

17. Others have previously made and developed the comparison between war and the automobile. See Mueller, *Retreat from Doomsday*, 267–269.

18. Number of soldiers killed in Iraq in 2003 calculated from data at the US Department of Defense, Directorate for Information Operation and Reports, Statistical Information Analysis Division, "Military Casualty Information," http://web1.whs.osd.mil/mmid/casualty/castop.htm.

19. Leo Tolstoy, "Last Message to Mankind," Address to the Swedish Peace Congress, Stockholm, 1909, http://www.wagingpeace.org.

20. Niall Ferguson, "The Next War of the World," *Foreign Affairs*, September/October 2006, 61–74.

21. Hans J. Morgenthau and Kenneth W. Thompson, *Politics Among Nations: The Struggle for Power and Peace*, 6th ed. (Knopf, 1985), 392–413.

22. "United States," *Encyclopedia Britannica*, http://search.eb.com.

23. "World War I," *Encyclopedia Britannica*, http://search.eb.com.

24. United States Strategic Bombing Survey, "The Effects of Atomic Bombs on Hiroshima and Nagasaki," 1946, http://www.ibiblio.org.

25. A Bomb WWW Museum, "Introduction: About the A Bomb," http://www.csi.ad.jp/ABOMB/data.html.

26. Thomas Schelling, *Arms and Influence* (Yale University Press, 1966), 191.

27. Samantha Power, *A Problem from Hell: America and the Age of Genocide* (Perennial, 2003), 334.

28. Bernard Brodie, *The Absolute Weapon: Atomic Power and World Order* (Harcourt, Brace, 1946), 76.

29. Soviet casualty numbers are still debated. See Rafael Reuveny and Aseem Prakash, "The Afghanistan War and the Breakdown of the Soviet Union," *Review of International Studies* 25 (1999): 696–697. For the number of Afghanis killed, see Human Rights Watch, "Backgrounder on Afghanistan: History of the War," October 2001, http://www.hrw.org.

30. International Rescue Committee, "IRC Study Reveals 31,000 Die Monthly in Congo Conflict," December 9, 2004, http://www.theirc.org.

31. Robert Windrem, "Is Egypt Ready to Go Nuclear," *MSNBS Online*, March 15, 2005.

32. See the debate on this question in Scott D. Sagan and Kenneth N. Waltz, *The Spread of Nuclear Weapons: A Debate Renewed* (Norton, 2002).

33. Monty G. Marshall, Center for Systemic Peace, "Global Conflict Trends," http://www.systemicpeace.org/conflicttrends.html.

34. John Lewis Gaddis, *The Long Peace: Inquiries into the History of the Cold War* (Oxford University Press, 1989).

35. Robert Jervis, "Theories of War in an Era of Leading-Power Peace," *American Political Science Review* 96:1 (2002): 1–14.

36. John Mearsheimer, "Back to the Future: Instability in Europe After the Cold War," *International Security* 15:4 (1990): 5–56.

37. Mearsheimer, *The Tragedy of Great Power Politics*, 338.

38. *International Herald Tribune*, February 5, 1999, http://www.iht.com.

39. Mearsheimer, *The Tragedy of Great Power Politics*, see especially ch. 10.

40. Bruce Russett and John Oneal, *Triangulating Peace: Democracy, Interdependence, and International Organizations* (Norton, 2001), 43.

41. See, for example, Larry Diamond, Juan J. Linz, and Seymour Martin Lipset, *Politics in Developing Countries*, 2nd ed. (Lynne Rienner, 1995), 6–7.

42. James Lee Ray, *Democracy and International Politics: An Evaluation of the Democratic Peace Proposition* (University of South Carolina Press, 1995), 125. Discussed in Russett and Oneal, *Triangulating Peace*, 47–48.

43. See Russett and Oneal, *Triangulating Peace*, 48.

44. Samuel Huntington, *The Third Wave: Democratization in the Late Twentieth Century* (University of Oklahoma Press, 1993).

45. Francis Fukuyama, "The End of History?" *National Interest* (Summer 1989): 3–18.

46. Freedom House, "Russia Downgraded to Not Free," December 20, 2004, http://www.freedomhouse.org.

47. John Mueller, *The Remnants of War* (Cornell University Press, 2004), 167–171.

48. Mueller, *Retreat from Doomsday*; Mueller, *The Remnants of War*, 2.

49. Martin van Creveld, *The Transformation of War* (Free Press, 1991), 197.

50. van Creveld, *The Transformation of War*, 203.

51. "President Clinton's March 25, 1999, Address to the Nation," *Teaching Human Rights Online*, Urban Morgan Institute for Human Rights, http://homepages.uc.edu.

52. "What's New with Smart Weapons," February 7, 2005, http://www.globalsecurity.org.

53. Michael Ignatieff, *Virtual War: Kosovo and Beyond* (Metropolitan Books, 2000).

54. Nick Cook, "War of Extremes," *Jane's Defense Weekly*, July 7, 1999, http://www.janes.com.

55. "Civilian Deaths in the NATO Air Campaign," Human Rights Watch, February 2000, http://www.hrw.org.

56. Reuters, July 21, 2010.

57. *The Independent*, August 27, 2014.

58. House of Commons Defence Committee, "Toward the Next Defence and Security Review: Part Two—NATO," Jul 31, 2014, see especially pp. 12–15, http://www.publications.parliament.uk/pa/cm201415/cmselect/cmdfence/358/358.pdf.

59. US Department of State, "Patterns of Global Terrorism 2003," April 29, 2004, http://www.state.gov.

60. Robert Pape, "The Strategic Logic of Suicide Terror," *American Political Science Review* 97:3 (August 2003): 343–361.

61. *Rand Database of Worldwide terrorist Incidents*, http://www.rand.org/nsrd/projects/terrorism-incidents.html.

62. Nick Wilson and George Thomson, "The Epidemiology of International Terrorism Involving Fatal Outcomes in Developed Countries (1994–2003)," *European Journal of Epidemiology* 20:5 (2005): 375–381.

63. National Consortium for the Study of Terrorism and Responses to Terrorism, "Annex of Statistical Information: Country Reports on Terrorism 2012," May 2013, pp. 3–4,

http://www.state.gov/documents/organization/210288.pdf.

64. Jessica Stern, *The Ultimate Terrorists* (Harvard University Press, 1999), 32–36.

65. Michael Walzer, *Just and Unjust Wars*, 3rd ed. (Basic Books, 2000), 197–200.

66. "Text of Fatwah Urging Jihad Against Americans," originally published in *Al-Quds Al-Arabi* on February 23, 1998. English translation available online at the International Policy Institute for Counter-Terrorism website, http://www.ict.org.il.

67. van Creveld, *The Transformation of War*, 192–205.

68. Mearsheimer, *The Tragedy of Great Power Politics*, 365.

Chapter 5

International Law and Organization

The Promise of Liberal Institutionalism

Barack Obama addresses the United Nations General Assembly in 2014. Liberals suggest that the UN provides a forum for successful cooperation among states to resolve global problems. Realists suggest that states use the UN as another instrument to advance their own interests. Who, in your judgment, is right?

 Learning Objectives

5-1 Identify the main sources of international law.

5-2 Explain the role of the World Court in international law adjudication and evaluate its effectiveness.

5-3 Identify the various approaches to international law enforcement.

5-4 Explain and evaluate the role of the United Nations in promoting law, order, and security in international relations.

As discussed in Chapter 1, realists see cooperative solutions to global problems as difficult since the anarchy of the international system mandates a concern with relative gains. In different ways, both constructivists and liberals take issue with that view and argue that realists underestimate the possibility and, indeed, the reality of cooperation among states.

For constructivists, the triumph of cooperation over conflict is rooted in the diffusion of powerful global norms favoring cooperative, nonviolent resolution of disputes. Those norms are manifested most powerfully among certain groups of states that have developed shared identities (e.g., the states of the Western security community), but they are also manifest more unevenly on a global scale. While those norms can be formalized as law and enforced by institutions, for constructivists it is the power and legitimacy of the norms themselves that shape state behavior.

For liberals, in contrast, the institutionalization of those norms in formal law and institutions is the key to cooperative behavior. Those liberal institutionalists accept the realist notion that war and violence in world politics result from the anarchy of the international system. Where they part company with realists, however, is in how they assess progress in overcoming anarchy via the creation of a system of international law and a set of international organizations that can promote order. In their view, the creation of enforceable rules provides the basis for an international society of states that can peacefully work out their differences via an accepted legal and institutional framework.

Realists are skeptical. While acknowledging the obvious proliferation of international laws and organizations, realists discount their effectiveness, and they would likely agree with Abba Eban, the first Israeli representative to the United Nations (UN), who commented, "International law is that law that the wicked do not obey and the righteous do not enforce."[1] The fact that laws exist does not mean they will be reliably obeyed or enforced. Neither does the establishment of even the most nobly intended international organization guarantee that its mission will succeed.

This chapter examines the record of international law and organization in the contemporary international system. In order to have a functioning legal order, one needs three things: a process of law-making, a process of law adjudication or courts to apply laws to individual cases, and a system of law enforcement whereby sanctions and punishments can be applied to those who violate the law. This chapter is organized around those three requirements. Along the way, special attention will be given to the United Nations and its key organs—the Security Council, the General Assembly, and the World Court—insofar as the UN is both the key international organization of the post–World War II era and the institutional linchpin of the contemporary system of international law. To the extent that these institutions appear to effectively constrain state sovereignty and reduce anarchy, the record will help confirm the liberal view of how the world works today. To the extent that these institutions appear to be weak and ineffective, the record will help reconfirm the traditional realist understanding of the world.

International Law-Making

5-1   Identify the main sources of international law.

Hugo Grotius (1583–1645) was a leading theorist and writer on the modern system of international law. As a Dutch jurist and legal thinker, he was concerned that the maritime power of England, Spain, and Portugal might threaten Holland's access to the open seas and its important trade routes. He argued that all countries must have the right to sail the seas and that powerful nations should not be allowed to deny that right to others.

This "Grotian notion of the ocean"[2] was a step in the direction of a larger system of international law. In his key work, *On the Law of War and Peace* (1625), Grotius accepts the concept of state sovereignty but argues that states must be a part of a larger international society with rules that govern their relations with one another. The first question that must be addressed, therefore, is where one turns to find these rules. In the domestic legal systems of most modern, democratic states, legislatures and parliaments typically establish such rules. In the United States, for example, the US Congress is the primary law-making body at the federal level, and state legislatures and their local equivalents (e.g., county legislatures, city councils) have primary responsibility for drafting and approving laws within their geographic spheres of jurisdiction.

At the global level, however, no such legislative body has the authority to make law. The closest approximation might be the UN General Assembly, and some observers look forward to the day when the General Assembly or some other global body might develop such law-making authority. However, as the UN's own International Law Commission—established by the General Assembly in 1947 to promote the development of international law—notes on its webpage, "The Governments participating in the drafting of the Charter of the United Nations were overwhelmingly opposed to conferring on the United Nations legislative power to enact binding rules of international law."[3]

Thus, the General Assembly's law-making authority is limited. According to Article 13 of the UN Charter, "The General Assembly shall initiate studies and make recommendations for the purpose of … encouraging the progressive development of international law and its codification." The General Assembly can provide a forum for discussion on matters of international law and can authorize, via the International Law Commission, the drafting of treaties and documents, but resolutions and declarations of the General Assembly are not legally binding on states. Therefore, one must look elsewhere for the sources of international law: treaties and conventions, international custom, general principles of law recognized by civilized nations, and judicial decisions and teachings of qualified jurists.

Treaties

International treaties are the most important source of international law. Today, hundreds of treaties govern relations among sovereign states. Some are **multilateral treaties**, the most significant of which may involve the majority of the world's countries. For example, 190 states are parties to the Nuclear Non-Proliferation Treaty—adopted in 1968 and extended indefinitely in 1995—that seeks to limit the spread of nuclear weapons to countries not already members of the nuclear club. Multilateral treaties are often intended to be norm-making— that is, to establish global standards that the parties view as a guide to beneficial behavior. In this respect, they are distinguishable from **bilateral treaties**, which apply narrowly to only two states. Bilateral treaties are, in effect, contracts between states and are not necessarily intended to establish norms for the international system as a whole. During the Cold War, for example, the United States and the Soviet Union signed a number of arms control treaties designed to regulate their bilateral arms race.

The international legal principle of *pacta sunt servanda* ("treaties must be respected") requires states to comply with the terms of treaties they have signed and ratified. When a broad majority of the world's states have signed and ratified a treaty, it can even put political pressure on nonsignatories to conform to treaty rules. However, under international law, only countries that have signed and then ratified a treaty are legally bound to observe its terms. The United States, which did not ratify the Kyoto Protocol on global warming, faced a lot of political heat for refusing to participate, but it was not legally required to comply with the treaty's regulations on emission of greenhouse gases. Likewise since India, Pakistan, and Israel did not sign and ratify the Non-Proliferation Treaty, they could legally acquire nuclear weapons despite the global consensus against nuclear proliferation.

Skeptical observers often note that treaties only bind states with their consent, and this, they say, is a major weakness of the international legal system. In their view, it is the equivalent of a domestic law that prohibits murder, but only for individuals who agree in advance to the prohibition. Even when states sign and ratify treaties, they often do so only after attaching **RUDs** (Reservations, Understandings, Declarations) whose purpose is to exclude or modify the applicability of specific provisions. Moreover, states often can formally withdraw from a treaty if they decide that compliance no longer serves their national interest. While such withdrawal is not always allowed, many treaties specifically provide a mechanism for doing so. For example, the Non-Proliferation Treaty provides that states can withdraw with three months' notice if "extraordinary events, related to the subject matter of this Treaty, have jeopardized the supreme interests of its country."[4] North Korea did precisely this in 2003, claiming the US posed a serious security threat to North Korea and citing as evidence of this threat US President George W. Bush's inclusion of North Korea as one of the three "axis of evil" countries (along with Iraq and Iran).

multilateral treaties
Also known as "norm-making treaties," these are agreements signed and ratified by many states—sometimes the vast majority of states.

bilateral treaties
Treaties between two states designed to regulate some aspect of their relationship with one another; legally binding on contracting parties.

pacta sunt servanda
(Latin for "treaties must be respected.") The international legal principle that requires states to comply with the terms of treaties they have formally signed and ratified.

RUDs
Formal reservations, understandings, and declarations attached to a state's ratification of a treaty intended to exclude or modify application of specific treaty provisions.

International Custom

customary international law
Long-established norms of behavior among states that, though not formalized in treaties, are routinely respected and come, over time, to be viewed as obligatory.

While treaties are the most important and most formalized source of international law, long-established norms of behavior among states can become a part of what is called **customary international law**. Customary law is established through a combination of (1) objective state practices or behaviors that show a consistent pattern of adherence to a rule over time, and (2) a subjective sense that states observe the rule because they view it as obligatory to do so. For example, the notion that unarmed fishing vessels should not be captured in warfare has long been a part of international customary law. More recently, it has been argued that customary international law, which has long recognized the right of states to defend themselves when threatened, may extend this right of self-defense to terrorist threats, including a right to engage in military response against states that harbor terrorists.[5]

Often customary law will be formalized through a treaty. For example, it was once the custom that the "cannon shot rule" defined a state's territorial waters. That rule said that coastal states could claim as sovereign territory waters three nautical miles from the shore—about the distance that cannons could fire when this rule was first formulated in the seventeenth century. As technology has changed and as states challenged the three-mile custom, the need for a more formalized treaty became clear and led to the 1994 Law of the Seas Treaty. That treaty extended territorial waters to 12 nautical miles and established economic zones of up to 200 miles within which coastal nations could claim exclusive rights to exploit fishing and other resources.

Other Sources of International Law

General principles of law recognized by civilized nations are a third source of international law. They refer to certain principles that are fundamental to the domestic legal systems of virtually all states, and they are sometimes referred to as "gap-fillers," insofar as they can provide a legal basis for decisions in cases where neither treaties nor customs offer conclusive guidance. These general principles often deal with legal procedures such as rules of evidence, but they can also relate to substantive matters such as human rights. The 1966 International Covenant on Civil and Political Rights, for example, which lays out a long list of human rights, is explicit in noting that "general principles of law recognized by the community of nations" must be respected.[6] Thus, if an individual violated human rights that were not explicitly covered in the 1966 treaty, that individual might still be prosecuted under international law if it could be shown that he or she had violated general principle covered by the domestic law of most civilized states.

Finally, judicial decisions and teachings of the most highly qualified jurists are considered subsidiary sources of international law. Rulings of the World Court and other judicial bodies, to the extent they apply and interpret the law, can contribute to the development of that law in much the way that domestic court rulings do. The same applies to the learned opinions of jurists and legal thinkers, whose interpretations of treaties and customs also contribute to the development of legal norms.

These various sources of international law provide a wide range of rules, procedures, obligations, and prohibitions that guide states as to acceptable and unacceptable behavior. Despite the absence of a global law-making legislature, it is hard to argue that the world lacks rules that, if observed, could reduce anarchy and increase order in the international system. Virtually every aspect of interstate relations, including the conduct of war, weapons proliferation, human rights, trade and investment, and the environment, are regulated by treaty or custom.

International Law Adjudication

5-2   **Explain the role of the World Court in international law adjudication and evaluate its effectiveness.**

An effective legal system not only requires a set of laws stated in advance but also a system of courts that can apply those laws. The courts must examine the circumstances of a case, determine if a law has been violated, and if so, decide who is responsible for that violation. In the international legal system, issue-specific institutions adjudicate some cases. The newly created International Criminal Court (ICC) tries cases that involve violations of human rights law (for more on the ICC, see Chapter 6). The World Trade Organization (WTO), though not a court per se, fulfills a quasi-judicial function in adjudicating disputes involving international trade law (for more on the WTO, see Chapter 7). However, the only general-purpose, global court with responsibility for resolving disputes among states under international law is the **International Court of Justice (ICJ)**, better known as the World Court.

International Court of Justice (ICJ)
Commonly known as the World Court; the general-purpose, global court with responsibility for resolving disputes among states under international law.

Structure and Functions of the ICJ

The World Court, located in The Hague, is a part of the United Nations system, and any state that is a member of the United Nations is automatically a party to the court. It has 15 judges, elected by the state parties, who serve nine-year renewable terms. The nationality of the judges has reflected an attempt to represent the global diversity of state parties while recognizing the uneven distribution of power in the international system. Thus, while no state can have more than one of its nationals sit on the court, the five permanent members of the UN Security Council (United States, Russia, France, Great Britain, and China) have generally always had a judge on the court, with the one exception of China from 1967 to 1984. However, the 15 judges who sit on the court are there not to represent their home country but to uphold and apply international law on an impartial basis.

The World Court has two primary functions. First, it can issue advisory opinions on matters of international law at the request of the UN Security Council, the UN General Assembly, or other more specialized UN agencies granted this right by the General Assembly. States, individuals, NGOs, and other international organizations outside the UN system cannot directly ask for such opinions. Note that ICJ advisory opinions are not considered legally binding. Instead, the opinion attempts to clarify the law and use the legal and political prestige of the court to influence world opinion.

One high-visibility advisory opinion had to do with the security wall built by the Israeli government to restrict Palestinians who might pose a threat to Israel. In October 2003, the UN General Assembly posed this question to the ICJ: "What are the legal consequences arising from the construction of the wall being built by Israel, the occupying Power, in the Occupied Palestinian Territory, including in and around East Jerusalem?"[7] The court, by a 14–1 majority in which the US judge was the lone dissenter, ruled that the wall is contrary to international law, that Israel must cease building the wall, dismantle what already exists, and make reparation for damage caused, and that the UN General Assembly and Security Council should consider further action to bring an end to this illegal situation.[8] In another controversial advisory opinion, the ICJ ruled in 2010 that Kosovo's 2008 declaration of independence from Serbia was legal. While some observers worried that this ruling would fuel separatist movements around the world, the court advised that there was no prohibition on declarations of independence in international law.

The second function of the ICJ is to hear and decide contentious cases between states. Only sovereign states can be parties to such a case; international organizations, NGOs, and individuals can neither bring contentious cases to the court nor be tried as defendants. Unlike advisory opinions, decisions in a contentious case are considered legally binding. However, for the Court to take a case in the first place and expect the parties to participate in court proceedings requires the prior consent of the states involved. In other words, the World Court lacks the power of **compulsory jurisdiction** that domestic courts typically possess and that allows those domestic courts to require parties to show up for court or face legal sanctions. Under international law jurisdiction is always by consent, and the World Court may acquire this consent to its jurisdiction in three ways:

compulsory jurisdiction
Power of a court to require parties in a dispute to participate in the court's proceedings and to accept its rulings.

1. *Special agreement:* Two states in conflict agree to take the case to the ICJ for resolution. Typically easiest to obtain where the stakes of the case are relatively low (e.g., minor border disputes, fishing rights) and the outcome of the court's deliberations is uncertain.
2. *Jurisdictional clause in a treaty:* Almost 300 treaties include a clause granting jurisdiction to the court in disputes over the interpretation of that treaty. Examples include the 1948 Convention on Genocide, the 1992 Convention on Climate Change, and the 1993 Chemical Weapons Convention.

Portion of the wall or barrier built by Israel to defend against terrorist attacks from Palestinian territories. The barrier remains despite a 2004 ICJ advisory decision that it was illegal. Yet liberals and constructivists might maintain that the ICJ decision was not irrelevant. Why might they argue that, and are they right?

3. *Article 36 of the ICJ charter:* Article 36, known as the **optional clause**, was intended as a compromise between those who wanted the World Court to have compulsory jurisdiction and those who rejected such a sweeping grant of jurisdiction in the name of protecting state sovereignty. A state that accepts the optional clause voluntarily accepts the ICJ's compulsory jurisdiction in any future case involving another country that has also declared such acceptance. As of 2015, 71 states accepted it.

optional clause
Article 36 of the charter of the ICJ; provides an opportunity for states to accept the jurisdiction of the ICJ in advance of any case to which they might be a party and in which the other involved parties have also accepted the court's jurisdiction.

The Impact of the ICJ

The World Court's dependence on the voluntary acquiescence of states to its jurisdiction is a weakness that even the most ardent supporters concede. In fact, state consent to ICJ jurisdiction via special agreements, treaties, and the optional clause often means less than meets the eye due to RUDs commonly attached to such consent.[9] For example, Australia exempts maritime boundary issues from its acceptance of the optional clause; Poland exempts disputes involving territory, state boundaries, and environmental protection; and the UK exempts disputes involving current or former British Commonwealth members.

The US relationship with the ICJ provides a good illustration of the problems inherent in the jurisdiction-by-consent approach. The US view of the Court has been ambivalent. On the one hand, as a status quo power the United States has had a stake in order and stability in the international system. To the extent that the ICJ and the larger system of international law preserve that order by providing a basis for peaceful resolution of disputes, it can benefit the United States. On the other hand, it is precisely because the main impact of law and courts is to limit the raw exercise of power that a superpower like the United States might find the World Court excessively constraining at times. As a result, though generally supportive of the ICJ in principle, in practice the United States has been reluctant to accept the ICJ's jurisdiction.

In the roughly 70-year history of the World Court, the United States agreed to submit a case to the court via special agreement on only one occasion. That was in 1981 when Canada and the United States agreed to seek a ruling on the relatively minor issue of the location of the maritime boundary between the two countries in the Gulf of Maine. Similarly, though the United States was among the first states to formally accept ICJ compulsory jurisdiction via the optional clause, a reservation attached to that acceptance, known as the Connelly Amendment, provided a huge loophole in stipulating that the "jurisdiction of the Court would not apply to matters which are essentially within the domestic jurisdiction of the United States as determined by the United States." Those last six words, *as determined by the United States*, drained all essential meaning from the US acceptance of compulsory jurisdiction.

The ambivalence of the United States toward the World Court is well illustrated by two cases: *The United States* v. *Iran* (1979–1981) and *Nicaragua* v. *the United States* (1984–1991).[10] The former case was brought by the United States to the ICJ in response to the hostage taking at the US embassy in Teheran. In November 1979, young militants stormed the US embassy and took approximately 70 Americans hostage. Here, the United States sought ICJ intervention, claiming, among other things, that the Iranian action violated the principle of diplomatic immunity. Despite Iran's refusal to participate in the proceedings, the ICJ ruled in May 1980 that Iran had violated international law, that it should immediately release the hostages, and that it must make reparations to the United States. That ruling notwithstanding, the hostages were not released until January 20, 1981, just minutes following newly elected President Ronald Reagan's inaugural address. The crisis had lasted for 444 days and had contributed to Jimmy Carter's defeat by Reagan in the 1980 election.

A few years later, in *Nicaragua* v. *the United States*, it was the turn of the United States to refuse to participate in ICJ proceedings. In this case, the left-leaning Sandinista regime of Nicaragua accused the United States of engaging in various illegal military actions intended to destabilize the Nicaraguan government, including laying mines to restrict access to ports. Despite having accepted the optional clause in 1946, the United States refused to recognize the jurisdiction of the Court. In April 1984, the United States submitted a notification that referred to the original 1946 acceptance of the optional clause: "The aforesaid declaration shall not apply to disputes with any Central American State or arising out of or related to events in Central America, any of which disputes shall be settled in such manner as the parties to them may agree."[11] The ICJ rejected the US arguments, asserted jurisdiction in this case, and in 1986 ruled against the United States on the substantive issues. In response, the United States terminated its acceptance of the optional clause, and rejected and ignored the substantive findings of the World Court.

US behavior toward the ICJ in these cases suggests that the adage about the World Court being "a place you can go but not be taken" is apt. Indeed, realists might argue that the World Court is a weak substitute for power and self-help in world politics. Not only does the ICJ lack the power to enforce its "legally binding rulings," but it cannot even compel state participation in court proceedings.

Despite those weaknesses, states do bring cases to the World Court. During the Cold War era (1947–1989), 81 cases were placed on the court's docket. Since the end of the Cold War, the World Court has become busier. Since 1990, 79 cases have been reached the court, all but 6 of them contentious cases.[12] If one couples these trends with the adjudication activities of such new tribunals as the International Criminal Court, the ad hoc tribunals created to consider human rights cases in the former Yugoslavia and Rwanda, and even the World Trade Organization (see Chapters 6 and 7), the global trend is toward more adjudication of international disputes.[13]

Clearly, states that bring cases to the World Court must see some purpose and value in doing so. At the very least, ICJ decisions can spill over into the larger court of world opinion, pressuring states that are in violation of international law even when they have failed to accept the World Court's jurisdiction. Moreover, ICJ rulings can provide part of the basis for other international organizations, in particular the UN Security Council, to act. Thus, the question of the effectiveness of international law is closely bound with the question of the effectiveness of the larger United Nations system.

International Law Enforcement

5-3   Identify the various approaches to international law enforcement.

One of the most common criticisms of the international legal system is related to the perceived weakness of law enforcement. In domestic systems, an individual convicted of a crime in a court of law faces immediately enforceable punishment, such as a fine or imprisonment. In the international system, the World Court might rule that a state has violated international law, but whether that state will terminate the law-violating behavior and make amends is an open question. In the cases noted above, Iran continued to hold US diplomats hostage for months following the World Court's ruling, while the United States effectively ignored the court's decision that US behavior toward Nicaragua was illegal. Yet, while the differences between domestic and international law in this respect are real and significant, one should not lose sight of the similarities.

Enforcement via Self-Help

In the domestic setting, law is often enforced without the overt intervention of public authorities. I refrain from parking my car on my neighbor's lawn not only because I fear the police will be summoned to fine or arrest me but also because the law prohibiting such a practice is one that I have internalized and respect. Moreover, I would have to contend with the damage to my reputation as a decent person and good neighbor that such behavior would likely produce. It is, as constructivists would argue, the power of widely accepted norms of behavior that keep me from behaving in an unneighborly way. If that isn't enough to deter me, my neighbor can impose more concrete costs. He might not invite me to his next Super Bowl party, or he might park his car on my lawn. In short, the situations in which the police and courts are called on represent only the most visible tip of domestic law enforcement.

The same is true of international law. Having signed a treaty, a state often respects it because of the power of the international norms of behavior and the reputational damage that would likely occur if the treaty is casually violated. States also have to consider the possibility of **reprisals** by other states. Often those reprisals, otherwise known as enforcement via self-help, involve perfectly legal actions by other states, including the recall of an ambassador, nonparticipation in an athletic competition, or the scaling back of a cultural exchange program. Other times, the reprisal might involve an action that would be illegal if unprovoked but that now is justified given the provocation. Thus, the terms of a treaty might not bind a state whose own rights under that treaty have been violated by another state. Likewise, a state that violates international trade agreements by limiting the import of another country's goods can expect to have its exports blocked in retaliation, often with the formal approval of the World Trade Organization, which functions as the court of international trade law.

Indeed, no legal system, domestic or international, could survive without a critical mass of actors who maintain voluntary respect for the law or who are at least deterred from violating the law by the prospect of reprisals. Without that critical mass, any legal system would collapse, as the police and other authorities would become overwhelmed. Of course, cases occur where neither concern for one's reputation nor fear of reprisal guarantee lawful behavior. The more powerful the actor, the more it can potentially withstand the threat of reprisals and contemplate illegal activity.

In such cases, the existence, or absence, of a "sheriff" to enforce the law will be most noticeable. Reliable enforcement by the sheriff is important to punish the few who break the law and to thereby reinforce the tendency of the many to obey it. As realists would stress, however, the international system has no sheriff with universal authority. The World Court might rule that a state violated the law, but it has no army to stop that violation.

One possible solution to policing the international system and enforcing international law is for a powerful state to take on this role. That state must possess three key attributes: (1) the capability, rooted in economic and military might; (2) a commitment to those rules in the belief that they serve the state's interests; and (3) the will to act when necessary. Such a state is capable of exercising hegemony, or dominance in the international system, and proponents of hegemonic stability theory (see Chapter 1) argue that stability and order in the

reprisals
In international law, acts of retaliation that might otherwise be illegal but that in response to violations of law by another state are legally justifiable.

international system are increased when such a powerful state or hegemon is able to take on this role.

At the end of the Cold War, some saw the United States taking on this role. This included President George H. W. Bush, who said, following the 1990 Iraqi invasion of Kuwait, "America and the world must support the rule of law. And we will." For Bush, standing up to Iraq was important not just to liberate Kuwait but also to send the larger message that violators of international law would have to face the wrath of the international community led by the United States.[14]

However, scholars disagree over whether hegemony, in the long run, supports or undermines the evolution of an effective international legal order. Some scholars argue that given the absence of effective global institutions, law enforcement by a hegemonic power is crucial. Others, however, see a tension between law and the interests of any single state, particularly one so powerful, which will invariably seek to enforce international law only when it suits that state's interests. Thus, for liberal institutionalists, international law enforcement ultimately depends on developing international organizations that can pick up the responsibility for law enforcement when enforcement via self-help reaches its limits.

The Role of International Organizations

International organizations are voluntary associations created to achieve a common purpose and with a membership that extends beyond the borders of a single state. International organizations are commonly divided into two subgroups: intergovernmental organizations and nongovernmental organizations.

An **intergovernmental organization (IGO)** is an organization whose membership is typically limited to states. There are three basic types of IGOs:

intergovernmental organization (IGO)
A voluntary association of sovereign states formally constituted for the purpose of achieving some common objective.

- *Global, general-purpose IGOs.* The most obvious example here is the United Nations, whose membership is virtually universal and whose organs and specialized agencies deal with the full gamut of global issues.
- *Regional IGOs.* These organizations can have multiple purposes, but membership is restricted regionally. Examples include the Organization of American States (OAS) and the African Union (AU). A special example of a regional IGO is the European Union (EU). As will be discussed in more detail in Chapter 7, the EU is unique because of the amount of sovereign authority its individual member states have ceded to EU-wide institutions.
- *Functional IGOs.* These functional or special-purpose organizations facilitate the achievement of some defined goal. Good examples are the Organization of Petroleum Exporting Countries (OPEC), created for the specific purpose of controlling oil prices; the Organization for Economic Cooperation and Development (OECD), which includes 34 of the most developed, democratic countries; and the International Whaling Commission, which monitors issues relating to the global whaling industry.

Whatever the type, IGOs seek to facilitate cooperation among members and thus can mitigate, if not eliminate, global anarchy. They can provide a forum for negotiation and a place to resolve disputes. They are often especially important in pooling the efforts and capabilities of their members to address challenges ranging from mutual defense (e.g., NATO) to economic development (e.g., the World Bank). Note that while states may be motivated to join at least in part by the common purpose that the IGO represents, they will also consider their state interests, and the votes they cast within the IGO will reflect those interests.

In their design and purpose, IGOs are closely linked with the development of international law. First, IGOs are themselves created by treaties among their members and are thus a product of international treaty law and also are bound by its obligations. Second, in some cases, IGOs are established to monitor compliance with a particular treaty. Third, IGOs can also provide a forum for negotiating new treaties among member states. Finally, IGOs can, in some cases, act as the enforcement arm of international law, with both the authority and the means to punish violators of the law.

nongovernmental organization (NGO)
Organization whose members are individuals rather than states, but whose membership and organizational apparatus extend across the borders of multiple states.

In contrast to an IGO, a **nongovernmental organization (NGO)** is an organization that is established and that operates independent of the formal control of governments. Its members are individuals rather than sovereign states. As a college student, you can become a member of an NGO like Amnesty International or Greenpeace by registering online and paying a membership fee, but you cannot join an IGO such as the United Nations. Like IGOs, NGOs are established to promote and achieve some common mission such as human rights, environmental protection, or global health. But unlike an IGO, in an NGO the interests of specific states are irrelevant. Instead, the larger cause is the sole concern.

In recent decades the number of NGOs has swelled. While the exact number is difficult to determine, estimates of tens of thousands of internationally operating NGOs are common. In pursuing their mission—whether it is promoting human rights, facilitating economic development, or combating climate change—NGOs pursue multiple strategies. They provide direct assistance to individuals and communities in need, they monitor and publicize the actions of governments, and they can lobby states to enact desired policy initiatives. Liberal, constructivist, and feminist scholars have pointed to this proliferation of NGOs as evidence that the realist, state-centric view of how the world works is increasingly dated.

An interesting trend in recent decades has been the expansion in cooperation between some IGOs and NGOs. This trend is most readily seen in the United Nations where NGOs can apply for and receive formal consultative status with UN agencies. The precedent for doing so was set early as 40 NGOs had received such consultative status by 1948, increasing to 180 by 1968, and then to 724 by 1992.[15] But it was really in the post–Cold War era that this trend escalated, with over 4,000 NGOs receiving formal UN consultative status by 2014.[16] For the NGOs, such status provides inside access to powerful IGOs, and the governments represented therein, with the power and resources to further

NGO objectives. It can also contribute to NGO prestige. For the IGOs, NGOs are a source of knowledge and expertise, and they can supplement limited IGO personnel by helping to implement and monitor compliance with international agreements[17] (see Theory in Practice 5.1).

Both IGOs and NGOs are central to the emergence and perpetuation of **international regimes**. A regime is a set of principles, norms, rules, and procedures that guides the behavior of states in a specific issue area. For example, the nuclear non-proliferation regime is centered on the basic principle that nuclear proliferation is destabilizing. Flowing from the principle are norms against the development, acquisition, or sharing of nuclear weapons technology; specific

international regime
A set of principles, norms, rules, and procedures that guides and shapes the behavior of states in a specific issue area.

Theory in Practice 5.1
NGOs in Afghanistan

The roles played by NGOs, and the promise and pitfalls associated with NGO efforts, are well illustrated by the situation in Afghanistan. Following the 2001 US invasion and the fall of the Taliban regime, the number of NGOs operating in Afghanistan proliferated. By 2009, as many as 2,000 NGOs were estimated to be in Afghanistan working in such diverse areas as education, human rights, the establishment of legal institutions, and economic development. Though most of those NGOs are Afghan, the largest and best-funded are international NGOs.

The NGOs have provided much needed assistance to a country reeling from the challenges of poverty, war, and civil strife. NGO personnel and resources have complemented those provided by the United Nations, the United States, and other national governments. At the same time, the NGO role in Afghanistan has not been without problems, not least of which has been the problem of security. In 2008 alone, 38 NGO staff workers (mostly Afghans) were killed by armed opposition groups. As if that is not enough to worry about, in May 2010 the Afghan government revoked the licenses of 172 NGOs (including 20 international NGOs) alleged to have engaged in misconduct.

Why have NGOs that have sought to help the Afghan people been targeted by the Afghan government? In part, the crackdown stemmed from a concern in some government circles that the weak Afghan government is too dependent on NGOs. But there is also more general disillusionment among many Afghans about the role of NGOs. The cooperative relationship that has developed in recent years between NGOs on the one hand, and IGOs and national governments on the other, has raised questions about the autonomy of NGOs. This concern can be especially acute in a place like Afghanistan where foreign troops are present. Moreover, there is a growing perception that many NGOs are out of touch with the needs of Afghanistan, and many Afghans have come to view NGOs as "the SUV (sports utility vehicle) community."

- In order to preserve their autonomy, should NGOs pull back from the trend toward close cooperation and formal consultation with IGOs and national governments?

- What factors might help explain the proliferation of NGOs in recent decades?

- Does the proliferation of NGOs undermine the realist, state-centric view of how the world works or not? How would realists respond to this claim?

SOURCES: Human Security Report Project, "Afghanistan Conflict Monitor," July 2010, http://www.afghanconflictmonitor.org/access.html and Nipa Banerjee, "Role of NGOs in Post-Taliban Afghanistan," *Asia Policy Briefs*, March 2009, http://exed.maxwell.syr.edu/exed/sites/policy/node/26.

rules stipulated formally in the Non-Proliferation Treaty and other international agreements; and procedures for monitoring non-proliferation, acquiring nuclear technology for peaceful purposes, and dealing with those who operate outside the norms and rules of the non-proliferation regime. Essential to this regime are the contributions of IGOs like the International Atomic Energy Agency (IAEA), along with numerous NGOs, in monitoring the non-proliferation regime.

The United Nations

5-4 Explain and evaluate the role of the United Nations in promoting law, order, and security in international relations.

Since the end of World War II, the single most important international organization has been the United Nations. The special significance of the UN is due to several factors. For one thing, it has almost universal membership, expanding from its original 51 members in 1945 to 193 members today. The only UN-recognized sovereign states that are not members are Vatican City and Palestine, both of which have a nonmember observer state status without a vote. The decision to grant that status to Palestine was made by the UN General Assembly in November 2012 over the objection of both the United States and Israel. Though possessing de facto attributes of sovereignty, the Republic of China (Taiwan) is not recognized by the UN as a sovereign state and thus lacks UN membership.

In addition, the UN is the only global, general-purpose organization in existence today. Through its organs and agencies, the UN deals with all matters of international affairs, including issues of war and peace, the global economy, human rights, environmental management, and global health management. Many key international agencies of the post–World War II era, including the International Monetary Fund (IMF), the World Bank, the World Health Organization (WHO), and the International Atomic Energy Agency (IAEA), are subsumed within the UN system.

Finally, the UN is the only international organization with the authority to use military power to promote global security and to enforce international law. While regional military alliances like NATO can use military power to protect the interests of their members, the UN is the only international body authorized to wield military power in the name of the international community.

UN Structure

Security Council
One of the principal organs of the United Nations, it has primary responsibility for maintaining international peace and security.

As specified in the UN Charter, and as shown in Figure 5.1, the structure and work of the United Nations is centered on its six principal organs:

1. The **Security Council** is the organ of the UN with primary responsibility for maintaining international peace and security. It is composed of five

Figure 5.1 The Structure of the United Nations

SOURCE: Adapted from http://en.wikipedia.org/wiki/United_Nations_System

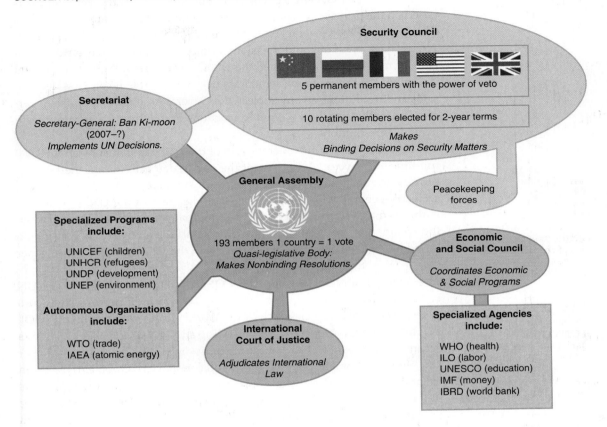

permanent members (the United States, Russia, China, Great Britain, and France) and 10 rotating members serving two-year terms. To act on any substantive measure, a supermajority of nine of the 15 members must agree, including all five of the permanent members. A single "no" vote, or veto, by one of the "Perm-5"—the five permanent members—effectively stymies Security Council action. The veto is related in part to the self-interested desire of the great powers after World War II to guard their sovereignty, but it also reflects the **great power unanimity principle**. The Perm-5 were the victors of World War II and, as a result, key players in the early postwar international system. For the Security Council to act without all five on board, and especially directly against the interests of one or more of them, would render the successful implementation of Security Council decisions highly problematic, thereby undermining the credibility of the council.

2. The **General Assembly** is the quasi-legislative organ of the UN, with the authority to issue nonbinding resolutions and declarations and to serve as

great power unanimity principle
The logic underlying the UN Security Council veto: that to be effective, the Security Council needs all the great powers on board.

General Assembly
Quasi-legislative organ of the United Nations with universal membership that has authority to issue nonbinding resolutions and declarations and to serve as a forum for discussion of international issues.

a forum for discussion of international issues. Its membership is universal, with all states that are members of the UN represented. Unlike the Security Council, the UN General Assembly is unhampered by the veto, and it is based on the principle of sovereign equality for all states. Thus, all members have a seat in the General Assembly; all, regardless of size, population, or power, have one vote; and decisions in most cases are based on the principle of majority rule. However, the UN Charter does not give the General Assembly the power to implement its decisions. While it can pass declarations and resolutions on any subject, the General Assembly cannot use coercive instruments such as economic sanctions or military power to put teeth behind its resolutions.

Secretariat
Bureaucratic arm of the United Nations, headed by the secretary-general, and staffed by about 9,000 full-time UN employees who carry out the daily activities of the UN and provide administrative support to other UN organs.

Economic and Social Council (ECOSOC)
One of the principal organs of the United Nations, it coordinates and oversees UN economic and social programs, including the work of various specialized, autonomous agencies.

Trusteeship Council
One of the original six primary organs of the UN established to supervise UN trust territories and facilitate their move to self-government. The work of this organ was suspended in 1994.

3. The **Secretariat** is the bureaucratic arm of the UN. It is staffed by about 9,000 full-time employees who carry out the day-to-day activities of the UN and provide administrative support to other UN organs. It is headed by the UN secretary-general, who is often viewed as the "face of the UN" and who is authorized to bring matters affecting international peace and security to the attention of the Security Council. Secretariat employees are considered international civil servants whose duty is to the UN and its mission, rather than to the state from which they come.

4. The **Economic and Social Council (ECOSOC)** coordinates and oversees UN economic and social programs, including the work of approximately two dozen specialized agencies such as the World Health Organization (WHO), the International Monetary Fund (IMF), and the World Bank. Though accountable to the ECOSOC, these agencies are largely autonomous. Major UN efforts to combat poverty, promote economic development, and control the spread of disease take place under the ECOSOC organizational umbrella. It is composed of 54 member countries elected to three-year terms. ECOSOC operates on the principle of one state, one vote, and decisions are taken by a simple majority.

5. The **International Court of Justice (ICJ)** or World Court, as previously discussed, is the primary court of international law.

6. The **Trusteeship Council** was originally created to supervise UN trust territories and their move toward self-government. The work of this organ was suspended in 1994 when Palau, the last remaining trust territory, gained its independence.

Through these principal organs, and the numerous agencies and programs whose work they authorize and coordinate, the UN plays an important role across a range of global issues. For example, the UN has been central to the development, monitoring, and enforcement of norms governing international human rights (see Chapter 6). The UN also plays an important role related to economic development and poverty reduction (see Chapter 7). And, as we have seen most recently in the response to climate change and H1N1 influenza, the UN has been directly involved in facilitating a cooperative response to global environmental and health challenges (see Chapter 8). However, the central debate between realists and liberal institutionalists regarding the performance and potential of the UN centers on the issues of promoting global security and enforcing international law and order. It is on these issues that the remainder of this chapter will focus.

UN Enforcement of Law and Order

The United Nations is empowered by its charter to enforce international law and order in a number of ways. Specifically, it can enforce decisions of the World Court, engage in collective security operations, and establish peacekeeping missions. In all these areas, the central actor is the Security Council, though the General Assembly sometimes plays a role as well.

ENFORCEMENT OF ICJ DECISIONS If one thinks of law enforcement in its most narrow sense, as the muscle behind the law as interpreted by courts, then the place to look in the UN Charter is Chapter XIV, Article 94, which addresses enforcement of World Court decisions:

> If any party to a case fails to perform the obligations incumbent upon it under a judgment rendered by the Court, the other party may have recourse to the Security Council, which may, if it deems necessary, make recommendations or decide upon measures to be taken to give effect to the judgment.[18]

Given this grant of authority to the Security Council, the requirements of an effective system of international law—a law-making process, a law adjudication process, and a law enforcement process—seem to all be in place. A broad array of laws created by treaty and custom are available for interpretation and application by the World Court, whose decisions are given teeth by the enforcement authority of the Security Council.

In practice, however, the law enforcement authority granted under Chapter XIV has been rarely used. Note that the wording of Article 94 gives the Security Council some discretion—that is, to enforce judgments of the ICJ only "if it deems necessary." Thus, the Security Council's enforcement of World Court decisions can be subject to political debates rather than strictly legal considerations. The result has been very few cases in which the Security Council has acted as the enforcement arm of the World Court under Article 94.

However, the law enforcement role of the Security Council is not limited to the execution of World Court decisions. In domestic legal systems, law enforcement is not limited to the punishment of criminals after conviction by a court. On the contrary, the most important law enforcement function of the police is to respond to calls regarding crimes in progress and to stop them before innocent individuals are hurt. The same is true of the UN Security Council, whose primary responsibility is to respond to threats to international peace and stability that are imminent or in progress. Like any good sheriff, the Security Council has a law enforcement role that precedes court action.

Chapter VII authority
Authority, granted to the Security Council by Chapter VII of the UN charter, to take both nonmilitary and military measures deemed necessary to reduce and eliminate threats to international peace and security.

COLLECTIVE SECURITY   Chapter VII of the UN Charter grants the Security Council the right to respond to "threats to the peace, breaches of the peace, and acts of aggression." Specifically, the Security Council is authorized, under what is often referred to simply as its **Chapter VII authority**, to (1) determine when such threats are occurring, (2) call on parties to take measures to prevent aggravation of the situation, (3) implement nonmilitary measures as required, and (4) if such measures prove inadequate, use military forces as necessary to restore peace and stability. In implementing military measures, UN members are obliged to make available to the Security Council the forces required. Thus, Chapter VII provides the basis for a system of collective security and another attempt at the Wilsonian approach to order represented by the failed League of Nations experiment (see Chapter 2).

However, while in principle the Security Council has significant authority to play that collective security role, in practice its record has been spotty. The main problem is the veto. From 1946 through 2014, the veto was exercised in the Security Council on 274 occasions. US and Soviet/Russian vetoes have accounted for close to 80 percent of all the vetoes cast, reflecting the realities of the bipolar Cold War era in which the United States and USSR were on opposite sides of virtually every significant international issue.

Over time, the pattern of veto usage by individual countries has shifted. Figure 5.2 breaks down the exercise of the veto into three periods. During the first two decades of the UN's existence, the veto was almost exclusively wielded by the USSR (106 times) without a single veto exercised by the United

Figure 5.2 The Security Council Veto (number of vetoes cast by period by each country)

SOURCES: Adapted from Global Policy Forum, "Changing Patterns in the Use of the Veto in the Security Council," http://www.globalpolicy.org and from "Veto List," Dag Hammarskjold Library Research Guides, United Nations, http://research.un.org/en/docs/sc/quick/veto.

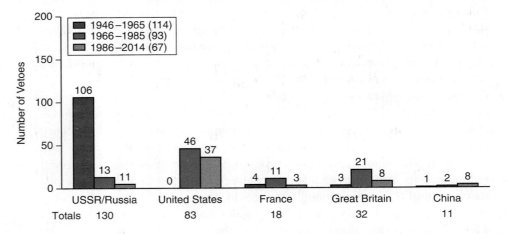

States and only a handful by the other three permanent members. That record reflects the fact that the UN of that era was dominated by the United States and its allies, who could control the agenda of the Security Council and thereby force the Soviet Union to repeatedly use its veto. Andrei Gromyko, the first Soviet ambassador to the UN, was sometimes referred to in the West as "Mr. Nyet" because of the number of vetoes he cast. Subsequently, Soviet vetoes declined while US vetoes increased. This shift reflected a larger shift in the membership of the UN and in international relations in general. By the 1970s, an increasingly large bloc of Communist states and newly independent states, the latter a legacy of the winding down of European colonialism, made it much more difficult for the United States to control the UN agenda. Thus, the United States increasingly used the veto to defend its interests and those of allies such as Israel.

As a result of the veto, only two collective security operations designed to enforce international law and order under Chapter VII authority have occurred. The first was the Korean War, which began in 1950 following the invasion of US-backed South Korea by Communist North Korea. A US-sponsored resolution demanding the withdrawal of North Korean forces from South Korea was passed without a dissenting vote in the Security Council and was followed by military intervention by UN forces under the direction of US General Douglas MacArthur. One might have expected a Soviet veto; however, the USSR had been boycotting Security Council meetings. They were protesting the refusal of the US-dominated body to transfer Chinese representation in the UN—including the permanent seat on the Security Council—from the US-backed Taiwanese government to the new Communist government. In essence, Security Council military intervention on the Korean peninsula was a fluke occasioned only by a tactical mistake on the part of the USSR.

It was not until four decades later that the second Security Council collective security operation took place, and that was in response to Iraq's August 1990 invasion of Kuwait. By international consensus, Iraq had clearly and flagrantly breached international law in violating the political sovereignty and territorial integrity of Kuwait. Concluding that diplomacy and economic sanctions would not reverse Iraq's invasion, the Bush administration got Security Council approval for Resolution 678, authorizing use of "all necessary means" to remove Iraq from Kuwait. With the understanding that "all necessary means" is often used as a diplomatic euphemism for military force, the United States was concerned about a possible veto by either China or the USSR. China ultimately abstained, while the USSR, in the midst of internal political and economic turmoil and badly in need of Western aid, voted in favor of the resolution.

Some hoped that Security Council cooperation in responding to the Kuwait situation marked a turning point and would usher in a new age of post–Cold

Former US Secretary of State Colin Powell addressing the UN Security Council in 2003 regarding Iraq's alleged weapons of mass destruction. Realist critics of the Security Council suggest that the US invasion of Iraq ended post-Cold War illusions about revived collective security. Are they right?

peacekeeping
UN military intervention intended to maintain a peace already established by the parties involved via negotiation or military stalemate. Also known as "first-generation peacekeeping."

War collective security. However, those hopes dissipated over the 1990s as post-Communist Russia reasserted its interests and its autonomy from the West and as China emerged as an economic, political, and, potentially, military power in East Asia. The 2003 US invasion of Iraq seemed effectively to end hopes for a revived system of UN collective security. Having failed to secure explicit UN Security Council authorization for military action against Iraq, and faced with the likelihood of a veto by Russia, China, or even France, the United States bypassed the UN and assembled an ad hoc "coalition of the willing" in going to war against Saddam Hussein.

PEACEKEEPING   Though UN collective security operations under Chapter VII have been rare, less ambitious UN peacekeeping operations have been frequent. **Peacekeeping** operations differ from collective security (or what are sometimes called **peace enforcement** actions) in a number of ways. In the collective security operations in Korea and Kuwait, the UN was, in effect, going to war against a country that violated international law and threatened international peace and stability by engaging in cross-border aggression. As a result, the UN forces needed to be large in number and heavily armed.

peace enforcement
UN military interventions, against aggressor states, intended to reverse cross-border aggression.

Figure 5.3 UN Peacekeeping Missions as of April 2015

NOTE: The date indicates the start of the ongoing mission.
SOURCE: United Nations, "List of Missions," http://www.un.org.

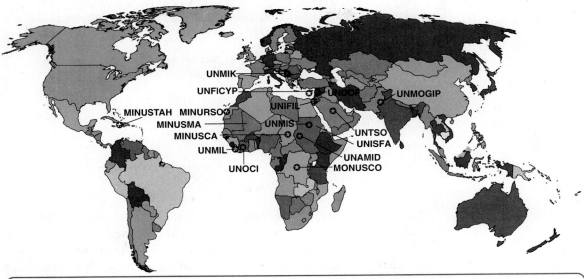

UNTSO—*UN Truce Supervision Organization*, 1948

UNMOGIP—*UN Military Observer Group in India and Pakistan*, 1949

UNFICYP—*UN Peacekeeping Force in Cyprus*, 1964

UNDOF—*UN Disengagement Force*, 1974

UNIFIL—*UN Interim Force in Lebanon*, 1978

MINURSO—*UN Mission for the Referendum in Western Sahara*, 1991

UNMIK—*UN Interim Administration Mission in Kosovo*,1999

UNMIL—*UN Mission in Liberia*, 2003

UNOCI—*UN Operation in Côte d'Ivoire*, 2004

MINUSTAH—*UN Stabilization Mission in Haiti*, 2004

UNMIS—*UN Mission in the Sudan*, 2005

UNAMID—*African Union/UN Hybrid Operation in Darfur*, 2007

MONUSCO—*UN Organization Stabilization Mission in the Democratic Republic of Congo*, 2010

UNISFA—*UN Interim Security Force for Abyei (Sudan)*, 2011

MINUSMA—*UN Multidimensional Integrated Stabilization Mission in Mali*, 2013

MINUSCA—*UN Multidimensional Integrated Stabilization Mission in Central African Republic*, 2014

In a peacekeeping operation, in contrast, the UN intervenes to maintain a peace already established via political negotiation or military stalemate. In such cases, the UN forces are typically there, with the prior consent of all parties, as an impartial buffer force. As a result, peacekeeping forces tend to be smaller in number and more lightly armed than collective security forces. There have been 69 UN peacekeeping missions from 1948 to 2014, with some, especially early on, initiated by the UN General Assembly, but most have been authorized by the UN Security Council. Following the collapse of the USSR and with the US–Soviet Cold War relegated to history, the Security Council became especially busy in this regard, initiating 51 of those peacekeeping missions since 1990. As illustrated in Figure 5.3, there were 16 missions in progress in 2015, 9 of which were in Africa.

Table 5.1 Three Types of UN Military Intervention

	Peace Enforcement (*collective security*)	Peacekeeping (*first-generation peacekeeping*)	Peacemaking (*second-generation peacekeeping*)
Purpose	Reverse cross-border aggression	Maintain a cease-fire	Impose a cease-fire
Parties to Conflict	States	States or subnational groups	Subnational groups
Consent of All Parties	No	Yes	Preferable, but not required
Impartiality of UN Forces	No	Yes	Preferable, but not required
Required UN Forces	Heavy	Light	Moderate

peacemaking
UN military intervention intended to impose a peace on parties in conflict, and used primarily to intervene in conflicts within states where humanitarian catastrophes are underway. Also known as "second-generation peacekeeping."

The goals of these peacekeeping missions also became more ambitious as the Security Council sent in UN forces—or "UN blue helmets" as they are often called—to intervene in countries such as Bosnia and Somalia to prevent humanitarian catastrophes caused by civil wars and ethnic conflicts. Thus, in contrast with traditional or first-generation peacekeeping, second-generation peacekeeping sees UN forces intervening without a prior cease-fire having been established. This second-generation peacekeeping is thus sometimes called **peacemaking**, insofar as the task is to impose a peace, with or without the consent of the parties. (See Table 5.1 for a summary comparison of the three main types of UN military interventions.) As a result, it therefore often requires a larger number of more heavily armed UN forces than first-generation peacekeeping.

The record of UN peacekeeping is mixed. Some prominent peacekeeping efforts have failed, including the well-publicized failure to stop genocide in Rwanda in 1994 (see Theory in Practice 5.2). Likewise, in the summer of 1995, in one of the bleakest moments of the conflict in the former Yugoslav republic of Bosnia, the 600 poorly equipped and outnumbered Dutch UN peacekeepers stood by as Serbian forces shelled and entered the Bosnian town of Srebrenica. Srebrenica had previously been designated as a UN "safe haven" where refugees from the fighting would be protected. However, UN forces there, fearful that they would be attacked or taken hostage, stood by as Serb forces rounded up and executed Bosnian Muslim men. Pleas for reinforcements and air support from the commander of the Dutch UN forces in Srebrenica went unheeded. In the end, some 7,000 Muslim men were killed, and the UN Protection Force (UNPROFOR) became known to many as the UN *Self*-Protection Force.[19]

On the other hand, there have been successes. The United Nations Mission in Sierra Leone (UNAMSIL) is a good example of a peacekeeping success. In 2001, the UN helped broker a cease-fire in the West African country's decade-long conflict between the government and the Revolutionary United Front (RUF).

Theory in Practice 5.2

Peacekeeping Versus Peacemaking in Rwanda

In the movie *Hotel Rwanda* there is a scene in which a reporter confronts a UN officer about the UN response to the 1994 genocide in which more than 800,000 ethnic Tutsis and moderate Hutus would ultimately be slaughtered. UN peacekeepers, already on the ground in Rwanda as the killing began, seemed to be doing little to stop it.

> REPORTER: "We have heard reports of reprisal massacres. Will the UN intervene to stop the bloodshed?"
>
> UN OFFICER: "We're here as peacekeepers, not as peacemakers. My orders are not to intervene."

In fact, that UN official was technically correct. The UN mission in Rwanda (UNAMIR) was, in theory, a textbook case of a peacekeeping mission. It was created to maintain the Arusha Accords, a 1993 peace agreement signed by the Hutu-dominated government and the mainly Tutsi Rwandan Patriotic Front (RPF) that had been fighting the government since 1990. In keeping with the goal of classic, first-generation peacekeeping, the UN mission was a relatively small, lightly equipped force placed in Rwanda to help two sides committed to peace successfully maintain peace.

However, hard-line Hutus had little intention of abiding by the Arusha Accords. The situation called for UN *peacemaking* rather than peacekeeping, and the greater commitment of forces, weapons, and will that the former requires. Romeo Dallaire, the commander of the UN mission in Rwanda, pleaded for such increased assistance. However, when 10 Belgian UN peacekeepers were slain by Hutu forces, the UN evacuated Westerners and then curtailed the UN mission, leaving the Tutsis to fend for themselves. For realists, the overriding lesson of this event is the weakness of international institutions like the United Nations. For liberal institutionalists, the lesson is the need to strengthen those institutions in order to avoid future Rwandas. For constructivists, Rwanda becomes a focal point for diffusion of norms about the obligation of the international community to act to stop genocide.

- One way to avoid the dilemma faced by the UN mission in Rwanda might be to deploy larger, better-equipped forces in peacekeeping operations. Is that a reasonable idea? Explain.

- Should the UN continue trying to help resolve internal conflicts like that in Rwanda, or should it focus instead on interstate wars?

- Realists claim that the UN mission's failure in Rwanda proves their point about the inherent weakness of international institutions. Do you agree? Why or why not?

A relatively large contingent of more than 17,000 UN peacekeeping forces maintained the cease-fire to the point that by 2002, relatively free and fair elections could be held. By the time the UNAMSIL peacekeeping mission ended in 2005, it had disarmed and demobilized tens of thousands of fighters and repatriated close to 300,000 refugees previously displaced by the war.[20] The UN also points to peacekeeping missions in Liberia and East Timor, among others, as success stories.

Moreover, supporters of UN peacekeeping note that the cost is relatively modest. The total budget for UN peacekeeping in fiscal year 2015 in support of 16 ongoing missions was 8.47 billion dollars.[21] That figure represents only a very small fraction of the 1,700 billion dollars in global defense expenditures in 2013.[22] Indeed, US defense spending alone has been roughly $600 billion per year in recent years, or about 70 times greater than the annual UN peacekeeping budget. Yet, despite those relatively low costs, the proliferation of UN peacekeeping in the post–Cold War era spread resources thin. The challenge was not only getting member states to raise their financial contributions to pay for the increased level of activity, but also in getting them to pay what they already committed. In February 2015 the UN estimated that there were about 2 billion dollars in payments in arrears for peacekeeping—not an insignificant amount in the context of an overall peacekeeping budget of 8.47 billion.[23]

This financial challenge was compounded beginning in the late 1990s when the United States (responsible for more than one-quarter of the UN peacekeeping budget) refused to pay all of its UN dues because of concerns regarding UN mismanagement of funds. Moreover, despite a 1999 compromise on this issue, which reduced assessments on the United States for both general UN funds and peacekeeping missions, the United States had, by 2008, still not completely caught up on what it owed. As of April 2008, the United States owed more than $2.8 billion in past dues, much of which was to fund overstretched UN peacekeeping missions.[24] That led UN Secretary-General Ban Ki-moon to label the United States as a "deadbeat donor,"[25] and to a subsequent commitment from the Obama administration to pay what the United States owes.

Reforming the United Nations

For those who would like to see the UN take a more assertive collective security role, the key structural problem is that the UN organ with coercive power (Security Council) is stymied by the veto, while the organ in which there is no veto power (General Assembly) has little coercive authority. This disjunction is no oversight or accident. Instead, it reflects that the UN represents a compromise between a desire to transcend self-help in the quest for international order and the continuing attachment to the principle of state sovereignty.

The 1950 Korean situation, however, revealed the limitations of this compromise. Had it not been for the fluke of the Soviet boycott, the UN collective security operation on the Korean Peninsula would surely have been vetoed. Given the realization that the USSR was unlikely to make such a tactical error again, in 1950 the United States sponsored the **Uniting for Peace Resolution**, which provided that the General Assembly could assume authority to act in matters of international peace and security (normally the Security Council's turf) if the Security Council is stymied by the veto. It was passed by an overwhelming 52–5 vote (with two abstentions) in the General Assembly, opposed only by the Soviet Union and a few of its allies. Although theoretically the resolution could be used to circumvent the US veto, at the time US dominance in the UN ensured that issues contrary to US interests would not make it onto the Security Council agenda. In principle, this resolution opened the possibility of the UN General Assembly taking on a collective security function. In practice, however, operations under the Uniting for Peace

Uniting for Peace Resolution
UN resolution sponsored by the United States and passed by the UN General Assembly in 1950 that allows authority on matters of international peace and security, including use of force, to be transferred to the General Assembly if Security Council action is blocked by the veto.

Resolution have been limited to peacekeeping operations, as the General Assembly has been largely unwilling to challenge the great powers on vital security matters.

Still, during the early 1990s, many felt renewed hope and optimism that the United Nations could finally fulfill its promise as an effective institution of collective security and enforcer of international law and order. The successful UN collective security action in the 1991 Persian Gulf War seemed to some to represent the promise of a new era. The disintegration of the USSR at the end of 1991 and the emergence of a more positive relationship between the United States and post-Communist Russia added to the sense that "great power unanimity" among the permanent members of the Security Council could become a reality. In fact, the UN Security Council did appear increasingly active in the 1990s, as it authorized military intervention in dozens of places around the world. However, those interventions were not collective security actions. Instead, all were peacekeeping or peacemaking missions whose record of success, as previously noted, was mixed.

By 2003 the inability of the United Nations to either deal effectively with Saddam Hussein or prevent the United States from bypassing the United Nations on its road to war in Iraq brought the optimism of the early 1990s to a decisive end.[26] Further tarnishing the reputation of the UN was a corruption scandal surrounding the UN's Oil-for-Food Programme, in which Iraq, under strict UN economic sanctions since the end of the Persian Gulf War, was allowed, beginning in 1995, to sell some of its oil in exchange for food and other humanitarian items. According to reports, the program was rife with corruption. Billions of dollars illegally made their way into Saddam Hussein's coffers, and UN officials and foreign governments faced accusations as well.

For realists, the shortcomings of the United Nations are symptomatic of the problems inherent in the concept of collective security. In the realist view, collective security is most successful when it is least needed—that is, when all the great powers are of one mind on an issue. However, when they disagree, especially when they disagree over vital interests, collective security is doomed, as was true in the case of the 2003 US war against Iraq.

Liberal supporters of the UN, however, argue that the problem is less with the concept itself than with its execution. In recent years, a variety of structural UN reforms have been proposed to make it more effective. Those reforms are intended to update the UN so that it reflects the changing realities of world politics 70 years after it was first created. Among the potentially most significant but controversial areas of reform are those related to the Security Council veto, Security Council enlargement, and the creation of a standing UN military force.

THE VETO   A frequent subject of discussion among those who want to empower the United Nations is the Security Council veto. Numerous commentators, including representatives of states who are not among the privileged five who possess the veto power, have suggested phasing out or restricting the issues on which the veto power can be exercised. In a December 2004 UN report prepared for the then secretary-general, Kofi Annan, it was noted that "the veto has an anachronistic character that is unsuitable for the institution in an increasingly democratic age."[27]

As indicated in Figure 5.2, the use of the veto has, in fact, dropped significantly over time. Nevertheless, the Perm-5 still see it as an important insurance policy and an effective tool in shaping Security Council discussions and resolutions via the mere threat of its use. The ability to get one's way by threatening to use the veto is known as the **closet veto**, and it greatly enhances the veto's impact. In light of this situation, the 2004 UN report noted above conceded that there is "no practical way of changing the existing members' veto powers."[28] Instead, the report settled for seeking nonbinding pledges from the Perm-5 that they would use the veto only when vital interests were truly at stake and reject its use when genocide or other serious human rights violations were at issue. Yet more than a decade later in 2015, Amnesty International said that the Security Council had "miserably failed" to protect civilian victims in places including Syria, Nigeria, and Ukraine, and it could only reiterate the call, without success, for the Perm-5 to waive their veto rights in cases of mass atrocities.[29]

closet veto
Implied threat to use the Security Council veto in order to shape Security Council agendas, discussions, and resolutions.

SECURITY COUNCIL ENLARGEMENT Another frequent topic of UN reform discussion is enlargement of the Security Council, specifically the addition of permanent members beyond the existing five. Supporters of enlargement argue that the world has changed significantly since 1946, as nations in Asia, Africa, and Latin America have emerged economically, politically, and, in some cases, militarily as significant players.

If we were creating the Security Council from scratch today, we might pass over France or Great Britain in favor of Japan, given its status as one of the world's largest economies, or in favor of India, given its size, population, nuclear weapons, and economic development prospects. A good case can be made that the Security Council's largely Eurocentric composition is out of step with current geopolitical realities and with the trajectory of twenty-first-century world trends.

In 2004, Kofi Annan urged UN members to address this issue, and he proposed two possible models of Security Council expansion (see Table 5.2). Model A envisioned six new permanent seats and three additional rotating seats. Model B envisioned no new permanent members but, instead, a new category of eight seats with four-year renewable terms, along with the addition of one nonrenewable two-year seat. Both models would raise the total membership of the Security Council from 15 to 24. Both models would assign the new seats on a regional basis to represent the geographic distribution of states in the United Nations as a whole. But both models, to avoid compounding the problem already represented by the veto, would limit the veto power to the original Perm-5.

Of course, designing such models of Security Council enlargement in the abstract is easier than filling in the countries that would hold the new seats. Model A would be particularly difficult in that regard, as it envisions six new

Table 5.2 Proposed Models of UN Security Council Enlargement

Model A					
Region	Number of States	Permanent Seats (current)	Proposed New Permanent Seats	Proposed Two-Year Seats (rotating)	Total
Africa	53	0	2	4	6
Asia/Pacific	56	1	2	3	6
Europe	47	3	1	2	6
Americas	35	1	1	4	6
Totals	191	5	6	13	24
Model B					
Region	Number of States	Permanent Seats (current)	Proposed Four-Year Renewable Seats	Proposed Two-Year Seats (rotating)	Total
Africa	53	0	2	4	6
Asia/Pacific	56	1	2	3	6
Europe	47	3	2	1	6
Americas	35	1	2	3	6
Totals	191	5	8	11	24

SOURCE: "In Larger Freedom: Toward Development, Security, and Human Rights for All," Report of UN Secretary-General, March 21, 2005, para. 170, http://www.un.org/largerfreedom/contents.htm.

permanent seats. While some candidates might be more or less obvious, such as Japan or India, every new addition would lead other countries to demand the same. For example, if India is added, then regional rival Pakistan would likely demand a permanent seat, but adding both India and Pakistan would use up the two new Asia/Pacific seats, leaving out Japan. If an expansion excluded Japan, then the prevailing assumption that Europe's additional seat would be granted to Germany on economic grounds would be called into question. Similarly, who would occupy the new seat for the Americas? Brazil has been campaigning for permanent seat status, and based on size alone, it might have a case. However, Mexico, Argentina, and others might have different ideas, and Brazil's singular status as a Portuguese-speaking country on a predominantly Spanish-speaking continent might become an issue.

Model B avoids some of these dilemmas by creating an entirely new category of renewable four-year seats. One might imagine some of those eight new seats taking on a quasi-permanent character, as key states have the potential for reelection on a continual basis. At the same time, the model has enough flexibility to appease those who might otherwise feel excluded. However, Model B perpetuates the status discrepancy between the Perm-5 and the rest of the Security Council. The former would retain the exclusive privilege of the veto and, unlike the newcomers, would face no risk of losing their Security Council seats. Thus for all the discussion of Security Council enlargement, the requisite consensus for action has not yet emerged.

A STANDING UN ARMY Yet another contentious Security Council reform idea is the creation of a standing UN military force. In many cases where urgent intervention has been required, the process of assembling a UN force from the contributions of member nations has been very slow, typically requiring three to six months after the Security Council decided to act. In cases of humanitarian emergency, this was often too late. Having a standby UN "rapid reaction force" could potentially cut down on the time involved from decision to deployment. Proposals for such an initiative typically involve a modest-sized force of 5,000 to 15,000 peacekeepers deployable by the secretary-general upon authorization from the Security Council.

During his term as UN secretary-general in the 1990s, Boutros Boutros-Ghali proposed this idea as the post–Cold War proliferation of UN peacekeeping missions was beginning. In 2000, his successor, Kofi Annan, convened a panel to review UN peacekeeping operations, and while cognizant of the resistance among member states to the creation of a standing UN military force, the final panel report noted that it would remain difficult to respond in a timely fashion to peacekeeping emergencies without it.[30] In 2014, Secretary-General Ban Ki-moon appointed yet another "High Level Independent Panel on Peace Operations," the first since 2000, to complete yet another comprehensive review, and the issue of a permanent UN brigade will almost certainly be discussed once again.[31]

A model for a future UN standing army was the multinational Standby High Readiness Brigade (SHIRBRIG). SHIRBRIG involved about 5,000 troops trained and available for peacekeeping missions. Sixteen mainly European states participated in the SHIRBRIG initiative. The concept had its limitations, however. It was a relatively small force in the context of the rapidly mounting number of peacekeeping missions; the troops remain based and scattered in their home countries and would be assembled for the first time only upon deployment for use in a particular crisis; and perhaps most significantly, the deployment of troops required case-by-case consent of the contributing countries.[32] Though it participated in several UN missions, it was disbanded in 2009.

While supporters of a standing UN force continue to press their case, most states remain reluctant to relinquish sovereign control over the decision to put their soldiers' lives in danger. For some critics of the idea, to do so would run afoul of domestic constitutional procedures required for sending citizens into conflict situations. In recent years, regional organizations like the African Union and the European Union have established their own peacekeeping forces, but even in the best of circumstances, those forces intervene only with the approval of contributing states.

Conclusion

The record of international law and the United Nations suggests some general points on which most observers agree. Clearly, international law and international organizations like the UN have a role to play in world politics. Those institutions provide mechanisms and opportunities for cooperation and problem-solving on a range of issues, and most observers see utility in state participation. The fact that membership in the United Nations is nearly universal, that the number of international organizations has expanded so dramatically in recent decades, and that states spend so much time and effort negotiating treaties provides testimony that states see such participation as worthwhile. At the same time, the record provides plenty of ammunition for disagreement and debate on how the world works. At the center of that debate, the question remains as to how effectively international law and institutions can constrain the behavior of states, especially the great powers, and especially when vital interests are at stake.

In this respect, noted realist thinker John Mearsheimer suggests that despite their differences, left-leaning liberal institutionalists in the United States share with right-wing neoconservatives a similar view of international law and institutions. Both groups assume that those institutions are able to "push states around" and constrain the behavior of even the greatest powers. The constraints can be seen as good—the liberal view—insofar as they commit states to rules that limit misbehavior. They can also be seen as bad—the neoconservative view—because they tie down even powerful states like the United States and complicate their ability to protect their interests. Realists reject both views. As Mearsheimer notes,

> Realists believe that institutions do not have the capability to push great powers around. If an institution tells the United States that it should do X, and the elites in the United States judge that doing X is not in the American national interest, the United States will either ignore the institution or rewrite the rules. But it will not do something that is not in its national interest. And that logic doesn't just apply to the United States, it applies to other great powers as well.[33]

In short, for realists, states use institutions to suit their own purposes. Thus, international law and institutions, in Mearsheimer's view, do not challenge the realist understanding of how the world works; they confirm it. The willingness of the United States to ignore the World Court when it has suited its purposes, the US decision to bypass the UN on the road to war in Iraq, and the general reluctance of the great powers to embrace reforms of the UN that would seriously challenge their state sovereignty all provide evidence to support the realist claim that institutional constraints on states are weak.

For liberal institutionalists, the response to the realists is partly descriptive and partly prescriptive. As a descriptive, empirical matter, they argue that realists underestimate the impact of international law and the UN. While states try to wield such institutions for their own purposes and flout the rules when it suits state needs, they often pay a price for doing so. Working through the UN system in the 1991 Persian Gulf War, for example, the United States garnered international support and legitimacy and emerged from the conflict with heightened prestige and influence. In working around the UN in the 2003 war against Iraq, however, the United States lacked such legitimacy, with a resultant decline in US prestige and influence around the world.

As a prescriptive matter, liberals suggest that institutions do need to be strengthened. Most would concede at least part of the realist argument that the ability of institutions to constrain misbehavior by the great powers is incomplete. International law, most agree, is a "primitive legal system" that falls far short of the standards set by the most effective domestic legal systems. However, for liberals, the appropriate response is to strengthen, not abandon, law and institutions. While realists see such efforts as a distraction from the effort to strengthen one's sovereign power in a dangerous, anarchic world, liberals see increasing global cooperation via such institutional development as the best bet human civilization can make to avoid future self-annihilation.

Review Questions

- To what extent can we say that the international legal system has effective and reliable law-making, law adjudication, and law enforcement processes? What are the accomplishments and limits in each of those three areas?
- To what extent can we say that the UN has fulfilled its purpose of maintaining peace and security in the international system? What reforms, if any, could help the UN do a better job in that respect?
- Does the record of international law and the UN do more to support realist or liberal understandings of the promise and limitations of international institutions in promoting international order and cooperation?

Key Terms

multilateral treaties
bilateral treaties
pacta sunt servanda
RUDs
customary international law
International Court of Justice (ICJ)
compulsory jurisdiction
optional clause
reprisals

intergovernmental organization (IGO)
nongovernmental organization (NGO)
international regime
Security Council
great power unanimity principle
General Assembly
Secretariat

Economic and Social Council (ECOSOC)
Trusteeship Council
Chapter VII authority
peacekeeping
peace enforcement
peacemaking
Uniting for Peace Resolution
closet veto

Endnotes

1. Widely attributed to Abba Eban, for example, in Robert J. Bunker in "Non-Lethal Weapons: A British View," *Military Review* 78 (July/August 1998): 86–87.
2. For this phrase, I am indebted to Professor Anthony C. Arend, Georgetown University.
3. UN International Law Commission, "Introduction," http://www.un.org/law/ilc/introfra.htm.
4. Nuclear Non-Proliferation Treaty, Article 10, http://www.state.gov/t/np/trty/16281.htm#treaty.

5. Shirley V. Scott, *International War in World Politics: An Introduction* (Lynne Rienner, 2004), 8–9.

6. International Covenant on Civil and Political Rights, Article 15, http://www.hrweb.org/legal/undocs.html.

7. "Legal Consequences of the Construction of a Wall in the Occupied Palestinian Territory," ICJ Advisory Opinion, July 9, 2004, http://www.icj-cij.org/icjwww/idocket/imwp/imwpframe.htm.

8. "Legal Consequences of the Construction of a Wall in the Occupied Palestinian Territory," ICJ Advisory Opinion.

9. For the text of all of the state acceptances of compulsory jurisdiction (optional clause), including any attached reservations, see ICJ, "Declarations Recognizing as Compulsory the Jurisdiction of the Court," http://www.icj-cij.org/jurisdiction/?p1=5&p2=1&p3=3.

10. The documents related to the two cases can be found on the ICJ website, http://www.icj-cij.org.

11. See the ICJ Judgment of November 26, 1984, regarding the jurisdiction of the court in this case, http://www.icj-cij.org.

12. See ICJ, "Cases," http://www.icj-cij.org/docket/index.php?p1=3&p2=2.

13. This general point is also made in Douglass Cassel, "Is There a New World Court?" *Northwestern University Journal of International Human Rights* 1 (Fall 2004), http://www.law.northwestern.edu/journals/jihr/v1/1/cassel.pdf.

14. George H. W. Bush, "Toward a New World Order," speech to joint session of Congress, September 11, 1990.

15. United Nations Department of Economic and Social Affairs, "Consultative Status with ECOSOC," http://csonet.org/content/documents/E-2014-INF-5%20Issued.pdf.

16. United Nations Department of Economic and Social Affairs, "Consultative Status with ECOSOC."

17. Jens Steffek, "Explaining Cooperation between IGOs and NGOs—Push Factors, Pull Factors and the Policy Cycle," Paper presented at the ISA's 49th Annual Convention, San Francisco, March 26, 2008, http://www.allacademic.com/meta/p252320_index.html.

18. Charter of the United Nations, http://www.un.org/aboutun/charter/index.html.

19. Samantha Power, *A Problem from Hell: America and the Age of Genocide* (Basic Books, 2002), ch. 11.

20. For the UN's own view of this success, see its UNAMSIL "End of Mission Press Kit," http://www.un.org.

21. "Fact Sheet: United Nations Peacekeeping Operations," February 28, 2015, http://www.un.org/en/peacekeeping/documents/bnote0215.pdf.

22. Stockholm International Peace Research Institute, April 14, 2014, http://www.sipri.org/media/pressreleases/2014/Milex_April_2014.

23. "Fact Sheet: United Nations Peacekeeping Operations," February 28, 2015, http://www.un.org/en/peacekeeping/documents/bnote0215.pdf.

24. "State Department and UN Officials Brief Congress on UN Funding, Peacekeeping," United Nations Association of the USA, April 3, 2008, http://www.unausa.org.

25. *Washington Times*, March 12, 2009, http://www.washingtontimes.com/news/2009/mar/12/un-chief-calls-us-deadbeat-donor/.

26. Michael Glennon, "Why the Security Council Failed," *Foreign Affair*, May/June 2003, 16–35.

27. "Report of the Secretary-General's High Level Panel on Threats, Challenges, and Change," para. 256, http://www.un.org.

28. "Report of the Secretary-General's High Level Panel," para. 256.

29. "Amnesty Urges UN Powers to Waive Vetoes on Genocide," France 24 International News, February 25, 2015, http://www.france24.com/en/20150225-amnesty-urges-un-security-council-drop-veto-genocide-conflict-2014-report/.

30. "Report of the Panel on United Nations Peacekeeping Operations," August 21, 2000,

http://www.un.org/en/ga/search/view _doc.asp?symbol=A/55/305.

31. "Secretary-General's Statement on Appointment of High-Level Independent Panel on Peacekeeping Operations," October 31, 2014, http://www.un.org/sg/statements/ index.asp?nid=8151.

32. H. Peter Langille, "SHIRBRIG: A Promising Step Toward a United Nations That Can Prevent Deadly Conflict," Global Policy Forum, Spring 2000, http://www .globalpolicy.org.

33. John Mearsheimer, "The World in 2020," presentation at Foreign Affairs Canada, April 2004, http://www.dfait-maeci.gc.ca/.

Chapter 6
The Human Rights Revolution

The Construction of International Norms

Genocide in Rwanda, 1994. Does the international community have an obligation to intervene in cases of genocide and other extreme human rights abuses?

 Learning Objectives

6-1 Identify and evaluate the main objections to the human rights revolution.

6-2 Explain the evolution and process of establishing human rights norms.

6-3 Describe and assess the mechanisms for monitoring compliance with human rights norms.

6-4 Analyze the record in practice of enforcing human rights norms.

6-5 Compare and contrast the strengths and weaknesses of the alternative ways of prosecuting individuals for human rights crimes.

What place do human rights have in the conduct of foreign policy? Realists argue that the overriding goal of foreign policy is to promote the national interest. Considerations of justice, morality, and human rights, though they might engage us as individuals and can surely be an important consideration in domestic affairs, have no role in international relations. In effect, for realists, human rights are a matter between a government and its citizens. The international community has little if any role to play. As one critic of the human rights emphasis put it, "Foreign policy is not social work."[1]

However, for global human rights activists and for many scholars, this realist view is not only a gross abdication of moral responsibility but is also increasingly outdated. As former US President Jimmy Carter, well-known for the human rights emphasis in his administration's foreign policy, argued: "All the signatories of the UN Charter have pledged themselves to observe and to respect basic human rights. Thus, no member of the United Nations can claim that mistreatment of its citizens is solely its own business."[2] In fact, since World War II the issue of human rights has received unprecedented attention from the international community. Constructivists and liberals would argue that the realist emphasis on national interest, state sovereignty, and self-help cannot explain this human rights trend.

The basic question of this chapter, therefore, is whether the new emphasis on human rights constitutes a revolution in our thinking about how the world works. If the noble words and aspirations have not been matched by behavioral changes, then the human rights revolution is an empty shell. If the record of global concern and action to protect human rights matches the rhetoric, then one might argue that the human rights revolution is real and that it challenges the principle of state sovereignty on which the Westphalian international system has been based. As constructivist scholar Kathryn Sikkink emphasizes, human rights norms are more than merely another issue in political science and international relations; they are, instead, "potent challenges to the central logic of the system of sovereign states."[3]

Reasons for Hesitation

human rights revolution

Post–World War II movement to make the internal human rights performance of states subject to international regulation, monitoring, and enforcement. Revolutionary insofar as this movement challenges state sovereignty.

6-1   Identify and evaluate the main objections to the human rights revolution.

Support for human rights would seem to be a no-brainer. Except for evil dictators concerned with guarding their ability to abuse their own citizens, who could be opposed? Most realists, presumably, prefer to see a world in which all leaders treat their subjects and citizens humanely. However, preferring a world in which human rights are respected and inserting them into the agenda of international relations are not one and the same. At least three concerns keep some observers from embracing the idea of a **human rights revolution** in which human rights would become the business of the international community: concern about international order, about the priority of the national interest, and about the dangers of cultural imperialism.

The International Order Argument

Perhaps the most compelling reason for hesitation in making human rights an issue of international politics is the potential impact on global order. As it is, states have a multitude of reasons to go to war with one another, including conflicts over territory, vital resources, and the balance of power. If we made the internal relationship between a government and its citizens a topic meriting international attention, then the occasions for conflict and war could expand greatly. Some states could use human rights concerns as a smokescreen for intervention and wars motivated by territorial conquest and political expansionism.

Insofar as war itself is a direct threat to many basic human rights, including most importantly the right to life, any expansion of war further threatens global human rights. In Kosovo, for example, the 1999 humanitarian intervention by NATO to protect ethnic Albanians from Serbian mistreatment produced almost 1 million Albanian refugees who fled to camps in neighboring countries to escape the conflict and possible retribution by Serbian forces. More than 200,000 Serbs and other non-Albanian minorities also left Kosovo following the intervention and the defeat of Serbian forces.[4]

To be sure, difficult trade-offs are involved. In the face of clear human rights violations, nonintervention leaves innocent people at the mercy of bad regimes. In Kosovo, deaths and displacements produced by the war must be weighed against the conflict's very real success in limiting government-sponsored human rights violations and prosecuting former Serbian dictator Slobodan Milošević for human rights abuses. However, as the unintended consequences of the Kosovo case suggest, one can make a moral case for the principles of sovereignty and nonintervention. To the extent that they contribute to global order, they can potentially help avoid wars and conflicts in which human rights would be greatly imperiled.

The National Interest Argument

A second reason for hesitation in internationalizing human rights has to do with prioritizing the national interest in foreign policy. Realists argue that resources are limited and should be reserved for the most clear-cut threats to state interests. Those limited resources include more than economic and military assets; citizens in democratic countries have limited tolerance for accepting the death of their soldiers in battle. In a dangerous, anarchic world where self-help is the key to survival, the expenditure of scarce military, economic, and political capital on "elective" wars for human rights could leave a nation unprepared when threats to vital interests appear. Moreover, given the logic of the balance of power system in which the enemy of your enemy can be your friend, cases may well arise in which servicing the national interest requires cooperation with regimes that have less-than-stellar human rights records.

During the Cold War, the United States often supported regimes with problematic human rights records because they were allies in resisting the spread of Communism. Even President Jimmy Carter sometimes found that his emphasis on human rights had to be trumped by more basic geopolitical security considerations. For example, he provided substantial financial aid to Egyptian dictator and former Soviet ally Anwar Sadat due to the strategic necessity of brokering peace in the Middle East and keeping Egypt in the pro-Western camp. And the strategic value of oil clearly drives America's long relationship with Saudi Arabia, a country consistently ranked by Freedom House as one of the world's worst violators of political rights and civil liberties.[5]

Again, trade-offs are involved. A single-minded focus on short-term national interests may not only abandon people in immediate human rights distress but may also ignore the potential long-term national security payoff that might accrue from promoting human rights. The persistent commitment to human rights manifested in US policy toward Eastern Europe during the Cold War produced a warm attitude toward the United States. Conversely, past support for oppressive dictators in the Middle East helped form the hostility toward the United States in evidence throughout that region today.

In general, the world's worst regimes from the point of view of human rights (e.g., North Korea) tend to be among the most authoritarian, least democratic regimes. To the extent that an emphasis on human rights challenges the legitimacy of those regimes and leads to their replacement by more open, less aggressive democratic regimes, human rights can indeed be good for the national interests and national security of fellow democratic states. Thus, a North Korea that respects the human rights of its citizens is less likely to pose a threat to South Korea, to other countries in East Asia, and therefore to the interests of the United States.

However, for states facing immediate, short-term national security challenges, such an enlightened, long-term view is often difficult to keep in focus. Moreover, realists would contend, cases will inevitably arise where national interests and human rights will not conveniently align. In such cases, where the national security stakes are high, national interests should and will prevail over considerations of human rights.

The Cultural Relativism Argument

cultural relativism
Argument that cultures will have differing human rights standards, and attempts to impose universal notions of human rights risk imposing standards alien to the local culture.

The idea of a revolution in human rights can also be challenged on the grounds of **cultural relativism**. The argument here is that different cultures have different perspectives on what constitutes a human right; therefore, any attempt to impose universal notions of human rights runs the risk of imposing alien standards. From this perspective, there can be no such thing as *universal* human rights. For some, in fact, the notion of universal human rights is seen as a smokescreen for imposing *Western* norms on other cultures. In the 1990s this cultural relativism perspective was articulated most clearly in the debate over "Asian values." Individuals like former Prime Minister Lee Kwan Yew of Singapore argued that the Western emphasis on the rights of the individual contrasts with the Asian emphasis on the needs of the larger community, and neither Westerners nor Asians should attempt to impose their concept of human rights on the other.

Not surprisingly, rights related to issues of women and gender roles are often a source of international contention, and they illustrate the tension between the idea of universal human rights and cultural diversity. Among the most controversial practices, sometimes defended on cultural grounds, is the practice of female genital mutilation. Still widespread in much of sub-Saharan Africa, in parts of the Middle East, and among some immigrant communities in developed nations, the practice involves removal of all or part of the female genitalia. According to Amnesty International, 135 million girls and women have undergone the procedure, with approximately 6,000 new procedures carried out each day.[6] While Amnesty International and most Western observers condemn the practice as barbaric and a violation of human rights, others see it as a cultural ritual to be defended. A former president of Kenya argued that the procedure is an important tribal initiation ritual and that "abolition … will destroy the tribal system."[7] An Egyptian woman, speaking of her daughters, noted: "Of course I shall have them circumcised exactly as their parents, grandparents, and sisters were circumcised. This is our custom."[8]

In an effort to reconcile the competing claims of universal human rights and tolerance of cultural diversity, at least one scholar has suggested a distinction between (1) an extreme, radical version of cultural relativism in which human rights are entirely culture bound, and (2) a weaker cultural relativism that accepts the universality of certain basic human rights while allowing some space for cultural difference.[9] While the second option might seem to allow for a meeting of minds, even a weak cultural relativism leaves much room for debate. Is female genital mutilation a practice that must be universally condemned, or can it fall under the category of protected cultural practices? What about arranged marriages, or the death penalty, or employment of very young children?

First Steps: Establishing Human Rights Norms

6-2 **Explain the evolution and process of establishing human rights norms.**

All three arguments for hesitation in internationalizing the issue of human rights raise reasonable concerns. The fact that dictators and other human rights abusers might use arguments about Asian values or international order as political and moral cover does not relieve us of the need to confront and consider those arguments. Nonetheless, certain human rights abuses are so extreme and abhorrent that those reasons for hesitation seem like a weak excuse for apathy and inaction.

The most obvious example is the Nazi Holocaust. Set against the historical backdrop of the systematic murder of 6 million men, women, and children for no reason other than their Jewish identity, arguments about order, interests, and cultural differences seem largely irrelevant. What disruption of international order could be worse than what the Nazis were already doing? What national interests could any moral individual appeal to in defense of inaction? As for the cultural relativism argument, could any culture sanction something like the Holocaust, and would such a culture deserve any deference or respect? In fact, the impetus for the post–World War II human rights revolution was at least, in part, driven by what happened to European Jews during the war and by the collective sense of global guilt at the failure of the international community to stop it.

In response to human rights tragedies like the Holocaust, we have witnessed the growth of transnational advocacy networks (see Chapter 1)—mixes of individuals and organizations with transnational representation "who are bound together by shared values, a common discourse, and dense exchanges of information and services."[10] In the view of constructivist scholars, such networks are crucial to both the development and diffusion of human rights norms on a global basis. Composed of varying combinations of individuals (e.g., prominent scholars, former government leaders, and well-known movie stars and pop singers) and nongovernmental organizations (e.g., religious organizations, the media, and NGOs like Amnesty International or Human Rights Watch), these networks may work with receptive individuals within governments and international organizations to achieve their agenda. Ultimately, transnational advocacy networks seek to influence the behavior of states and international organizations and, as liberals would emphasize, to formalize human rights norms in international agreements.

The first very hesitant step in this direction after World War II can be found in the UN Charter. The charter, as well as the United Nations itself, was largely concerned with buttressing rather than undermining state sovereignty. Article 2.7 of the charter affirms the principle of sovereignty in noting: "Nothing contained in the present Charter shall authorize the United Nations to intervene in matters which are essentially within the domestic jurisdiction of any state."[11] In 1965, General Assembly Resolution 2131 underlined the point: "No State or group of States has the right to intervene or interfere in any form or *for any reason whatsoever* [emphasis added] in the internal and external affairs of other States."[12] Privileging the idea of state sovereignty in this way seems to rule out intervention in the name of human rights.

At the same time, the charter does not entirely ignore human rights. The preamble affirms that the peoples of the UN are determined "to reaffirm faith in fundamental human rights," Article 1 declares that one purpose of the UN is "promoting and encouraging respect for human rights and for fundamental freedoms," and Article 68 requires the UN Economic and Social Council to establish a formal commission "for the promotion of human rights."[13] The inclusion of that human rights language was no accident; it was the result of lobbying

"Last Jew in Vinnitsa"—an iconic photo showing a German soldier about to shoot a Jewish man at a mass grave in Vinnitsa, Ukraine, during World War II. After the Holocaust the world said "never again." How have we done in that regard since then?

efforts by the American Jewish Committee together with representatives of business associations, labor unions, and religious groups who wanted the newly created United Nations to pay attention to human rights. As one scholar noted, it was the efforts of this advocacy network of important NGOs that "was, to a large extent, the key to human rights advancement."[14]

It was in 1948, however, that the post–World War II human rights revolution really began. In that year, the international community adopted two breakthrough human rights documents; one of them was the Universal Declaration of

Human Rights. Drafted by the newly established UN Commission on Human Rights under the leadership of Eleanor Roosevelt, supported by a host of transnational NGOs, and adopted by the UN General Assembly, the declaration spells out a variety of rights to which every human is entitled. Those rights include **negative rights** (those that prohibit certain government actions) such as freedom from torture, the right of free movement, the right to practice one's religion, and the right of free expression, and **positive rights** (those guaranteed by government action) such as the right to education and to an adequate standard of living.

negative rights
Human rights whose achievement and endurance depend on prohibiting certain government actions, for example, freedom of speech, freedom of religion, freedom from torture.

The original idea was that the Universal Declaration would be formalized in a legally binding treaty on human rights to be signed and ratified by individual states (remember that a General Assembly resolution is not itself legally binding). For the better part of two decades, however, this process was caught up in Cold War politics. The United States wanted a treaty that would emphasize negative rights such as freedom of speech and press, as those were the kinds of rights spelled out in the US Bill of Rights and on which US performance was relatively good. The Soviet Union, in contrast, emphasized positive rights, especially economic rights such as the right to employment, since it arguably performed better in those areas than on negative rights.

positive rights
Human rights that depend on positive government action, such as the right to education and the right to adequate health care.

The impasse was broken in 1966 with the adoption of two separate treaties: (1) the International Covenant on Civil and Political Rights (CCPR), and (2) the International Covenant on Economic, Social and Cultural Rights (CESCR).[15] The former was largely, though not exclusively, concerned with negative rights, while the latter emphasized positive rights. As of 2015, 168 countries had become states parties to the CCPR, and 164 had become states parties to the CESCR. The United States signed both treaties in 1977 and ratified the CCPR in 1992, but it has yet to ratify the CESCR. American hesitation to sign and ratify these treaties reflects a general concern about loss of state sovereignty, and in the case of the CESCR, about the legitimacy of the positive, economic rights that make up much of that treaty.

Aside from the Universal Declaration of Human Rights, the other major human rights event of 1948 was the adoption of the Convention on Genocide. **Genocide**, according to the language of the treaty, refers to "acts committed with intent to destroy, in whole or in part, a national, ethnical, racial, or religious group."[16] The treaty provides that genocide shall be treated as a crime under international law (Article 1), that those accused of genocide shall be tried and punished under the auspices of an appropriate international tribunal (Article 6), and that parties to the treaty should prevent and punish genocide (Article 1), including calling on organs of the United Nations to prevent and suppress acts of genocide under way (Article 8).

genocide
According to the 1948 Genocide Convention, "acts committed with intent to destroy, in whole or in part, a national, ethnical, racial, or religious group."

The Genocide Convention was just the first of a series of international treaties intended to treat in much greater detail key issues of human rights. Subsequent human rights treaties deal with issues ranging from torture to racial discrimination to the rights of women and children (see Table 6.1).

Table 6.1 Major International Human Rights Treaties: US Ratification and Global Status

Treaty	Adopted	Entry in Force	US Signature	US Ratification	Number of States Parties
Convention on Genocide	1948	1951	1948	1988	146
Covenant on Economic, Social and Cultural Rights	1966	1976	1977	No	164
Covenant on Civil and Political Rights	1966	1976	1977	1992	168
Convention on Elimination of Racial Discrimination	1965	1969	1966	1994	177
Convention on Elimination of Discrimination Against Women	1979	1981	1980	No	189
Convention Against Torture	1984	1987	1988	1994	158
Convention on Rights of the Child	1989	1990	1995	No	196
Convention on Protection of Migrant Workers and Families	1990	2003	No	No	48
Convention on the Rights of Persons with Disabilities	2006	2008	2009	No	159

SOURCE: United Nations Treaty Collection, Chapter IV: Human Rights, as of October 2015, https://treaties.un.org/pages/Treaties.

Transnational advocacy networks were crucial to the adoption of most of these treaties. The 1984 Convention Against Torture, for example, owed much to Amnesty International's 1973 "Campaign Against Torture," while the Genocide Convention was adopted largely due to the work of one man, Raphael Lemkin, a Polish Jew who fled the Nazis and settled in the United States.[17] Lemkin's greatest struggle was to get the United States to ratify the treaty. At the time, NGOs like Amnesty International or Human Rights Watch did not yet exist. However, Lemkin was aided in his efforts by a network of advocates including the American Jewish Committee, the Federal Council of Churches of Christ, labor unions, and the National Council of Women.[18] Eventually, they garnered the support of Senator William Proxmire of Wisconsin, who, beginning in January 1967, gave a speech per day on the floor of the Senate advocating ratification. Nineteen years and 3,211 speeches later, the Genocide Convention was finally ratified.

Taken as a whole, what is most significant about all these documents is the challenge they pose to those who resist the internationalization of human rights. Every independent, sovereign state has ratified at least one human rights treaty, and most have signed and ratified many of them. To take one example, 196 states are parties to the Convention on Rights of the Child (the only exception is the United States). In so doing, those states have, in effect, voluntarily signed away their sovereign right to treat children in their own territory in ways that violate the terms of the treaty, no matter what national interest might lead them to behave otherwise. Similarly, the fact that 196 states have ratified the treaty

Figure 6.1 The Human Rights Revolution

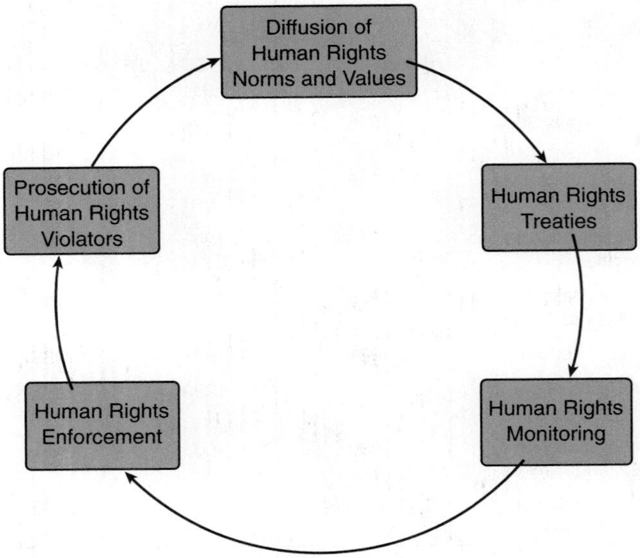

seems to concede, arguments about cultural relativism notwithstanding, that some basic human rights can be accepted on a virtually universal basis.

Realists and other human rights skeptics, however, might counter that signing treaties is one thing; enforcing them and conforming to their provisions are quite another. After all, a serial human rights violator like North Korea is a party to the Convention on Civil and Political Rights. Saudi Arabia, where women who walk unaccompanied are at risk of arrest on moral offenses, has ratified the Convention on Elimination of Discrimination Against Women. And Iraq was a party to the Genocide Convention when Saddam Hussein was dropping mustard gas and other chemical agents on Iraqi Kurds in 1988. Such contradictions undermine claims of a revolution in human rights.

Indeed, setting human rights standards is only the starting point of the human rights revolution. As illustrated in Figure 6.1, successful completion of that revolution also requires (1) effective human rights monitoring, (2) effective human rights enforcement, and (3) effective prosecution of those who violate human rights standards.

Monitoring Human Rights

6-3 **Describe and assess the mechanisms for monitoring compliance with human rights norms.**

Monitoring of human rights compliance is crucial in order to give those who can do something about human rights abuses the information on which to act.

In the world today, this monitoring function is carried out via UN-based bodies, NGOs, and national and regional reporting systems.

UN Monitoring

UN-based human rights oversight bodies are simultaneously among the most important and the most criticized human rights organizations in place today. They are most important, as they constitute the core of a truly global human rights regime working under the mandate of the United Nations and its state members. Thus, they have a formal legitimacy that other monitoring mechanisms do not enjoy. They are most criticized, however, because many see their successes as incomplete at best.

Created in 1946, the first dedicated UN human rights institution and the centerpiece of UN human rights monitoring for 60 years was the **UN Commission on Human Rights**. Its original purpose was to develop human rights standards, and it was the setting within which the 1948 Universal Declaration of Human Rights was hammered out. Its members were 53 states that belonged to the United Nations, elected for three-year, renewable terms by the UN Economic and Social Council (ECOSOC). But it was not until 1967 that the commission acquired a monitoring function that, for the first time, gave it the authority to investigate allegations of gross and systematic abuses of human rights. It could appoint either an individual expert known as a "special rapporteur" or a panel of experts called a "working group" to investigate. Still, the effectiveness of the Commission on Human Rights was mitigated by several factors.

First, although the names of countries whose human rights practices were under discussion were publicly announced, and while most countries did what they could to avoid being placed on this "black list," there was a lack of full transparency as specific allegations and deliberations took place out of public view. Second, the commission members were not independent human rights experts or activists; instead, they were sovereign states with interests to protect and scores to settle. Indeed, some member states of the commission were countries with very poor human rights records. For example, in 2005, Sudan was a member of the commission as it faced accusations of genocide against non-Arab inhabitants in its Darfur region. Finally, the commission often could not keep pace with fast-developing human rights tragedies. A case in point was the 1994 genocide in Rwanda, in which almost a million people were killed in approximately 100 days. Signs of trouble in Rwanda long preceded these tragic events, yet it was only on May 25, 1994, seven weeks after the killing began, that a rapporteur was appointed to investigate and report back to the commission.[19]

At a September 2005 UN World Summit covering a broad range of issues, it was resolved to create a new **Human Rights Council (HRC)** to promote human rights and to coordinate UN activities in that area.[20] In 2006, the UN General Assembly followed through and formally created that new body, abolishing the UN Commission on Human Rights in the process.[21] Central to the HRC's

UN Commission on Human Rights
Original UN human rights body, created in 1946 to promote the development and, later, the monitoring of global human rights norms; replaced in 2005 with a new UN Human Rights Council.

Human Rights Council (HRC)
UN body established in 2005 to monitor human rights practices of states. Intended as a more effective successor to the UN Commission on Human Rights.

work is the new Universal Periodic Review (UPR), which establishes a process for review of the human rights record of all UN member states. By 2011, all UN States had been evaluated in the first cycle of reviews with the second cycle (2012–2016) beginning immediately thereafter.[22]

Despite some success by NGOs such as Human Rights Watch to keep countries with poor human rights records off the HRC (e.g., Belarus was defeated in its bid for election to the HRC in 2007, and Sri Lanka suffered the same fate in 2008),[23] other states on the HRC continue to have questionable human rights records. In 2015, members of the HRC included countries with pretty dismal track records on human rights, including Russia, China, Saudi Arabia, and Kazakhstan. Skeptical as to the merits of the HRC, the United States initially refused to be considered for membership. However, the Obama administration reversed that Bush administration policy, seeking and achieving election to the council in 2009.

The monitoring work of the Human Rights Council is supplemented by the individual treaty-monitoring bodies created in conjunction with the human rights treaties adopted since 1948. Seven such bodies currently exist, including the Human Rights Committee (set up to monitor compliance with the 1966 Covenant on Civil and Political Rights), the Committee Against Torture, and the Committee on the Rights of the Child. In addition, in 1993 the UN General Assembly established the Office of the High Commissioner for Human Rights (OHCHR). The creation of this new office and the appointment of a **high commissioner for human rights** were intended to put a public face on UN human rights monitoring, drawing attention to human rights issues and abuses as needed to galvanize the international community. In September 2014, Zeid Ra'ad Al Hussein of Jordan became the seventh high commissioner and the first Asian, Muslim, and Arab to occupy the position.[24]

high commissioner for human rights

The principal UN human rights official; puts a public face on UN human rights monitoring, drawing attention to general human rights issues and specific abuses.

NGO Monitoring

The UN human rights monitoring system is slow, cumbersome, and dependent for its success on states with interests at stake and even questionable human rights records of their own. However, the UN system is not the only source of information on human rights practices around the world. While NGOs sometimes help develop human rights norms, they are probably even better known for tracking compliance with those norms once established.

Among the human rights NGOs, the two most noteworthy are Amnesty International and Human Rights Watch. Amnesty International is headquartered in London, and Human Rights Watch is headquartered in New York, though each has offices, chapters, and members throughout the world. In their efforts to shed light on human rights practices and abuses, they focus on individual cases of abuse and on the general records of states.

Central to the work of both these NGOs is the publication of their annual country reports, providing detailed discussion of human rights trends in each of the world's sovereign states.[25] The seriousness with which those reports are taken is manifested in the often swift and harsh reaction of governments to what is found therein. For example, Amnesty International's 2005 criticism of the United States for its treatment of detainees in the war on terror at Guantanamo and elsewhere provoked a swift and stinging rebuke from the highest levels of the US government. Asked about the Amnesty International report at a White House briefing, President George W. Bush called it "absurd."[26] Given the reach and global authority of Amnesty International, no leader, and especially not the leader of a country whose global influence is based in part on a reputation of respect for human rights, can afford to ignore it.

Complementing the publicity given to human rights abuses by human rights organizations are the actions of the global media. Though not dedicated human rights monitors per se, the media play a crucial role in two respects. First, they amplify the reports of human rights organizations. Amnesty International can publicize human rights abuses on its webpage and in its publications, but most people learn about them only through media coverage of the reports. Second, the media often do investigative work and reporting on human rights abuses, thereby serving a monitoring function of their own.

At times, one picture in a newspaper will be enough to shame the international community into action. In 1999 the front page of the *New York Times* carried a color photo of a victim of the ethnic conflict in Kosovo, providing the catalyst for NATO intervention after many months of hesitation. If a picture is

One of many photos of abuse and torture of Iraqi detainees by US personnel at the Abu Ghraib prison outside of Baghdad. How did publication of these photos affect the conduct of the war, and to what extent do they illustrate the "CNN effect" and the role of public opinion in foreign policy?

CNN effect
Impact and power of images of human rights abuses transmitted via the media in galvanizing world opinion to pressure governments to do something about human rights abuses.

worth a thousand words, a video clip carried on a global television network is worth even more. In what has been called the **CNN effect**, footage of genocide, ethnic cleansing, or torture can galvanize world opinion against abusers.

National and Regional Monitoring

Along with UN bodies and NGOs, regional organizations and even individual governments provide yet another layer of human rights monitoring. The US Department of State, for example, provides a yearly, systematic review of human rights practices in countries around the world that parallels reports issued annually by Human Rights Watch and Amnesty International.[27] Though most other governments do not publish such a systematic yearly review, they often monitor and call attention to human rights abuses.

While bias in such reports might be expected, their utility cannot be summarily dismissed. Although the US State Department report is unlikely to agree entirely with assessments found in reports from Amnesty International or Human Rights Watch, it is often critical of human rights practices in countries where the United States has strategic interests and good government-to-government relations. For example, the 2013 State Department *Human Rights Report* clearly identified human rights abuses in such countries as Saudi Arabia (despite US strategic interest in Saudi oil), in Pakistan and Uzbekistan (despite their importance to the United States as frontline states in the war against terror), and even in Israel (despite its status as America's closest ally in the Middle East).

Finally, one must note the monitoring and reporting systems of various regional human rights regimes. The most developed of these is in Europe, where the European Commission on Human Rights is empowered to receive, review, and report on complaints from individuals, NGOs, and sovereign states. Variations on this regional approach are found in the Inter-American Commission on Human Rights and the African Commission on Human and Peoples' Rights. However, compared with the European system, these other regional commissions and their reporting and monitoring systems tend to be weak and undeveloped.

Taken individually, none of the mechanisms of monitoring and reporting on human rights is without its flaws and biases. But the ultimate success of the global human rights monitoring system is found precisely in the layers of overlapping reporting done by states, NGOs, the media, and international organizations at the global and regional levels.

Ideally, the publicity given to human rights violations and the damage thereby done to the violators would be enough to deter most human rights abuses. Regrettably, we have little evidence that bad publicity alone equals deterrence. The potential of the human rights revolution must also rest on enforcement. The international community must be able to enforce the standards it has set if the human rights revolution is to be taken seriously.

Enforcing Human Rights

6-4   **Analyze the record in practice of enforcing human rights norms.**

Faced with reports and evidence of serious human rights abuses, the first and lowest-cost response of concerned states is noncoercive diplomacy. Public and private communications among governments, expressions of diplomatic concern, or symbolic gestures such as recall of an ambassador, cancellation of government-to-government meetings, or withdrawal of participation in some cultural or athletic event might, in some cases, get the offending government's attention. However, in many cases such diplomatic pressures succeed only if backed by the threat of measures that can cause the offending government real pain. Those measures are economic sanctions and military intervention.

Economic Sanctions

Economic sanctions involve the imposition of limitations or prohibitions on trade, investment, or aid in order to get a country to change its policies. Sanctions are a popular tool of coercive diplomacy, as they can satisfy the desire to "do something" in response to a challenge or provocation. Especially since World War II, the United States has used economic sanctions as an instrument of foreign policy more than any other country, leading former President Bill Clinton, who applied sanctions to a number of countries, to remark with an element of regret that the United States was becoming "sanctions happy."[28]

economic sanctions
The limitation and prohibition of trade, investment, or aid with a target country in order to get that country to change its policies.

Not all the economic sanctions imposed by the United States or other countries have been motivated strictly by human rights enforcement. In fact, the purposes have been varied and have included fighting terrorism, discouraging weapons proliferation, punishing interstate aggression, and stemming the trade in illicit drugs.

Perhaps the best known and most successful use of economic sanctions in the service of human rights was the case of South Africa. Following World War II, the Afrikaner National Party came to power in South Africa and created a system of racial segregation and separation known as **apartheid** that denied the black majority the political and economic rights and privileges held by the small white minority. By the 1960s, global calls to end apartheid were being backed by economic sanctions. The UN General Assembly called on member countries to engage in a trade embargo with South Africa, the Security Council called for an arms embargo, and many countries followed through with those measures. At the same time, private businesses came under increasing pressure to disinvest from South Africa and to eliminate any new economic investment there.

apartheid
Post–World War II era system of racial segregation imposed by the white Afrikaner National Party in South Africa.

By the 1990s the system of apartheid was unraveling, and in 1994 Nelson Mandela, former political prisoner and head of the antiapartheid African National Congress, was elected as the country's first black president. To the extent that sanctions made a difference in South Africa, the fact that they had

constructive engagement
View that the best way to improve human rights in countries where abuses exist is to maintain economic and political relations in order to influence and exert leverage on the country in question.

broad global support certainly helped. Not every country participated with equal enthusiasm. The United States, for example, was relatively slow to get on the sanctions bandwagon. Some in the US government argued that the best way to improve the human rights situation in South Africa and elsewhere was through **constructive engagement**. These individuals argued that the United States could better influence human rights by maintaining economic relations. Those relations would allow US companies in South Africa, via policies of equal treatment of black South Africans, to set an example for emulation. Moreover, such involvement would contribute to economic development, which in the view of some was the path to a more enlightened order. Still, US hesitation notwithstanding, the South African sanctions had more global support than virtually any other set of post–World War II sanctions.

Without global support, sanctions imposed by one country can be easily undermined by the actions of others. One study found that of the 39 cases involving unilateral US sanctions between 1970 and 1990, only five (13 percent) produced a desired policy change on the part of the target country.[29] Multilateral sanctions are only slightly more successful. Between 1970 and 1999 only about 20 percent of all US sanctions (unilateral and multilateral combined) achieved even partial success.[30] Thus, the overall record of sanctions is not especially promising.

Perhaps even more troubling than the question of the effectiveness of economic sanctions is the issue of their human cost. The essence of sanctions logic is to cause economic pain in the target country and lead the target country's government to make a rational calculation that sanctions cost more than altering current policy. Depending on the nature of the sanctions, ordinary citizens often bear, directly or indirectly, much of the economic pain. This always raises ethical issues, but especially so when the purpose of the sanctions is to address human rights violations. That is why, while many prominent South African critics of apartheid (most notably the black South African archbishop Desmond Tutu) supported the imposition of economic sanctions, other antiapartheid leaders opposed them.

A good illustration of the moral ambiguities of economic sanctions is found in the comprehensive UN economic sanctions imposed on Iraq on August 6, 1990. These sanctions came as a response to Iraq's invasion of Kuwait, but they were maintained following Iraq's 1991 expulsion from Kuwait to pressure Saddam Hussein to eliminate weapons of mass destruction and to comply with other cease-fire terms. The Iraqi sanctions debate is filled with hyperbole. On one end of the spectrum are claims that more than 500,000 children under five years of age died in the 1990s due solely to the economic sanctions. At the other end are those who dismiss such numbers or who blame such deaths on Iraqi leader Saddam Hussein's regime for both refusing to comply with the conditions that would have lifted sanctions and misusing available economic resources.

Getting at the truth in a case such as this is not easy. One widely cited study concluded that the number of excess child deaths in Iraq from 1991 to 1998 was somewhere between 100,000 and 227,000. Richard Garfield, the author of the study, suggests that about one-quarter of those deaths were a legacy of the 1991

Persian Gulf War, with the remainder attributable to sanctions.[31] Even at the low end, that would mean 75,000 children under five died as a result of UN sanctions policy. To be sure, Saddam Hussein must be held at least partly to blame. While ordinary Iraqis were dying without adequate food, medical care, and sanitation, he was paying for his military and building palaces. On the other hand, as a leader with such an atrocious human rights record—among other things, he used chemical weapons against his own people—it is hardly surprising that deaths of ordinary Iraqis produced by sanctions were not a major concern for him.

Increasingly sensitive to this problem, sanctions were eventually adjusted. The UN Oil-for-Food Programme allowed limited oil sales by Iraq that, in turn, allowed for the import of certain food and medical supplies. This was a step in the direction of the **smart sanctions** that the UN Security Council, at the urging of the United States and Great Britain, adopted in May 2002. These sanctions loosened or eliminated the ban on Iraqi import of civilian goods, while tightening restrictions on imports of arms and other goods essential for the Iraqi regime. However, the long-term impact of those smart sanctions in Iraq was never really tested. The outbreak of war the following year cut them short, and the program had been rife with corruption as proceeds were funneled both to Iraqi leaders and to UN officials.

smart sanctions
Economic sanctions targeted at things most valued by the political leaders of a country, while allowing essential civilian goods and humanitarian assistance to reach people in need.

Military Intervention

The use of the military in response to human rights abuses is often referred to as **humanitarian intervention**. Though human rights abuses often provoke international outrage, governments and their citizens only reluctantly put their own soldiers in harm's way unless clearly identified national interests are on the line. That said, exceptional cases occur, and two recent examples are the NATO interventions in Kosovo (1999) and Libya (2011).

humanitarian intervention
Use of military measures by the international community to end human rights abuses in an otherwise sovereign state.

KOSOVO   When the former Communist-led state of Yugoslavia disintegrated in the early 1990s, it was replaced by five newly sovereign states: Slovenia, Croatia, Macedonia, Bosnia, and Serbia and Montenegro. (Serbia and Montenegro would later separate into two sovereign states as well; see Figure 6.2.) Redrawing the map of the region did not proceed peacefully. Given both latent ethnic and religious suspicions and nationalist politicians like Serbian leader Slobodan Milošević who purposely stoked those suspicions for political gain, the 1990s were a decade of bloodshed in the Balkans.

Bloodiest of all was the conflict in Bosnia, where no one ethnic group constituted a majority and where decades of intermingling and intermarriage had produced an ethnic mosaic once hailed as a triumph of interethnic peace and cooperation. In the 1990s the idea of ethnic integration was now replaced by **ethnic cleansing**, whose goal was to rid an area of an unwanted ethnic group. The tactics were often brutal, including attacks on school buses, marketplaces, and other places where innocent men, women, and children went about their daily business. In the perverse logic of those who perpetrated such offenses, the

ethnic cleansing
Practice of ridding an area of members of an unwanted ethnic group through acts of violence that make life so dangerous that they choose to flee, thereby "cleansing" the region and making it ethnically pure.

Figure 6.2 The Former Yugoslavia

SOURCE: United Nations, http://www.un.org.

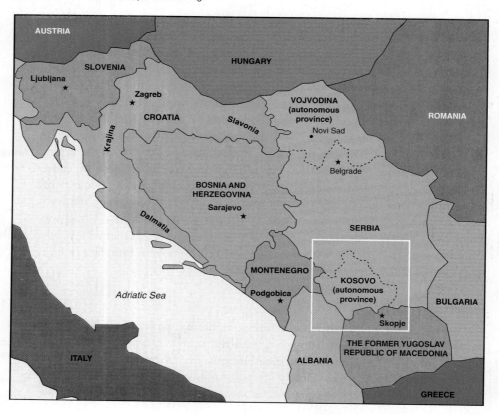

situation would become so dangerous that the unwanted would feel compelled to flee, thereby "cleansing" the region and rendering it ethnically pure. By 1994 approximately 250,000 had been killed, with another 2 million rendered homeless.

Meanwhile, the region of Kosovo, a part of Serbia but with a population of 2 million that was 90 percent Albanian and Muslim (Serbs were Eastern Orthodox Christian), was ready to explode. Though small in size and population, nationalist Serbs viewed Kosovo as the cradle of Serbian civilization, a region that needed to be kept as part of a greater Serbia and, for some, a region that had to be cleansed of non-Serbs.

By early 1999 the atrocities and deaths compelled the Clinton administration to act. Sensitive to criticism that the international response to the horrors of Bosnia had come too late, the Clinton administration tried one last time to convince Serbian leader Milošević to accept NATO peacekeepers in Kosovo. Milošević refused, and on March 24, 1999, Clinton, acting without UN authorization, announced that NATO airstrikes against Serbian targets had begun. In so doing, he discussed the American national interest in putting an end to the conflict in the Balkans and preventing the possible eruption of a larger war. However, at the core of Clinton's justification for war in Kosovo were human rights. As he put it, "Ending this tragedy is a moral imperative."[32]

On June 10, 1999, Clinton pronounced victory in Kosovo. Serbia had agreed to remove its forces from Kosovo, and an international peacekeeping force, which included US troops, took their place. Milošević remained in power, but his loss in Kosovo undermined his authority. In 2000 the political opposition ousted him, and in 2001 the new Serbian government handed him over to the UN International Criminal Tribunal for the Former Yugoslavia, where he was tried on numerous charges of human rights violations committed in Bosnia and Kosovo. While the situation there remains far from perfect, Kosovo illustrates effective international human rights enforcement.

The Kosovo case set a precedent for intervention to protect human rights within the boundaries of a sovereign state. Here was a case, in contrast to the "realist" view of how the world works, where justice trumped power and where state sovereignty took a back seat to human rights. As former British Prime Minister Tony Blair noted: "Non-interference has long been considered an important principle of international order.... But the principle of non-interference must be qualified in important respects. Acts of genocide can never be a purely internal matter."[33]

LIBYA The Arab Spring uprisings in Tunisia (December 2010) and Egypt (January 2011) had by February 2011 stimulated a rebellion against the regime of Libyan dictator Muammar Qaddafi. Early on, regime opponents seemed to have the upper hand gaining control of large swaths of the country. In response, Qaddafi fought back with military forces, and by mid-March those regime forces were mobilizing a large number of men and armored vehicles outside of the city of Benghazi—where the main concentration of anti-regime fighters was gathered. That regime military buildup around Benghazi, combined with Qaddafi's characterization of his opponents as "rats" and "cockroaches" and threats to "cleanse Libya house by house," led world leaders to fear an impending bloodbath.[34]

On March 17, the UN Security Council, by a 10-0 vote with five abstentions (Brazil, China, Germany, India, Russia) authorized a no-fly zone along with "all necessary measures" to protect the civilian population from the Libyan government.[35] The United States and NATO followed through with air strikes against Libyan government forces. By the end of October 2011 the NATO operation ended as Qaddafi was captured and killed and his forces defeated.

Supporters of the NATO operation in Libya have called it a "model intervention" and a "textbook example" of how the relatively new idea of a "responsibility to protect" ought to be applied, but critics are not so sure. While the intervention did demonstrate a renewed will to intervene in the name of human rights and successfully ended Qaddafi's ruthless regime, it also, according to the critics, extended the fighting, increased the death count, and replaced Qaddafi with a failed state that has served as an incubator for radical Islamists.[36]

responsibility to protect (R2P)
Global norm, endorsed by the UN, that states have responsibility to protect their citizens from human rights abuses and that, when states fail to do so, the international community has both a right and responsibility to intervene.

A RESPONSIBILITY TO PROTECT? The concept of a **responsibility to protect (R2P)** had been under discussion for several years and was formally endorsed at the 2005 UN World Summit attended by leaders from around the world. As noted in the summit's official outcome document, each individual state has the primary responsibility to protect its population from genocide, war crimes, ethnic cleansing, and crimes against humanity. However, when states fail to do so, the responsibility to protect falls to the international community working through the United Nations.[37] Thus, R2P sought to promote a new global norm establishing that a state's claim to sovereignty cannot be considered absolute protection from external intervention if it is committing or allowing extreme human rights abuses to occur on its territory.

R2P was a direct response to the international community's inconsistent actions in the face of human rights emergencies. In Rwanda, in the spring of 1994, as 800,000 ethnic Tutsis were, in the span of 100 days, butchered with machetes and other weapons by majority Hutus, the main concern of the United States and other countries seemed limited to withdrawing their own citizens safely. In fact, US government officials went to great lengths to avoid using the word "genocide" to label the events in Rwanda precisely because it would arguably trigger the obligation, under article one of the Genocide Convention, to take action "to prevent and to punish" (see Theory in Practice 6.1).

Yet, even as global leaders were discussing and establishing the new responsibility to protect norm, human rights atrocities were under way in the African state of Sudan. Beginning in 2003, regime-backed Arab militias were destroying villages in the largely black African Darfur region, raping inhabitants, killing perhaps hundreds of thousands, and displacing more than 2 million people. However, the response of the international community was both slow and modest. A small contingent of African Union (AU) troops has been on the ground in Sudan since 2004, and European Union troops were sent to neighboring countries to deal with the flow of refugees from Darfur. In July 2007 the UN Security Council established a UN/African Union hybrid mission in Darfur (UNAMID) and authorized a larger contingent of 26,000 peacekeeping troops. By spring 2008, only a third of those troops had been deployed, and the UN secretary-general declared the situation in Darfur to be "going from bad to worse."[38] As of spring 2015, the security situation for civilians in Darfur remained bleak, with violence against and displacement of civilians continuing unabated.

Likewise, UN and NATO action in Libya stands in stark contrast to the glaring failure of the international community to defend human rights in Syria and Iraq. Confronted first in 2011 with a ruthless attempt by the Syrian regime of Bashar al-Assad to suppress protest and then by the barbarism of ISIS militants, 200,000 Syrians were killed and millions had become refugees by the end of 2014. In March 2015, UN human rights investigators accused ISIS of war crimes and genocide, the latter particularly in light of attacks against the Yazidis—a religious minority which ISIS has vowed "to destroy … as a group."[39] Indeed, the atrocities (mass rapes, executions, beheadings, kidnappings, etc.) committed in

Theory in Practice 6.1

The "G-Word"

The 1948 Convention on Genocide requires the international community to act if genocide is deemed in progress anywhere in the world. For that reason, US and other world leaders and officials have been reluctant to use the "g-word" lest they commit themselves to an intervention that they and their citizens wish to avoid. Consider, for example, the following exchange that took place at a press briefing from State Department spokesperson Christine Shelly on June 10, 1994, after hundreds of thousands had been killed in Rwanda. While realists would say that the following exchange confirms the reluctance of states to follow through with human rights enforcement, constructivist scholars would see in this the power of words and ideas (in this case, the word and idea of "genocide") to impact world politics.

Q: How would you describe the events taking place in Rwanda?

Ms. SHELLY: Based on the evidence we have seen from observations on the ground, we have every reason to believe that acts of genocide have occurred in Rwanda.

Q: What's the difference between "acts of genocide" and "genocide"?

Ms. SHELLY: As you know, there is a legal definition of this. There has been a lot of discussion about how the definition applies under the definition of "genocide" contained in the 1948 convention…. What we have seen so far, as best as we can, and based, again, on the evidence, we have every reason to believe that acts of genocide have occurred.

Q: How many acts of genocide does it take to make genocide?

Ms. SHELLY: Alan, that's just not a question that I'm in a position to answer.

Q: Well, is it true that you have specific guidance not to use the word "genocide" in isolation but always to preface it with these words "acts of"?

Ms. SHELLY: I have guidance which I try to use as best as I can. There are formulations that we are using that we are trying to be consistent of our use of. I don't have an absolute categorical prescription against something, but I have the definitions. I have phraseology which has been carefully examined and arrived at as best as we can apply to exactly the situation and the actions which have taken place.

Q: Well, what is an act of genocide, Christine?

Ms. SHELLY: As defined in the 1948 Genocide Convention, the crime of genocide occurs when certain acts are committed against members of a national, ethnic, racial or religious group with the intent of destroying that group in whole or in part.

Q: You say genocide happens when certain acts happen, and you say that these acts have happened in Rwanda, so why can't you say that genocide has happened?

Ms. SHELLY: Because, Alan, there is a reason for the selection of words that we have made, and I'm not a lawyer.

- Is calling a human rights disaster "genocide" and then not acting sufficiently to stop it (the US position vis-à-vis Darfur) worse than refusing to use the word when conditions merit it (the US position vis-à-vis Rwanda)? Explain.

- What might be legitimate reasons for well-intentioned individuals or governments to disagree as to whether situations like those found in Rwanda, Kosovo, or Darfur qualify as genocide?

- Some have suggested that the international community is especially slow in responding to genocide in Africa. Is that true? If so, why? If not, why not?

SOURCE: US Department of State Daily Press Briefing, June 10, 1994, http://dosfan.lib.uic.edu/ERC/briefing/daily_briefings/1994/9406/940610db.html.

both Syria and Iraq by ISIS make whatever crimes were committed by Qaddafi in 2011 seem relatively minor by comparison. Alan Kuperman, one of the critics who has argued that the Libyan intervention was both unnecessary and counterproductive, suggests that fears of a bloodbath in Libya were overstated and that without NATO intervention approximately 1,100 Libyans (largely combatants) would have died.[40] While tragic, that is far less than have died at the hands of ISIS. Though the Obama administration began bombing raids against ISIS in 2014, that was three years after the fighting started there. As for the United Nations, no Libya-type resolution authorizing intervention against ISIS in Iraq and Syria was in place as of mid-2015.

Humanitarian intervention skeptics have argued that this inconsistency is predictable. Charles Krauthammer, for example, has suggested that the idea of war for human rights is doomed by what he calls the "iron law of humanitarian war," which he defines as the notion that, "Humanitarian war requires means that are inherently inadequate to its ends."[41] States and their citizens, in other words, are reluctant to sacrifice much, and especially not the lives of their own soldiers, unless clearly defined national interests are at stake. In a case like Kosovo, where NATO won by bombing from high altitudes, without use of ground forces, and without losing a single soldier, humanitarian war might be possible. Likewise, in Libya where NATO can fight a war from the skies and leave the ground battles to local rebels, intervention was also possible. But few conflicts will conform to this pattern, and where the expectation of a clean, bloodless war on the side of those interveners cannot be assured—in places like Rwanda, Darfur, or Syria—effective humanitarian intervention is unlikely.

Prosecuting Human Rights Violators

6-5 **Compare and contrast the strengths and weaknesses of the alternative ways of prosecuting individuals for human rights crimes.**

Ultimately, the success of the human rights revolution also depends on bringing violators to justice. This is especially true given the spotty record of the world community when it comes to stopping those violations while in progress. Even where humanitarian intervention succeeds, justice would be incomplete if the perpetrators remained in power or retired quietly to some country dacha or seaside haven.

In some cases, justice will be administered internally, in the country where the human rights abuses occurred. In many countries where severe human rights abuses occurred, **truth commissions** have been established to investigate, but the reach and power of those commissions vary considerably. Because many domestic justice efforts are weak, and also because perpetrators often have flagrantly violated international human rights treaties, prosecution at the international level is also an option. There are, at present, three paths to international prosecution: (1) universal jurisdiction, (2) ad hoc tribunals, and (3) the International Criminal Court.

truth commissions
Domestic bodies charged with investigating, publicizing, and prosecuting those responsible for human rights violations in states emerging from periods of authoritarian rule or severe human rights abuses.

Universal Jurisdiction

On October 16, 1998, 82-year-old former Chilean dictator Augusto Pinochet was arrested in his London hospital bed, where he was recuperating from surgery on a herniated disc. Pinochet had come to power in Chile in 1973 in a violent military coup that overthrew the democratically elected socialist leader Salvador Allende. Though some credit Pinochet's policies with creating one of Latin America's most successful economies, his 17 years in power were also characterized by significant human rights violations. The Rettig Report issued by Chile's Truth and Reconciliation Commission in 1991 documented more than 2,000 deaths and more than a thousand "disappearances" linked to the Pinochet regime. A subsequent report issued in 2003 by Chile's National Commission for Political Imprisonment and Torture established that the use of torture by the Pinochet regime was systematic state policy, documenting more than 28,000 cases.[42]

Despite those abuses, Pinochet avoided domestic prosecution. The Truth and Reconciliation Commission was intended to establish and document the record of human rights abuses rather than to prosecute. Moreover, a 1978 Chilean amnesty law protected those accused of human rights violations, and when Pinochet stepped down in 1990, he was made a senator for life, which, under the terms of the constitution he drafted, came with a grant of lifetime immunity.

The London arrest in 1998 thus resulted not from actions taken by Chilean authorities, but instead from an indictment handed down by a Spanish judge alleging human rights abuses including genocide, terrorism, and torture. The judge requested that the British government extradite Pinochet to Spain for trial. More than a year of legal debate followed, during which time Pinochet remained under house arrest in Great Britain. In the end, the British House of Lords proceeded with the extradition, only to be overruled by a decision of the government to return Pinochet to Chile, given the fragile state of his health.

Pinochet died in 2006 without ever being convicted or punished. However, the 1998 indictment, arrest, and agreement in principle to extradite Pinochet to Spain set a precedent for **universal jurisdiction** in matters of international human rights law. According to this principle, in some especially grave crimes, the duly recognized judicial bodies of a state may exercise jurisdiction without regard to the territory where the crime was committed or the nationality of the perpetrators or victims. In the Pinochet case, though crimes against Spanish citizens were noted in the indictment, a Spanish judge indicted and the British police arrested a Chilean citizen and ex-president for crimes committed on Chilean territory against Chilean citizens as well.

Universal jurisdiction is highly controversial, as it directly challenges state sovereignty. However, it is not without basis in international law. All four of the 1949 Geneva Conventions on war embrace the idea of universal jurisdiction in instances of "grave breaches" of these conventions.[43] Likewise, the 1984 Convention Against Torture provides first that jurisdiction should be established

universal jurisdiction
Idea that in the case of grave violations of human rights, the judicial bodies of a sovereign state may exercise jurisdiction without regard to the territory where the crime was committed or the nationality of the perpetrators or victims.

in torture cases by states directly impacted. However, Section 2 extends jurisdiction universally:

> Each State Party shall likewise take such measures as may be necessary to establish its jurisdiction over such offences in cases where the alleged offender is present in any territory under its jurisdiction and it does not extradite him pursuant to article 8 to any of the States mentioned in Paragraph 1 of this article.[44]

Most recently, Article 6, Section 4, of the 1998 International Convention for the Suppression of Terrorist Bombings adopts the above language from the Convention Against Torture almost word for word, thereby extending universal jurisdiction to that area as well.[45]

Supporters of universal jurisdiction hail it as a trend toward further prosecution of human rights abusers. Critics, however, worry that it is a principle ripe for abuse insofar as states, or even individual judges, could use it to settle political and ideological scores. In recognition of this dilemma, some human rights advocates have emphasized the need for international tribunals duly authorized by the world community to prosecute human rights violators. International courts, in principle, could end the ability of such individuals to escape prosecution by hiding behind the walls of state sovereignty while avoiding the potential for abuse inherent in the universal jurisdiction approach.

Ad Hoc Tribunals

ad hoc tribunals
Temporary courts established by UN Security Council to prosecute human rights abuses.

Nuremberg Tribunal
Tribunal established by the victors of World War II to prosecute Nazi officials for crimes against peace, war crimes, and crimes against humanity.

The precedent for creating temporary or **ad hoc tribunals** to prosecute individuals for human rights violations was the **Nuremberg Tribunal**, established by the victorious Allies after World War II. The Nuremberg Charter authorized the prosecution of Nazi officials for crimes against peace, war crimes, and crimes against humanity. It was the last of these three areas of jurisdiction that was most controversial. The charter defined crimes against humanity as:

> murder, extermination, enslavement, deportation, and other inhumane acts committed against any civilian population, before or during the war; or persecutions on political, racial, or religious grounds in execution of or in connection with any crime within the jurisdiction of the Tribunal, whether or not in violation of the domestic law of the country where perpetrated.[46]

Thus, in a direct challenge to state sovereignty, the door was opened to prosecuting individuals for human rights abuses against their own citizens and irrespective of domestic law.

The Nuremberg precedent was followed in the 1990s, first with the establishment of the International Criminal Tribunal for the former Yugoslavia (ICTY) in 1993 and then with the creation of the International Criminal Tribunal for Rwanda (ICTR) in 1994. Unlike Nuremberg, where the authorization for the proceedings came from agreement among the victorious Allied powers, the 1990s tribunals were established under the authority of the UN Security Council and were thereby more effectively insulated from the claims of "victor's justice" sometimes used to critique Nuremberg.

In both the Yugoslav and Rwandan tribunals, dozens of people were indicted, many have been put on trial and convicted, and prison sentences are being served. The most famous defendant was former Serbian leader Slobodan Milošević. He was first indicted in 1999 for war crimes and crimes against humanity, but a charge of genocide was added in 2002 for his part in authorizing ethnic cleansing in Bosnia. In 2001 he was arrested by the new Serbian government on domestic corruption charges and subsequently transferred to The Hague, where the ICTY conducts its proceedings and where his trial, which began in February 2002, ended due to his death in 2006.

The establishment of both the Yugoslav and Rwanda tribunals was, in principle, a significant step in putting some muscle behind international human rights law, in making individuals responsible for flagrant violations accountable, and in sending the message that future violators will be brought to justice. However, the Yugoslav and Rwanda cases also demonstrate the shortcomings of the ad hoc approach.

First, the record of both tribunals is mixed. While many indictments have been handed down, not all of those indicted have been apprehended and tried. In both cases, but especially in the Rwandan case, progress was initially very slow. In the first seven years of the ICTR's work, verdicts were issued on only nine individuals, with many more of those responsible living freely around the world. Moreover, those verdicts did not come cheaply. The ICTR had 800 employees and a budget of more than $90 million.[47] To some extent, the slow pace was understandable, as these tribunals were blazing new trails. Over time, things improved. By the time it wrapped up its last case in 2012 (a few cases are still pending appeal) the ICTR had indicted 91 individuals of whom 61 were convicted and sentenced.[48] Meanwhile, the ICTY, which is expected to wrap up its last case by no later than 2017, indicted 161 individuals and sentenced 80.[49]

Second, and more fundamentally, the ad hoc tribunal approach is inherently noncomprehensive. Charged with attending to human rights cases in Rwanda and the former Yugoslavia, the 1990s tribunals have no authority to try cases of severe human rights violations anywhere else in the world. Interest in creating additional tribunals is low, as the cost and slow pace of the Yugoslav and Rwandan proceedings have created a "tribunal fatigue."

The combination of promise and limitations manifested in the work of the Yugoslav and Rwandan tribunals contributed to the interest in establishing a more global and permanent solution to the challenge of prosecuting human rights violators. Thus was revived the idea of an international criminal court.

The International Criminal Court

The idea for a permanent international court of human rights is rooted not only in the lessons of the ad hoc tribunals, but also in the record of permanent human rights courts that have been operating at regional levels. The most significant of these is the European Court of Human Rights (ECHR), established by the 1950 European Convention on Human Rights and set up to begin hearing cases in 1959. The ECHR has been increasingly busy in recent years. As of December 31, 2014, 69,900 applications to the court to hear a case, almost all from individuals, were pending, with the majority of the complaints lodged against four countries—Ukraine, Italy, Russia, and Turkey. [50] That huge number belies the fact that it is, by design, a regional court whose jurisdiction is confined to Europe.

International Criminal Court (ICC)
Established in 1998 by the Rome Statute, it is the court of international human rights law intended to try individuals (not states) accused of genocide, war crimes, or crimes against humanity.

In contrast, the Rome Statute establishing the **International Criminal Court (ICC)** was intended to create a body with truly global reach. It was adopted in 1998 by a vote of 120–7 (with 21 abstentions).[51] The seven negative votes came from Iraq, Qatar, Yemen, Libya, Israel, China, and the United States. The statute provided that the ICC could begin to operate when 60 countries ratified, and that occurred by July 1, 2002; as of July 2015, 123 countries had joined the court (see Theory in Practice 6.2).

Unlike the International Court of Justice (World Court), where parties to cases are always states, the purpose of the ICC is to try cases against individuals. The Rome Statute gives the court authority to hear cases in three areas: (1) genocide, (2) war crimes, and (3) crimes against humanity. Court authority to try crimes of aggression was also debated, but it was decided to postpone inclusion for at least seven years until agreement on a definition of aggression could be reached. In 2010 the state parties agreed, under limited circumstances, to allow the court to try cases involving aggression beginning in 2017.

In all areas where the court is authorized to adjudicate, its jurisdiction includes both crimes committed by nationals of countries that have ratified and crimes committed by anyone (whether their country is a party to the ICC or not) in the territory of states that have ratified. In addition, the UN Security Council can authorize, given nine votes and the absence of a veto, ICC investigation and jurisdiction even if neither the parties to a crime nor the territory where it was committed belong to states that have ratified the ICC. Conversely, the Security Council can also halt ICC proceedings if those proceedings are deemed to imperil efforts to make and secure peace. Such Security Council action also requires a supermajority of nine votes, including all of the five permanent members. Thus, only with a significant consensus in the Security Council can ICC proceedings be halted.

As of mid-2015, the ICC has conducted formal investigations of 9 situations (all in Africa) and 22 cases have reached the Court for adjudication. All told, 36 people have been indicted; proceedings for 12 have ended, with two convictions and one acquittal (the others either had their charges dismissed or have died).[52] One case of note is that of Sudanese president Omar al-Bashir. Though Sudan is not a member of the ICC, in 2005 the Security Council authorized the ICC prosecutor to investigate the situation in Darfur, and in 2009 and 2010 arrest warrants were issued for al-Bashir on charges of war crimes, crimes against humanity, and genocide. Despite the indictments, as of July 2015 al-Bashir remained in office.

Theory in Practice 6.2
Palestine and the International Criminal Court

On April 1, 2015, Palestine, over strong opposition from Israel and the United States, became the 123rd member of the ICC. The Palestinian authority had long been seeking membership, but it had been denied since membership is limited to sovereign states. That changed in November 2012 when the UN General Assembly, by an overwhelming 133–9 vote (with 41 abstentions), upgraded Palestine's UN status to that of "non member observer state." That word "state" is crucial as it made the Palestinians eligible for membership in the ICC and a host of other international organizations.

As a new member of the ICC, Palestine can now request that the Court investigate alleged war crimes committed by Israel during the 2014 Gaza War and, conceivably, the continued building of Israeli settlements in the West Bank. That is possible despite the fact that Israel is not a member of the Court since the ICC has the authority to investigate crimes committed by anyone, even nonmembers, on member state territory.

That said, it is up to the chief prosecutor of the ICC to decide whether or not there are grounds for indictment and prosecution. Putting aside the legal merits of the situation, the Court is likely to be torn between

avoiding such a contentious issue as Israeli war crimes and taking it up precisely because the Court needs to adjudicate an important legal case outside of Africa (where all of its other prosecutions have focused to date). It is also important to note that once an investigation begins, the Court can investigate, indict, and prosecute all parties to a situation. Thus, it is likely that the Court would not only investigate accusations of Israeli war crimes, but also Israeli accusations that Hamas put Palestinians at risk by illegally using civilians as human shields and failing to adequately identify their fighters with military insignia. According to the laws of war, the latter is required so that opposing soldiers can distinguish combatants from civilians.

- Should the United States and Israel be worried about Palestinian membership in the ICC? Why or why not?
- The United States is among the shrinking minority of states that are not members of the ICC. Should it join?
- How would realists, liberals, and constructivists differ in their understanding of the significance of the ICC?

In refusing to ratify the Rome Statute, the United States has cited a number of defects with the ICC. In general, US critics have argued that it lacks accountability, both because of the broad powers of investigation and indictment given to ICC prosecutors and because it shifts power away from the UN Security Council. Under the ad hoc tribunal system, prosecution, indictment, and trial could not begin until a Security Council majority without veto so authorized. Under the ICC system, it takes the same majority without veto to *halt* court action. As the United States is a permanent member of the Security Council with veto power, its influence on international human rights adjudication would be notably reduced under the ICC approach.

Some ICC critics worry that US superpower status and the global reach of US policy could make Americans tempting targets of ICC prosecution and harassment. For example, some fear it could lead to indictments of US soldiers and even US officials for war crimes allegedly committed in internationally unpopular wars like that in Iraq. Likewise, it could lead to indictments against

Israel for crimes against humanity related to its treatment of Palestinians. The vague definitions of the crimes that the ICC is authorized to investigate and prosecute add to the concern over the possible politicization of the court.

Supporters of the ICC and of US participation counter that the United States is protected by the principle of **complementarity**, which provides that the ICC steps in only if national courts are unable or unwilling to investigate and prosecute. One should emphasize that the principle of complementarity does not require findings of guilt or even indictments of suspected human rights violators. As long as the United States investigates and prosecutes alleged human rights violations in good faith through the American judicial system, the ICC would not have jurisdiction.

Even though the United States is a nonparty to the ICC, US citizens can be prosecuted if their crimes occur on the territory of states that are parties. Thus, supporters argue, it is indeed in the US interest to participate in selecting and removing prosecutors and judges and in helping to define the future role of the court. Such participation requires US ratification. More fundamentally, supporters argue that as a country with a global commitment to human rights, the United States needs to be out in front of the pack, not lagging behind, in putting an end to the ability of human rights violators to act with impunity.

Though supportive of the idea of the ICC in principle, the Clinton administration refused to submit the treaty to the US Senate for ratification until US concerns were addressed. The Bush administration went even further, ending all US participation in ICC negotiations on May 6, 2002, and refusing to participate as an observer state along with other nonparties to the court, such as Russia, China, and Israel. In the early years of the Obama administration, the United States ended its policy of noncooperation with the ICC. In January 2009 Secretary of State Hillary Clinton said, "We will end hostility toward the ICC and look for opportunities to encourage effective ICC action in ways that promote US interests by bringing war criminals to justice."[53] In June 2010 the United States participated as an observer in the first-ever ICC review conference held in Kampala, Uganda. However, given that that full-fledged US membership in the ICC would require ratification of the Rome Treaty by the US Senate—a body that is highly polarized along ideological lines—full membership in the ICC is not likely anytime soon.

complementarity
Principle that the International Criminal Court will not hear a case unless the domestic judicial system of the state in question is unwilling or unable to adjudicate the case in good faith.

Conclusion

The debate over the International Criminal Court is a debate over the larger human rights revolution in microcosm. On the one hand, evidence suggests that over the past half-century or so, the idea of human rights has affected how the world works in important ways. The ICC has been created, and, by mid-2015, 123 states had become members. The first ICC case involving human rights abuses in Uganda was undertaken in late 2005, and individuals accused of human rights violations on the territory of member states face indictment and prosecution irrespective of whether their country has ratified the Rome Statute. In 1999, NATO warplanes launched a war against Serbia over human rights in Kosovo, and Serb leaders eventually went on trial at the ICTY for genocide, war crimes, and crimes against humanity. Likewise, Augusto Pinochet felt the reach of the human rights revolution in his hospital bed in London, and other former leaders with human rights skeletons in their closets may still face consequences for their past actions.

On the other hand, the human rights revolution is incomplete. Several of the world's great powers—the United States, Russia, China—have refused to ratify the Rome Statute establishing the ICC. Ethnic cleansing and genocide in places like Chechnya, Sudan, and Syria have occurred with minimal intervention by the international community. And following the events of September 11, 2001, terrorists and the fight against them pose new challenges to human rights. In 2005 even the secretary-general of Amnesty International noted a "lethal combination of indifference, erosion and impunity that marks the human rights landscape today. Human rights are not only a promise unfulfilled, they are a promise betrayed…. Sixty years ago, out of the ashes of the Second World War, a new world order came into being, putting respect for human rights alongside peace, security and development as the primary objectives of the UN. Today, the UN appears unable and unwilling to hold its member states to account."[54] These same trends led Michael Ignatieff, a scholar of human rights, to ask back in 2002, "Is the human rights era ending?"[55]

In short, the human rights revolution has not completely ended the ability of human rights abusers to act with impunity. However, we can still see a change in the balance between state sovereignty and human rights in world politics. Thus, we can find sufficient human rights successes and failures to support the views of both realists and their critics. In pointing to the limits of the revolution, realists suggest that the world continues to work in essentially the same way it always has, as sovereignty and national interest continue to trump global concern with human rights. In pointing to the revolution's successes, constructivist and liberal scholars, as well as human rights activists, note the power of human rights norms, treaties, and institutions to shape not only the way we think the world *should* work but also, in some cases, how it actually *does* work.

Review Questions

- Why might an otherwise moral and ethical individual doubt the wisdom of the "human rights revolution"? To what extent are those doubts justified?
- Because the United States has been slow to ratify some human rights treaties, hesitated to embrace the new Human Rights Council, and has refused to become a party to the International Criminal Court, some see it as failing to do its part to promote human rights. Others argue that in refusing to participate in flawed institutions, the United States is seeking to elevate concern with human rights. Who is right and why?
- How much of a change to "business as usual" in world politics, as understood by realists, has the "human rights revolution" produced? Does the record of the international community on human rights support or undermine the realist view of how the world works?

Key Terms

human rights revolution
cultural relativism
negative rights
positive rights
genocide
UN Commission on Human Rights
Human Rights Council (HRC)
high commissioner for human rights

CNN effect
economic sanctions
apartheid
constructive engagement
smart sanctions
humanitarian intervention
ethnic cleansing
responsibility to protect (R2P)
truth commissions
universal jurisdiction

ad hoc tribunals
Nuremberg Tribunal
International Criminal Court (ICC)
complementarity

Endnotes

1. Charles Krauthammer, "Liberal Democrats' Perverse Foreign Policy," *Washington Post*, July 11, 2003, http://www.washingtonpost.com.

2. Jimmy Carter, "Address Before the General Assembly, March 17, 1977," *The American Presidency Project*, http://www.presidency.ucsb.edu.

3. Kathryn Sikkink, "Transnational Politics, International Relations Theory, and Human Rights," *PS: Political Science and Politics* 31:3 (1998): 517.

4. "Kosovo/Serbia and Montenegro: Joint Statement on the Status of Internally Displaced and Refugee Minorities from Kosovo," Human Rights Watch, June 16, 2004, http://hrw.org.

5. "The Worst of the Worst 2012: The World's Most Repressive Societies," Freedom House, https://freedomhouse.org/report/special-reports/worst-worst-2012-worlds-most-repressive-societies#.VSdyzROUdXY.

6. Amnesty International, "Female Genital Mutilation," http://www.amnesty.org.

7. Amnesty International, "Female Genital Mutilation."

8. Amnesty International, "Female Genital Mutilation."

9. Jack Donnelly, *Universal Human Rights: In Theory and Practice*, 2nd ed. (Cornell University Press, 2003), 89–90.

10. The term and definition are adopted from Margaret E. Keck and Kathryn Sikkink, *Activists Beyond Borders: Advocacy Networks in International Politics* (Cornell University Press, 1998).

11. Charter of the United Nations, http://www.un.org.

12. General Assembly Resolution 2131: Declaration on the Inadmissibility of Intervention in the Domestic Affairs of States and the Protection of Their Independence and Sovereignty, December 21, 1965, http://jurist.law.pitt.edu/2131.htm.

13. Charter of the United Nations, http://www.un.org.

14. William Korey, *NGOs and the Universal Declaration of Human Rights: "A Curious Grapevine"* (Palgrave Macmillan, 2001), 39.

15. The full text of these two treaties (and other major human rights treaties) can be found online at http://www.hrweb.org/legal/undocs.html.

16. Convention on the Prevention and Punishment of the Crime of Genocide, http://www.hrweb.org/legal/genocide.html.

17. Sikkink, "Transnational Politics, International Relations Theory, and Human Rights," 519.

18. Samantha Power, *A Problem from Hell: America and the Age of Genocide* (Perennial Books, 2003), 72.

19. Donnelly, *Universal Human Rights*, 133.

20. UN General Assembly Resolution 60/1, "2005 World Summit Outcome," September 16, 2005, http://daccess-dds-ny.un.org/doc/UNDOC/GEN/N05/487/60/PDF/N0548760.pdf?OpenElement.

21. UN General Assembly Resolution 60/251, "Human Rights Council," March 15, 2006, http://daccess-dds-ny.un.org/doc/UNDOC/GEN/N05/502/66/PDF/N0550266.pdf?OpenElement.

22. UN Office of the High Commissioner for Human Rights, "Universal Periodic Review," http://www.ohchr.org/EN/HRBodies/UPR/Pages/UPRmain.aspx.

23. See "NGOs Campaign on the 2008 HRC Elections," http://www.hrw.org.

24. UN Office of the High Commissioner for Human Rights, http://www.ohchr.org/EN/AboutUs/Pages/HighCommissioner.aspx.

25. Amnesty International, https://www.amnesty.org/en/countries and Human Rights Watch, *World Report 2014*, http://www.hrw.org/world-report/2014.

26. BBC News, "Bush Says Amnesty Report Absurd," May 31, 2005, http://news.bbc.co.uk/2/hi/americas/4598109.stm.

27. The annual US Department of State *Human Rights Report* is available at http://www.state.gov/g/drl/rls/hrrpt/.

28. Gary Clyde Hufbauer, "Sanctions-Happy USA," Institute for International Economics Policy Brief 98-4, July 1998, http://www.iie.com.

29. Kimberly Ann Elliott, "Evidence on the Costs and Benefits of Economic Sanctions," speech given before the Subcommittee on Trade Committee on Ways and Means, US House of Representatives, Washington, DC, October 23, 1997; available online at Institute for International Economics, http://www.iie.com.

30. Gary Hufbauer and Barbara Oegg, "A Short Survey of Economic Sanctions," Institute for International Economics, *CIAO Case Studies*, http://www.ciaonet.org/casestudy/hug01/.

31. Richard Garfield, "Morbidity and Mortality Among Iraqi Children from 1990 through 1998: Assessing the Impact of the Gulf War and Economic Sanctions," 1999, http://www.casi.org.uk.

32. William J. Clinton, Address to the Nation on Airstrikes against Serbian Targets in the Federal Republic of Yugoslavia (Serbia and Montenegro) March 24, 1999, *Weekly Compilation of Presidential Documents*, March 29, 1999, 516–518.

33. Tony Blair, "The Blair Doctrine," speech before the Chicago Economic Club, April 22, 1999; available online at Global Policy Forum, http://www.globalpolicy.org.

34. "Libya Protests: Defiant Gaddafi Refuses to Quit," BBC News, February 22, 2011, http://www.bbc.com/news/world-middle-east-12544624.

35. United Nations Security Council Resolution 1973, March 17, 2011, http://www.nato.int/nato_static/assets/pdf/pdf_2011_03/20110927_110311-UNSCR-1973.pdf.

36. Supporters of the Libyan intervention include Ivo H. Daalder and James G. Stavridis, "NATO's Victory in Libya: The Right Way to Run an Intervention," *Foreign Affairs* 91:2 (March–April 2012); Gareth Evans, "R2P Is Breaking New Ground in the Development of Global Governance," *YaleGlobal*, April 15, 2011, http://yaleglobal.yale.edu/content/gareth-evans-responsibility-protect-transcript. A harsh critic of the Libya intervention is Alan Kuperman, "A Model Humanitarian Intervention? Reassessing NATO's Libya Campaign," *International Security* 38:1 (Summer 2013).

37. *2005 World Summit Outcome Document*, para. 138–139, http://www.un.org/summit2005/documents.html.

38. *Christian Science Monitor*, April 9, 2008, http://www.csmonitor.com.

39. "United Nations Investigators Accuse ISIS of Genocide Over Attacks on Yazidis," *New York Times*, March 19, 2015, http://www.nytimes.com/2015/03/20/world/middleeast/isis-genocide-yazidis-iraq-un-panel.html?_r=0.

40. Kuperman, "A Model Humanitarian Intervention?, 118–119.

41. Charles Krauthammer, "The Short, Unhappy Life of Humanitarian War," *National Interest*, Fall 1999, http://nationalinterest.org/article/the-short-unhappy-life-of-humanitarian-war-835.

42. Amnesty International Press Release, November 30, 2004, http://web.amnesty.org.

43. Geneva Conventions for the Amelioration of the Condition of the Wounded and Sick in Armed Forces in the Field, for the Amelioration of the Condition of Wounded, Sick and Shipwrecked Members of Armed Forces at Sea, Relative to the Treatment of Prisoners of War, and Relative to the Protection of Civilian Persons in Time of War. This language is contained in all four of the Geneva Conventions on war. See, for example, Article 146 of the fourth convention. Available online at http://www.globalissuesgroup.com/geneva/convention4.html.

44. Convention Against Torture, http://www.hrweb.org.

45. International Convention for the Suppression of Terrorist Bombings, United Nations Office on Drugs and Crime, http://www.unodc.org.

46. Charter of the International Military Tribunal, Article 6; available at Avalon Project, Yale Law School, http://www.yale.edu.

47. International Crisis Group, "International Criminal Tribunal for Rwanda: Justice Delayed," *Africa Report No. 30*, June 7, 2001, http://www.crisisgroup.org.

48. "The ICTR in Brief," http://www.unictr.org/en/tribunal.

49. UN ICTY, "Key Figures of the Cases," http://www.icty.org/sid/24.

50. "The ECHR in Fact and Figures 2014," http://www.echr.coe.int/Documents/Facts_Figures_2014_ENG.pdf.

51. The Rome Statute of the International Criminal Court, http://www.un.org.

52. See the webpage of the ICC at http://www.icc-cpi.int/en_menus/icc/situations%20and%20cases/Pages/situations%20and%20cases.aspx.

53. Briefing on the International Criminal Court Conference in Kampala, Uganda, US Department of State, June 2, 2010, http://www.state.gov/s/wci/us_releases/remarks/142585.htm.

54. Irene Khan, *Amnesty International Report 2005: Foreword*, http://web.amnesty.org.

55. Michael Ignatieff, "Is the Human Rights Era Ending," *New York Times*, February 5, 2002.

Chapter 7

Economic Globalization

The Consequences of Liberal Commercialism

Shanghai's Pudong district: 1989...and today. How would realists and liberals differ in their assessment of the geopolitical consequences of China's rapid economic development? Who is right?

 Learning Objectives

7-1 Compare and contrast the realist, liberal, and neo-Marxist perspectives on the global economy.

7-2 Explain the key attributes and accomplishments of the Bretton Woods system in the areas of trade, money, development, and regional integration.

7-3 Explain the phenomenon of globalization and discuss the arguments of both its supporters and critics.

7-4 Identify and evaluate the factors that could lead to the reversal of globalization.

Traditionally, scholars of international relations have distinguished between "high politics" and "low politics." High politics is concerned with the competition between states for power and geopolitical influence, while low politics has to do with the interactions among states and nonstate actors in relation to global economic, environmental, demographic, and other nonmilitary issues. The terms reflect a realist bias that the primary concern of international relations is the military and political power struggle, while such issues as global trade, finance, and migration, though important in their own right, are secondary to the core security interests of states.

In the 1990s, however, the end of Cold War military competition combined with the increasing trend toward global economic integration led to a resurgent interest in low politics. The more optimistic adherents of the liberal commercialist paradigm (see Chapter 1) argue that globalization is rendering high politics obsolete. Those optimists assert that the benefits of global economic interdependence and the consequent cost of disrupting it are making war and the realist preoccupation with military power increasingly unthinkable. To the extent that globalization is, as one observer has argued, as unstoppable as the dawn,[1] one might conclude that the entire realist view of how the world works is becoming passé.

For realists, however, the celebration of globalization and the acceptance of its inevitability, both so fashionable in the 1990s, were shortsighted.[2] States can slow or even reverse the forces of economic globalization if it appears contrary to their interests. Rather than an unambiguous force for peace, globalization also contains the seeds of interstate conflict. From a different perspective, neo-Marxists also challenge liberal views of economic globalization. Like realists, neo-Marxists believe that international economic relations produce both winners and losers and are as likely to lead to conflict as cooperation in world politics.

This chapter begins with a comparison of realist, liberal, and neo-Marxist perspectives on the global economy. From there we will turn to an examination of the key issues and institutions of the international economic order as they have evolved from World War II to the present. Though the world economy has changed significantly over recent decades, many features of the international economic order established in the 1940s continue to shape international economic relations today. The chapter will culminate with an extended discussion of the globalization debate. As we will see, globalization is the logical extension of the liberal paradigm, and it provides a powerful challenge to the realist understanding of how the world works. Thus, while this chapter will examine the nuts and bolts of how the world of international economic relations works, the larger goal is to help you assess the merits of that challenge to the realist paradigm.

Perspectives on the Global Economy

7-1 Compare and contrast the realist, liberal, and neo-Marxist perspectives on the global economy.

The three paradigms that have the most to say about the global economy are realism, liberalism, and neo-Marxism. Although each was discussed in general terms in Chapter 1, here we focus on those elements of each paradigm most directly related to understanding how the world of international economic relations works.

Realism

The controversy that currently swirls around the phenomenon of globalization is to a large extent a variation on a much older debate between mercantilist supporters of protectionism and liberal proponents of free trade. In its classic sixteenth-century conception, mercantilism was a policy aimed at increasing the national wealth via the accumulation of precious metals like gold and silver. Modern mercantilism, or **neomercantilism**, is focused instead on accumulation of national wealth via a trade surplus, which is the result of exporting more than one imports. When a country has a trade surplus, it both accumulates monetary reserves and promotes the development of domestic industries.

This neomercantilist concern with national wealth accumulation is consistent with the realist emphasis on national power, and many scholars view mercantilism as the realist paradigm applied to international economic relations. For many realists, mercantilist policies that promote a nation's economic wealth and power are essential, as military power ultimately rests on a strong economic foundation. As noted in Chapter 1, relative gains are key to realists. Even if all states become more prosperous as a result of global trade (absolute gains), those who enjoy the greatest boost (relative gains) will be advantaged in the global balance of power. Thus, for realists, the world economy is essentially a **zero sum game** in which every gain for one country is a loss for another.

The realist or neomercantilist approach to the world economy requires that governments play an activist role in promoting and protecting their national industries from foreign competition. Such policies of **protectionism** can take many forms. The most straightforward is via tariffs. A **tariff** is a tax levied on imported goods and services. If importers of such goods pass the cost of that tax on to consumers, it will raise the price of imports and make domestic goods more price-competitive and attractive to consumers.

Used to similar effect are a variety of **nontariff barriers (NTBs)**, which include any protectionist barriers that are not tariffs. The most common nontariff barrier is a **quota**, or a limit imposed on the amount of a particular good that can be imported within a given time period. By limiting the supply of that product, the effect is, like a tariff, to raise the price of the import and make domestic products more competitive. Governments can sometimes be very

neomercantilism
Approach to the global economy that aims for the accumulation of national wealth via a trade surplus.

zero sum game
Set of interactions that produces winners and losers and in which every gain by one party must be a loss for other parties so that net winnings and losses equal zero.

protectionism
Any policy pursued by a government to insulate domestic industries from foreign competition.

tariff
Tax levied on imports to raise their cost to domestic consumers, thereby making domestic-made goods more price-competitive.

nontariff barrier (NTB)
Government-imposed measure that is not a tariff but that makes it more difficult and costly to import foreign goods and services. Examples are quotas and strict health and safety standards.

quota
A quantitative limit imposed on the number or amount of a particular good that can be imported within a given period.

creative in devising nontariff barriers. For example, strict health and safety inspections required for imports can often work well in protecting domestic industries. Likewise, governments can help domestic industries by providing **subsidies**—grants of money or other valuable assets designed to lower the cost of production—with the goal, once again, of making domestic products more desirable than foreign imports.

subsidies
Grants of money or other valuable assets to domestic industries intended to lower the cost of production and to make those industries more competitive against foreign competitors.

Protectionist policies often have a populist appeal. Even today, many citizens and politicians would have no trouble identifying with the anti–free trade sentiments of President Abraham Lincoln, who is reported to have said: "I don't know much about the tariff. But I know this much. When we buy manufactured goods abroad, we get the goods and the foreigner gets the money. When we buy the manufactured goods at home, we get both the goods and the money."[3]

beggar thy neighbor
Government policies such as trade barriers and currency devaluations designed to solve domestic economic problems at the expense of one's trade partners.

Protectionist views are likely to be especially strong and hold political sway in periods of economic recession or depression, when unemployment is high. In such circumstances, restrictions on imports can seem like a quick way to solve unemployment problems. Such **beggar-thy-neighbor** policies—by which one country seeks a solution to its economic problems at the expense of other countries—were pervasive among industrial nations during the Great Depression of the 1930s.

Liberalism

comparative advantage
Theory developed by nineteenth-century economist David Ricardo that says countries should produce the goods and services they can produce most efficiently in comparison to other goods and services.

Standing in stark contrast to neomercantilism and realism is economic liberalism. Rooted in the eighteenth-century views of classical economists like Adam Smith, economic liberals today believe in minimizing government intervention in the free market. Applied to the global economy, the liberal perspective argues that governments should refrain from interfering in the free flow of goods and services across international borders.

The case for the liberal position rests on the theory of **comparative advantage** as developed in the early nineteenth century by British economist David Ricardo. According to that theory, countries should produce those goods that they can manufacture most efficiently in comparison to other goods. Ricardo's key insight was that even when a country has an **absolute advantage** in the production of a good—that is, it can produce a good more cheaply than other countries can—it would still benefit by producing the goods that it can produce most efficiently in comparison to other goods. In effect, comparative advantage is concerned with **opportunity cost**—the cost of an alternative foregone. The opportunity cost of reading this textbook is studying for an exam in another course, while the opportunity cost of using scarce resources to produce steel is the use of the resources to produce computers.

absolute advantage
Situation in which one country can produce a good or service more cheaply than another country. A theory of trade developed by Adam Smith but superseded by Ricardo's theory of comparative advantage.

Gregory Mankiw, former head of President George W. Bush's Council of Economic Advisors and author of a best-selling economics textbook, nicely illustrates the concepts of opportunity cost, comparative advantage, and absolute advantage when he asks, "Should Michael Jordan mow his own lawn?"[4]

opportunity cost
The value of an alternative foregone.

In his day, Jordan was one of the world's top athletes (today it might be LeBron James), and the physical strength and athleticism that allowed for his basketball prowess would surely have enabled him to mow his lawn more efficiently than anyone he might hire to do the job for him. He arguably had an absolute advantage in both basketball and lawn mowing. However, the opportunity cost of Jordan mowing his own lawn might be working on his jump shot or doing a TV endorsement, and the added money made from the additional hour gained to practice basketball or film a television commercial would be more than enough to outsource the lawn mowing to a landscaper or even to a 13-year-old kid. Thus, despite the fact that Jordan had an *absolute advantage* in both basketball and lawn mowing, his *comparative advantage* was basketball, and both Jordan and the local landscaping company benefit when he concentrates on that activity.

The same argument can be made about national economies. In comparison to a world in which every country follows a policy of **autarky**, or economic self-sufficiency, the theory of comparative advantage suggests that specialization and trade minimize costs of production and raise the standard of living for the world as a whole and the individual countries involved in trade. Liberals believe that trade leads to absolute gains for all countries and therefore see international relations as a **positive sum game**, where everyone who participates benefits.

In some circumstances, the liberal case for trade and for opposing protectionism can seem obvious and intuitive. While it is theoretically possible, for example, to grow bananas in the harsh climate of northern Minnesota by constructing enormous greenhouses and then protecting that expensive local production with high tariffs against imported bananas from Central America, the opportunity cost would be very high. Consumers who would continue to buy bananas at their newly expensive price levels would find their standard of living in decline as disposable income to buy other goods and services diminished. Meanwhile, workers in other Minnesota industries could, as a result, lose their jobs as high-priced bananas squeeze out purchases of the goods and services they produce. The resources devoted to banana production would be better allocated to other sectors where there was a comparative advantage—biotechnology, perhaps.

The liberal case for free trade in steel or textiles or any other manufactured good does not differ in any essential way from the case for free trade in bananas. In all those cases, the call for tariffs or nontariff barriers is simply a way to shield from foreign competition an industry that lacks a comparative advantage. Yet as compelling as the case against banana tariffs appears to be, many people endorse comparable tariffs designed to protect domestic industries such as steel, automobiles, or textiles from import competition. Some might argue that there is a difference—while one cannot grow bananas in Minnesota one can produce steel there. However, it is possible, with the use of greenhouses, to produce bananas in Minnesota as well. The issue is not whether growing bananas in Minnesota is possible, but at what cost.

autarky
Policy that rejects participation in the global economy in favor of economic self-sufficiency.

positive sum game
Set of interactions in which all participants can come out ahead. The interactions increase the total pool of benefits available to all who participate.

Neo-Marxism

The neo-Marxist perspective on international economic relations has its roots in the writings of Karl Marx, the nineteenth-century German philosopher (see Chapter 1), and Vladimir Lenin, the leader of the 1917 Russian Revolution. Writing during the era of Europe's Industrial Revolution, Marx noted the poor living and working conditions of Europe's new industrial working class. He noted also that the wealth and profit produced by industrialization remained with the capitalists who owned the means of production, while workers, including children, toiled long hours for little pay in dirty, unsafe conditions. Marx predicted that this exploitation of the working class would eventually lead to Communist revolutions throughout Europe in which workers would rise up to overthrow the capitalist system.

The revolutions that Marx predicted, however, did not materialize. Lenin explained this failed prophecy by citing **imperialism**, which Marxists define as a policy of extending national power over other states and peoples for economic gain. According to Lenin, the rich capitalist states of Western Europe acquired colonies in Asia, Africa, and Latin America where labor and resources could be exploited. The profits obtained by these imperial ventures were then used to improve conditions for workers at home just enough to temporarily prevent the domestic class struggle from spilling over into revolution. However, while class conflict at home was moderated for a time, imperialism gave rise to two kinds of conflict at the international level: (1) conflict between rich capitalist countries and the colonies they exploited and (2) conflict between rich capitalist states as they competed over access to those colonies.

imperialism
The extension of national power over other states and people for the purpose of economic gain.

Most contemporary neo-Marxists have abandoned predictions of worker revolution and renounced the kind of political regimes created in places like Russia and China in the twentieth century in the name of Marx and Lenin. However, the understanding of international economic relations rooted in the words of Marx and Lenin remains central to their analysis in three areas.

First, neo-Marxists see the global economy as characterized by a constant economic rivalry among developed capitalist states. While European states once struggled to establish direct colonial rule, in our postcolonial era states seek more indirect access to and control of resources, markets, and places for investment. Thus, neo-Marxists would view economic and trade disputes among the capitalist powers—the United States, Western Europe, and Japan—as part of the unavoidable logic of global capitalism. While some commentators have welcomed China's embrace of market capitalism as promising better Chinese relations with the developed Western countries, neo-Marxists anticipate increased tensions. They say this because China, the newest player in this global intracapitalist struggle, challenges the economic position of those Western countries.

Second, neo-Marxists continue to emphasize the exploitation of poor countries by the developed capitalist states. While liberals tend to see poverty and economic underdevelopment as the result of poor internal policy choices, neo-Marxists place the blame on external factors—specifically, the exploitation of poor countries by rich developed ones. A version of this argument known as **dependency theory** was popular in the 1960s and 1970s. According to this theory, poor countries were poor precisely because they were victims first of overt colonial rule and then of less direct control via investment, trade, and aid relations with developed countries, giving the advantage to the developed countries at the expense of the poor, which became dependent.

Third, neo-Marxists argue that whatever success a country's capitalists have in their intracapitalist struggle or in their exploitation of poor countries around the world, the benefits will not necessarily trickle down to workers within those capitalist countries. On the contrary, neo-Marxists argue, the more integrated the global economy, the more workers in developed economies will lose, as they now are in a global competition for jobs with workers in low-wage countries thousands of miles away.

In short, neo-Marxists share with realists a rejection of the liberal view that international economic relations are a positive sum game in which all involved will benefit. Like realists, neo-Marxists see the global economy producing both winners and losers. The difference is that while realists assess the world economy in terms of the relative advantages or losses it produces for different states, neo-Marxists are more interested in the advantages and losses it produces for social classes. From this perspective, an American firm that establishes a profitable factory in Mexico may benefit its corporate bottom line at the expense of both Mexican workers and US workers.

dependency theory
Set of theories that explain poverty and underdevelopment in less-developed countries as a consequence of the integration of the poor into the larger world economy and their consequent exploitation by the rich.

The Bretton Woods System

7-2 **Explain the key attributes and accomplishments of the Bretton Woods system in the areas of trade, money, development, and regional integration.**

During the Great Depression of the 1930s, powerful neomercantilist pressures developed around the world as countries sought to solve their economic problems on the backs of their neighbors. Tariffs and other protectionist measures proliferated, the volume of international trade plummeted, and political tensions escalated. The Depression, combined with the subsequent economic devastation produced by World War II, also provided a significant boost to Marxist and Communist parties in many West European nations. As the war was ending, economic liberalism was under challenge from both mercantilist and neo-Marxist constituencies in many countries.

Determined to avoid another round of beggar-thy-neighbor policies, the United States—the world's dominant postwar military and economic power—pushed for the creation of a postwar economic order based on liberal principles of free markets and free trade. In July 1944, representatives from the United States and the other 43 Allied countries met at the Mount Washington Hotel nestled at the base of the White Mountains in Bretton Woods, New Hampshire. The purpose of the meeting was to establish rules and institutions that would govern the postwar international economic order. Those rules and institutions, collectively referred to as the **Bretton Woods system**, were intended to prevent the global economy from sliding back toward self-defeating neomercantilist policies. Though many of the original features of the Bretton Woods system have evolved or been replaced over time, many of the decisions made and institutions created in the 1940s continue to influence international economic relations in the twenty-first century.

The International Trade Regime

As you will recall from Chapter 5, a regime is a set of principles, norms, rules, and procedures guiding international behavior in a specific issue area. At the core of the original Bretton Woods trade regime was the **General Agreement on Tariffs and Trade**, better known as GATT. Less a formal organization than an international treaty, the 1947 GATT aimed to realize the liberal vision of a world of free trade. It did so by providing a forum within which countries committed to free trade could negotiate a reduction of protectionist barriers. In 1995 it was replaced by a more formal organization, the **World Trade Organization (WTO)**.

GATT and the WTO share in common the norm of **nondiscrimination** in providing other GATT/WTO members equal access to one's home market. That norm requires that all states that are members of GATT/WTO grant other members **most favored nation (MFN)** status (now called Permanent Normal Trade Relations or PNTR). So, for example, if Canada imposed a 10 percent tariff on shoes imported from Italy, it must impose a 10 percent tariff on shoes imported from all other GATT countries. Canada cannot discriminate either in favor of or against Italian shoes. The goal is to deter bilateral trade wars between member countries.

Of course, the aim was not just to have equal tariff levels among countries, but lower tariff levels as well. Thus, the GATT/WTO process is based on a series of discussions or "rounds" in which further liberalization of world trade is pursued. During the GATT era, eight such rounds were completed, the last of which was the Uruguay Round, which got under way in Uruguay in 1986 and which lasted seven and one-half years. By the end of the Uruguay Round, GATT had achieved significant success. The number of GATT member countries increased from the original 23 founders to 123, tariffs on industrialized goods declined to a global average in the single digits, and the volume of world trade increased dramatically.

At the same time, GATT had less success in freeing up trade in agricultural goods and services, where domestic lobbies, especially farmers long protected from foreign competition, objected and made trade liberalization in such areas politically risky for national leaders. Even in manufactured goods, countries often compensated for GATT-mandated reductions of tariffs by erecting

Bretton Woods system
Post–World War II international economic system established by the US and its Allies and intended to support the development of a liberal economic order.

General Agreement on Tariffs and Trade (GATT)
The 1947 treaty that sought to promote the liberal idea of free trade by providing a forum through which countries could negotiate a reduction of protectionist barriers.

World Trade Organization (WTO)
The 1995 successor to GATT, it is the international forum for negotiating trade agreements and the de facto court for resolving trade disputes among member nations.

nondiscrimination
Trade principle that requires all GATT and WTO members to provide all other members equal access to their home market.

most favored nation (MFN)
Nation whose goods and services receive the most "favorable" treatment in trade, so they face the lowest tariffs and nontariff barriers. MFN has recently come to be known as "normal trade relations."

nontariff barriers to protect domestic industries. Often portrayed as health and safety regulations to protect consumers, or as regulations to protect the environment, these nontariff barriers were often difficult to identify and regulate. During the 1970s, as high oil prices and slowed economic growth led to rising levels of unemployment in many countries, those nontariff barriers were often the protectionist instrument of choice as they allowed for protection of the domestic economy without violating GATT rules governing tariffs.

The first round of global trade talks of the WTO era, the Doha Round, began in 2001 and was still in progress as of 2015. Aside from continuing GATT era efforts in such areas as freeing up trade in services and further regulating nontariff barriers, a central objective has been to promote development in poorer countries. A key to achieving this objective is reducing agricultural protectionism in developed countries, so that the developing countries can compete. This move involves cutting high agricultural tariffs in Japan and the EU and reducing the large domestic subsidies to farmers that characterize both the EU and the United States. However, as of 2015, the Doha Round talks were essentially stalled as the now 160 members of the WTO remained unable to find consensus on these issues.

What most distinguishes the WTO from GATT is a legally binding WTO "dispute settlement process." GATT provided no mechanism for resolution of interstate trade disputes. If one state believed another was engaging in protectionist practices in violation of GATT agreements, there was no place to take one's complaint for redress. That omission has been addressed in the WTO; members who believe that a trading partner is violating international trade agreements can take the case to the WTO for a hearing. Should the dispute

A call center in India servicing American consumers. How would a mercantilist, a liberal, and a Marxist differ in their assessment of the trend for American companies to move services like call centers offshore to places like India?

Theory in Practice 7.1

The Banana War: WTO Dispute Settlement in Practice

One of the early tests of the WTO dispute settlement process was the US–EU banana war. In 1993 the EU placed quotas on banana imports coming from outside its North African preferential trade zone. Although the United States has no domestic banana production, US-based multinational corporations such as Dole and Chiquita operating in Central America were affected. The United States therefore filed a complaint against the EU at the WTO and was joined in that complaint by Mexico, Honduras, and Ecuador.

A WTO dispute settlement panel was formed in 1996 to hear the case. In 1997 the panel ruled in favor of the United States. The EU appealed, but that appeal was rejected, forcing the EU to change its banana regime. The United States complained that the changes were cosmetic, and in April 1999 the WTO once again ruled against the EU, authorizing retaliatory trade sanctions against certain EU products (mainly imported luxury goods such as designer shoes, smoked salmon, expensive coffeemakers, etc.). Those sanctions remained in place until April 2001, when the EU finally caved.

This case reveals both the strengths and limitations of the WTO dispute settlement process and provides ammunition for both liberal and realist interpretations of the WTO. On the one hand, the EU could not avoid the process and the negative publicity attached to it. It eventually had to change its banana policy, and international trade law was upheld. In the GATT era, it would have been much less likely that the EU policy would have been changed. Liberals would thus argue that the case illustrates the power of institutions (in this case, the WTO) to regulate and constrain state behavior for the benefit of the world economy as a whole.

On the other hand, the process took a long time—five years from the establishment of the dispute settlement panel until final resolution, and even longer if you go back to the initial establishment of the EU banana regime. Moreover, one can only speculate whether the EU would have changed its policy if the United States had not been involved as one plaintiff in the case, in turn denying the EU access to the lucrative US market for the sanctioned European goods. Thus, realists might argue that it was US power and US interests that drove this decision. Whether Honduran sanctions alone, in combination with the legal status of a WTO ruling, would have been enough remains an open question.

- To what extent would you agree that the banana case represents a WTO success story?

- Should we be worried or pleased that the WTO has dispute settlement power? Explain.

- Does the banana case undermine or support the realist view of international relations? Explain.

settlement panel, which is composed of trade experts and authorized by the larger body to hear the case, rule in favor of the plaintiff, the WTO can demand the end of the illegal trade practices and, if necessary, authorize the aggrieved parties to impose retaliatory sanctions (see Theory in Practice 7.1). In short, the WTO functions as a court of international trade law, and its authority to apply sanctions makes it in some ways more powerful than even the long-established International Court of Justice.

The International Monetary Regime

In a world with multiple national currencies, how those currencies are valued in relation to one another is a key issue. An American student studying in Europe, for example, will need to have euros in order to buy European goods and services. The student will perhaps visit a currency exchange booth in an airport and buy euros with American dollars. How many US dollars it costs to buy those euros will be partly affected by the nature of the exchange rate system. The choices are essentially two: a floating or a fixed exchange rate system.

In a **floating exchange rate system**, the relative value of currencies fluctuates in response to supply and demand. For example, if Americans were buying large amounts of European goods and services, leading to a US trade deficit with the Europe, demand for the euros necessary to buy those goods and services would increase. Thus, the relative cost of the euro in US dollars would increase, making European goods more expensive for American consumers and American goods cheaper for Europeans. In a **fixed exchange rate system**, in contrast, the relative values of national currencies are set at preestablished levels in relation to one another or a precious metal like gold, and they are not allowed to fluctuate regardless of supply and demand.

The original Bretton Woods monetary regime was based on a fixed exchange rate system. But in the 1970s that fixed exchange system collapsed as the United States, faced with mounting balance of payments pressures, announced a devaluation of the US dollar in relation to other currencies and a withdrawal of its long-standing commitment to exchange dollars for gold. A floating exchange system gradually emerged, and today most countries allow their currencies to float.

The choice of exchange rate system is important because it influences the response to balance of payments problems. **Balance of payments** refers to the net flow of money into and out of a country in connection with activities such as trade, investment, and foreign aid. When more money flows into a country than out, the country is said to be enjoying a surplus in its balance of payments. Conversely, when more money is flowing out than in, that country is experiencing a deficit in its balance of payments. While it is possible to endure balance of payments deficits for a time by borrowing, in the long run large deficits are unsustainable for most countries. Countries with large deficits will eventually find themselves unable to borrow the additional funds needed to finance their imports of foreign goods and services.

In a floating system, balance of payments deficits are partly self-correcting. A country experiencing high deficits will see the value of its currency fall in relation to others. That, in turn, would help correct the deficit since it would make foreign goods more expensive and reduce foreign imports. To correct these problems in a fixed exchange rate system requires painful domestic measures like reduction in both government and consumer spending.

To help countries with severe balance of payments problems, the Bretton Woods monetary regime included the establishment of the **International Monetary Fund (IMF)**. The IMF offers loans to countries facing deep and persistent balance of payments difficulties. The money for such loans comes from the member countries, each of which is required to contribute its "quota," based on the relative size of its economy, to the pool of money available for lending. As the world's largest economy, the United States has always been the world's

floating exchange rate system
System in which the relative value of national currencies fluctuates in response to supply and demand.

fixed exchange rate system
System in which the relative values of national currencies are set at preestablished levels in relation to one another or a precious metal like gold, and they are not allowed to fluctuate regardless of supply and demand.

balance of payments
Net flow of money into and out of a country as a result of trade, investment, aid, and other transactions over a specified period.

International Monetary Fund (IMF)
Bretton Woods institution that provides loans to countries facing persistent balance of payments difficulties on the condition that recipient countries adopt economic policies prescribed by the IMF.

largest contributor to the IMF, accounting for 17.69 percent of IMF funding in 2015.[5] In turn, the IMF's weighted voting system gives countries voting power roughly commensurate with their quota. Thus, US voting power in 2015 was 16.75 percent.[6]

When it makes loans to countries in need, the IMF normally attaches conditions. Specifically, countries receiving IMF loans will be required to adopt **structural adjustment programs**—programs designed to make changes in economic policy to eliminate the source of the country's financial difficulties. In the 1990s the reforms recommended by the IMF were known collectively as the **Washington consensus**, due to the support those recommendations had from the United States. They included reduction of state economic regulation, privatization of state industries, elimination of protectionist trade barriers, reduced restrictions on foreign investment, and reductions in government spending—all of which emphasized replacing state intervention with free market forces.

The IMF and its policies have always been controversial and subject to criticism on several counts. Even IMF supporters concede that the economic medicine prescribed can be bitter, with the anticipated long-term gain preceded by considerable short-term pain. Moreover, the critics argue that the one-size-fits-all advice provided by the IMF often ignores the specific political, economic, and cultural context of countries in economic crisis.

For example, the IMF faced harsh criticism in response to its handling of the East Asian financial crisis of 1997. In previous decades, governments had loosened restrictions on the flow of capital across national borders. As a result, up-and-coming "emerging market economies" in places like Southeast Asia received billions of dollars of capital from Western investors looking to earn higher rates of interest than they could at home. This cash infusion proved a boon to those recipient countries and accelerated a dynamic expansion of their economies, including a surge of investment in infrastructure projects, real estate, and construction activity.

In the summer of 1997, however, doubts set in about the future of these economies, and money began to flow out of the region as quickly as it had once arrived. The result was economic turmoil. Growth stalled, construction projects were halted, jobs were lost, and local currencies declined in value. Some suggested that the 1997 crisis was an inherent problem of the unregulated global market in capital that had come to characterize the world economy by the 1990s. The IMF largely blamed internal factors such as corruption, and it offered to bail out the countries in the region only if they implemented the usual Washington consensus. Critics argued that for countries facing economic collapse, the IMF medicine was the wrong prescription. Neo-Marxists argued that this crisis was just one more illustration of the IMF and Western nations trying to reconstruct others in their own image and dominate developing countries' economies whatever the local cost. Even less radical critics of the IMF argued that this was not one of the IMF's most shining moments.

structural adjustment programs
Economic policy changes that countries are required to adopt as a condition of receiving IMF loans.

Washington consensus
Collective term for a set of economic prescriptions, emphasizing reduced state intervention and favoring market forces, recommended by the IMF, the World Bank, and the US government to countries in distress.

The Challenge of Development

In addition to the GATT and the IMF, the 1944 Bretton Woods conference led to the establishment of a third institution, the **World Bank**. "The Bank," as it is frequently called, is an independently governed institution within the larger UN system. Like the IMF, it acts as lender of last resort for countries with demonstrated need. However, while the IMF traditionally emphasizes short-term loans for countries facing balance of payments crises, the World Bank focuses on making loans to finance longer-term economic development projects. It is composed of the International Bank for Reconstruction and Development (IBRD), created in 1945 to facilitate post–World War II reconstruction, and the International Development Association (IDA), established in 1960 to help the poorest nations with interest-free loans and, in some cases, outright grants.[7] Like the IMF, the World Bank has adopted a weighted voting system that gives predominant authority to the developed countries.

Initially, the focus of the Bank was on the reconstruction of postwar Europe. But as Europe recovered, the Bank's attention shifted to the challenge of economic development in the global South (the poor countries of Africa, Asia, and Latin America). In the early days, the emphasis was on financing dams, road construction, and other large-scale physical infrastructure projects. More recently, it has turned to poverty reduction and human development initiatives. In 2000 this new emphasis was reflected in the Bank's adoption of the UN's **Millennium Development Goals (MDGs):**

1. Eradicate extreme poverty and hunger.
2. Achieve universal primary education.
3. Promote gender equality and empower women.
4. Reduce child mortality.
5. Improve maternal health.
6. Combat HIV/AIDS, malaria, and other diseases.
7. Ensure environmental sustainability.
8. Develop a Global Partnership for Development.

In 2002, the secretary-general of the United Nations, Kofi Annan, commissioned the Millennium Project to develop a concrete plan for implementing the eight goals, and he called on Harvard economist Jeffrey Sachs to head the project. In that capacity, Sachs advocated that developed countries make available as much as $195 billion per year from 2005 to 2015, with the ultimate goal of "ending poverty in our time," by the year 2025.[8] The foreword to Sachs's 2005 book *The End of Poverty* was written by the rock star Bono, who referred to Sachs as "my professor." The professor and the rock star joined forces to promote the global fight against poverty, traveling together around the world, giving speeches, and calling on governments to combat extreme poverty in keeping with their commitment to the Millennium Goals. For each goal, specific objectives were set, with a target date of 2015 and with plans for a September 2015

World Bank
International institution created after World War II whose main function is to provide low-interest loans for economic development projects to countries with demonstrated need.

Millennium Development Goals (MDGs)
Set of eight UN-established goals focusing on poverty reduction, primary education, gender equality, child mortality, maternal health, disease, environmental sustainability, and economic development.

Table 7.1 The Distribution of Global Poverty by Region (in 2005 PPP)

	% of Population Living at $1.25 per Day or Less (PPP) in 1990	% of Population Living at $1.25 per Day or Less (PPP) in 2011
Europe and Central Asia	1.5	0.5
Middle East and North Africa	5.8	1.7
Latin America and Caribbean	12.0	4.6
East Asia and Pacific	58.2	7.9
South Asia	53.2	24.5
Sub-Saharan Africa	56.6	46.8
World	36.4	14.5

NOTE: PPP or "purchasing power parity" figures adjust for the fact that the US dollar will buy more goods in poor countries than in the United States.

SOURCE: The World Bank, "Global Monitoring Report 2014/2015: Ending Poverty and Sharing Prosperity," 2015, http://www.worldbank.org/content/dam/Worldbank/gmr/gmr2014/GMR_2014_Full_Report.pdf.

UN Summit meeting to assess progress and to establish a post-2015 development agenda.

Not everyone is taken with the MDG approach. William Easterly, an economist and former senior economic advisor at the World Bank, argues that the record of the World Bank and the IMF in fostering economic development has been bleak. Between 1960 and 2000, more than $500 billion in aid to went to Africa, far more than to any other region, but that continent is still stuck in poverty.[9] As indicated in Table 7.1, almost half the population of sub-Saharan Africa is living in "extreme poverty," which the World Bank defines as living on less than US$1.25 per day. Levels of poverty in South Asia are also high. Easterly is especially critical of the Millennium Development Goal approach, which he describes as a "utopian plan" aimed more at satisfying the "something is being done" needs of rich Western countries than at serving the needs of the world's poor.[10]

The debate over the record of the World Bank and the potential of the Millennium Development Goals provides a window into a much larger debate over the causes of and solutions to the poverty and economic underdevelopment characteristic of much of the global South. Liberals, mercantilists, and neo-Marxists each have a different perspective on these issues.

For liberals, the keys to closing the North–South development gap and reducing global poverty are policy adjustments taken by the poor countries themselves. Back in the 1950s and 1960s many less-developed economies developed a strategy of development known as **import substitution industrialization (ISI)**, which sought to promote industrialization by erecting barriers to imports and serving the local market through domestic production. Liberals argue that countries that rejected the ISI approach, took advantage of their comparative advantage in labor-intensive industries, and adopted an export-led growth approach have reaped the greatest rewards. As Table 7.1 makes clear, in

import substitution industrialization (ISI)

Development strategy that seeks to stimulate industrialization by erecting barriers to imports and serving the local market through domestic production.

1990 both South Asia and East Asia had levels of poverty comparable to those of sub-Saharan Africa, but by 2011 they had made far greater progress (especially dramatic in East Asia) through a development approach that, as liberals would argue, stresses "trade not aid." According to Easterly: "As ... ministers and rock stars fussed about a few billion dollars here or there for African governments, the citizens of India and China (where foreign aid is a microscopic share of income) were busy increasing their own incomes by $715 billion in 2005."[11]

In addition to greater integration into the global economy, liberals also argue the need for good governance within countries. An example of an effort to emphasize good governance as the key to growth was the establishment of the **Millennium Challenge Corporation (MCC)** by the Bush administration in 2004. The MCC administered a fund of development aid available from the US government. Eligibility to receive that aid would depend on countries' scores on 17 selection indicators. One of those indictors was trade policy—more specifically, the openness to world trade as discussed above. But the rest of the indictors all dealt with domestic policy and governance issues such as rule of law, control of corruption, government effectiveness, civil liberties, political rights, public expenditure on health, and natural resource management.[12] In tying aid to domestic reforms, the MCC approach was clearly not rejecting aid as a part of the solution to the problem of global poverty. Instead of "trade not aid," the MCC strategy is "trade plus aid plus good governance."

Millennium Challenge Corporation (MCC) US aid program, initiated during the Bush administration, linking eligibility for development aid to a set of indicators of good governance and commitment to free markets.

While liberals argue that the key to development is integration into the global economy and the adoption of Western policy prescriptions for domestic governance, neo-Marxists take issue with that view. Many argue that the disparity of wealth and power between poor Southern countries and the rich governments and private-sector actors of the North causes interaction between poor countries and the developed economies to do more to perpetuate than to eradicate the North–South development gap. Consider the following:

- The IMF's and World Bank's weighted voting system gives developed countries effective control over those institutions. In 2010 "developing and transition countries" received a boost in their World Bank voting power, bringing them up to 47.19 percent, but that still leaves developed countries with majority control.[13] Moreover, a similar reform of IMF voting agreed to in principle in 2010 has yet to be implemented because of US opposition.[14]
- While the GATT/WTO process has significantly lowered trade barriers on most manufactured goods since the 1940s, the record on agricultural goods and other primary commodities, many of which are important sources of income in poor countries, is much less positive. The Doha Round discussions have stalled in large part precisely because Europe and the United States have been unable to agree to reductions of subsidies to agriculture in their own countries.
- While developing countries often seek the capital, jobs, and technology provided by Western companies looking to invest abroad, those countries

often need to make concessions in order to attract those companies. In many cases, Southern countries are dealing with large multinational corporations with annual sales greater than the country's gross national product.

- At a 2002 conference in Monterrey, developed countries agreed to work toward a target of foreign economic assistance of 0.7 percent of GNP. That **Monterrey Consensus** goal has yet to be met by most rich countries. With few exceptions (the Netherlands, Luxembourg, and the Scandinavian countries), developed countries have not met the target. The United States (despite the Millennium Challenge initiative discussed above) devoted approximately 0.2 percent of GNP to foreign economic assistance in 2014.[15]

Monterrey Consensus
Informal 2002 agreement among developed countries to devote at least 0.7 percent of GNP to foreign economic assistance.

One need not be a neo-Marxist to be concerned with these problems. Many mainstream economists and policy advocates also argue for increasing foreign development aid, reforming international institutions, and opening up developed state markets to developing country exports. The difference is that while those mainstream observers accept the possibility of such reform, their more radical neo-Marxist counterparts suggest that the system is not reformable and that exploitation of the poor by the rich is inherent in the world capitalist system.

The mercantilist view of development differs from that of both liberals and neo-Marxists. Unlike the neo-Marxists, mercantilists do not see an inherently exploitative relationship between rich and poor in the world economy. But unlike liberals, their strategy for development is not open borders and adoption of the Washington consensus policies advocated by the IMF, the World Bank, and the US government. In fact, the mercantilist reading of economic history is that the most successful developers were those that combined an embrace of export-led growth with significant protection of newly developing domestic industries from foreign competition. For example, while liberals sometimes cite the successful development of East Asia (including Japan, South Korea, Taiwan, and China) as evidence of the success of the liberal development strategy, mercantilists argue that in each of those cases growth occurred behind protectionist policies that included tariffs, nontariff barriers, and government subsidies to new industries. In fact, they argue that even developed countries like the United States and Britain had a long history of mercantilism that gave way to liberalism only once those countries had successfully developed.

infant industry protectionism
Protectionist policies designed to shield new industries from competition with established companies in the global marketplace until they can survive and compete on their own.

The mercantilist development strategy is based in part on the concept of **infant industry protectionism**. The idea is that a new industry needs some nurturing and protection in its formative years before it can compete with established companies in the global marketplace. Some have suggested that China has practiced a version of this approach. In 2010, for example, the Chinese government announced a new series of regulations governing the emerging e-book reader market. Some observers have suggested that those regulations were an attempt to protect emerging Chinese producers of that technology from established foreign competitors.[16] In fact, one might argue that the Chinese policy of keeping the value of its currency, the RMB, artificially low against the US dollar provides the most comprehensive protection for the Chinese economy as a whole. The low value of the RMB makes Chinese goods relatively cheap for US consumers, thereby stimulating Chinese industry and adding to the US trade deficit with China.

Regional Integration

While the Bretton Woods system created the GATT, the IMF, and the World Bank to focus on global approaches to trade, monetary relations, and economic development, it also made a place for regional organizations designed to promote trade liberalization and economic integration among smaller groups of countries. The nature and degree of regional economic integration can vary considerably and result in three basic types of arrangements:

1. **Free trade agreement:** an agreement in which a group of countries eliminates (or at least largely eliminates) barriers to trade among themselves.
2. **Customs union:** an arrangement in which trade barriers are eliminated among member countries, and the member countries adopt common external tariffs toward nonmembers.
3. **Economic union:** the highest form of integration between countries, in which member countries eliminate internal trade barriers; implement a common external tariff; and harmonize economic, social, and environmental rules and policies. Members can freely move goods and services as well as labor and capital across national borders with other member countries, and ultimately they adopt a common currency and common monetary and fiscal policies.

Technically speaking, all three forms violate the GATT/WTO principle of nondiscrimination, since imports from fellow members of a regional organization are treated more favorably than those of nonmembers. However, the original GATT agreement exempted such regional organizations from the nondiscrimination rule on the grounds that, on balance, these organizations liberalized trade and could provide, in combination with GATT, a dual-track approach to the same free trade goal. The successes and limitations of this regional approach can be illustrated by two cases: the European Union and the North American Free Trade Agreement.

THE EUROPEAN UNION   The European Union (EU) originated in the European Economic Community (EEC) created in 1957 by the Treaty of Rome. The EEC was originally composed of six countries: Germany, Italy, France, Belgium, Luxembourg, and the Netherlands. In eliminating most barriers to trade among its members and in imposing a common external tariff on nonmembers, it was a textbook example of a customs union. The founders were motivated by economic and political objectives. Economically, European integration promised a fast track to prosperity because it took advantage of the efficiencies of specialization and trade identified by the theory of comparative advantage. Politically, as the liberal

free trade agreement

An agreement in which a group of countries eliminates, or significantly reduces, barriers to trade among member countries.

customs union

Group of countries that have eliminated barriers to trade among themselves and have adopted a common external tariff toward nonmembers.

economic union

Group of countries that eliminate internal trade barriers; adopt a common external tariff; harmonize domestic policies; allow free movement of labor and capital; and, ultimately, adopt a common currency and common monetary and fiscal policies.

commercialist perspective on international relations would predict, integration promised more peaceful relations, as economic interdependence would make the cost of war among member states too great to contemplate.

The 1992 Treaty of Maastricht officially changed the name of the organization to the European Union. The change in name symbolized both the broadening and deepening of European integration. The most recent enlargement in 2013 increased the total membership to 28 states, including almost all the countries of Western and Northern Europe and a number of post-Communist states of Central and Eastern Europe (see Figure 7.1), and future additions continue to be discussed. Moreover, the level of integration among member states has deepened. Over the years, the members have moved from a customs union in the direction of an economic union, marked most notably by the adoption of a common currency, the euro, which by 2015 had replaced the traditional national currencies in 19 EU countries.

Figure 7.1 The European Union

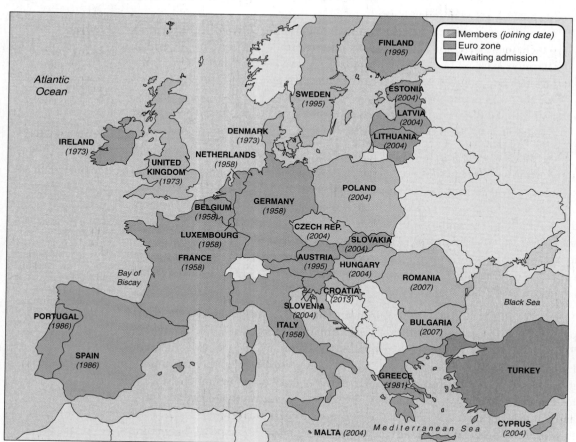

The results of economic integration in Europe have been notable. Although accounting for only 7 percent of the world's population, EU countries account for approximately 20 percent of global trade.[17] The heavy trade orientation of the EU countries is in large part due to the absence of protectionist barriers among members, and is reflected in the fact that about two-thirds of the trade of EU countries is with other EU members.[18] Partly as a result of economic integration, the EU economies have grown and prospered, with a collective GNP larger than that of the United States. Today, its per capita GNP and standard of living make Europe among the most prosperous places on the planet.

Beyond its economic successes, the EU has been uniquely successful in inducing countries to give up elements of their sovereignty. The EU long ago transcended the limits of an international organization within which sovereign states interact and pursue their interests. Instead, it is better categorized as a **supranational organization**, as it has both significant authority and an elaborate governance structure separate from that of its constituent state members. That structure includes the European Commission, which is the executive branch of the EU, charged with proposing and implementing legislation; the EU Council of Ministers and the European Parliament, which are the legislative arms of the EU; and the European Court of Justice, which is the supreme court of the EU.

Perhaps the most notable success of the EU is that its member states have remained at peace with one another for the past half-century. Realists might attribute this peace to the hegemonic role played by the United States in Europe or to the need to collectively balance the power of the common external threat posed by the Soviet Union. Liberals, in contrast, argue that the EU represents the most successful manifestation of the Kantian triangle (see Chapter 1). These successes notwithstanding, the EU faces some real challenges:

- **A lag in political integration:** Economic integration has greatly outpaced political integration in the EU. Unlike domestic legislatures, the European Parliament cannot initiate legislation, and the 28 members of the European Commission are appointed by their member governments rather than directly elected. Decisions made by EU bureaucrats in Brussels, the de facto capital of the EU, lack the degree of legislative and popular oversight common in the domestic politics of democratic states.

- **Tensions with external trading partners:** From the point of view of Europe's external trading partners, the EU success in promoting intra-EU trade has come at the expense of countries and industries left on the outside looking in. For example, as US goods have come to face greater competitive challenges in the global economy, US industries and policy-makers have become more concerned about the discriminatory impact of EU trading practices.

- **The challenge of globalization:** The EU provides impressive protections of workers' rights and generous government social programs. This system came to define continental Western Europe's "third way"—an approach between the Eastern European Communist economies and the

supranational organization
An international organization in which significant powers and elements of sovereignty of member states have been surrendered to the larger organization.

Anglo-American ones that emphasize markets over government. Now challenged by low-cost Asian producers, the European model may no longer be tenable, and efforts to trim back workers' rights and social programs have led to sharp domestic political battles.

- **Broadening versus deepening:** The success of the EU in broadening its membership to 28 has made deepening the integration more difficult. This is due partly to the political challenge of reaching consensus among a larger group of members. Perhaps even more fundamentally, it reflects the fact that economic integration is inherently more difficult among states that are at different levels of economic development.

The global financial crisis that began in 2008 exposed many of these underlying challenges. Despite beginning in the United States, the impact of that crisis has been deeper and more long-lived in Europe. Cutbacks in bank lending contributed to a deep recession from which Europe has yet to recover. In 2009, real gross domestic product (GDP) in the EU fell by 4.4 percent, and, despite a very modest rebound, growth in 2014 was a paltry 1.3 percent. Things were worse in the 19 Eurozone countries who experienced a 2014 growth rate of only 0.9 percent.[19] Unemployment in the EU remained at over 10 percent in 2014, with Greece and Spain experiencing unemployment of approximately 25 percent. [20]

Making matters worse has been the high amount of government debt characterizing some Eurozone countries—in particular, Greece. Battered by the global recession, by 2010 Greece was plagued by enormous budget deficits and the prospect of default on its debt obligations. Some observers speculated that Greece would have to drop out of the Eurozone. By the spring of 2010 a joint EU-IMF bailout package estimated at 110 billion euros (145 billion dollars) was cobbled together, temporarily mitigating the possibility of the worst-case scenario. The price, however, was that Greece promised to initiate a program of economic austerity involving deep cuts in government spending, including government pensions and salaries, that were very painful for Greeks to endure. Thus, in January 2015 Greek voters elected the leftist Syriza party led by Alexis Tsipras who campaigned on a promise of abandoning austerity.

As prime minister, Tsipras spent much of early 2015 engaged in a game of brinksmanship with the Germans who threatened to end aid to Greece unless Greece got its fiscal act together. The prospect of a Greek exit from the Eurozone or "Grexit" was higher than ever, and it threatened to begin the unraveling of the grand experiment with the common currency, especially as the public and politicians in other countries such as Italy and Spain were also beginning to have second thoughts about the euro. The Germans, supported by other northern European countries held firm, and in the summer of 2015, the leftist Greek government, in a stunning about-face, accepted another EU bailout on very strict terms that included selling off Greek state assets to help guarantee loan repayment.

However the Greek situation plays out, the Eurozone crisis highlighted the risks associated with a common currency and monetary policy in a region where national governments still control fiscal policy (i.e., government spending and tax policy) and where national politicians are still beholden to their domestic constituents first and to the EU second. From that tension, one can draw two opposing lessons: (1) that the EU needs to complete its process of integration by creating a United States of Europe where a single European polity catches up with the single European economy, or (2) that the EU needs to rethink the overambitious idea of the Eurozone. The first, at least in the short term, is highly unlikely; the second threatens to unravel the grand, and, in many ways, remarkably successful experiment in European integration that has been associated with peace and prosperity in Europe for over half a century.

THE NORTH AMERICAN FREE TRADE AGREEMENT   The North American Free Trade Agreement (NAFTA), which went into effect on January 1, 1994, is a classic example of a free trade agreement. Its three members, the United States, Canada, and Mexico, agreed to phase out tariffs and other trade barriers among themselves. Unlike the EU, it is not a customs union with a common external tariff, nor does NAFTA aspire to become an economic union.

The creation of NAFTA was very controversial, not least in the United States, where it became an important issue in the 1992 presidential election campaign. Third-party candidate Ross Perot received almost 19 percent of the popular vote in that election, making him the most successful third-party candidate since Theodore Roosevelt in 1912. A good part of his success was due to his opposition to NAFTA. He argued that NAFTA would produce a "giant sucking sound" of jobs leaving the United States for Mexico. In his opposition to NAFTA, he was joined by a politically and ideologically diverse group of critics: consumer advocate Ralph Nader, the AFL-CIO, pro-labor Democrats in the US Congress, and conservative Republicans like cable news commentator Pat Buchanan. What united this diverse group were concerns that US industries would be unable to compete, given Mexico's low wages and lax environmental protection enforcement, and that the sovereignty of the United States would be compromised.

On the other hand, NAFTA had the support of Republican incumbent President George H. W. Bush, his Democratic opponent Bill Clinton, and important representatives of the US business community. In large part, the NAFTA discussion reprised old arguments about the costs and benefits of free trade. While critics emphasized the threats to domestic jobs and industries, NAFTA supporters pointed to the potential benefits to consumers. Because NAFTA would allow US companies to invest in Mexico, they could reduce costs and more effectively compete with Asian producers. Moreover, opening the borders to free trade would stimulate economic development in Mexico itself, providing benefits for both Mexico and the United States. Some suggested that NAFTA would reduce illegal Mexican immigration, as more jobs would be available in Mexico.

After more than two decades, NAFTA remains controversial. NAFTA did lead to a surge in intra-American trade as its supporters had hoped. Since the agreement went into effect, the absolute volume of trade among the United States, Canada, and Mexico more than tripled, jumping from $287 billion in 1993 to over $1 trillion by 2011.[21] US trade with Mexico grew by 522 percent from 1993 to 2013; by comparison US trade with countries outside of NAFTA grew by only 279 percent during that same period.[22] However, as some US critics feared, Mexican exports to both Canada and the United States have soared. In 1993, the United States had a small trade surplus of $1.7 billion with Mexico, but in 2013 the United States had a trade deficit with Mexico of $54.3 billion.[23]

Meanwhile, the United States, Canada, and Mexico have all been involved (along with Australia, Brunei, Chile, Japan, Malaysia, New Zealand, Peru, Singapore, Vietnam) in negotiating a new **Trans-Pacific Partnership (TPP)** designed to further free trade and investment among those states. Some have dubbed the TPP "NAFTA on steroids" both because of the larger number of states involved and because the TPP promises, for better (in the view of its supporters) or worse (in the view of its critics) to extend the level of economic integration among the included countries even deeper than that established by NAFTA.

Trans-Pacific Partnership (TPP)

A free trade agreement under negotiation among 12 nations, including the United States, designed to reduce barriers to trade and investment.

The Globalization Debate

7-3 **Explain the phenomenon of globalization and discuss the arguments of both its supporters and critics.**

Regional agreements like the EU, NAFTA, and TPP represent important, but still only partial components of the much larger phenomenon of globalization. In the past few decades, use of the term "globalization" has proliferated. Googling "globalization" produces millions of hits, and an Amazon.com search of the word produces a list of thousands of books. The frequency with which the term is employed has led some to suggest that it has become little more than a buzz-word, "the most abused word of the 21st century."[24] Yet the term does capture something important about the world of the early twenty-first century.

What Is Globalization?

globalization

Process of integration and increasing inter-dependence among economies, societies, and cultures on a global level.

Globalization refers to the process of integration and increasing interdependence among economies, societies, and cultures on a global level. Think of globalization in contrast to the notion of sovereignty. Sovereignty assumes that national borders matter, because within those borders are distinctly national societies, economies, and cultures governable by national political institutions. Globalization is a direct challenge to sovereignty in all those respects, as it entangles national and local economies, societies, and cultures within a web that national governments are increasingly unable to control. The assault on sovereignty inherent in globalization is one reason that critics view the realist paradigm, and its privileging of the position of the sovereign state, as increasingly antiquated.

As an economic phenomenon, globalization involves the expansion of international trade, production, and finance. Whether taken individually or as a group, none of these things is entirely new. Nations have traded with one another for centuries. **Multinational corporations (MNCs)**—corporations based in one country but with production facilities scattered across other nations— have been around for decades. Such familiar brand names as Coca-Cola, Ford, and General Motors were globally traded and produced long before the current globalization era. Moreover, as long as international trade and investment have taken place, a system of international finance has existed to support this movement of real goods. Three things, however, distinguish the contemporary globalization era from the international economic interaction of previous eras.

First, there is a difference of degree. The volume of global trade and overseas investment is at an all-time high. The only comparable period is what many refer to as the "first era of globalization" (approximately 1880–1914), when international trade and investment also surged. However, that early-twentieth-century globalization era might be considered part of a single, long globalizing trend that was interrupted for a few decades by the two great twentieth-century wars. Thought of in these terms, the world has been moving along a globalizing trajectory for the better part of a century.

Second, there is a difference in speed. Modern telecommunications technology links far-flung parts of the globe instantaneously. We see this most clearly in the speed with which financial transactions now take place. At the click of a computer mouse, millions of dollars can be moved around the world to buy and sell stocks, national currencies, government securities, and other assets. Thomas Friedman has referred to the people moving this money as the "electronic herd."[25] As Friedman notes, these instant financial movements across computer screens can have enormous real-world consequences, bringing capital and prosperity to places the electronic herd sees as good bets, and also quickly bringing down economies and governments if the herd senses trouble and moves its money out.

Third, and perhaps most significantly, there is a difference in scope. More than ever before, the global economy is truly "global." Even in the pre–World War I phase of globalization, the "world" economy essentially involved Europe and European-settled countries like the United States. When countries in places like Asia or Africa were integrated into the global economy at that time, it was largely as colonies and economic subjects of the Europeans. Today, non-European states like China and India are becoming influential economic players. Moreover, the post-Communist states of Central and Eastern Europe, which were for decades isolated from the rest of the global economy, are slowly being integrated into the world economy—further broadening its geographic reach.

multinational corporation (MNC)
A corporation based in one country but with production of goods or services that takes place in at least one other.

Why Globalization?

Globalization is a product of both technological change and policy choices. Advances in technology have facilitated globalization. The late-nineteenth- and early-twentieth-century phases of globalization were made possible by railroads and steamships that could transport goods over long distances more cheaply and faster than ever before, rapidly expanding both global trade and global production. The midcentury rise of air travel was yet another step in the transportation revolution, further shrinking and integrating the world. More recently, the computer-based communications revolution stimulated globalization by allowing buyers and sellers, employers and employees, and the various branches and subsidiaries of far-flung multinational companies to stay in touch almost as easily as if they were located in the same office building.

While technology is an important part of the story, and while the kind of globalization just described could not take place without it, policy choices also play a part in globalization. In the early post–World War II era, both the US commitment to a liberal international economic order and its leadership in creating the Bretton Woods institutions to support that order were crucial in reigniting the globalization cut short in previous decades. This political commitment to globalization was backed up by American military power, which could protect shipping lanes or threaten regimes that sought to nationalize the holdings of US-based MNCs.

For realist scholars such as Robert Gilpin, the US role is central to understanding the globalizing trends of the post–World War II era.[26] In his view, US efforts to contain Soviet Communism led US policy-makers to conclude that a vibrant, integrated international economic system binding the United States, Western Europe, and Japan together served US national interests. At the same time, US power and hegemony enforced the rules of the integrated Western world economy that the United States sought to establish.

By the 1980s and 1990s an increasing number of countries were participating in the larger global economy via trade and foreign investment, while those trying to resist the globalization trend (e.g., North Korea) were dwindling to a few. In much of the developing world the inward-looking strategy of import substitution industrialization was abandoned as countries sought to reap the benefits of global trade. Similarly, in the Communist world, from China to Russia to Eastern Europe, markets and economic liberalization came into fashion, and joining GATT (later the WTO) became a common objective. For its part, the United States, through the IMF and World Bank, encouraged and promoted these trends by tying multilateral aid to the adoption of Washington consensus polices of liberalization.

Cause for Celebration?

For many observers, globalization provides reason for celebration. Supporters argue that it has increased economic efficiency, productivity, and growth, resulting in higher standards of living for people around the globe. For liberal economists, the "secret" of globalization is that it unleashes the power of comparative advantage on a worldwide scope. As barriers to trade and investment are reduced and as more of the world joins the global economy, the efficiency and productivity gains expand. In short, from this perspective, twenty-first-century economists can tell us little that Adam Smith and David Ricardo had not anticipated more than two centuries ago.

For citizens of developed countries like the United States, the benefits of economic globalization are, perhaps, most apparent in the low prices of imported goods, especially those from China and East Asia, which are commonly found on the shelves of Walmart and almost any other retailer (see Theory in Practice 7.2). Indeed, the low inflation rates characteristic of the United States and other developed economies in the 1990s and in the first two decades of the twenty-first century have been attributable, at least in part, to inexpensive foreign imports.

The case in favor of globalization also rests on the success of developing countries catching up with the developed world in many areas. Jagdish Bhagwati, a well-known trade economist and defender of globalization, puts the argument very succinctly: "Trade is associated with higher growth, and that

Theory in Practice 7.2
The Walmart Phenomenon: A Globalization Success Story?

Starting out with a single store in 1962, Walmart has become the largest retailer in the world with over 11,000 stores in 27 countries and total sales in fiscal year 2015 of $482 billion. It employs 2.2 million people worldwide, and its 1.3 million American workers make it the largest private employer in the United States.

This "Walmart phenomenon" is directly tied to globalization. Beginning in the 1980s, Walmart began to feature large numbers of imported goods at rock-bottom prices. By Walmart's own estimates, in 2003 it accounted for about $15 billion in Chinese imports, or about 10 percent of the US trade deficit with China. By 2006, another study found that Walmart's Chinese imports had jumped to $27 billion. Walmart works closely with Chinese companies, telling them what to produce to meet Walmart's needs, and even in some cases teaching the Chinese how to produce those goods to Walmart's specifications.

For liberals, the measure of economic success is the impact of economic activity on individual consumers. From this perspective, the Walmart/China connection benefits consumers with low prices, and that is why 100 million shoppers per week visit American Walmart stores. Indeed, excluding auto sales, fuel, and restaurants, Walmart accounts for over 11 percent of total US retail sales. For realists who look at the world through a mercantilist lens, the better measure of economic success is how much one produces. To the extent that Walmart's China connection drives US manufacturers to shift their production overseas or go out of business because they can't compete with "the China price," our gains as consumers, according to both realist and neo-Marxist critics, are outweighed by our losses as producers and workers.

- Is Walmart good for America? Is Walmart good for China? Explain.
- What should be the more important measure of economic success: levels of consumption or levels of production? Why?
- In what ways is the debate over Walmart a reflection of a larger debate about globalization?

SOURCES: PBS *Frontline*, "Is Wal-Mart Good for America?"; Wal-Mart website, http://news.walmart.com/walmart-facts/; Robert E. Scott, "The Wal-Mart Effect," *Economic Policy Institute*, June 25, 2007, http://www.epi.org/publication/ib235/; *Supply Chain Digest*, July 26, 2013, http://www.scdigest.com/assets/newsviews/13-07-26-1.php?cid=7260.

higher growth is associated with reduced poverty. Hence, growth reduces poverty."[27] In fact, in developing countries, a surge in economic growth produced average annual increases of 2.9 percent in per capita gross domestic product (GDP) from 1990 to 2003.[28] As reported by the World Bank, that growth, in turn, has produced lasting progress in other areas of human development:[29]

- *Poverty.* The percentage of the world population living in extreme poverty (living on less than one US$1.25 a day) fell from 43.4 percent in 1990 to 17 percent in 2011.
- *Child mortality.* Child mortality rates in developing countries fell from 99 per 1000 in 1990 to 50 per 1000 in 2013.
- *Primary school completion.* The percentage of children in developing countries that completed primary education rose from 77 to 91 percent from 1990 to 2012.
- *Child malnutrition.* Rates of child malnutrition fell from 28 to 17 percent between 1990 and 2013.

Developing countries have much ground still to make up, as achievement in all the areas noted above continues to lag considerably behind the developed world. Millions of people across the world still have inadequate levels of income, education, and health care; even people who have managed to rise slightly above the very low, $1.25 per day cutoff for "extreme poverty" remain very poor by standards of the developed world. However, as the UN report concludes, "On average, people born in a developing country today can anticipate being wealthier, healthier, and better educated than their parents' generation."[30]

The poster child for those who argue the merits of globalization is China. When Mao Zedong, the leader of the 1949 Chinese Revolution and founder of the Chinese Communist regime, died in 1976, China was an inward-looking country, largely isolated from the global economy. Trade and investment relations with the developed countries of the West were limited, and its internal economy was largely state-owned and controlled. However, beginning in the late 1970s, under the leadership of Deng Xiaoping, China began to reform. Domestically, the role of the state was reduced, and markets and private ownership were allowed to emerge. Internationally, China began to look to the world economy as a source of investment and as a place to sell Chinese-made goods. Ever the pragmatist, Deng responded to those who cautioned against abandoning Communism for capitalism with such responses as "To get rich is glorious" and "Whether a cat is black or white makes no difference. As long as it catches mice, it is a good cat."

The results have been stunning. Since the reform and opening of its economy in the late 1970s, China has been the world's fastest-growing economy, with average annual growth rates of close to 10 percent, leading to an overall per capita GDP growth of approximately 900 percent.[31] Despite some moderation in that growth rate in recent years, the impact in reducing poverty and improving the quality of life for Chinese citizens has been, as Bhagwati predicted, dramatic. From 1981 to 2010 the percentage of the Chinese population subsisting on

Anti-WTO protest, Seattle 1999. Why has the WTO sparked so much protest over the years, and how would mercantilists, liberals, and Marxists differ in their assessment of the legitimacy of the complaints lodged against the WTO? Who is right?

$1.25 per day or less fell from 84 to 10 percent—that is a reduction of 680 million people living in extreme poverty.[32] The reduction of extreme poverty in China accounts for three-quarters of global poverty reduction over the past 30 years, and that accomplishment, according to supporters of globalization, was produced largely via Chinese integration into the global economy.

To be sure, China remains a developing country based on its per capita levels of income and GDP, as the gross output and income of the Chinese economy have to support the world's largest population—1.3 billion people. Nevertheless, the economic growth has been breathtaking, and the resultant impact on living standards for millions of Chinese has been undeniable. Moreover, China is not the only globalization success story. Some argue that India, with its long-established democratic political system, its strong and growing high-tech sector, and its abundance of highly educated and highly skilled workers, may have a bigger upside than China.

A Backlash to Globalization?

Despite the successes to which proponents of globalization point, it has been a lightning rod for controversy. In 1999, for example, thousands gathered in Seattle to protest a WTO meeting. The protests, some of which grew violent, required cancellation of the opening ceremonies and largely overshadowed the meetings. The protesters were a diverse group, including representatives of US labor unions, environmental and animal rights groups, human rights organizations, farmers' groups, industry associations, civil rights organizations, and women's groups. Ideologically, the protesters ranged from anarchists and anticapitalist leftists to people who, on many issues, would fit comfortably within the US

Democratic or Republican Parties. Since 1999 the WTO has become the central institutional symbol of the globalization era, and similar protests have occurred at subsequent WTO meetings both in the United States and around the world.

While the pro-globalization writer and journalist Thomas Friedman dismissed the protesters as "senseless in Seattle,"[33] others suggested that the Seattle backlash against globalization and other subsequent protests are rooted in legitimate complaints. The complaints are many, but most fall into one of three categories: inequality, the privileging of economic efficiency over other values, and the corruption and distortion of political processes.

1. *Inequality.* Critics might acknowledge the economic growth associated with globalization and the benefits that such growth provides, but they emphasize that those benefits are unevenly distributed. For example, in the 1980s and 1990s, as China was growing at an annual double-digit rate, sub-Saharan Africa was economically stagnant, experiencing negative growth for much of that period. As Bhagwati anticipated, this differential has produced very different results in terms of poverty reduction. As we saw in Table 7.1, in East Asia, led by China, the share of the population living on less than $1.25 per day fell from 58.2 percent in 1990 to 7.9 percent in 2011, but in sub-Saharan Africa, the population at that extreme level of poverty declined much more modestly from 56.6 to 46.8 percent during that same period. Though economic growth rates in sub-Saharan Africa since the late 1990s have improved substantially and progress in reducing poverty there might finally be underway (indeed most of the modest poverty reduction in Africa suggested by the numbers above has occurred since the late 1990s), Africa stills lags far behind in this area.[34]

   According to critics, globalization has increased inequality not only across national boundaries but also within countries. This result would not surprise neo-Marxists, who see the world economy as driven primarily by the pursuit and clash of class interests. However, one need not be a neo-Marxist to note, for example, that average real wages (i.e., wages adjusted for inflation) in the United States have been stagnant since the 1980s. Meanwhile, the income of the richest 1 percent of the US population has increased significantly in the globalization era, and that top 1 percent now earns 20 percent of US income, the highest level of income inequality since the 1920s.[35] A good part of this trend has been attributed to globalization, which has created an integrated labor market in which workers in developed, high-wage nations compete for jobs with workers in Shanghai, where labor costs are far lower. To take advantage of those low overseas labor costs, companies now routinely engage in **outsourcing**, subcontracting parts of a company's business activity to suppliers abroad. To distinguish this behavior from domestic outsourcing, a new term, "offshore outsourcing," or **offshoring**, has been coined. The result is downward pressure on developed country wages.

   This increased inequality is not limited to developed countries like the United States. Although China and India are dynamic emerging economies,

outsourcing
The subcontracting of parts of a company's business activity to outside suppliers.

offshoring
Offshore outsourcing; subcontracting parts of a company's business activity to suppliers outside the company's home country.

not all who live there benefit equally. In China, an enormous gap in income, growth, and quality of life exists between the bustling coastal regions and the still largely rural and poor interior of the country. As for India, our image of a globalization success story with high-tech call centers, a growing middle class, and highly educated, technically proficient citizens who pose a competitive challenge to US workers is in large part true in the urban areas of the south. In large swaths of northern and rural India, however, extreme poverty, high rates of child mortality, and illiteracy prevail.[36]

2. *Privileging economic efficiency.* Critics complain that with globalization, a range of noneconomic values are sacrificed on the altar of economic efficiency. Environmental protection, animal rights, human rights, and local cultural traditions all take a back seat to the goal of increasing economic efficiency via free trade. As the philosopher Peter Singer puts it, in the current era of globalization, economics "trumps" all of these other considerations.[37] In the United States and Canada, for example, many producers of beef add growth hormones to the diet of cattle. If you are a North American consumer who eats beef, you almost certainly, unless you make a conscious effort to avoid it, eat beef containing growth hormones. The US government and beef industry argue that growth hormones are not only perfectly safe, but that cattle fed hormone supplements grow more quickly and with less fat in their flesh, making their beef cheaper and healthier. EU officials, however, have suggested that we lack evidence for the long-term health implications of consuming beef hormones, especially for vulnerable populations such as the very young, pregnant mothers, or older people. Thus, beginning in the 1980s, the EU banned imports of hormone-fed beef.

   The United States took the case to the WTO, which in the late 1990s ruled against the EU and authorized retaliatory sanctions on the grounds that the EU ban amounted to a policy of protectionism that violated international trade law. In fact, Article 20 of the original GATT treaty allows the WTO to uphold trade restrictions based on such considerations as animal rights, human health, and environmental protection. In practice, however, the WTO has been reluctant to act on that basis, fearing that trade discrimination based on differing values could be a slippery slope in which countries disguise simple trade protectionism behind those more noble-sounding objectives. The result, according to WTO critics, is that globalization and its goal of free trade have run roughshod over real differences in values across nations and cultures.

3. *Political distortions.* Supporters claim that globalization is associated with democracy and good government. States that are most highly integrated into the global economy tend to be the most democratic and least corrupt. In contrast, states with closed, isolated economies tend to be disproportionately corrupt and authoritarian.[38] Of course, correlation is not causation. Democracy and good government might lead to integration into the global economy rather than the reverse. Or globalization and democracy might both be caused by some third variable.

For critics, however, a deeper problem lies in the relationship between democracy and globalization. Even if globalization is associated with the formal institutions of democratic government, it weakens the sovereign control those governments have over policies central to their citizens' well-being and values. This problem results in cases where the WTO intervenes, as noted above, to strike down national laws protecting the environment, animal rights, or public morals in the interest of free trade. Even without WTO intervention, governments seen as excessively regulating business and industry or imposing excessive taxation to finance national policy goals could find that business and industry flee to more hospitable business environments. Thus, critics often claim that globalization leads not only to a "race to the bottom" as countries try to attract business by lowering regulatory standards, but also to a "democratic deficit" as democratic governments become unable to regulate an increasingly globalized economy.

One solution is regulation at the global level. Pascal Lamy, director-general of the World Trade Organization from 2005 to 2013, was an advocate of efforts to "humanize" globalization.[39] He has suggested that the Washington consensus with its narrow emphasis on free trade and free markets should be replaced by a new Geneva consensus (Geneva is the headquarters of the WTO), which takes into account the costs that free trade imposes on labor and the environment. To accomplish this humanizing agenda, Lamy proposed movement toward global governance and global regulation, for he believes it is only at the global level that these costs of economic globalization can be adequately addressed.[40]

Lamy's position at least partially accepts some of the criticisms made by the Seattle protesters, but resistance to this Geneva consensus is strong. It stems not only from the natural proclivity of global corporations to resist regulation but also from governments of developing countries. The latter see efforts to regulate global labor and environmental standards as a challenge to their national sovereignty and as an attempt by rich countries to undermine the competitive position of poorer countries that is based largely on cheap labor and lax regulatory standards. Thus, the quest to "humanize" globalization via global regulation often leads to an odd alliance of human rights activists, labor unions, and some developed country governments against an equally odd alliance of global corporations and many developing country governments.

Geopolitics and the Future of Globalization

7-4 Identify and evaluate the factors that could lead to the reversal of globalization.

The debate that swirls around globalization is not limited to its economic and social consequences. Considerable disagreement also surrounds the relationship of globalization and geopolitics. Indeed, the geopolitical consequences of globalization most directly challenge the realist paradigm. According to liberal commercialists, the political impact of economic globalization has the potential to change international relations and world politics as realists have tradition- ally understood them. Specifically, liberals argue that the resulting web of **interdependence**, defined as a set of mutual relationships that would be costly to break, has bound states and societies together in a manner that will cause them to avoid military conflict and war.

Liberals argue that this theory of peace has been most convincingly demon- strated in Western Europe. This now largely peaceful and prosperous chunk of the world's real estate was once, not too many years ago, one of the bloodiest places on Earth. The two most horrific wars in world history, measured by the death and destruction produced in a relatively compressed period, were the two world wars of the twentieth century, and both were fought largely on European territory.

Today, the idea of another war between such historic adversaries as France and Germany is almost inconceivable. More than half a century of economic integration has transformed those two countries and 26 of their neighbors into a single economic union, with many sharing the same currency. In fact, a primary motivator for the original architects of post–World War II European economic integration was the desire to make another world war on European soil unthink- able. Jean Monnet, a French economist and leading proponent of European inte- gration, argued: "To create Europe is to create peace."[41]

The pacifying impact of trade and economic interdependence extends, according to liberals, beyond the EU. Political scientist Robert Jervis has sug- gested that Western Europe, the United States, and Japan are part of a "security community" in which war is no longer an option for settling interstate disputes among themselves (see Chapter 4). Although Jervis identifies many possible explanations for this development, liberals would include mutual economic dependence.

For neo-Marxists and for realists, however, this liberal optimism is naive. While they disagree on the nature of world politics, both neo-Marxists and real- ists would agree that economic interdependence and globalization, far from guaranteeing international peace and stability, could contribute to international political tensions and even to interstate war. For neo-Marxists, such conflicts would be rooted in global inequalities and competition among capitalists in developed countries to dominate world markets and resources. For realists, economic globalization reveals and exacerbates fundamental differences in national interests.

A good illustration of these differences can be found in competing assess- ments of the geopolitical impact of China's recent economic boom. For liberals, economic development and integration into the global economy will motivate China to develop a stake in global stability and in good relations with its trading partners, including the United States. Conflict with the United States would risk access to the US consumer market on which much of China's economic miracle has been based.

interdependence
The web of mutually beneficial relation- ships that bind together states and societies and that would be highly costly to break.

Even the Taiwan Strait, long a world hot spot (see Chapter 4), looks less dangerous to liberals in the globalization era. If the Chinese attack Taiwan, they risk, as Thomas Friedman argues, $100 billion in Taiwanese investments in China, access to the Taiwanese experts who are crucial in the mainland's emerging high-tech sector, and disruption of global supply chains for many industries that are central to continued Chinese economic growth.[42] Moreover, the United States, Japan, and the EU would likely impose economic sanctions. Given these potential disruptions, could China afford to contemplate serious military action against Taiwan? Would any state in the integrated global economy take such a risk?

Skeptics would note that countries have taken such risks before. The economic interdependence of the early twentieth century did not deter the outbreak of World War I. Neo-Marxists would argue that World War I emerged precisely from the competition among capitalists of the developed countries to reap the benefits of globalization. Realists would suggest that the economic development of Germany contributed to war because Germany sought political status commensurate with its emerging economic strength, and because neighboring states felt threatened.

Contemporary China, some realists have suggested, may be the Germany of today, and Asia could become the center of geopolitical conflict in the twenty-first century, just as Europe was in the twentieth. Indeed, China's rapid economic development has been accompanied by a significant modernization of Chinese military capability, raising concerns not just in Washington, but also in Tokyo, Seoul, Hanoi, and other Asian capitals. Likewise, China's rapid economic development has forced the Chinese to dramatically increase imports of oil, another potential source of conflict in a twenty-first-century world where energy supplies are, at best, uncertain. Thus, while for liberals Chinese economic growth is a positive development, for realists it represents the potential emergence of a world power capable of challenging the interests of its neighbors and the geopolitical hegemony of the United States in Asia and elsewhere. Even a limited war over Taiwan would belie the liberal assumption that globalization equals peace, and as World War I did to the early-twentieth-century phase of globalization, it could halt globalizing trends for decades.

Short of major war, one might imagine still other circumstances under which globalization might be slowed, if not completely reversed. Those circumstances could involve continuing security issues, a slow erosion of support for globalization in key countries, or a deepening of the recent global economic crisis.

1. *Security considerations.* Following the terrorist attacks of September 11, 2001, border security was given a new priority. One area of special concern has been the cargo coming into US ports on container ships. Approximately 7,500 ships make 51,000 port calls on a yearly basis, delivering more than 6 million containers filled with goods from around the world.[43] Although some fear that one of those containers might one day deliver a weapon of mass destruction, to this point the percentage of containers subject to

inspection has been very small. The cost of greater vigilance would be very high, and the demands of security from such a terrorist threat have to be balanced against the interruption of global commerce that could result. However, if another spectacular attack were to occur, and in particular, if the worst fear was to materialize in the form of a nuclear device smuggled into a US port, then one might easily imagine a recalibration of the security versus commerce trade-off that could considerably slow the process of globalization.

In 2006 we got an early glimpse of this security/commerce trade-off when a company, Dubai Ports World (DPW), owned by the government of the United Arab Emirates, acquired a British firm that had been managing several major US port facilities. While supporters of the acquisition, including the Bush administration, pointed to the strong track record of DPW, US critics were concerned about a company owned by even a friendly Arab government overseeing port management. Facing strong congressional criticism, DPW sold its control over US ports to a US company. Supporters of the original deal argued that this episode sent a bad signal to the rest of the world regarding American commitment to globalization, and that it undermined US interests by chilling foreign investors that the United States wants to attract.

2. *Changing attitudes.* While a spectacular terrorist attack could dramatically reverse globalization, the more likely threat may be an erosion of support for globalization in key countries. The new competitive challenge from Asia coupled with national security considerations may lead to a realignment of domestic political forces in the United States and Europe against globalization. One irony of this situation is that, for years, many critics assumed globalization was a policy and economic order that served the interests of the richest nations at the rest of the world's expense. Indeed, the United States, the richest and most powerful country of all, has long been globalization's most important promoter.

Yet it is precisely in the United States where second thoughts about globalization have been most notable in recent years, with evidence of that trend preceding the global economic crisis that began in 2008. Between October 1999 and January 2004 the proportion of Americans who viewed globalization as "positive" fell from 53 to 40 percent.[44] This shift in American attitudes toward globalization has been shaped by enormous trade deficits, offshoring of jobs, rising illegal immigration, and fear of terrorism. In 2014 the United States had a trade deficit in goods of $737 billion, of which $343 billion (or 46 percent) was a result of the American bilateral trade deficit with China.[45] It is, thus, no wonder that while 89 percent of Chinese citizens surveyed thought global trade and business ties were good for their country and 67 percent thought trade created jobs, only 68 percent of the American respondents thought trade was good for the United States and a mere 20 percent though it led to job creation. And Americans are not alone in their skepticism as citizens of other advanced economies—most notably Japan, Italy, and France—also increasingly question the benefits of trade.[46]

In fact, asked to name the world's leading economic power, more Americans now say it is China (41 percent) rather than the United States (38 percent).[47] Adding to this sense of a shift in global economic power was the 2015 launch of the new, Chinese-led Asian Infrastructure Investment Bank (AIIB). The AIIB seemed poised to rival the US led World Bank, especially given that important US allies such as Germany and Britain, over the opposition of the United States, had applied to join. Given that China is still a relatively poor country with a 2013 GDP per capita of only $6,807 (compared to $53,042 in the United States), that perception of Chinese dominance is, at the very least, exaggerated and premature.[48] But it does reflect a growing perception, both in the United States and around the world, of relative US decline, and that, in turn, can continue to erode US support for globalization.

3. *Global Economic Crisis.* A change in attitudes toward globalization would be accelerated by global economic crisis. The early twentieth century round of globalization was brought to a halt when the post–World War I economic boom gave way to the stock market crash of 1929 and the worldwide economic depression that ensued. Governments began to impose protectionist measures. The Smoot–Hawley Tariff Act of 1930 raised US tariffs on manufactured goods to almost 60 percent, leading to a dramatic drop in imports and retaliation by trading partners.

The economic crisis that first manifested itself in 2008 has posed the greatest threat to the global economy since the 1930s. The problem originally centered on mortgage loans, which US financial institutions made to high-risk borrowers. Once those borrowers were hit with declining home values and escalating payments on adjustable rate mortgages, they began to default on their loans. Those defaults reverberated throughout the US economy as banks cut back on lending and as the glut of houses in default further depressed home values in many parts of the country. Because of the declining value of their homes, homeowners felt less wealthy, and faced also with soaring energy prices, they began to cut back spending in other areas. These problems could not be confined to the US economy. Foreign banks owned a good chunk of the subprime loans extended to US borrowers. Moreover, any recession in the United States was bound to impact other economies that depended on US consumers to buy their goods.

Efforts to contain the crisis included at least three primary lines of attack. First, the United States and other governments spent trillions of dollars to bail out financial institutions in crisis to prevent them from collapsing. Second, led by the United States, many governments implemented large stimulus programs designed to spur economic activity. In the United States, the Obama stimulus plan, formally the American Recovery and Reinvestment Act of 2009, provided for a combination of tax relief and government spending totaling almost $800 billion.[49] Third, some governments, including the United States, have considered new regulations on financial institutions designed to prevent similar crises in the future.

While worst-case scenarios of a global economic meltdown have been averted, as of early 2015 the world economy was still far from recovery. As previously discussed, the European Union remains mired in an economic slump characterized by anemic economic growth, high unemployment, fears of price deflation, and, in many countries, an unsustainable amount of public debt. That, in turn, has given rise, in many European countries, to political movements of both the right and left that have increasingly questioned the merits of globalization in general and the EU project in particular. The United States has done better with a slow but steady decline in unemployment levels and modest economic growth of 3.1 and 2.4 percent in 2013 and 2014 respectively,[50] but US wages remain stagnant and income inequality is at record high levels. By 2015, even China was experiencing, by its recent standards, slowed growth, deflationary pressures, and reduced trade expansion, raising concerns both about how China would handle this new situation and the potential ripple effects on the global economy.[51]

Despite some indications of protectionist responses to the 2008 crisis, trade wars reminiscent of the 1930s did not materialize. We have today a more elaborate system of international trade rules and an institution, the WTO, whose job is to ensure that a repeat of 1930s protectionism does not reoccur. However, we have already seen that WTO successes in reversing illegal protectionist policies can be slow and complicated (refer again to Theory in Practice 7.1), and in the face of a global crisis on the order of the 1930s, the WTO dispute-settlement mechanism could easily become overwhelmed by global protectionist sentiments and policies.

Indeed, even some supporters of globalization have argued that "globalization has gone too far," and they worry that excessive deregulation of the global economy, especially in the area of money and finance, not only has contributed to growing global inequality but also raises the prospect of another financial crisis.[52] In 2015, worry was growing in some quarters that we were repeating some of the same mistakes that led to the 2008 crisis—lax regulation, excessive financial speculation, increasing debt—and that an even worse crisis than 2008 was looming. Should those worries come to pass, the challenge to globalization might be difficult to resist.

Conclusion

In 1960 a spokesperson for the IBM Corporation is reported to have observed: "For business purposes the boundaries that separate one nation from another are no more real than the equator ... they do not define business requirements or consumer trends.... The world outside the home country is no longer viewed as a series of disconnected customers ... but as an extension of a single market." That same individual added: "The world's political structures are completely obsolete. They have not changed in at least 100 years and are woefully out of tune with technological process. The critical issue of our time is the conceptual conflict between the search for global optimization of resources and the independence of nation-states."[53]

Although articulated half a century ago, those words were prescient. They anticipated the view that globalizing trends of the late twentieth century fundamentally challenge an international political order that dates back not 100 years (as suggested in the quote) but all the way back to the 1648 Peace of Westphalia and the beginning of the nation-state system.

Liberals, realists, and neo-Marxists would differ in their responses to the IBM spokesperson. The most optimistic of contemporary liberal commercialists would anticipate that economics and technology will indeed prevail. Further, they would say that nation-states, their parochial interests, their inclination to interfere with the efficient operation of markets, and their tendency to use war and violence as the means to assert those interests will become obsolete. In short, for liberals, globalization is changing the way the world works.

Realists, in contrast, would suggest that international economic relations have always been the servant rather than the master of state interests.

Trade and globalization prevail when powerful states see it in their interests. When that is not the case, globalization will be reversed. For these realists, security trumps prosperity, national prosperity trumps global prosperity, and military power, still largely a state monopoly, ultimately trumps all other forms of influence. For neo-Marxists, the words of the IBM spokesperson reflect the class interests of capitalists, specifically, their desire to eliminate political restrictions on their ability to exploit a nation's workers and its resources for their own benefit.

For many observers, reality incorporates a mixture of these perspectives. Indeed, we can generally conclude without much debate and controversy that global economic integration and interdependence have increased in recent decades, that globalization has challenged but not replaced nation-states and military power, and that national, class, and individual interests are all affected by trends in the global economy. Where observers disagree is over the trajectory of these globalizing forces in the twenty-first century, and the extent to which they are permanently transforming how the world works.

Review Questions

- Many suggest that the Bretton Woods system institutionalized the liberal perspective on the global economy. How so? How might realists and neo-Marxists interpret the nature and purpose of the Bretton Woods institutions differently from liberals?

- In what ways is globalization altering how the world of geopolitics works? Does globalization undermine the assumptions of the realist paradigm?
- Is globalization, in your view, fundamentally a positive or negative phenomenon? Why do you think so?

Key Terms

neomercantilism
zero sum game
protectionism
tariff
nontariff barrier (NTB)
quota
subsidies

beggar thy neighbor
comparative advantage
absolute advantage
opportunity cost
autarky
positive sum game
imperialism

dependency theory
Bretton Woods system
General Agreement on Tariffs
    and Trade (GATT)
World Trade Organization
    (WTO)
nondiscrimination

most favored nation (MFN)
floating exchange rate system
fixed exchange rate system
balance of payments
International Monetary Fund
(IMF)
structural adjustment programs
Washington consensus
World Bank

Millennium Development
Goals (MDGs)
import substitution industrialization (ISI)
Millennium Challenge
Corporation (MCC)
Monterrey Consensus
infant industry protectionism
free trade agreement

customs union
economic union
supranational organization
Trans-Pacific Partnership (TPP)
globalization
multinational corporation (MNC)
outsourcing
offshoring
interdependence

Endnotes

1. Thomas Friedman, *The Lexus and the Olive Tree* (Farrar, Straus and Giroux, 1999), xviii.
2. See, for example, David Rieff, "Globalization 2.0," *New York Times Magazine*, March 26, 2006.
3. Cited in Dani Rodrik, "Symposium on Globalization in Perspective: An Introduction," *Journal of Economic Perspectives* 12:4 (1998): 3.
4. N. Gregory Mankiw, *Principles of Economics*, 3rd ed. (South-Western, 2003), ch. 3.
5. International Monetary Fund, "IMF Members' Quotas and Voting Power, and IMF Board of Governors," April 17, 2015, https://www.imf.org/external/np/sec/memdir/members.aspx#C.
6. International Monetary Fund, "IMF Members' Quotas and Voting Power."
7. Note that three additional institutions—the International Finance Corporation (IFC), the Multilateral Investment Guarantee Agency (MIGA), and the International Centre for Settlement of Investment Disputes (ICSID)—are also closely associated with the bank and constitute the larger "World Bank Group."
8. Jeffrey D. Sachs, *The End of Poverty: Economic Possibilities for Our Time* (Penguin, 2005).
9. William Easterly, "The Utopian Nightmare," *Foreign Policy*, September/October 2005, 58–64.
10. William Easterly, "The Utopian Nightmare."
11. William Easterly, "The West Can't Save Africa," *Washington Post*, February 13, 2006,

http://www.washingtonpost.com. Also see William Easterly, *The White Man's Burden* (Penguin, 2006).
12. For the full list of selection indicators, see Millennium Challenge Corporation, "Selection Indicators," http://www.mcc.gov/mcc/selection/indicators/index.shtml.
13. World Bank, "World Bank Reforms Voting Power, Gets $86 Billion Boost," April 25, 2010, http://web.worldbank.org.
14. Edwin M. Truman, "IMF Governance Reform: Unfinished Business for the 113th Congress," Peterson Institute for International Economics, November 12, 2014, http://blogs.piie.com/realtime/?p=4607.
15. "ODA from Major Economies Stable at $135 Billion," *UN Tribune*, April 8, 2015, http://untribune.com/oda-from-major-economies-stable-at-135-billion/.
16. Stan Abrams, "Ebook Readers and China's Infant Industry Argument," http://www.chinahearsay.com/ebook-readers-china-infant-industry-argument/.
17. Europa (official EU website), "Facts and Figures: The Economy," http://europa.eu/about-eu/facts-figures/economy/index_en.htm.
18. Europa, "Facts and Figures: The Economy."
19. Eurostat, "Real GDP Growth Rate," http://ec.europa.eu/eurostat/tgm/table.do?tab=table&init=1&language=en&pcode=tec00115&plugin=1.

20. IMF, *World Economic Outlook 2015*, p. 51, http://www.imf.org/external/pubs/ft/weo/2015/01/.

21. Office of the US Trade Representative, "Trade Facts," March 2006,; M. Angeles Villarreal and Ian F. Fergusson, "NAFTA at 20: Overview and Trade Effects," *Congressional Research Service*, April 28, 2014 https://fas.org/sgp/crs/row/R42965.pdf, p. 10

22. Villarreal and Fergusson, "NAFTA at 20," p. 10.

23. Villarreal and Fergusson, "NAFTA at 20," p. 14.

24. Quote attributed to the *Economist* magazine by Nayan Chanda, "What Is Globalization?" *Yale Global Online*, November 19, 2002, http://yaleglobal.yale.edu.

25. Friedman, *The Lexus and the Olive Tree*, ch. 7.

26. See Robert Gilpin, *US Power and the Multinational Corporation* (Basic Books, 1975).

27. Jagdish Bhagwati, *In Defense of Globalization* (Oxford University Press, 2004), 64.

28. *Human Development Report 2005*, UN Development Programme, http://hdr.undp.org.

29. World Bank, *World Development Indicators 2015*, http://data.worldbank.org/products/wdi.

30. *Human Development Report 2005*, 19.

31. Data on China in this paragraph are from C. Fred Bergsten et al., *China: The Balance Sheet* (Public Affairs, 2006), 18.

32. "Towards the End of Poverty," *The Economist*, June 1, 2013, http://www.economist.com/news/leaders/21578665-nearly-1-billion-people-have-been-taken-out-extreme-poverty-20-years-world-should-aim.

33. Thomas Friedman, "Senseless in Seattle," *New York Times*, December 1, 1999, http://www.nytimes.com.

34. *Africa's Pulse*, April 2013, World Bank, pp. 14–15, http://www.worldbank.org/content/dam/Worldbank/document/Africa/Report/Africas-Pulse-brochure_Vol7.pdf.

35. Colin Gordon, "Income Share of Top 1 Percent: 1912–2012," Center for Economic and Policy Research, September 30, 2013, http://www.cepr.net/index.php/graphic-economics/graphic-economics/income-share-of-the-top-1-percent-1913-2012-annotated.

36. *Human Development Report 2005*, 30–31.

37. Peter Singer, *One World: The Ethics of Globalization* (Yale University Press, 2002), 57.

38. "Measuring Globalization," *Foreign Policy*, May/June 2005, 59.

39. Pascal Lamy, "Humanizing Globalization," speech given in Santiago, Chile, January 30, 2006, http://www.wto.org.

40. Pascal Lamy, "Toward Global Governance," Master of Public Affairs inaugural lecture at the Institut d'Etudes Politiques de Paris, October 21, 2005, http://www.wto.org.

41. Jeremy N. Smith, "The Father of Europe," *Great Moments in World Trade*, http://www.worldtrademag-digital.com.

42. Thomas Friedman, *The World Is Flat* (Farrar, Straus and Giroux, 2005), 423.

43. David Eberhart, "Container Ships: The Next Terrorist Weapon," *Newsmax*, April 15, 2002, http://www.newsmax.com.

44. Public Opinion on International Affairs, "America and the World: Globalization," http://www.americans-world.org.

45. US Census Bureau, https://www.census.gov/foreign-trade/statistics/historical/gands.pdf.

46. "Faith and Skepticism about Trade, Foreign Investment." Pew Research Center, September 16, 2014, http://www.pewglobal.org/files/2014/09/Pew-Research-Center-Trade-Report-FINAL-September-16-2014.pdf.

47. Pew Research Center, "22-Nation Global Attitudes Survey," June 17, 2010, p. 41, http://pewglobal.org/.

48. The World Bank, http://data.worldbank.org/indicator/NY.GDP.PCAP.CD.

49. See the US government's official website "Recovery.gov" to track stimulus spending at http://www.recovery.gov/Pages/home.aspx.

50. US Department of Commerce, Bureau of Economic Analysis, https://www.bea.gov/newsreleases/national/gdp/gdpnewsrelease.htm.

51. "China Walks a Tightrope as Its Growth Rate Declines," *Wall Street Journal*, January 20, 2015, http://www.wsj.com/articles/china-walks-a-tightrope-as-its-growth-rate-declines-1421776903.

52. See for example, Dani Rodrik, *The Globalization Paradox* (Oxford University Press, 2012). Also see his earlier book, *Has Globalization Gone Too Far?* (Institute for International Economics, 1997).

53. Cited in Richard J. Barnet and Ronald E. Muller, *Global Reach: The Power of the Multinational Corporations* (Simon & Schuster, 1975), 14, 19.

Chapter 8

Transnational Challenges

The State System Under Stress

Canadian icebreaker in Arctic waters. Climate change is opening up Arctic waters to commercial shipping and military vessels of countries competing to claim the resources of the region. Will cooperative solutions to climate change and Artic management be found, or will tension and conflict over those challenges prevail? What would the various IR paradigms predict?

Learning Objectives

8-1 Compare and contrast the concepts of national security and human security.

8-2 Explain how transnational environmental problems pose a challenge to sovereign states, and assess how states cope with that challenge in the three response scenarios discussed in this section.

8-3 Explain how infectious diseases challenge the essence of the state system, and discuss how globalization has contributed to that challenge.

8-4 Explain how the Internet poses a threat to state sovereignty, and assess the ability of states to respond to that threat.

In the Cold War era and, indeed, throughout much of the past several centuries, world politics has been about the competitive struggle among states, especially the great powers, to acquire land, people, wealth, and influence. Security and survival were determined largely by one's success, often through military means, in capturing those valuable assets more effectively than other states. In the view of many scholars, however, the twenty-first century is presenting new kinds of challenges that come not from the armies of other states but from an array of transnational (or what Maryann Cusimano aptly labels "transsovereign") problems, including environmental pollution, illegal immigration, infectious diseases, drug smuggling, and terrorism.[1] These challenges play havoc with the idea of state sovereignty and, by implication, with the realist understanding of how the world works. That is a view that liberals, constructivists, feminists, and neo-Marxists would tend to share.

For realist scholars such as Stephen Krasner, however, these issues threaten neither the sovereignty of the state nor the traditional realist understanding of the world. As he sees it, the global problems noted above are not entirely unique, and states continue to have the resourcefulness to respond to them. States, he notes, have a "keen instinct for survival," and, thus, "those who proclaim the death of sovereignty misread history."[2] It thereby follows that as long as we continue to organize human societies within the institution of the state, concern over national security and the state's relative power will remain the driving force in international life.

The range of global issues over which this debate can be waged is extensive. For the purposes of this chapter, three issues will be addressed as representative of the debate. They are the global environment, global health and disease, and the flow of information over the Internet. In each case, we will first describe the challenge posed and will then assess how well sovereign states are dealing with the problem. This analysis will provide you with both an understanding of each issue and an appreciation of how you might view these issues within the debate over how the world works. First, however, we will examine the theoretical issues at stake.

From National Security to Human Security

8-1 Compare and contrast the concepts of national security and human security.

Even the most dyed-in-the-wool realist would likely acknowledge the reality of global problems such as pollution, infectious disease, or international criminal organizations and would accept the need for remedial action in response. To be a realist does not require one to be indifferent to global warming or the spread of a disease such as AIDS. The differences between realists and their critics relate to whether they believe these problems require rethinking certain fundamental assumptions about how the world works.

First, in the realist view, the main threats and challenges faced by states emanate from other states—in particular, the threat posed by the use, or potential use, of military power. However, as scholars like Cusimano argue, the new global challenges like pollution and AIDS neither emanate from other states nor are military in character. They result from the actions of an array of nonstate actors pursuing their individual or organizational interests. These new transnational forces pay little heed to state interests or boundaries, and if recent world trends are any indication, it may be harder for a state to defend its borders from these challenges than from foreign armies.

Second, the traditional realist approach to defending the national interest has been self-help, specifically, the accumulation of military power. However, critics suggest that individual states acting alone cannot adequately respond to these new threats, as they mock the notion of the sovereign border and require cooperative, global responses that extend far beyond self-help. As for military power, it seems largely irrelevant to problems such as environmental degradation or infectious disease.

Third, the main goals of statecraft and foreign policy have traditionally been defense of sovereignty and the promotion of national security. However, to critics of realism, these new transnational challenges suggest a need not only to sacrifice some national sovereignty but also to think beyond national security to a more inclusive notion of **human security**. This new concept focuses on the security of individual humans facing a wide range of political, military, economic, and environmental threats, not all of which directly emanate from other states (see Figure 8.1).

human security
View of security emphasizing protection of individuals from political, military, economic, and environmental threats; challenges the idea of "national security" as too state-centric.

The idea of human security achieved prominence in 1994, when it emerged as the central organizing theme of that year's United Nations Human Development Report. The report argued that the traditional notion of security interpreted "as security of territory from external aggression or as protection of national interests in foreign policy" is too narrow, as it overlooks "the legitimate concerns of ordinary people who sought security in their daily lives" from threats such as crime, hunger, disease, and environmental hazards.[3]

Skeptics have suggested that this idea of human security, encompassing as it does such a diverse range of problems, is too broad and vague to be useful either to international relations theorists or to policy-makers. However, to the extent that "human security" refers to more than a list of global problems but is also intended, as suggested above, as a new way to think about the essential nature of world politics, it presents a theoretical challenge to realism and a new perspective on how the world works. In examining the issues of the environment, disease, and the Internet in the following pages, these theoretical issues can be more clearly illustrated.

Figure 8.1 Two Approaches to Security

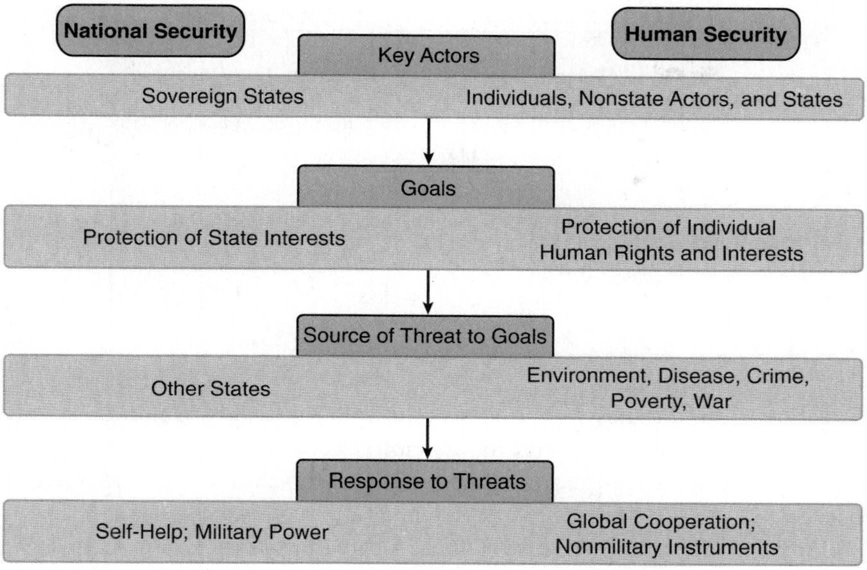

National Security	Key Actors	Human Security
Sovereign States		Individuals, Nonstate Actors, and States

	Goals	
Protection of State Interests		Protection of Individual Human Rights and Interests

	Source of Threat to Goals	
Other States		Environment, Disease, Crime, Poverty, War

	Response to Threats	
Self-Help; Military Power		Global Cooperation; Nonmilitary Instruments

The Global Environment

8-2 **Explain how transnational environmental problems pose a challenge to sovereign states, and assess how states cope with that challenge in the three response scenarios discussed in this section.**

In 1798 an English scholar by the name of Thomas Malthus penned his influential "An Essay on the Principle of Population." Malthus argued that the supply of food would not be able to keep up with growth in population and that only moral constraint limiting reproduction, combined with human disasters such as war, disease, and famine, would keep population growth in check. Today the **Malthusian** label can be loosely attached to those who argue that we live in a world of finite resources and limits to growth. Jettisoning Malthus's specific predictions and time lines, these contemporary Malthusians make two interrelated points: (1) growing demand for the earth's finite resources—energy, minerals, fresh water—is raising serious questions about future availability of those resources, and (2) the increasingly intensive exploitation of those resources is degrading the quality of the earth's environment.

In coming to terms with these Malthusian challenges, it is helpful to begin by distinguishing four different types of goods that people regularly consume: private goods, public goods, common pool resources, and club goods. Those four types of goods are distinguished from one another along two different

Malthusian
One influenced by Thomas Malthus who argued that the supply of food would not be able to keep up with the world population. Contemporary Malthusians argue that we live in a world of finite resources and that there are limits to growth.

Figure 8.2 Four Types of Goods

	Excludable	Non-Excludable
Rival	**Private Good** (food, clothing, cars)	**Common Pool Resource** (fisheries, well water)
Non-Rival	**Club Good** (cable TV)	**Public Good** (Wikipedia, public radio)

public good

A good or service whose benefits are freely available to all without possibility of exclusion and whose consumption by one individual does not limit the ability of others to consume that same good or service.

free-rider problem

The tendency of individuals or organizations to fail to contribute to the production of a public good or service, since those who do not contribute can continue to benefit from that good or service.

common pool resource

A good or service which is not excludable but whose supply is finite, thus causing one person's consumption to limit the ability of others to consume it.

tragedy of the commons

Concept popularized by ecologist Garrett Hardin, in which a common pool resource is exploited without anyone feeling a responsibility to protect it.

dimensions. First, are they excludable—that is, is it possible or not to exclude people from consuming the good in question? Second, are they rival—that is, does one person's consumption of that good limit the ability of others to enjoy its use?

Figure 8.2 illustrates these distinctions. A private good (e.g., a pizza) is both excludable and rival. People unwilling to pay can be excluded from eating a pizza, and a pizza is rival since my consumption of a slice means that slice is not available for others to eat. The opposite of a private good is a **public good**, which is both non-excludable and non-rival. A good example is Wikipedia. Whether or not you contribute to one of Wikipedia's periodic fundraising campaigns, you can continue to use the product, and your use of it does not limit anyone else's ability to do so. Such public goods are susceptible to the **free-rider problem**, whereby some benefit, without contribution, from the efforts of others. The two other types of goods are a club good, which is excludable but non-rival (e.g., cable TV), and a **common pool resource**, which is rival but not excludable (e.g., ocean fisheries). Common pool resources are susceptible to what ecologist Garrett Hardin termed the **tragedy of the commons**, in which a commonly available resource like a fishery is abused, exploited, and overused without anyone feeling a responsibility to protect it.[4]

Global environmental politics is all about common pool resources and public goods. For example, ocean fisheries or oil deposits in international waters are good examples of common pool resources (non-excludable but rival). To the extent that most natural resources are finite and rival, one might argue that they generally can be considered common pool resources. At the same time, the concept of a "global public good" has been increasingly utilized over the past decade or so to refer to things like a clean environment or the eradication of infectious diseases. According to the World Health Organization: "Public goods become global … in nature when the benefits flow to more than one country and no country can effectively be denied access to those benefits."[5] Countries can free-ride just as individuals do. Thus, the central global environmental challenge is rooted in finding ways to avoid the tragedy of the commons and the free-rider problem characteristic of common pool resources and global public goods. To illustrate that challenge, we will focus on two central and interrelated issues: energy and climate change. The discussion of those issues will then be followed by an examination of approaches to coping with the challenge presented. Are the Malthusians right, or is their pessimism overstated?

The Energy Challenge

Of all the world's scarce resources, none is more fundamental to economic growth and human well-being than energy. All aspects of human activity, including food production, manufacturing, transportation, and communications, depend on reliable sources of energy. Since the beginning of the industrial age, human economic activity has heavily depended for its energy needs on fossil fuels—coal, natural gas, and petroleum. While coal originally was the most important of the three, government and industry turned increasingly to petroleum as the primary energy source during the twentieth century. Compared to coal, oil was easier to transport, often cheaper, and it burned cleaner, thereby releasing fewer harmful toxins into the atmosphere. The rise of the automobile and the internal combustion engine, which relied on gasoline derived from petroleum, rapidly increased dependence on oil; by the last decades of the twentieth century, oil had become the lifeblood of all developed economies and crucial for all others seeking to develop.

The challenge for the twenty-first century is satisfying a rapidly increasing global demand for energy. According to US government data, global consumption of energy almost doubled between 1980 and 2012, and if you exclude the United States, Canada, Europe, and Japan, consumption in the rest of the world over that same period increased 450 percent.[6] Rapid economic growth in China and other developing countries is fueling the bulk of the increase in global energy demand. Between 1980 and 2012, Chinese energy consumption increased 600 percent, and in 2012 China was the world's largest energy user accounting for about 20 percent of global energy consumption.[7]

At the same time that demand is increasing, some contemporary Malthusians worry about the future supply of energy, especially oil. In recent years, some experts have suggested that the world is approaching **peak oil**, the point when global oil production reaches its peak and then starts to decline. While that decline is expected to be gradual, it would signal a turning point in the global energy economy that could set off a speculative panic and a rise in oil prices even beyond what the supply and demand situation would anticipate. Though some have predicted that peak oil will occur within a matter of years, a major study of world energy resources conducted by the United States Geological Survey (USGS), an agency of the US government, has suggested that the peak would not occur until the middle of the century.[8]

peak oil
The point at which the global production of oil peaks and then starts to decline.

Declining global oil prices in 2014 cooled some of the worry about peak oil, with many observers pointing to new technologies like fracking as the antidote to Malthusian pessimism. Yet even under the more optimistic scenarios, a continuing source of concern is the location of many of the world's most prolific oil fields in politically unstable regions. A 2014 report from the US Energy Information Administration, while noting that world supplies of oil should be adequate for at least the next 25 years, also notes that such projections are uncertain and assume the absence of geopolitical events capable of undercutting supply.[9] At the beginning of the twenty-first century, eight states in the politically volatile Persian Gulf/North African region (Saudi Arabia, Kuwait, the United Arab Emirates, Qatar, Iran, Iraq, Libya, Nigeria) accounted for approximately 69 percent of the world's proven reserves of oil. Add to that the 7.4 percent of proven world reserves found in Russia and several unstable former Soviet states along the Caspian Sea, and another 7.4 percent in Venezuela and one ends up with over 80 percent of global oil reserves in places where it is not hard to imagine politically generated disruptions of supply.[10]

Organization of Petroleum Exporting Countries (OPEC)

Cartel of oil-producing states, many located in the Middle East and Persian Gulf, who through the establishment of production quotas for member states seek to control the global supply and price of oil.

In fact, much recent volatility in world oil supplies and prices has been rooted in political causes. In the mid-1970s the first of the great oil shocks to hit the global economy was due to the effectiveness of the **Organization of Petroleum Exporting Countries (OPEC)** in artificially raising the global price of oil. Composed largely of Middle Eastern and Persian Gulf oil states, OPEC established production quotas for its member states that limited the amount of oil produced, reduced the global supply of oil available for export, and thereby raised both the price of oil and the revenues of oil-exporting countries. In 1979 the Soviet invasion of Afghanistan combined with the Iranian Revolution, which replaced the US-backed shah of Iran with an Islamic fundamentalist regime, led to a second politically inspired oil shock. By the end of the decade, a barrel of Persian Gulf oil, available for a couple of dollars at the beginning of the 1970s, hovered in the 40 dollar range.

In the early years of the twenty-first century, a combination of economic, political, and geological factors once again focused global attention on oil supplies and prices. The sustained growth in the Chinese thirst for oil continued to put long-term pressure on global oil supplies and prices. The terrorist attacks of September 11, 2001, the subsequent war on terror launched by the Bush administration, and the war in Iraq together reminded the world of how much it depended for the bulk of its oil on the politically unstable Middle East and Persian Gulf region. And the April 2010 explosion of British Petroleum's ultra-deepwater offshore drilling rig, Deepwater Horizon, and the subsequent disastrous oil spill into the Gulf of Mexico led some to suggest that even if we are not in an era of "peak oil," it is an era of "tough oil" as the search for new supplies will necessitate drilling in less accessible and more environmentally fragile locations.

The Climate Change Challenge

In 1995, US President Bill Clinton had an intriguing conversation with his Chinese counterpart, Jiang Zemin. In an interview with New York Times columnist Thomas Friedman, Clinton noted that the Chinese president asked about US attitudes and intentions toward China. Clinton surprised the Chinese president in noting that the greatest security concern posed by China to the United States had little to do with Chinese military power or policy toward Taiwan, but, instead, that the Chinese people "will want to get rich in exactly the same way we got rich." Clinton went on to talk about the impact of more than one billion Chinese driving cars and emitting greenhouse gases on a scale matching that of individual Americans, and he suggested that would lead to environmental catastrophe.[11]

In the years since that conversation, concern over the environmental challenge posed by fossil fuel emissions and their impact both on air quality and climate change has grown more intense. Since most scientists believe that burning fossil fuels contributes to climate change, any solution to the energy challenge that is based on finding and using more oil, gas, or coal will likely exacerbate this problem.

Climate change refers to any extended alteration in Earth's climate produced by natural factors, human activities, or some combination of the two. Currently, the central climate change concern is **global warming**—the increase in the average temperature of Earth's lower atmosphere. Experts disagree on specific dimensions of the challenge: how much warming we might anticipate, how severe the consequences might be, and what the time line is for all these developments. However, widespread consensus exists among climate scientists on certain basic questions.

First, most scientists agree that the Earth is warming. The US Environmental Protection Agency (EPA) notes that from 1901 to 2013, the surface temperature of Earth has increased at an average rate of 0.15°F per decade—a total increase in temperature over that period of roughly 1.65°F—and that 2001–2010 was the warmest decade on record since thermometer-based observations began.[12] Furthermore, the EPA expects the pace of warming in the twenty-first century to accelerate, with average global temperature increasing another 2–11.5°F by 2100, depending on the pace of greenhouse gas emissions and the climate projection model utilized.[13] In 2013 the Intergovernmental Panel on Climate Change (IPCC) established by the United Nations confirmed the assessment that "warming of the climate system is unequivocal," that "each of the last three decades has been successively warmer at the Earth's surface than any preceding decade since 1850," and that "in the Northern Hemisphere, 1983–2012 was likely the warmest 30-year period of the last 1400 years."[14]

Second, the scientific consensus is that this global warming cannot be explained entirely by natural factors. This view was confirmed by the IPCC, which suggests both that it is "extremely likely" that over half of the observed increase in

climate change
An extended alteration in Earth's climate produced by natural factors, human activities, or some combination of the two.

global warming
An increase in the average temperature of Earth's atmosphere produced by natural factors, human activities, or some combination of the two.

surface temperature from 1951 to 2010 was anthropogenic (human generated) and that the evidence of the anthropogenic sources of climate change has increased over time.[15] The major human contributions to global warming come from burning fossil fuels and from deforestation. Burning fossil fuels in cars, homes, and businesses emits carbon dioxide, methane, and other greenhouse gases that trap heat in our atmosphere. While some quantity of such gases is natural and, indeed, essential to keep Earth warm enough for human survival, over the past two centuries the Industrial Revolution has produced a rapid increase in the presence of such gases. This trend has been further exacerbated by deforestation, which has reduced the presence of trees and other plant life that absorb carbon dioxide.

Third, there is concern that climate change, if unabated, will have costly effects on human health and life. For example, warming is already melting glaciers and polar ice caps, which in turn leads to rising sea levels and potential flooding and permanent submersion of coastal territories. Global warming could also shift patterns of human agriculture, bringing longer growing seasons to some locations but excessive heat and drought to others. Warming can also impact the spread of climate-sensitive diseases, especially those spread via insects, as it can extend the geographic range of disease transmission as well as the duration of disease transmission seasons.[16] Some see these effects as potentially catastrophic, while others caution against exaggeration and hysteria, but almost all scientific observers believe that significant potential exists for harmful effects if global warming is left unchecked.

This climate change consensus came under attack in late 2009 when hundreds of private e-mail messages and scientific documents on the server of a prominent British university were unearthed by computer hackers. The e-mails discussed tactics for combating climate change skeptics, derisive comments about those critics, and, perhaps most damning, discussion of how to engage in statistical "tricks" to hide some recent evidence of a decline in temperatures.[17] While some have argued that the e-mails provide cause to seriously undermine the prevailing climate change orthodoxy, others, indeed the vast majority of scientists, have argued that notwithstanding the questionable behavior of a few of their colleagues, the evidence remains overwhelming that the climate change threat is both real and serious.

While oil shortages and climate change are perhaps the most dramatic and widely discussed resource and environmental threats facing Earth and its human inhabitants, they are not the only such challenges we face. On the resource front, some observers expect that in parts of the world, shortages of water may soon rival shortages of energy as a reason for concern. On the pollution front, smog, degradation of lakes and streams, and acid rain, though lacking the drama of global climate change, also have significant adverse health, economic, and quality-of-life consequences.

Most important, what all these environmental challenges share is a disregard for sovereign borders. Pollution from factories in Detroit produces acid rain across the border in Canada; increased energy consumption in India raises the price of oil in the United States; new coal-fired plants being built in China at a rate of one per week will increase the emissions of greenhouse gases that may nullify European Union efforts to combat global warming. In 2006 an "Asian brown cloud" produced largely by Chinese pollution drifted over the Korean Peninsula before making its way across the Pacific Ocean. Using a US satellite to track the cloud as it made its way over US territory, scientists detected a rise in dangerous pollutants associated with cancer, heart disease, and respiratory ailments. One scientist found that filters deployed to measure pollution in the mountains of eastern California were "the darkest that we've seen" outside urban areas.[18] In 2008 concerns ran high that pollution would harm the health and performance of athletes participating in the Beijing Olympics. While air quality during the games was the best Beijing had experienced in years, that was only because the Chinese government had temporarily closed many factories and placed restrictions on automobiles in the weeks preceding the start of the games. In 2012, a new study suggested that the annual drifting of the Asian brown cloud to the United States could warm the United States by 0.4°C (0.72°F) by 2024.[19]

Responses to the Challenge: Three Scenarios

Experts have imagined a wide range of possible responses to the myriad and often interlinked global environmental challenges of the twenty-first century. However, most scenarios fall into one of three broad categories: (1) geopolitical conflict, (2) markets and technology to the rescue, or (3) effective global regulation. While many observers might emphasize the greater likelihood of one outcome over the others, they are not necessarily mutually exclusive.

GLOBAL CONFLICT   The realist paradigm does not, of course, offer any opinion on the relative scarcity or abundance of a resource such as petroleum or on the causes or severity of global climate change. What realism does contribute to the discussion is an expectation that states will attempt to respond to these challenges by putting their own interests first even if, as is likely, that comes at the expense of other states. Thus, realists see global environmental problems as yet another potential source of international tension and conflict. The most immediate source of that conflict is likely to be competition for scarce resources.

Geopolitical conflict over resources is hardly a novel development. Japan's surprise attack on the US fleet at Pearl Harbor on December 7, 1941, was intended to preempt a US naval response to seizure of oil fields in Southeast Asia. Iraq's August 1990 attack on Kuwait aimed at control over the rich Kuwaiti oil fields and the revenues they generate. The US-led global military coalition that evicted Iraqi forces from Kuwait in the 1991 Persian Gulf War sought to ensure that Saddam Hussein did not seize control of Persian Gulf oil.

The United States is not the only outside power with a vital stake in access to global oil supplies and other important resources. Japan, the European

Union, Russia, and China have interests in this area. Anticipating that by 2025 approximately 75 percent of its thirst for oil will have to be met via imports, China has actively forged political ties with oil-producing states. Meanwhile, its state-owned firms have been heavily investing in foreign oil fields from Africa to Latin America and securing, in the process, long-term contracts for oil deliveries. In places like Sudan, where China has sought to buffer a genocidal regime from foreign sanctions, and in oil-rich Venezuela, where it has signed energy deals with the overtly anti-American regime, China is going head to head with the United States both economically and politically. Short of a major breakthrough in alternative energy supplies, pessimistic observers see the United States and China on an oil-slicked collision course.

That collision course potentially extends to the farthest regions of the Earth. In late 2014, Chinese President XI Jinping was on an icebreaker close to Antarctica pledging an expansion of Chinese efforts to study and explore the continent, with many observers working on the assumption that his main interest is the region's untapped resources.[20] Similarly, one recent study estimated that a quarter of the world's undiscovered petroleum might be in the Arctic region, and that is certainly one reason why Russia, in late 2014, established a new Arctic Military Command to coordinate the defense of Russian national interests in the region.[21]

Climate change could also have negative geopolitical consequences. In fact, one of the reasons that the Arctic has received so much attention of late is precisely because polar melting has opened up sea lanes and increased the prospects for tapping Arctic resources. More generally, a 2004 report released by the US Department of Defense's internal think tank, the Office of Net Assessments, caused a stir with its scenario for abrupt climate change. The report envisions dramatic annual temperature increases of 4°F in much of the Southern Hemisphere, along with even greater drops in temperature in much of the Northern Hemisphere, including Europe and the United States. These sudden changes would produce drought, food shortages, decreased availability of fresh water, and disruption of access to energy supplies (see Theory in Practice 8.1).

The authors of the report stress that they were painting a worst-case scenario, not necessarily predicting that this scenario would occur. Nonetheless, the report speculates about the geopolitical conflict that climate change could engender:

> As famine, disease, and weather-related disasters strike due to the abrupt climate change, many countries' needs will exceed their carrying capacity. This will create a sense of desperation, which is likely to lead to offensive aggression in order to reclaim balance. Imagine eastern European countries, struggling to feed their populations with a falling supply of food, water, and energy, eyeing Russia, whose population is already in decline, for access to its grain, minerals, and energy supply. Or, picture Japan, suffering from flooding along its coastal cities and contamination of its fresh water supply, eyeing Russia's Sakhalin Island oil and gas reserves as an

Theory in Practice 8.1
Climate Change and the Darfur Conflict

The conflict that has raged in the Darfur region of Sudan since 2003 has taken hundreds of thousands of lives and has displaced millions more. It is most often interpreted as yet another case of unfathomable ethnic or racial hatred pitting Arabs against black Africans. Yet according to journalist Stephan Faris, the roots of the conflict, and the genocidal results it has produced, might be traceable to global warming.

According to this interpretation, the black African farmers and the nomadic Arabs on their horses and camels once lived in peace with one another. The latter grazed their animals on the hillsides between the farmers' crops, generally without conflict and often sharing water from the farmers' wells. However, as drought descended on the region in the 1980s, farmers began to fence off their land, making it difficult for the Arabs to graze their animals. Some Arabs attempted to seize land from the farmers. By the late 1980s the language of racial superiority was being used to justify such actions, and it was around this time that the Janjaweed—the Arab militias responsible for much of the killing—was born.

The drought that sparked this conflict was once thought to be a result of poor farming techniques and land use by the region's inhabitants. But Faris cites expert studies pointing out that most of the deteriorating conditions can be attributed to changes in ocean temperatures out of the control of the people and the state of Sudan. Thus, the Darfur crisis illustrates both the limitations and continued persistence of a state-centric approach to understanding world politics. The original cause of the crisis was climate change, a global trend that no single state can control. This challenges the realist emphasis on the continued power and centrality of the sovereign state. At the same time, at many turns, the Sudanese government effectively blocked the international response to the bloodshed in Darfur by claiming sovereign control over events happening in its territory. So realists might cite the Darfur case as evidence that states and the international community still take sovereignty seriously.

- To what extent do developed countries that have contributed most to climate change owe assistance to poor countries in dealing with the impact of that climate change?

- Is the global challenge posed by climate change more likely to lead to international conflict or cooperation? Explain.

- Does the Darfur case do more to support or challenge the realist perspective on world politics? Explain.

SOURCE: Stephan Faris, "The Real Roots of Darfur," *Atlantic Monthly*, April 2007, 67–69.

---

energy source to power desalination plants and energy-intensive agricultural processes. Envision Pakistan, India, and China—all armed with nuclear weapons—skirmishing at their borders over refugees, access to shared rivers, and arable land. Spanish and Portuguese fishermen might fight over fishing rights—leading to conflicts at sea.[22]

While the report envisions the United States managing the challenges of abrupt climate change better than many other countries, that in itself, the report suggests, will pose a security challenge, as it will invite a dramatic surge in both refugees and resentment from the rest of the world.

In short, for realists, the expectation that global environmental crisis will lead to cooperative responses is both naive and contrary to the record of human history. If the Pentagon report is any indication of how states will behave in the face of an acute environmental crisis, then the future looks bleak. Thus, for environmental activists and others who seek to avoid that pessimistic scenario, global cooperation now, while we still have time, is essential.

GLOBAL REGULATION   While realists see global environmental challenges as another potential source of interstate conflict, liberals and constructivists see the potential for cooperation and regulation to address common global problems. Government regulation, such as the establishment of emissions standards for business, industry, and transportation is, of course, a common domestic approach to environmental free-riding. Coupled with threats of fines or imprisonment, regulation can help ensure that all relevant actors contribute to a public good (clean air). Many argue, however, that regulation at the nation-state level is not enough. States can also free-ride on global public goods. If, hypothetically, Brazil has strict air pollution standards but Argentina does not, then Argentina benefits from Brazil's high standards, while Brazilians are negatively impacted by Argentinean pollution.

There have been some noteworthy efforts at global regulation. In 1985 the Vienna Convention for the Protection of the Ozone Layer was adopted and provided the framework for the 1987 **Montreal Protocol**, which aimed to phase out use of substances that were depleting the atmosphere's ozone layer. Ozone is crucial to protect Earth from the sun's harmful ultraviolet rays. By 2009 all countries in the United Nations were party to the protocol. Most significantly, the original 1987 treaty together with its six subsequent revisions have significantly reduced the amount of ozone-depleting CFCs (chlorofluorocarbons) in the atmosphere. Former UN Secretary-General Kofi Annan once suggested that this agreement was "perhaps the most successful environmental agreement to date."[23]

Unfortunately, HFCs (hydrofluorocarbons) have replaced CFCs for such uses as refrigerants in air conditioners and propellants in aerosol cans, and while they have no negative ozone-depleting impact, they do contribute to global warming—indeed, much more so than the now banned CFCs. HFCs are one of six greenhouse gases (GHGs) targeted for reduced use by another global agreement, the **Kyoto Protocol** adopted in 1997. Kyoto was an update of the 1992 United Nations Framework Convention on Climate Change (UNFCCC), and it set national targets for reductions in GHG emissions. It went into force in 2005, when the requisite 55 states ratified the agreement—with the number of ratifications eventually expanding to 192.[24] Kyoto created an **emissions trading**, or "cap and trade," system that combines government regulation with market incentives. National caps are set on the allowed levels of GHG emissions. For developed countries (so-called Annex 1 states) those caps are legally binding; for developing counties (non-annex countries) they are nonbinding goals. Countries and firms whose emissions are below the cap can sell unused emissions credits to other countries and firms having difficulty meeting their established caps. The rationale is that climate change is a global problem, and it does not matter where in the world emissions are reduced as long as total global emissions decline.

Montreal Protocol

The 1987 agreement whereby countries aimed to phase out the use of substances depleting the ozone layer.

Kyoto Protocol

The 1997 agreement updating the 1992 UN Framework Convention on Climate Change. Kyoto set national targets for reductions in greenhouse gas emissions.

emissions trading

System whereby countries whose greenhouse gas emissions are below the cap set by Kyoto Protocol can sell unused emissions credits to other countries and firms having difficulty meeting their caps. Also known as a "cap and trade" system.

A major nonparticipant in the Kyoto Protocol was the United States. US refusal to ratify was rooted in two primary concerns: the perceived cost to the US economy of compliance with the Kyoto targets and the exemption granted to developing countries from binding requirements. Given that in 2006 China bypassed the United States as the world's greatest annual GHG emitter and has become, by far, the world's single largest source of new GHG emissions (see Figure 8.3), the United States objected particularly strenuously to China's status as a non-annex country without legally binding emissions caps.[25] In response, China and other developing countries argue that developed countries like the United States should bear the greater burden both because they are responsible for the bulk of the GHGs already emitted and because developed countries tend to be the worst emitters on a per capita basis. For example, while China was responsible for more total emissions in 2010 than was the United States, on a per capita basis US emissions were almost 300 percent higher than China (17.6 vs. 6.2 metric tons per person).[26]

With the Kyoto Protocol set to expire in 2012, the December 2009 Copenhagen Climate Summit, formally the Fifteenth Session of the Conference of the Parties to the United Nations Framework Convention on Climate Change (COP15), took place with the goal of agreeing to a framework for further mitigation of climate change. From the beginning, the summit was marked by acrimony as developed and developing countries disagreed over who should bear the burden for combating climate change. China, in particular, was reluctant to accept any agreement with strict, binding emissions limits that might impinge on its "right to develop." Anxious to salvage an agreement, the Obama administration pledged to work with other developed countries to raise $100 billion to help developing countries adjust to stricter climate standards, and Obama himself made an eleventh-hour trip to Copenhagen to help negotiate a deal. Despite such efforts, those who had hoped for a tough, legally binding agreement were disappointed. The final Copenhagen Accord was less ambitious in setting goals for reducing emissions and future global temperature increases than many environmentalists thought necessary, and the agreement itself was a political statement of aspirations rather than the legally binding treaty that many hoped would replace the Kyoto Protocol.

At COP18 held in Doha in 2012, a more formal agreement emerged. The "Doha Amendment" revised the list of greenhouse gases to be included in country reporting, it established new commitments of GHG reductions for the developed, Annex 1 countries to meet, and, most importantly, it established a "second commitment period" that would extend Kyoto from 2013 to 2020. The idea was to maintain momentum in the effort to reduce greenhouse gases pending negotiation of an entirely new treaty to cover the period after 2020. However, as of April 2015 only 28 countries representing less than 20 percent of global GHG emissions (and far less than even that if you only count Annex 1 ratifications) had ratified the Doha Amendment—far short of the 144 ratifications necessary for the agreement to enter into force.[27] Some countries, most notably the United

Figure 8.3 Contributors to Global Warming, 2012

Note: Percentages calculated from data available from US Department of Energy, Energy Information Administration, *Total Carbon Dioxide Emissions from the Consumption of Energy (Million Metric Tons)*, http://www.eia.gov/cfapps/ipdbproject/IEDIndex3 .cfm?tid=90&pid=44&aid=8.

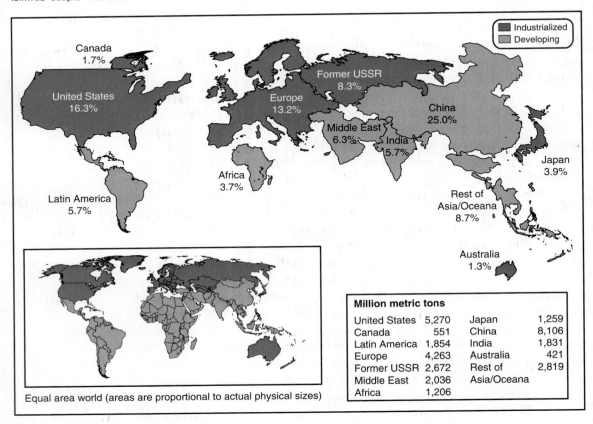

Million metric tons			
United States	5,270	Japan	1,259
Canada	551	China	8,106
Latin America	1,854	India	1,831
Europe	4,263	Australia	421
Former USSR	2,672	Rest of	2,819
Middle East	2,036	Asia/Oceana	
Africa	1,206		

Equal area world (areas are proportional to actual physical sizes)

States, Russia, Japan, Canada, and New Zealand have, in fact, served notice that they would not be participating in the Doha Amendment. Canada, in fact, facing penalties for failing to meet its binding Kyoto emission reduction commitments, withdrew from the Kyoto Protocol in 2011.

The overall record of Kyoto is mixed. On the one hand, the developed countries with binding emissions limits succeeded, on average, in meeting their required emission reductions as required by Kyoto. That success is mitigated, however, by three factors: (1) the nonparticipation of the United States, (2) the fact that the 2008 global economic crisis slowed both growth and associated emissions, and (3) the fact that some of the calculated reduction was due to economic slowdowns in economies in transition (post-Communist states). More generally, the UN's Intergovernmental Panel on Climate Change (IPCC) reports that despite Kyoto and other national climate change reduction policies, anthropogenic GHG emissions have continued to grow.[28] Meanwhile, the path forward to a post-Kyoto agreement remains uncertain at best. In short, what one might say is that while the situation would likely be worse in the absence of Kyoto, one cannot yet say that Kyoto, or global regulation in general, has solved the climate change challenge.

MARKETS AND TECHNOLOGY   As previously discussed, Malthusians argue that increasingly intense exploitation of the world's finite resources is putting unsustainable stress on the earth's environment. Critics, however, note that this Malthusian pessimism has been frequently proven wrong because it underestimates the combined power of markets and technological innovation. Put simply, the argument is that when a resource becomes scarce, its price rises, thereby providing an incentive for investors—both public and private—to find new supplies or substitutes for that resource or to develop technologies that use the resource more efficiently. For example, stimulated by concerns about global food shortages, the **green revolution** of the post–World War II era relied on a mix of private and public funding to discover and introduce new strains of high-yielding rice, wheat, and other crops, significantly increasing agricultural production throughout much of the developing world.

green revolution
Post–World War II introduction of new strains of high-yielding rice, wheat, and other crops resulting in significant increases in agricultural production.

Stimulated by the rising oil prices of the immediate post-9/11 era, oil companies developed technologies to extract large supplies of oil that they once left behind because the cost of extraction would have been higher than the market price for that oil. Thus, while a 2000 US government study estimated that the world held about 3.3 trillion recoverable barrels of oil, a subsequent study by a private research firm revised that estimate upward to 4.8 trillion barrels. Similarly, some observers suggest that Saudi Arabia's officially declared reserves of 260 billion barrels may be underestimated, and that recoverable reserves are two or even three times that official figure.[29]

Perhaps the most significant new technology to come along and shape global energy markets in recent years has been hydraulic fracturing, more

Fracking wells on Colorado's Roan Plateau. What are the costs and benefits of fracking (economic, environmental, and geopolitical), and which, in your judgment, are more significant?

fracking

Process that involves injecting water under high pressure deep under the ground into low-permeability rocks like shale or tight sandstone in order to increase the flow of oil or gas.

commonly known as fracking. **Fracking** is a process that involves injecting water under high pressure deep under the ground into low-permeability rocks like shale or tight sandstone in order to increase the flow of oil or gas.[30] Use of the process is most advanced in the United States where it has revolutionized the energy industry. Due in large part to resulting increases in domestic energy production, imports in 2013 accounted for only 13 percent of total US energy consumption, compared to 30 percent in 2005.[31] The impact is not limited to the United States, as the increase in the global supply of energy represented by this new American production has increased global supplies and contributed to a fall in global prices of oil and other fossil fuels.

Fracking proponents argue that the technique is a perfect illustration of how the combination of markets and innovation have belied claims of global energy shortage and have, once again, made Malthusian pessimism seem short-sighted. In contributing to falling energy prices, fracking supporters argue that it has been an economic boon to the United States and other energy-importing countries—many of which are poor countries in the developing world. It has also had a geopolitical impact insofar as it lessens US dependence on Middle Eastern oil and undercuts the geopolitical hand of US adversaries like Russia and Iran—both of which are highly dependent on high energy prices to balance their budgets. In addition, supporters argue that fracking is a green technology because it is a "coal killer." Cheaper gas produced via fracking has replaced much less environmentally friendly coal, and that has contributed directly to a decline in carbon emissions in the United States that is greater than in any other country in recent years.[32] However, fracking opponents dispute its characterization as a green technology. The fracking process itself has been criticized for leading both to groundwater contamination and increased risk of earthquakes. Perhaps even more significant is the fear that in lowering the cost of fossil fuels, fracking will undercut the incentive both to develop alternative sources of energy to replace fossil fuels and to invest in the development of more energy efficient products.

In the United States, transportation is by far the biggest user of petroleum; 40 percent of all petroleum used by Americans goes to fuel our cars, SUVs, vans, and pick-ups.[33] New technologies already in use that reduce oil consumption include hybrid vehicles, which run on a combination of gasoline and electric batteries along with **biofuels** produced from crops like corn, soy beans, or sugar cane. The world leader in the movement toward biofuels has been Brazil, where half of all cars can run fully on ethanol, mainly produced in Brazil from sugar cane, and where biofuels have replaced more than a third of gasoline consumption. A more radical new technology for the future may be hydrogen fuel cells.

biofuels

Fuels produced from biomass, including crops like corn, soybeans, or sugar cane, which can be converted into liquid and combined with petroleum-based fuels to provide energy for transportation.

Innovation in sectors besides transportation is also important. Industry and agriculture along with the energy needs of homes, businesses, and government offices for heat and electricity make up the bulk of our overall energy consumption.[34] Some observers, including influential *New York Times* columnist Thomas Friedman, suggest that China, whose rapid economic development has created many of the world's most polluted cities, may take the lead in developing new green technologies in all these areas. US President Barack Obama made the development of "green technology" one of his early priorities as well, arguing not only that it is environmentally urgent but also a major source of twenty-first-century industry and jobs.

To be sure, big questions surround these innovations. Hydrogen fuel cells remain a very expensive and, at this point, largely theoretical replacement for the internal combustion engine, with no assurance that they will ever be feasible for mass use. Expansion of biofuel usage on a global scale increases the demand for crops such as corn and soy and, absent increased production, leads to higher prices for food that hurt the poor especially hard. At the same time, expanded agricultural production raises land use and deforestation problems, with their own severe environmental effects. Still, market-oriented optimists suggest that while we don't yet have the specific technological solutions to the climate change challenge, the historical record provides reason to believe that human ingenuity combined with the right incentives may provide a solution that no one now can fully envision.

Global Health and Disease

8-3 **Explain how infectious diseases challenge the essence of the state system, and discuss how globalization has contributed to that challenge.**

Like greenhouse gases and other pollutants, the viruses and bacteria that cause human disease, along with the birds and other animals that help spread them, have never paid any attention to the political boundaries that humans superimpose on the map of the world. Though effective domestic health-care policies, including sound nutrition, vaccinations, early detection, and pharmacological treatments, can limit the impact and spread of many diseases, such policies cannot completely insulate even the most advanced countries from health threats outside their borders. Traditional instruments of national security, including soldiers, guns, and tanks, provide little protection. In the globalization era, the increasing interconnectedness of the world has magnified the challenge of global disease.

The Reemergence of Infectious Disease

The transnational movement of birds, animals, soldiers, and travelers has always facilitated the migration of disease. The bubonic plague, or "black death," that swept Europe in the fourteenth century killed an estimated 25 million people as it was transmitted from rats to fleas to people without concern for nationality or sovereign borders. More recently, the influenza pandemic that swept the world from 1918 to 1920 killed approximately 50 million, more than twice the estimates of military and civilian deaths produced by World War I.

In the post–World War II era, however, infectious diseases were thought to be a thing of the past. In the most developed countries, antibiotics and immunizations, combined with improvements in health care, hygiene, and nutrition, all but eliminated the fear of such diseases as tuberculosis and polio. Meanwhile, in the developing world, the use of insecticides to combat disease-carrying mosquitoes and the efforts of international organizations like the **World Health Organization (WHO)** to vaccinate the poor and improve the water supply seemed to promise an end to "poor people's diseases" like cholera and malaria.

By the 1980s, however, such optimism began to look very naive. On the one hand, several old diseases reemerged as global health threats:

World Health Organization (WHO)
Agency of the UN with responsibility for directing and coordinating international efforts to maintain and improve global health.

- **Tuberculosis:** If the introduction of antibiotics seemed to promise an end to tuberculosis (TB) in the years following World War II, that promise has been left unfulfilled. According to the WHO, 9 million people contracted and 1.5 million people died from TB in 2013.[35] Most worrisome has been the emergence of drug-resistant varieties of the TB bacterium.
- **Malaria:** What antibiotics promised to do for tuberculosis eradication, DDT and other insecticides promised to do for the fight against malaria. By the 1980s, however, the goal of worldwide eradication was abandoned and replaced by the more modest objectives of control and treatment. The good news since then is that malaria death rates have fallen by almost half since 2000. The bad news is that there were still 198 million cases in 2013, with over a half million deaths—mainly among African children.[36]
- **Cholera:** The WHO estimates that there are still 3–5 million cases per year producing over 100,000 deaths.[37] People catch the disease mainly by drinking infected water, but treatment of cholera has also been complicated by the emergence of drug-resistant strains.

While the failure to eradicate these old diseases has been a source of concern, perhaps even more alarming has been the emergence of new infectious diseases. According to scientists, new, deadly disease-causing pathogens are being identified at an unprecedented rate of one per year.[38] The primary concern is that some of those diseases could develop into a **pandemic**—the global spread of an infectious disease among humans who, because the pathogen is new, lack any natural immunity. Among these new diseases are the following:

pandemic
The global spread of an infectious disease, typically the result of the emergence of a new pathogen to which people lack any natural immunity.

- **HIV/AIDS:** Since it was first detected in 1981, approximately 39 million people worldwide have died of AIDS.[39] Though progress has been made in treating AIDS and in slowing new transmissions, the problem remains acute. In 2013 alone, the WHO estimated that 35 million people were infected with the HIV virus, 2.1 million of them were newly infected that year, and 1.5 million died of AIDS and its complications. The hardest hit region is sub-Saharan Africa, which accounts for about 70 percent of the world population currently infected by the virus, but globally there is no region unaffected by the epidemic (see Figure 8.4).

Figure 8.4 Global HIV Distribution: Adults and Children Living with HIV in 2013

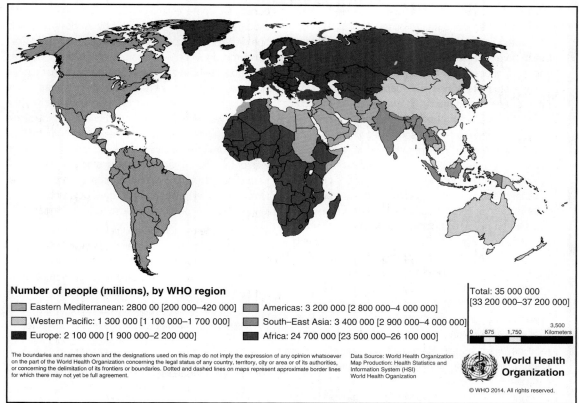

**Adults and children estimated to be living with HIV, 2013
By WHO region**

Number of people (millions), by WHO region

- Eastern Mediterranean: 2800 00 [200 000–420 000]
- Western Pacific: 1 300 000 [1 100 000–1 700 000]
- Europe: 2 100 000 [1 900 000–2 200 000]
- Americas: 3 200 000 [2 800 000–4 000 000]
- South–East Asia: 3 400 000 [2 900 000–4 000 000]
- Africa: 24 700 000 [23 500 000–26 100 000]

Total: 35 000 000
[33 200 000–37 200 000]

0   875   1,750   3,500 Kilometers

Data Source: World Health Organization
Map Production: Health Statistics and Information System (HSI)
World Health Oganization

**World Health
Organization**

- **Ebola:** Ebola made its first appearance in 1976. It is a severe disease characterized by vomiting, diarrhea, and sometimes internal and external bleeding. Average fatality rate is 50 percent, but can range as high as 90 percent in some outbreaks.[40] The most recent outbreak that began in West Africa in March 2014 was the most serious yet, producing (as of February 2015) more cases (22,790) and deaths (9,151) than all previous outbreaks combined. Human to human transmission, to this point, requires direct contact with the blood or bodily fluids of infected people, thus most transmissions have been to family members, health-care workers, and other caregivers.

- **New strains of influenza:** While influenza is not a new disease, new strains, to which humans have no immunity, are emerging all of the time.

Theory in Practice 8.2

Ebola vs. the Flu: The Risks of a Pandemic

Despite only a handful of US Ebola cases and just two confirmed deaths, the 2014 Ebola outbreak caused panic in the United States. For much of 2014 Ebola dominated US headlines, controversial quarantines of health-care workers returning from West Africa were imposed, and schools and universities were hesitating to enroll students or host guest speakers coming from parts of Africa. In contrast, 2014 seldom saw discussions of pandemic flu reach the front page, and it was treated by the public with a sense of complacency.

The difference in perception is understandable. Ebola is an exotic disease that produces horrible symptoms and, especially in its most recent outbreak, is usually fatal. The flu, in contrast, is a disease that, in its milder varieties, most people have endured and survived on numerous occasions. Moreover, pervious warnings from experts of possible flu pandemics (e.g., the 2009 scare over H1N1 swine flu) were not followed by anything approaching the worst-case scenarios, leading to a "cried wolf" attitude among the public.

Yet the threat of pandemic flu is considered by experts to be far greater than Ebola. Compared to the flu, Ebola is not highly contagious. Ebola transmission requires direct human to human contact with bodily fluids, unlike flu which is an airborne pathogen that can be transmitted via a cough or a sneeze. If you are sitting in an airplane, you are in much greater danger if the person sitting next to you has H5N1 flu than if he has Ebola. Thus Ebola outbreaks tend to be more localized, especially in poorer places where basic health-care procedures and equipment are lacking. The chances of an outbreak of Ebola on the scale of the recent West African outbreak in a developed country like the United States is highly remote.

In contrast, the 1918 Spanish flu outbreak produced, by some estimates, 50 million deaths worldwide (more deaths than caused by World War I), and one well-known expert speculated that a global H5N1 pandemic could be even more deadly with as many as 16 million deaths in the United States alone. That is more Americans dead than were killed in all of the wars fought in US history. Indeed, a 2015 report published by the British government identified pandemic flu as the single most significant civil emergency risk faced, greater than flooding, drought, other emerging diseases, civil unrest, war, or terrorism. That report suggested that the magnitude of pandemic flu would be as great as a catastrophic terror attack using weapons of mass destruction, but it judged the likelihood of pandemic flu to be higher.

- Given the magnitude and risk of a pandemic flu outbreak as described above, would it make sense to divert resources from traditional military expenditures to research and prevention efforts on influenza and other infectious diseases?

- Does the threat of a global pandemic require a reversal of the globalization that has characterized the world in recent decades? Could we reverse it even if we wanted to?

- Should global disease considerations lead students and universities to scale back student exchanges and study-abroad programs?

SOURCES: Laurie Garrett, "The Next Pandemic?" *Foreign Affairs*, July/August 2005, http://www.foreignaffairs.org; Cabinet Office, "National Risk Register for Civil Emergencies," March 27, 2015, https://www.gov.uk/government/publications/national-risk-register-for-civil-emergencies-2015-edition.

One of the more worrisome strains in recent years is a subtype of avian influenza, or "bird flu," known as H5N1, which emerged in Asia in 2003. From 2003 to March 2015 there were 826 confirmed human cases of H5N1 leading to 440 deaths in 16 different countries.[41] While the numbers remain relatively low, the high mortality rate among those infected makes it a continuing cause of concern among health experts (see Theory in Practice 8.2).

The emergence of these diseases should not be surprising. History has always involved a struggle between new, frequently mutating, disease-causing microbes and their human hosts. However, what makes infectious diseases today potentially more challenging is the new context of globalization in which they emerge.

Globalization and Disease

The policies and technologies that have facilitated the trade, investment, travel, and cultural interaction characteristic of globalization also provide a perfect environment for the emergence of global pandemics. The most obvious connection is the expansion of air travel. As people crisscross the globe, they can, along with their luggage and briefcases, carry microbes that spread disease. In the fifteenth and sixteenth centuries, it took about a year for an infectious disease like smallpox to spread around the world; today, air travel allows an infection to move from one spot to any other on the planet in 36 hours or less. Given the incubation periods—the period between infection and development of symptoms—an infected traveler can hop on a plane and travel across the globe, infecting others along the way without realizing that he or she is sick.[42]

An interesting study took advantage of the shifts in the volume of air travel produced by the 9/11 terror attacks by comparing the speed of global influenza transmission before and afterwards. During the 1997–1998 flu season, it took 26 days for influenza to spread from abroad to the United States; with increased air travel, during the 2000–2001 season, that time period fell to 11 days. In the 2001–2002 season, air traffic volume to the United States declined significantly due to post-9/11 fears and restrictions, and, as a result, the time it took for influenza to spread to the United States crept up a bit, to 16 days. In France, where such restrictions were not imposed, the spread of influenza did not slow.[43]

The 50 million killed by the Spanish flu pandemic of 1918 can also be understood in connection to globalization. While international travel by civilians during the first globalization era of the early twentieth century was still, in comparison to twenty-first-century standards, very limited, international travel of another sort was made necessary by World War I. It was the international movement of soldiers back and forth to the battlefields of Europe that, according to some recent studies, facilitated the spread of influenza.[44]

Increased global travel is not the only way in which globalization facilitates the transnational spread of disease. The globalization era has also witnessed a massive increase in food trade. Roughly 20 percent of the US food supply is imported, including about a third of fresh produce and over two thirds of seafood.[45] While consumers can now eat nectarines and peaches year-round, this convenience comes with risks. Here are a few documented examples of global transmission of disease via food, as noted by the World Health Organization:[46]

- In Latin America, the reemergence and spread of cholera in the 1990s after a century free of the disease were due, at least in part, to contamination of imported seafood.

- Bovine spongiform encephalopathy (BSE), or "mad cow disease," was first discovered in the United Kingdom in 1982, and it then spread via food exports to the rest of the EU and Japan. Human affliction has been concentrated in the United Kingdom, but cases elsewhere have been reported.
- The *E. coli* bacteria is an emerging pathogen first noted and described in 1982. It is spread mainly via beef consumption but sometimes through lettuce, alfalfa sprouts, and other foods. Outbreaks have occurred in Australia, Canada, Japan, the United States, the EU, and South Africa.
- In 1996–1997, a large outbreak of cyclosporiasis occurred in North America. The source was traced to contaminated raspberries imported from South America.

In a 2012 report, the US Center for Disease Control (CDC) reported that illness in the United States from imported food was on the rise, with 39 outbreaks and 2,348 illnesses linked to imported foods.[47]

Of course, while globalization can and does contribute to the extent and speed of disease transmission, it also provides opportunities for globalized responses to, and perhaps eradication of, diseases. Especially for poor countries without sufficient resources, this global response can be crucial.

Responses to Global Disease

The good news is that in recent years, attention and resources devoted to fighting infectious disease have surged. In no small part, this trend has been driven by a sense of moral obligation as 24-hour cable news channels and broadband Internet connections deliver reports and photos of human suffering around the world to the homes of people in wealthy countries. At the same time, those in the wealthiest countries recognize that air travel, food imports, and other dimensions of globalization put all of us at some risk when infectious disease in faraway places goes unchecked. Thus, this combination of moral obligation and self-interest has given new prominence to the global fight against infectious disease.

Evidence of this trend is seen in the behavior of IOs, national governments, and NGOs. Of the eight Millennium Development Goals adopted by the United Nations in 2000 (see Chapter 7), one explicitly targets infectious disease. Goal number six is to "Combat HIV/AIDS, malaria, and other diseases." The targets for 2015 were to halt and begin to reverse the spread of these and other major diseases. To that end, considerable financial resources have been marshaled not only by obvious global institutions like the WHO but also by IOs like the World Bank, which for most of its existence saw health and disease as external to its central mission of fostering economic development. Spurred on by the Millennium Development Goals, the World Bank's spending on health surged, and it began to compete with the WHO for the title of the world's largest spender on AIDS programs.[48] National governments are also spending money with new urgency. In his 2003 State of the Union address, US President George W. Bush announced his "President's Emergency Plan for Aids Relief" (PEPFAR).

The plan called on the US Congress to allocate $15 billion over five years for international AIDS care, treatment, and prevention, with most of the effort directed at 14 focus countries in Africa and the Caribbean. By 2014, over $46 billion had been allocated to AIDs relief by PEPFAR in one of the most significant efforts by a single government targeting a single disease.[49]

NGOs and private-sector actors have also gotten into the act. The Bill and Melinda Gates Foundation, the world's most richly endowed private philanthropic foundation, devotes approximately 60 percent of its yearly expenditures to global health, with much of that focused on what Bill Gates calls the "big three" diseases of AIDS, malaria, and tuberculosis.[50] Established in 1994, the foundation made grants totaling more than $6 billion in its first 10 years to a variety of organizations committed to fighting global disease.[51] That level of spending approximately equals the budget of the WHO during that same period. In 2004, the foundation launched its Grand Challenges in Global Health which awards grants to scientists to solve basic health research questions such as the development of vaccines that do not require refrigeration or single-dose vaccines that can be used soon after birth.[52]

All this new attention and money have produced some success stories. For example, the UN reported in 2014 that since 2001 the number of new HIV infections had fallen by 38 percent overall and by 58 percent among children. Similarly, the number of AIDS-related deaths has fallen by 35 percent from the peak in 2005, largely as a result of access to antiretroviral therapy that is estimated to have saved 6.6 million lives since 1995.[53] Likewise, between 2000 and 2012, malaria mortality rates fell 42 percent, averting an estimated 3 million deaths.[54]

Nevertheless, the global response to infectious disease faces many problems and limitations. Some critics have argued that much spending on global health challenges has been misdirected toward a few "celebrity diseases" rather than the diseases and programs that can have the greatest impact. This results in what has been called "the 10/90 problem," where an estimated 10 percent of global health research resources are spent on conditions accounting for 90 percent of global disease. A good case in point is global AIDS spending. In 1990, AIDS was already clearly a growing world problem, yet measured in terms of number of years of healthy life lost, it was only the twenty-sixth leading cause, contributing 0.84 percent of the total disease burden. As the AIDS epidemic spread, it has become a larger share of the problem, and it is estimated that by 2020 it will be the tenth leading disease burden for developing countries.[55] Still, it will lag behind other less visible, and less well-funded, diseases, including pneumonia and dysentery.

Even when focused solely on AIDS funding, some criticize priorities. Most money spent on AIDS in the developing world is directed toward treatment programs, including expensive "cocktails" of antiretroviral drugs. The WHO estimates that even with the use of the least expensive generic forms of the drugs, the cost of extending the life of one AIDS patient for one year is approximately $1,500. Meanwhile, only 20 percent of the US PEPFAR program is directed at

AIDS prevention. The result is that even in countries with measurable success in treating AIDS patients, new infections continue at an unacceptably high rate. Moreover, in some countries, backsliding has occurred on other indicators of public health. While one might argue that the solution is more money spent on all areas of global health, the political reality is that resources will always be limited, and difficult choices will have to be made about how best to allocate them.

The Internet and Global Communications

8-4   Explain how the Internet poses a threat to state sovereignty, and assess the ability of states to respond to that threat.

It might appear odd to include discussion of the Internet in a chapter that considers global challenges like environmental degradation and disease. While pollution and disease are clearly problems, the Internet is generally seen as a positive development that links the world and makes our lives easier in countless ways. Still, in one very important respect, the Internet resembles pollution and disease: it has an inherent disregard for political borders and challenges the ability of sovereign states to control what happens on their territory. In that sense, the Internet is yet one more transnational challenge to the state system.

The early development of the Internet was promoted and, to a large extent, made possible by the US government. The network of interlinked computers we today use for both serious work and research and for communicating with friends, checking sports scores, or ordering a hot pizza was originally stimulated by a US government research program. Back in the 1960s and early 1970s the thinking was that creating such a network would stimulate and promote scientific research to help the United States keep and even expand its technological edge over the Soviet Union and other competitors. Perhaps even more important, experts were concerned that in case of a war with the USSR, a war with a high probability of going nuclear, traditional centralized means of government communication and military command and control could be jeopardized. To this end, the US government, via the Defense Department's Advanced Research Products Agency or ARPA (later renamed DARPA), funded work on this decentralized computer network project at US universities and corporations.

This early history of the Internet fits very well within the realist framework. In classic "self-help" fashion, the US government, motivated by national security concerns, funded a program to strengthen its military preparedness. Indeed, ARPA was a direct product of the Cold War, created in response to the 1957 Soviet launch of *Sputnik*, the first satellite to orbit Earth. The military applications of satellite technology were well known, so the *Sputnik* success not only surprised but also alarmed the US government and led to ARPA and many other programs designed to meet this new Soviet technological challenge.

Yet despite this early government involvement, "Very little of the current Internet is owned, operated, or even controlled by governmental bodies."[56] Indeed, the Internet appears, in the eyes of some, to have taken on a Frankenstein-like quality, challenging the authority and power of states around the world.

The Challenge to State Authority

Governmental authority typically implies control over a particular chunk of the world's real estate. In international law, formal recognition of a state and all that goes with that recognition (e.g., diplomatic missions, seats in the UN) assumes state control over a defined geographic territory. In contrast, when we talk about Internet communications taking place in cyberspace, it implies a release from geography. While the computers at which we work and play are obviously rooted in time and place, the words, ideas, and pictures we create with them float above and beyond the location where they were first created. Unlike other products, from automobiles to clothing, which are always located somewhere, information on the Internet, once created, is simultaneously everywhere. This situation challenges the authority of sovereign states in three interrelated ways.

CONTROL OVER INFORMATION   The Internet challenges governmental control over the flow of information. This poses a problem for authoritarian regimes, which depend on limiting and carefully controlling access to information that might undermine regime stability. The Communist regime in the former Soviet Union is a good case in point. During the Soviet period, the state owned and managed all means of mass communication—including newspapers, magazines, television, radio, and book publishers. To ensure that some intrepid reporter, writer, broadcaster, or editor at one of these state-owned information outlets did not stray from the official Communist Party line, government censors read and edited everything prior to dissemination.

By the end of the twentieth century, new information technologies made the job tougher for state censors. In 1989, when Chinese students were demonstrating against corruption and repression in Tiananmen Square in Beijing, Chinese students studying abroad used fax machines to keep the demonstrators back home up to date on world reaction and even on developments in China that were largely absent from the official Chinese news sources. When Russian hard-liners launched a coup in August 1991 to topple the reformist leadership of Mikhail Gorbachev, CNN satellite TV broadcast images from the streets of Moscow to viewers around the world. The reluctance of the coup plotters to go all the way and smash resistance with overwhelming force may have had something to do with the fact that the world was watching them.

By the time of the Arab Spring of 2010–2011, it was not the fax machine, satellite TV, or even e-mail that was the key politically disruptive technology but, instead, social media. According to a study done soon after the events of 2011, social media were crucial in shaping political debates, in spreading democratic

Anti-government protester near Cairo's Tahrir Square where the Egyptian stage of the "Arab Spring" began on January 25, 2011. Can authoritarian governments survive indefinitely in the era of the Internet and social media?

ideas, and in driving the revolutionary movements in various Arab countries.[57] Indeed, the efforts of regimes in the region to try to block Facebook and other social media sites were indications of the role those new forms of communication were playing. For example, when Wael Ghonim, a Google employee in Egypt, started a Facebook group to honor an anti-regime blogger who was beaten to death by police, his group rapidly expanded to over 300,000 before Ghonim was arrested, and by then it was too late for the regime. Similarly, by the time of Egyptian President Mubarak's resignation, the number of tweets about political events in the country swelled to 230,000 per day, with most originating inside Egypt itself. Those tweets not only kept Egyptians informed about the course of events, but helped spread the message of revolution to other countries in the region.

For authoritarian regimes bent on maintaining their information monopoly, the Internet and social media represent the worst of two worlds. On the one hand, they are, like television or radio, media well-suited for the mass broadcast of information. On the other hand, unlike TV or radio, no one needs an expensive TV studio or transmission tower to distribute information via the Internet. One individual with a smartphone and a Facebook or Twitter account can distribute information to thousands in a matter of seconds. Thus, the Internet combines the mass audience of TV or radio with the ease of access and relatively low cost of mail or telephone communication.

Given this new technology, many Western observers have anticipated the end of authoritarian regimes and the ushering in of a new era of global democracy. Colin Powell, who was secretary of state during the George W. Bush administration, reflected this view when he noted: "The rise of democracy and the power of the information revolution combine to leverage each other."[58]

President Bush was even more direct when he asserted during a campaign debate in 1999: "Imagine if the Internet took hold in China. Imagine how freedom would spread."[59] Underlying these assumptions was the belief that better and more accurate information about their own countries and the world at large, combined with the **demonstration effects** of seeing citizens in other countries rise to topple their repressive regimes, would make survival unlikely for the world's remaining dictators.

At the same time, some observers have suggested that it is not only authoritarian states that are challenged by the Internet. While those regimes face special challenges in controlling political news, even the most democratic regimes may seek, often with popular support, to control access to certain kinds of information or images. The most obvious example here is pornography, and especially that subgenre of porn that involves the abuse of children. With few exceptions, even the most ardent civil libertarians accept restrictions on access to such material. However, even if laws strictly regulate the posting of such images on websites from servers located in the regulating state's territory, limiting access to such images from servers located abroad and beyond the reach of domestic law is far more challenging. A similar challenge is faced by states that want to regulate or prohibit online gambling run from servers in extraterritorial locations.

In 2010 the Internet challenge to state control of information was once again illustrated by the publication via "WikiLeaks" of more than 90,000 classified documents related to the US war effort in Afghanistan. Online since 2007, the WikiLeaks website indicates that its goal is to "provide an innovative, secure and anonymous way for sources to leak information to our journalists."[60] What makes it such a challenge to state authority is that, unlike a newspaper or TV network, WikiLeaks and its staff operate largely outside the reach of governments inclined to prosecute and punish for unauthorized publication of state secrets, illustrating once again the potential of modern telecommunications technology to chip away at the sovereignty of even the most open, democratic states.

EMPOWERMENT OF NONSTATE ACTORS   Another challenge posed by the Internet to state sovereignty is its contribution to the empowerment of nonstate actors, including individuals and NGOs. Most estimates suggest that tens of thousands of NGOs are active across national borders. From Amnesty International to al-Qaeda, the telecommunications revolution of the late twentieth century has greatly empowered these organizations. First, because the Internet has diversified and democratized the dissemination of information, nonstate actors are in a better position to challenge official state interpretations and positions on important issues. To the extent that "information is power," the weakening of what was once a near state monopoly on information readjusts the balance of power between states and nonstate actors. Use of the Internet allows both al-Qaeda and Amnesty International to quickly and efficiently diffuse information around the world.

Second, the Internet creates a sense of community that extends across national borders. It brings together human rights activists or environmentalists

demonstration effects
Impact on behavior produced by observing the behavior of others. An example is the spread of popular revolutions produced by observing successful revolutions in other countries.

or anti-US terrorists in a way that can make their transnational associations and interests more significant to them than their national identities and interests. Some observers have spoken of the emergence of a **global civil society**. As defined by the Centre for the Study of Global Governance at the London School of Economics, global civil society is the "sphere of people, events, organisations, networks—and the values and ideas they represent—that exist between the family, the state and the market, and which operate beyond the confines of national societies in a transnational arena."[61] For states around the world, what this means is that their policies and actions are subject to challenge not only by their own citizens or by the official policies of other states, but also by increasingly active transnational issue networks and organizations that are connected by the Internet.

One of the best illustrations of the empowerment of global civil society via the Internet is the case of the International Campaign to Ban Landmines (ICBL). In the early 1990s frustration grew among activists at the slow pace of addressing the problem of landmines. As states negotiated the Convention on Conventional Weapons (CCW)—a 1980 treaty dealing with a range of matters that affect the safety of noncombatants in warfare—millions of landmines were killing and injuring thousands of civilians on a yearly basis.

In response, the ICBL was founded in 1992 as a network linking over a thousand NGOs in dozens of countries that wanted to push for an immediate and comprehensive ban on antipersonnel landmines. At a 1996 conference in Ottawa, Canada, the ICBL worked closely with the Canadian government to jump-start a new and separate Mine Ban Treaty, breaking with the slower and less comprehensive CCW approach. Central to the ICBL effort was effective use of the Internet. In the period leading up to the Ottawa conference, the ICBL orchestrated a campaign via e-mail and the World Wide Web to link supporters around the world and to arm them with data, talking points, and other useful tactical tips. At the same time, the ICBL used this technology to appeal directly to governments and their citizens with information and images designed to illustrate the harm done by landmines.

The ICBL effort was very successful. The Mine Ban Treaty was adopted in 1997, received the requisite number of state ratifications to go into effect in 1999, and, as of mid-2015, 162 states were parties to the treaty. Today, the ICBL continues to use the Internet to pressure the states that have not yet ratified the treaty (including the United States, Russia, and China). As the Canadian foreign minister noted back in 1997, the success of the ICBL suggests that "NGOs can no longer be relegated to simple advisory or advocacy roles. They are now part of the way decisions have to be made." Indeed, that very success has worried some who argue that the marriage of global NGOs and modern telecommunications technology is undermining the ability of states to do what is necessary to protect vital national interests.[62]

CYBERTERRORISM In recent years, concern has risen that terrorists might take advantage of cyberspace to advance their political agendas. The term **cyberterrorism** has been defined as "unlawful attacks and threats of attacks against

---

global civil society
Network of social, economic, and political organizations, constituted on a transnational basis, that are separate from and often challenge the power and authority of state institutions and policies.

cyberterrorism
Attacks on computer networks intended to intimidate governments and their citizens as a means to force a change of policy and achieve political objectives.

computers, networks and the information stored therein when done to intimidate or coerce a government or its people in furtherance of political or social objectives."[63] Cyberterrorism can include massive spam attacks, dissemination of computer viruses, and other efforts to interfere with the computer networks and webpages that are so crucial to contemporary life. Even more alarming is the fear that cyberterrorists can hack into and take control of computer systems regulating anything from air traffic control, to dams, to electricity grids with the intention of threatening basic economic infrastructure and human life.

As is true of terrorism in general (recall the discussion in Chapter 4), the distinction between cyberterrorism and ordinary computer crime is the presence or absence of political motive. By far, most viruses, spam, and hacking into computer networks are done for reasons of personal economic gain or merely for "sport" and would not qualify as terrorism. In fact, some observers have suggested that the threat of cyberterrorism has been greatly exaggerated. Governments, however, take the threat seriously and cite some significant examples of suspected cyberterrorism.

In Estonia in May 2007, websites of government agencies, private companies, banks, and political parties were subjected to a massive three-week attack that forced many offline. The timing coincided with the removal of a Soviet-era war memorial from the capital city of this former Soviet republic. While the Russian government has denied responsibility, the political motives driving those attacks led some to suggest that, whoever was responsible, it was an unambiguous example of a cyber attack against a state.[64] The fact that it could be carried out presumably from computers located outside the borders of Estonia made it difficult for Estonian leaders to control or punish those who were responsible.

While the cyber attack on Estonia was limited to disruption of cyber communications, the Stuxnet worm, which surfaced in 2010, raised the ante even higher as it was aimed at producing physical damage in the real world. The Stuxnet attack, presumably hatched in Israel or the United States, was aimed primarily at Iran's Natanz nuclear facility where it damaged centrifuges by causing them to spin out of control. If one can use computer code to affect the behavior of centrifuges, then one can imagine a cyber attack that shuts down an electricity grid, causes a critical dam to fail, or interferes with air traffic control.

The 2015 the *Worldwide Threat Assessment of the US Intelligence Community* put cyber threats at the top of its list of threats to US national security. The message was reinforced when the US Director of National Intelligence, James Clapper, began his presentation of the Assessment to the Senate Armed Services Committee by noting the increasing "frequency, scale, sophistication, and severity of impact" of the cyber threat.[65] Some of that cyber threat comes from governments, and thus might be viewed by realists as yet another weapon, along with guns, tanks, soldiers, and bombs, in the arsenals of states. Russia and China (along with the United States) have very sophisticated cyber capabilities, as do many other states. According to Clapper, "the most damaging cyber attack on US interests to date" was the 2014 attack on Sony presumed to have come from

North Korea.[66] The attack rendered many Sony computers inoperable, and led to the release of a trove highly sensitive corporate and personal information.

At the same time, Clapper noted the need not only to be concerned with the threat of cyber attacks from other states, but also from terrorists, organized crime groups, and even individuals with both the capability and motive to attack the United States in this manner. For example, he noted that the so-called "Cyber Caliphate," acting in support of ISIS, successfully hacked into the Twitter account and YouTube page of the United States Central Command (CENTCOM), which coordinates the US military's activities in the Middle East, North Africa, and Central Asia. In fact, one of the challenges of cyber attacks is attribution—it is often hard to be sure who is responsible for the attacks. Thus not only do those attacks easily penetrate the borders of sovereign states, it is hard to defend those borders and to deter future attacks both because of the nature of the attacks and because of doubts over who initiated them.

The State Strikes Back

The Internet clearly presents a new kind of challenge to the sovereign state. At the same time, states are not completely helpless in the face of this challenge. Their leverage comes from the possibility of tracking real people making use of real hardware found in real countries associated with all the information and images created, disseminated, and consumed on the Internet's information superhighway.[67]

On one end of the information flow is the information source. For a subversive political tract, a pornographic image, or a gambling site to be available online, someone sitting in front of a computer has to upload the document. If the government of the state where that individual is located wants to stop such uploading, it can track and find the server and even the computer from which the document emanated. That is exactly why purveyors of illegal child pornography or Internet gambling sites who want to reach the US market operate outside the United States. If they operated inside the United States, where such activities are illegal, they would be arrested and their hardware confiscated.

These offshore illegal activities may be out of reach of local authorities, but those who consume these illegal activities in countries where they are banned remain vulnerable. Even though US authorities cannot prosecute someone in Russia who uploads child porn, they can prosecute Americans who download those images in the United States. At the same time, states can regulate what goes on in cyberspace by focusing on the intermediate actors who provide the essential links between the original source and ultimate consumer of Internet documents.

Anyone who uses the Internet is familiar with those crucial intermediaries. First, there is the Internet service provider or ISP. Cable companies like Comcast and phone companies like Verizon provide both the hardware (cables and wires) and software without which one computer could not access another. While their product might be composed of electrons that almost magically appear as text and images on computer screens around the world, their company headquarters, office, trucks, personnel, cables, and routers are all solid objects that exist on the territory of sovereign states. Second is the search engine. Without sites like Google to help us find our way through the billions of webpages that have been created, the World Wide Web would be an unusable jungle of information. Third, there are the financial intermediaries. Anytime a fee is charged, someone has to record the transaction, and collect and transfer the appropriate funds. This is most often a credit card company or a specialized Internet payment service such as PayPal. All these intermediaries represent points where governments can limit what end users access on their computers.

A good illustration comes from China. Despite hopes and expectations that the Internet would undercut the authoritarian Chinese state, the Chinese state has demonstrated considerable resilience in taming the Internet. Today's version of the Great Wall of China is an Internet firewall that blocks information from flagged websites or e-mails with certain words in them. An estimated army of 50,000 people patrols the Chinese web on behalf of the government, looking for sites on politically sensitive topics. According to one political scientist, those 50,000 censors are particularly concerned with blocking access to anything urging public activism and collective citizen action, and they are remarkably effective in their efforts.[68] Complementing the "Great Firewall" is the "Great Cannon," which directs a flood of Internet traffic to sites like GitHub, an encrypted site that helps those looking to slip through the Great Firewall.[69] Unless and until the offending pages are removed, the Great Cannon can cause costly disruptions of service at targeted sites.

Similarly, the Chinese government has effectively pressured search engines like Google to screen the results of Internet searches for information and topics deemed a threat to Chinese authorities. In 2006, Google's relationship to China received a great deal of attention when the search engine, whose motto is "do no evil," agreed to censor the results of searches conducted by individuals in China. An irony here is that Google made this announcement in January 2006, just shortly after it indicated that it would resist a call from the Bush administration to turn over Internet search records as part of a US government effort to crack down on Internet pornography. In the Chinese case, Google officials argued they had no choice: either conform to the demands of the Chinese government or fail to receive the license required to operate in the Chinese market. As a senior counsel for Google put it on the company's blog at the time, "Filtering our search results clearly compromises our mission. Failing to offer Google search at all to a fifth of the world's population, however, does so far more severely."[70]

In January 2010 the tension between Google and the Chinese government escalated when Google reported that it was the victim of a sophisticated Chinese cyber attack specifically targeting the Gmail accounts of Chinese human rights activists. Those attacks, in combination with the Chinese government's persistent blocking of social networking sites such as Facebook, Twitter, and YouTube, led Google to announce in March 2010 that it was ending its policy of censoring searches on its Chinese search engine (Google.cn) and redirecting users to its Hong Kong search engine (Google.com.hk) for uncensored searches.[71] The Chinese government, in turn, continued efforts to filter results mainland users could see from Hong Kong-based searches, and it began to pressure Google in other ways, including threats to cancel plans to place Google on the mobile Internet homepage of China's biggest cellular communications company.

Since that time, the tug of war between China and Google has continued, as have Chinese efforts to limit access to Western social media sites. Aware of the role of social media in the Arab Spring, the Chinese government has continued to block access to Facebook and Twitter in favor of more compliant Chinese alternatives. So too with Google. Throughout 2014 all of Google services in China were subject to at least temporary disruptions, and at the end of the year, users of Google in China were reporting that both their search attempts and access to Gmail were being blocked. This seems to be part of a Chinese strategy to get Chinese users to switch to the Chinese search engine, Baidu, and the strategy has been working. Measured by revenue, Baidu had 80 percent market share in the fourth quarter of 2014 compared to Google's 12 percent.[72] While Google still dominates the global search market with a 54.7 percent share in 2014, the limitations on Google operations in the fast-growing Chinese market are leading Google's global market share to slowly decline.[73]

The Chinese case suggests that, contrary to conventional wisdom, the threat to state sovereignty posed by the Internet may be greater in democracies than in authoritarian regimes like China. That is because to a considerable extent, state control of the Internet and its content is less a question of technical ability than political will. In a democratic regime, with its tradition of the free flow of information, marshaling the political and legal consensus to censor the Internet will be difficult. When the Bush administration sought in the years following 9/11 to require Internet service providers and search engines to keep records of customers' online activities, it faced resistance from Google and an outcry from civil libertarians. Similarly, US National Security Agency (NSA) interception of telephone metadata of every American, condemned by many on both the political left and right as a threat to the privacy and civil liberties of American citizens, has been the source of much public debate since revealed by Edward Snowden, a former NSA employee, beginning in 2013. And in 2015, a Federal Appeals Court ruled the NSA program to be illegal.

In an authoritarian regime like China, in contrast, web censorship and electronic monitoring of citizen communications are simply a couple more in a long list of government controls over information deemed harmful to the state. Indeed, the China case suggests that determined governments can eat their cake and have it too. By 2014 the number of Chinese web surfers exceeded 600 million, more than double the number of users in the United States, and 22 percent of global users, all without undermining the political grip of the one-party Chinese state.[74]

Conclusion

The three issue areas discussed in this chapter—the environment, disease, and the Internet—illustrate the tensions surrounding the traditional state-centric view of the world that is at the core of the realist paradigm. If we had instead examined international crime, drug smuggling, or refugee and migration flows, the details would have been different, but the larger story would be essentially the same. In all these cases, the overriding story is the tension between the system of sovereign states and an array of new, transsovereign forces and actors that seem to challenge that state system.

Political scientist James Rosenau has suggested that these tensions are leading to what he calls the "bifurcation" of world politics.[75] On the one hand, there is the sphere of high politics and military security, which remains essentially state-centric. In this sphere, the world still looks and operates much as it has since 1648. On the other hand, there is the more "multicentric" world, in which states are merely one of many kinds of actors (individuals, NGOs, IOs, terrorists, criminal gangs). In this world, states play a role, but they do not dominate, and their sovereignty is continually challenged.

Both realists and their critics recognize the distinction between these two worlds, but they see their relationship playing out in different ways. In this regard, realists would make two central points. First, they would argue that the state-centric realm matters most, for it is in that world where the game of world politics is played for the highest stakes, life and death, and with the most potent instruments, guns and bombs. Second, to the extent that issues in the multicentric world—such as global warming, resource scarcity, or infectious disease—come to be perceived as having high stakes themselves, then states will pay greater attention and incorporate them into their state-centric world. As illustrated by the Chinese relationship to the Internet, realists would argue that if and when states decide to exercise control over transsovereign forces, they have a good chance of succeeding.

Critics challenge realists on both counts. First, they question the hierarchy of importance that realists assign to global problems. From the perspective of such critics, climate change and disease are at least as great a threat to humankind as are military weapons in a neighboring state's arsenal. Second, the critics are much less confident than are realists that the instruments at the disposal of sovereign states are adequate for dealing with these new transsovereign challenges. Despite all their military might, states are ill equipped on their own to respond adequately to a global problem such as ocean warming or pandemic flu.

In short, one might imagine three alternative paths for world politics in the twenty-first century. One is the continued expansion of Rosenau's "multicentric" world and a clearer movement into a post-Westphalian era. A second scenario is that states adapt to the new challenges and incorporate them into their state-centric world. Both these scenarios assume that Rosenau's bifurcated world is a temporary characteristic of a world in transition. A third possibility is that this messier, bifurcated world will remain for the indefinite future. In this world, states are neither powerful enough to exercise hegemony over world politics nor challenged enough to lose their position as first among equals. This chapter provides enough evidence for informed observers to disagree as to how the world of the future is, in fact, most likely to work.

Review Questions

- What is "human security," and how does that concept challenge traditional realist conceptions of "national security"?
- In what ways do issues such as the global environment, disease, and the Internet challenge state sovereignty? To what extent is this challenge new?

- Would you agree with the view that the Westphalian era based on the sovereign state is over? Or, to paraphrase Mark Twain, are the rumors of the demise of the sovereign state greatly exaggerated? Explain your reasoning.

Key Terms

human security
Malthusian
public good
free-rider problem
common pool resource
tragedy of the commons
peak oil
Organization of Petroleum Exporting Countries (OPEC)

climate change
global warming
Montreal Protocol
Kyoto Protocol
emissions trading
green revolution
fracking
biofuels

World Health Organization (WHO)
pandemic
demonstration effects
global civil society
cyberterrorism

Endnotes

1. Maryann K. Cusimano, *Beyond Sovereignty: Issues for a Global Agenda* (Bedford/ St. Martin's, 2000), 3.
2. Stephen D. Krasner, "Think Again: Sovereignty," *Foreign Policy*, January/February 2001, 20, 24.
3. United Nations, *Human Development Report 1994*, 22, http://hdr.undp.org.
4. Garrett Hardin, "The Tragedy of the Commons," *Science*, December 13, 1968, 1243–1248, http://www.sciencemag.org.
5. "Global Public Goods," The World Health Organization, http://www.who.int/trade/glossary/story041/en/.
6. Energy Information Administration, *International Energy Statistics*, http://www.eia.gov/cfapps/ipdbproject/iedindex3.cfm?tid=44&pid=44&aid=2&cid=regions&syid=1980&eyid=2012&unit=QBTU.
7. Energy Information Administration, *International Energy Statistics*.
8. John Wood, Gary Long, and David Morehouse, "Long-Term World Oil Supply Scenarios," Energy Information Administration, http://www.eia.doe.gov.
9. "International Energy Outlook 2014," US Energy Information Administration, http://www.eia.gov/forecasts/ieo/more_overview.cfm.
10. Data in this paragraph are from Michael Klare, *Blood and Oil*, (Metropolitan Books, 2004), 19.
11. Bill Clinton as related to Thomas Friedman, "Gardening with Beijing," *New York Times*, April 17, 1996, http://www.nytimes.com.
12. US Environmental Protection Agency, "Climate Change Indicators in the United States: U.S. and Global Temperature,"

http://www.epa.gov/climatechange/science/indicators/weather-climate/temperature.html.

13. US Environmental Protection Agency, "Future Climate Change," http://www.epa.gov/climatechange/science/future.html.

14. Intergovernmental Panel on Climate Change, "Climate Change 2013: The Physical Science Basis: Summary for Policy-Makers," pp. 4–5, http://www.ipcc.ch/report/ar5/wg1/.

15. Intergovernmental Panel on Climate Change, "Climate Change 2013," p. 17.

16. US Environmental Protection Agency, "Climate Change: Health and Environmental Effects," http://www.epa.gov.

17. Andrew Revkin, "Hacked E-Mail Is New Fodder for Climate Dispute," *New York Times*, November 20, 2009, http://www.nytimes.com/2009/11/21/science/earth/21climate.html.

18. *New York Times*, June 11, 2006, http://www.nytimes.com.

19. Sid Perkins, "Asian Brown Cloud Threatens U.S.," *Science: AAAS*, May 25, 2012, http://news.sciencemag.org/asia/2012/05/asian-brown-cloud-threatens-u.s.

20. Jane Perlez, "China, Pursuing Strategic Interests, Builds Presence in Antarctica," *New York Times*, May 3, 2015, http://www.nytimes.com/2015/05/04/world/asia/china-pursuing-strategic-interests-builds-presence-in-antarctica.html?_r=0.

21. Council on Foreign Relations, "The Emerging Arctic," http://www.cfr.org/arctic/emerging-arctic/p32620#!/; Roger McDermott, "Russia Creates Arctic Military Command," *Eurasia Daily Monitor* 11:215, The Jamestown Foundation, December 3, 2014, http://www.jamestown.org/single/?tx_ttnews%5Btt_news%5D=43144&no_cache=1#.VUdrkY6qpHw.

22. Peter Schwartz and Doug Randall, "An Abrupt Climate Change Scenario and Its Implications for United States National Security," October 2003, prepared for US Department of Defense, Office of Net Assessments, http://www.grist.org.

23. *We the Peoples: The Role of the United Nations in the 21st Century* (United Nations Department of Public Information, 2000), 56, http://www.un.org.

24. "Status of Ratification," United Nations Framework Convention on Climate Change, http://unfccc.int/kyoto_protocol/status_of_ratification/items/2613.php/.

25. Union of Concerned Scientists, "Each Country's Share of CO2 Emissions," http://www.ucsusa.org/global_warming/science_and_impacts/science/each-countrys-share-of-co2.html.

26. The World Bank, http://data.worldbank.org/indicator/EN.ATM.CO2E.PC?order=wbapi_data_value_2010+wbapi_data_value+wbapi_data_value-first&sort=desc.

27. "Status of Doha Amendment," United Nations Framework Convention on Climate Change, http://unfccc.int/kyoto_protocol/doha_amendment/items/7362.php.

28. *Climate Change 2014: Mitigation of Climate Change*, Intergovernmental Panel on Climate Change," https://www.ipcc.ch/report/ar5/wg3/.

29. *New York Times*, March 5, 2007, A-1, A-11.

30. US Geological Society, http://energy.usgs.gov/OilGas/UnconventionalOilGas/HydraulicFracturing.aspx.

31. *Annual Energy Outlook 2015*, US Energy Information Administration, http://www.eia.gov/forecasts/aeo/section_energyprod.cfm.

32. Alex Trembath, Max Luke, Michael Shellenberger, and Ted Nordhaus, *Coal Killer: How Natural Gas Fuels the Clean Energy Revolution*, Breakthrough Institute, June 2013, p. 4, http://thebreakthrough.org/images/main_image/Breakthrough_Institute_Coal_Killer.pdf.

33. National Environmental Trust, "The Facts About Raising Auto Fuel Efficiency," http://www.net.org.

34. Tim Folger, "Blueprint for Disaster?" National Resources Defense Council, http://www.nrdc.org.

35. *Global Tuberculosis Report 2014,* World Health Organization, http://apps.who.int/iris/bitstream/10665/137094/1/9789241564809_eng.pdf.

36. World Health Organization, http://www.who.int/mediacentre/factsheets/fs094/en/.

37. World Health Organization, http://www.who.int/mediacentre/factsheets/fs107/en/.

38. BBC Online, http://news.bbc.co.uk.

39. Data in this paragraph are from the World Health Organization's HIV/AIDS Factsheet # 360, November 2014, http://www.who.int/mediacentre/factsheets/fs360/en/.

40. Data in this paragraph are from the World Health Organization's Ebola Virus Disease Factsheet #103, April 2015, http://www.who.int/mediacentre/factsheets/fs103/en/ and World Health Organization, "Ebola Virus Disease in West Africa," February 2015, http://www.afro.who.int/en/search.html?searchword=ebola&ordering=&searchphrase=all.

41. "Influenza at the Human-Animal Interface," World Health Organization, March 31, 2015, http://www.who.int/influenza/human_animal_interface/Influenza_Summary_IRA_HA_interface_31_March_2015.pdf.

42. Carnegie Endowment, "Globalization 101: Diseases Go Global," http://www.globalization101.org.

43. "Airline Travel Speeds Flu Spread, *Journal Watch,* http://infectious-diseases.jwatch.org.

44. Mark Osborne Humphries, "Paths of Infection: The First World War and the Origins of the 1918 Influenza Pandemic," *War in History* 21:1 (2013): 55–81.

45. "CDC Worried About Imported Food Safety? Fails to Factor in Volume of Imports, Reports are Meaningless," FDAImports.com Blog, http://www.fdaimports.com/blog/cdc-imported-food-safety-meaningless-2/.

46. World Health Organization, "Foodborne Diseases, Emerging," http://www.who.int.

47. Centers for Disease Control Press Release, March 14, 2012, http://www.cdc.gov/media/releases/2012/p0314_foodborne.html.

48. See Laurie Garrett, "The Challenge of Global Health," *Foreign Affairs,* January/February 2007, http://www.foreignaffairs.org. Also see William Easterly, *The White Man's Burden* (Penguin, 2006), 242–243.

49. *The United States President's Emergency Plan for Aids Relief,* http://www.pepfar.gov/funding/budget/.

50. CNN Money, June 25, 2006, http://money.cnn.com.

51. Bill and Melinda Gates Foundation, "Global Health Program Fact Sheet," http://www.gatesfoundation.org.

52. Bill and Melinda Gates Foundation, "Grand Challenges in Global Health," http://gcgh.grandchallenges.org/about/Pages/Overview.aspx.

53. "UN AIDS Factsheet 2014," http://www.unaids.org/en/resources/campaigns/2014/2014gapreport/factsheet; "The Millennium Development Goals Report 2014," United Nations, 2014, p. 36, http://www.un.org/millenniumgoals/2014%20MDG%20report/MDG%202014%20English%20web.pdf.

54. "The Millennium Development Goals Report 2014," p. 37.

55. Nicholas Prescott, "Setting Priorities for Government Involvement with Antiretrovirals," in *The Implications of Antiretroviral Treatments: Informal Consultation,* ed. Eric van Praag, Susan Fernyak, and Alison Martin Katz (World Health Organization in collaboration with UNAIDS, April 1997), 57–62, http://www.worldbank.org.

56. Robert E. Kahn, "The Role of Government in the Evolution of the Internet," in *Revolution in the U.S. Information Infrastructure* (National Academy of Sciences, 1994), http://books.nap.edu.

57. All of the information in this paragraph is from Philip N. Howard, et al., "Opening Closed Regimes: What Was the Role of Social Media During the Arab Spring?" Project on Information Technology and Political Islam, Working paper

2011.1, http://pitpi.org/wp-content/uploads/2013/02/2011_Howard-Duffy-Freelon-Hussain-Mari-Mazaid_pITPI.pdf.

58. Cited in Shanthi Kalathil and Taylor C. Boas, "The Internet and State Control in Authoritarian Regimes," Carnegie Foundation for International Peace, 2001, http://outreach.lib.uic.edu.

59. "George W. Bush on China," *On the Issues*, http://www.issues2000.org.

60. Wikileaks, http://wikileaks.org/wiki/WikiLeaks:About.

61. The Centre for the Study of Global Governance, "Global Civil Society," http://www.lse.ac.uk.

62. Cited in John F. Troxell, "Landmines: Why the Korea Exception Should Be the Rule," *Parameters*, Spring 2000, 82–101, http://carlisle-www.army.mil.

63. Dorothy E. Denning, "Cyberterrorism," Testimony Before the Special Oversight Panel on Terrorism Committee on Armed Services, US House of Representatives, May 23, 2000, http://www.cs.georgetown.edu.

64. *Guardian*, May 17, 2007, http://www.guardian.co.uk.

65. *Worldwide Threat Assessment of the U.S. Intelligence Community for the Senate Select Committee on Intelligence*, February 26, 2015, http://www.dni.gov/files/documents/Unclassified_2015_ATA_SFR_-_SASC_FINAL.pdf; James R. Clapper, "Opening Statement to Worldwide Threat Assessment Hearing, Senate Armed Service Committee," February 26, 2015, http://www.dni.gov/files/documents/2015%20WWTA%20As%20Delivered%20DNI%20Oral%20Statement.pdf.

66. James R. Clapper, "Opening Statement to Worldwide Threat Assessment Hearing."

67. A detailed treatment of the issues discussed below is found in Jack Goldsmith and Tim Wu, *Who Controls the Internet?* (Oxford University Press, 2006).

68. Kentaro Toyama, "How Internet Censorship Actually Works in China," *The Atlantic*, October 2, 2013, http://www.theatlantic.com/china/archive/2013/10/how-internet-censorship-actually-works-in-china/280188/.

69. Nicole Perlroth, "China Is Said to Use Powerful New Weapon to Censor Internet," *New York Times*, April 10, 2015, http://www.nytimes.com/2015/04/11/technology/china-is-said-to-use-powerful-new-weapon-to-censor-internet.html?_r=0.

70. Andrew McLaughlin, "Google in China," *The Official Google Blog*, January 27, 2006, http://googleblog.blogspot.com/2006/01/google-in-china.html.

71. "A New Approch to China: An Update," *The Official Google Blog*, March 22, 2010, http://googleblog.blogspot.com/2010/03/new-approach-to-china-update.html.

72. "China Search Engine Market Overview in 2014," *China Internet Watch*, March 16, 2015, http://www.chinainternetwatch.com/12678/search-engine-market-overview-2014/.

73. Ginny Marvin, "Google Still Dominant, but Baidu Benefitting from Google Ban in China Says eMarketer," March 31, 2015, http://searchengineland.com/google-still-dominant-but-baidu-benefitting-from-google-ban-in-china-says-emarketer-217745.

74. "Internet Users by Country (2014)," http://www.internetlivestats.com/internet-users-by-country/.

75. James Rosenau, *Turbulence in World Politics* (Princeton University Press, 1990).

Chapter 9
Global Futures
Competing Visions of the Twenty-First Century

One image of the global future. In 2015, the *Bulletin of Atomic Scientists* reset its Doomsday Clock to 3 minutes to midnight. The clock conveys a judgment as to how close we are to destroying civilization through nuclear war, climate change, and other actions of our own making. During the optimistic 1990s, the clock stood at 17 minutes to midnight. Are you an optimist or a pessimist about the global future? Why?

 ## Learning Objectives

9-1 Identify the key assumptions of the "end of history" vision of the global future, and evaluate the plausibility of that vision.

9-2 Identify the key assumptions of the "one world" vision of the global future, and evaluate the plausibility of that vision.

9-3 Identify the key assumptions of the "world state" vision of the global future, and evaluate the plausibility of that vision.

9-4 Identify the key assumptions of the "cascading norm against war" vision of the global future, and evaluate the plausibility of that vision.

9-5 Identify the key assumptions of the "engendered peace" vision of the global future, and evaluate the plausibility of that vision.

9-6 Identify the key assumptions of the "clash of civilizations" vision of the global future, and evaluate the plausibility of that vision.

9-7 Identify the key assumptions of the "great power war" vision of the global future, and evaluate the plausibility of that vision.

If a modern-day Rip Van Winkle went to sleep sometime in the 1980s only to awaken today, he or she, much like the original character in Washington Irving's story, might struggle to understand the changes that have taken place in the world. While that person slept, the Berlin Wall fell, the Soviet Union collapsed, Germany reunified, foreign terrorists carried out a major attack in the United States, much of Europe adopted a single currency, and relatively poor and isolated China had become a political and economic power. Upon awakening, this individual would have no idea of the significance of such individuals as George W. Bush, Osama bin Laden, Vladimir Putin, Angela Merkel, Xi Jinping, Barack Obama, or Edward Snowden, and the names of such organizations as al-Qaeda, ISIS, Hamas, or the World Trade Organization (WTO) would convey little if any meaning. If asked to identify America's major trade rival, this individual would likely say Japan rather than China, and he or she would have little clue about the debate over outsourcing. Unless he or she was a careful student of geography before going to sleep, this individual might have a hard time locating Kosovo, Rwanda, or Crimea on a map, and if you suggested "googling" those places, you would likely get a blank stare.

The world is always in flux, and change, as the old adage teaches us, is the only constant. However, many observers of the past few decades believe that the world is changing in a way that is more fundamental than usual. The end of the bipolar Cold War era, the deepening of economic globalization, the emergence of several Asian economic powers, the rise of new nonstate actors, and revolutionary changes in information technology all suggest a watershed era in world politics. That these changes just happened to be coinciding with the beginning of a new millennium probably contributes to the perception, if not the reality, that we are entering a new era.

These developments have spawned a number of efforts to anticipate where the major trends are leading. Painting with broad brushes, scholars have produced "big books" with provocative and competing images of our global future. Many of their ideas are rooted in the basic perspectives on world politics laid out in Chapter 1 of this text. While the various nonrealist perspectives on the global future differ among themselves, they all share the sense that change is trumping continuity in world politics. Realists, in contrast, would tend to agree with the maxim that the more things appear to change the more they remain the same. As one realist has suggested, while we might like to believe that there are "new ideas that, once discovered, could usher in a new era of peace and amity among nations," that is an illusion, as all the alternatives to realist power politics have already been tried without success.[1]

This chapter will compare and contrast seven competing visions of the global future, each of which draws upon and extends the logic of one of the competing paradigms discussed in Chapter 1. While each vision presented is, thus, an exaggerated restatement of one of the major paradigms, highly regarded scholars, cited in the discussion of each vision, have articulated precisely the seven images of the global future to be considered. We will proceed by first articulating each vision of the global future, followed by a critique that raises questions about the likelihood of events unfolding as described.

Future I: The End of History

9-1 **Identify the key assumptions of the "end of history" vision of the global future, and evaluate the plausibility of that vision.**

The Vision: As discussed in Chapter 4, the "third wave" of democratization began in the 1970s in Southern Europe before moving through Latin America and on to much of Asia and parts of sub-Saharan Africa. By the late 1980s and early 1990s, this democratic wave had also transformed the map of Eastern Europe, including the Soviet Union, as it washed away one-party Communist regimes and replaced them with competitive multiparty systems. The fall of the Berlin Wall in 1989 and the dissolution of the USSR and its Communist regime in late 1991 radically transformed the world that had existed at least since World War II. By the 1990s both the percentage of the world's countries and the percentage of the world's population living under democratic rule were higher than they had ever been in human history.

Despite the geographic and cultural diversity of the world's democracies, the assumption of democratic peace theorists that democratic states would not fight wars with one another has largely held. Worries expressed by some that the end of the "Soviet threat" would deprive the Western democracies of a common enemy and restart old rivalries proved groundless, as major democratic states did not return to an era of selecting the military option for resolving disputes among themselves.[2] Moreover, in the immediate post-Communist era, relations between Russia and the West seemed to be in line with what democratic peace theory would predict. As Russia, under the leadership of Boris Yeltsin, democratized in the early 1990s, its relations with the United States and Western Europe improved to the point where both sides could think of themselves as partners rather than adversaries. Contrary to what realists might have expected, the Cold War rivalry was ended not by military victory but through a change in the character of domestic politics within Russia.

The optimism generated by these developments was most clearly captured in Francis Fukuyama's argument that we had reached the "end of history."[3] Writing precisely as Eastern European and Soviet Communism collapsed, Fukuyama argued that the end of history was the point at which all the great debates about how human beings should organize themselves politically and economically were resolved. As Fukuyama saw it, the end of the Soviet Communist system was part of a larger global trend toward accepting the idea that democracy and market capitalism were the only viable alternatives. That, in turn, he concluded, would inevitably lead to changes in how states conduct their relations with one another, and the "unreality of realism" in the twenty-first century world would soon become apparent.[4]

To be sure, as Fukuyama recognized, in the late twentieth and early twenty-first centuries some countries have remained mired "in history." The Islamic countries of the Middle East have remained largely untouched by the democratic wave. While the Arab Spring raised hopes of a fourth wave of democratization in the region that would once and for all end the arguments about whether Islamic and Arab culture were compatible with democracy, those hopes were soon dashed. Instead of democracy, the region in 2015 was characterized by war, dictatorship, failed states, and the rise of the brutal ISIS movement. Meanwhile, with one-quarter of the world's population living within its borders, the People's Republic of China (PRC) remains a one-party, authoritarian state. Despite economic liberalization, the Chinese Communist Party remains determined (as we saw in the discussion of its efforts to control the Internet) to resist calls for substantive democratic reform.

Yet even in those democratic backwaters, there are optimistic notes. While Chinese Communist leaders continue to gamble that economic growth will remain compatible with, and even justify and solidify, one-party rule, many political scientists are not so sure. According to **modernization theory**, wherever economic development occurs, a more educated, middle-class population emerges and demands the opportunity for democratic participation in the political process. In retrospect, and viewed in this light, the pro-democracy Tiananmen Square protests of 1989, though crushed by Chinese government tanks, were an early indicator of democratic pressures, produced by economic modernization, bubbling up from below. Likewise, though the democratic aspirations of the Arab Spring were unfulfilled, the events of 2010–2011 suggest that Arabs and Muslims are not immune to the desire for more liberal and democratic forms of government.

In short, although the world of 2015 is not 100 percent democratic, and although conflict and small-scale wars do flare up, it is arguably premature to be proclaiming "the end of the end of history."[5] After all, the world of 2015, as discussed in Chapter 4, is still more democratic than at any time in history, and, despite the global problems reported daily in the news, interstate wars remain, by historical standards, a relatively rare occurrence. While the path to a more democratic and, thus, more peaceful future is not a straight line but more a case of two steps forward and one step back, the vision of a global future defined by democratic peace remains a viable one.

The Critique: This liberal internationalist vision of democratic peace may have been understandable in the optimistic context of the immediate post–Cold War years. However, recent developments have led to a good deal more caution. Three trends, in particular, have emerged in the early twenty-first century to sober things up.

First, even if one ultimately accepts the thesis that stable, consolidated democracies do not fight wars with one another, some scholars have argued that the transition from authoritarianism to democracy can increase the propensity for war.[6] This tendency occurs because, during these transitions, those in power sometimes need to rally divided societies around the regime. Identification of, and perhaps even conflict with, an external enemy can sometimes serve this unifying purpose.

modernization theory
Theory that economic development leads to the emergence of a more educated, middle-class population, which in turn demands increased opportunity for democratic participation in the political process.

Second, and even more fundamental, some now see evidence that the third wave of democratization that began in the 1970s may have ended with much of the world still not on board, including China, most of the Middle East, and large swaths of sub-Saharan Africa and Asia. As we saw in Chapter 4, the democratic gains of the late twentieth century, though significant, appear to have stalled out in the twenty-first century. The assumption, indeed the hope, of some observers that China and the Middle East will be part of a fourth wave of democratization may not hold. Furthermore, just as some countries slid back into authoritarian habits following the first and second waves of democratization, others may do so today. Most significant has been the authoritarian backsliding in Russia under Vladimir Putin. The Putin era has been characterized by a systematic retreat from democratic processes and ruthless efforts to isolate and silence opposition parties, nongovernmental activists, and journalists (see Theory in Practice 9.1).

Theory in Practice 9.1

The End of History?: The Russian Case

When the Soviet Union collapsed at the end of 1991 and Boris Yeltsin became the president of Russia, many democrats in both Russia and the West hoped that Russia was on the path to liberal democracy. In many ways, Russia in the 1990s was a more open and democratic society than it had been under Communist rule. Competitive multiparty elections replaced the single-candidate electoral charade that had passed as "socialist democracy" during the Soviet period, and a diverse media culture representing a wide range of perspectives replaced the state-controlled media of the Communist era. However, corruption and economic turmoil also characterized Yeltsin's Russia. By the end of the decade, Yeltsin's health and popularity were in steep decline, and Russian citizens longed for security, order, and economic prosperity.

Yeltsin resigned on December 31, 1999, and his successor according to the Russian constitution would be his prime minister, Vladimir Putin. Putin was the former head of the Russian intelligence agency that replaced the Communist-era KGB. He was subsequently elected to full terms in 2000 and 2004. Under Putin, the Russian economy stabilized, and political stability increased. The price, according to critics of Putin, has been a retreat on democracy and civil liberties. The media, especially television, has once again come under close state control. Nominally competitive elections have become less democratic. And opponents of Putin have been prosecuted and harassed by state authorities. Some have ended up dead under suspicious circumstances.

Because the Russian constitution limits the president to two consecutive terms in office, Putin could not run again in the March 2008 election. However, his successor, Dmitry Medvedev, appointed Putin to the post of prime minister, and from that position Putin continued to be the center of power in Russia until he successfully ran for president again in 2012. While democrats bemoan the decline of Russian democracy on Putin's watch, Putin remains very popular in Russia, and that popularity surged following the 2014 invasion of Crimea. Indeed, the return to authoritarianism in Russia, the invasion of Ukraine, and the popularity of Putin seem to undercut every element of the "end of history" thesis.

- Despite short-term setbacks like that in Russia, does the long term still favor the spread of democracy on a global basis? Why or why not?

- To what extent should democracy promotion be a goal of foreign policy?

- Will history ever end in the sense meant by Fukuyama?

Finally, and cutting closest to the core of democratic peace theory, is new evidence that may undercut the notion that democracies will not fight one another. Democratization of politics in Lebanon and in the Palestinian Territories has empowered the militantly anti-Israel Hezbollah and Hamas movements, and has arguably made peace in the Middle East less rather than more likely. Indeed, given that many Muslims in the region associate the concept of democracy with what they view as unjust American wars in Iraq and Afghanistan, democratization in the current Middle East would likely bring to power radical, anti-Western Islamist parties who see war with Israel as the only solution to their problems.

In short, more than a quarter century after the Berlin Wall fell and Fukuyama's celebratory "end of history" article was published, the mood surrounding discussions of democratic peace theory has turned more cautious. The stalling of the third wave of democratization; the authoritarianism of great powers such as Russia and China; the apparent staying power of their regimes;[7] the relative decline of America's global influence; the tarnishing of the idea of democracy in the eyes of many around the world; and the illiberal, militant forces that have benefited from democratic elections in parts of the Middle East have all combined to raise doubts as to whether democracy is the silver bullet that will vanquish power politics and war.

Future II: One World

9-2 **Identify the key assumptions of the "one world" vision of the global future, and evaluate the plausibility of that vision.**

The Vision: In the early years of the twenty-first century, post–Cold War euphoria about the "end of history" and the "democratic peace" has begun to fade. China continues to defy predictions that economic development will lead to political liberalization, Russia continues its authoritarian backsliding, and the failure of Arab Spring has dashed hopes for democratic peace and stability in the Middle East. Optimism has turned to pessimism, and observers have even begun to worry again about the prospects of war among the great powers. Tensions have escalated between the United States and Russia over Ukraine and between the United States and China over Chinese attempts to assert its sovereignty in the South China Sea.

While this pessimism is to some extent understandable, some observers argue that it will ultimately be proven wrong given the pacifying impact of economic globalization. Despite deep differences in culture and politics among the great powers of the twenty-first century, their fates and interests are increasingly bound together in an interdependent global economy. Facilitated by the revolution in information technology that makes distance and geography largely irrelevant to business and commerce, the global economy has become essentially one world, in which production, trade, and commerce no longer have much relationship to geography or culture. In this new world, allegiances and interests that cut across the formal boundaries of states are replacing the nationalism and patriotism of a bygone era.

Though the global financial and economic crisis that began in 2008 led some to predict that the era of globalization was coming to an end, in the long run the forces of global economic integration are likely to prevail. The trade wars and return of beggar-thy-neighbor polices that some anticipated post-2008 never really materialized. Instead, the response has been to double down on efforts at global integration as represented by the negotiations underway in mid-2015 to expand economic integration via the Trans-Pacific Partnership (TPP). Of course, not everyone is pleased by the emergence of this one world. Cultural preservationists, unskilled workers in high-wage countries, labor unions, and many politicians lament the loss of sovereignty and control associated with globalization. Globalization continues to create both winners and losers.

However, as commentators like Thomas Friedman have argued, trying to stop globalization is like trying to stop the sun from rising in the morning.[8] Moreover, in a grand sense, humanity has benefited enormously, not only from the global efficiencies and prosperity produced by globalization, but also from the global peace to which it has undeniably contributed.

A third world war between the United States and China is unthinkable not only because war in the nuclear age would be horrific but also because such a war would be one in which the belligerents would be destroying their own assets. US attacks on China would destroy American-owned factories that provide goods to American consumers, while a Chinese attack on the United States would be an attack on the trade and investment partner on which the

Starbucks opened its first store on mainland China in 1999, expanding to 1700 stores in 90 Chinese cities by 2015. Can two countries whose citizens drink Caramel Frappuccinos at Starbucks fight wars with one another?

Chinese economic miracle of the late twentieth and early twenty-first century has depended. Of course, differences of interest between the United States and China, and among states generally, will remain. But twentieth-century-style total war among the great powers in now largely unthinkable because rational people understand that war would be bad for global commerce and would undercut global prosperity. In the end, economic interdependence trumps out-moded notions of geopolitics.

The Critique: As noted in Chapter 7, the liberal commercialist argument that economic interdependence makes war unthinkable is not new to the early twenty-first century. At the beginning of the twentieth century similar argu-ments were made in response to the first wave of globalization. The most famous proponent of this view at that time was journalist and eventual Nobel Peace Prize winner Norman Angell. In his 1910 book *The Great Illusion*, Angell took issue with the argument, common at that time among many Marxist crit-ics of capitalism and among some defenders of capitalism, that war could be good for the economy.[9] On the contrary, Angell argued, war would be extremely costly, and the economies of Europe were integrated enough that no reasonable person could consider war a realistic option any longer.

Of course, the publication of Angell's book was followed a few years later by the most destructive war that the Europeans had ever known. The flaw in his argument, and its twenty-first-century variants, is threefold. First, it assumes that continued global economic integration is a given. However, another "great recession" or global financial crisis like that of 2008 may lead countries to turn inward, retreat from their commitment to globalization, and return to protec-tionist policies. This is precisely what happened in the 1930s, and many fear it could happen again.

Second, Angell saw humans as rational creatures. However, as we saw in Chapter 3 of this text, not only are individuals limited in their capacity to ratio-nally identify and link ends and means, but single individuals rarely control foreign policy decision-making. Instead, policy is often formulated via a pull-ing and hauling among a wide variety of individual, bureaucratic, and societal interests. Moreover, decision-making takes place in an environment of limited knowledge, where miscalculation is always possible, and where cognitive biases shape decisions. Indeed, many view World War I as a war into which the states of Europe stumbled almost against their will.

Finally, and perhaps most significant, Angell's argument assumes that humans are motivated first and foremost by economic well-being and pros-perity. Plenty of evidence indicates that this view of humanity is too limited, as people often have willingly sacrificed economic comfort to fight for liberty, democracy, sovereignty, national pride, honor, or religious values.

Thomas Friedman is undeniably correct when he asserts that leaders in Beijing would have to think not once, not twice, but three times before using military force to reunite the island of Taiwan with the mainland.[10] Taiwan is an important market for mainland Chinese goods, a rich source of investment funds for mainland industries, and a crucial provider of high-tech inputs in the supply chain feeding mainland industries. Moreover, as Friedman notes, any attack on Taiwan could compromise Chinese economic relations with the United States, Europe, and Japan, who might respond with economic sanctions or perhaps even military force. That said, Beijing may at some point have a leadership that values national unity over economic prosperity, or that calculates, correctly or incorrectly, that the world, following a few symbolic protests, will accept the Chinese action out of a fear that war with China would negatively impact their own prosperity.

Angell, Friedman, and the liberal commercialist argument in general are indisputably correct on one basic point: war has high economic costs. World War I, as Angell anticipated, proved to be extremely destructive economically to all the European powers caught in its grip. In the twenty-first century, given both the kinds of weapons available and the integration of the global economy, the costs of a global war would be unprecedented and hard to limit to the losing side. Yet time and again, states have gone to war in spite of those costs.

Future III: A World State

9-3 Identify the key assumptions of the "world state" vision of the global future, and evaluate the plausibility of that vision.

The Vision: By the end of the twentieth century many scholars and journalists were writing about the mismatch between the "the fixed geography of states and the nonterritorial nature of today's problems and solutions."[11] Such problems as environmental degradation, infectious disease, and transnational crime are increasingly recognized as beyond the capacity of individual sovereign states to address. Likewise, in the increasingly integrated global economy, notions of national economies and national economic policies are becoming obsolete. Indeed, those problems and trends directly challenge the notion of state sovereignty, as they demonstrate the limited ability of states to control events taking place on their own territory.

For some scholars, this challenge to state sovereignty is seen as leading to a **new medievalism** in which a wide array of substate and nonstate actors share power with diminished states. States coexist and compete for influence with multinational corporations, terrorist groups, transnational religious organizations, and a host of other nongovernmental and international organizations. The diminishment of state power is seen as leading not to the elimination of states or their replacement with another single type of organization but, rather, to a new pluralism of actors in which states had been reduced to simply one of many.

However, what the new global problems and trends arguably require is not merely a diminishment of state authority but the creation of new institutions at the supranational level with authority beyond that of the sovereign state. Already in the early twenty-first century international institutions exist

new medievalism

View of an emerging world in which state authority, sovereignty, and power are replaced by an overlapping mix of states, subnational actors, nonstate actors, and supranational organizations, all competing for the loyalty and allegiance of individuals.

that aim at global governance. At the regional level, institutions such as the European Union have been created to address issues on a supranational level. At the global level, the UN, the WTO, the International Criminal Court (ICC), and a host of specialized agencies, many associated with the UN, exist to shape global solutions to global problems. However, these efforts are limited in two main ways: they depend in most cases on the voluntary acquiescence of still nominally sovereign states, and they deal primarily with issues of low politics. The state's monopoly on the use of violence in world politics is left essentially unchanged. But some scholars anticipate that this too will change.

Writing in 2003, political scientist Alexander Wendt predicted that a world state, defined as a supranational organization with a monopoly on the legitimate use of violence in world politics, will exist within 100 years.[12] He anticipates that movement in the direction of the world state will proceed in five stages:

1. *Sovereign state system.* This is the Hobbesian world, based on state sovereignty, characteristic of the Westphalian era.
2. *Society of states.* This is essentially still a system of sovereign states but with rules and international law regulating interstate relations. This Grotian-type system (see Chapter 5) was attempted, with limited success, over much of the twentieth century.
3. *World society.* This is essentially a world security community in which states, on their own, rule out violence as a way of resolving problems with one another. Such a security community was first created among the states of North America, Western Europe, and Japan in the late twentieth century (see Chapter 4). It is still a system of state sovereignty, however, insofar as it has no organization to enforce the norms of the security community on a supranational level.
4. *Collective security.* At this stage, states not only agree to forgo the use of force in resolving disputes but also accept the duty to defend others should a rogue state violate the norms of the security community. Primitive precursors of this collective security community emerged by the mid-twentieth century. They were the post–World War II NATO alliance (limited to only a handful of nations) and, on a more global scale, the flawed United Nations system.
5. *World state.* At this stage, the monopoly on the legitimate use of violence resides in a single supranational actor (the world state).

Wendt's world state prediction might seem unrealistic, especially given the persistent appeal of nationalism in the early twenty-first century, but it might be possible to create some sort of federalist system that still allows for local (state-level) decisions on a range of issues, while transferring exclusive authority for the use of violence to the world state. In so doing, one would thereby definitively write the closing chapter on the Westphalian era and the system of state sovereignty that defined that period. Doing so is arguably necessary both to solve global problems and to avoid the calamity of a third world war among the great powers.

global governance
Collective efforts on a global basis to address issues, problems, and challenges that transcend the boundaries of individual states and that cannot be adequately addressed by states acting autonomously.

The Critique: The idea that solving global problems and ensuring global peace depends on power evolving in the direction of supranational institutions is hardly new. A rich literature exists on issues of **global governance**, defined as "collective efforts to identify, understand, or address worldwide problems that go beyond the capacity of individual states to solve."[13] In practice, those efforts have often involved formal institutions such as the European Union, the WTO, the ICC, and various agencies of the UN that, once created by states, have been given at least limited supranational authority. As discussed in various chapters of this text, those institutions have managed varying degrees of success.

The idea of a world state, however, takes this liberal institutionalist argument to its logical and extreme conclusion, noting that the exercise of supranational authority on issues like trade, the environment, and human rights depends, in the final analysis, on overriding the sovereign state's monopoly on the use of force. The question is whether a world state is, in fact, an idea whose time has come or a utopian fantasy.

Critiques of the world state idea involve questions of both desirability and feasibility. For some critics, a world state is something to be feared. A global entity with the exclusive right to exercise force in world politics would arguably threaten local norms, traditions, and cultures. It also raises questions about the practices and institutions of democracy. The experience of the European Union in this regard is instructive, as the transfer of power and authority to the supranational EU bureaucracy in Brussels has far outpaced the transfer of democratic oversight to an effective European Parliament. If the same were to occur with a world state, the resulting **democratic deficit** would likely be even more noticeable, because of the even greater scale and diversity of the world as a whole.

democratic deficit
The loss of democratic accountability that results from the transfer of authority from democratically elected legislatures of sovereign states to unelected bureaucracies of supranational organizations.

These issues of desirability are directly related to the issue of feasibility. Again, the experience of the European Union may be instructive, as residual feelings of nationalism combined with the challenges of the post-2008 economic crisis not only have highlighted the limits of European political integration but also have raised concerns about the future of European monetary and economic integration. Elsewhere in the world, national and tribal allegiances are arguably stronger still. From the Balkans to Iraq to Palestine, one can see violent evidence of the continuing pull of these national identities. Short of a major global crisis, such as a devastating war, it is difficult to imagine the abandonment of nationalism and sovereignty that the creation of a world state would entail.

Finally, the increasing number of civil wars taking place today (see Chapter 4) raises the question of whether a world state would be in a perpetual state of civil war as local entities pushed back against a distant world government judged insensitive to local needs. The difficulty that states today have in finding and smashing small terrorist cells hidden in caves along the Afghan–Pakistani border is an indication of the kinds of challenges that revolutionaries or freedom fighters or terrorists would potentially pose in asymmetrical wars they might wage against the world state. Thus, the creation of a world state, rather than solving the problem of war and violence in world politics, may simply change the character of warfare.

Future IV: A Cascading Norm Against War

9-4   Identify the key assumptions of the "cascading norm against war" vision of the global future, and evaluate the plausibility of that vision.

The Vision: In the late twentieth century, international relations scholars working within the liberal tradition anticipated a decline in the frequency of war and discussed the possibility that great power war, in particular, might become a thing of the past. While some of these scholars rooted their optimism in the spread of democratic government, others counted on the pacifying effects of economic interdependence or on the creation of international institutions that could constrain the behavior of states. While differing from one another in important ways, all these international relations liberals shared an assumption that the path to global peace began with structural changes in world politics—changes in domestic regimes, in the pattern of international economic relations, or in international institutions. Global peace, it was assumed, could only be assured on the basis of change in one or the other (or some combination of all three) of these elements of the Kantian triangle.

For some scholars, in contrast, peace among nations does not depend on any of those structural factors. It is, instead, rooted in the growing global consensus, or what constructivists would call a **norm cascade**,[14] at least among developed states, that war is an idea whose time has passed. The clearest representative of this view is political scientist John Mueller.[15] Mueller notes that other practices once considered acceptable, such as dueling and slavery, long ago had gone out of fashion. By the end of the twentieth century anyone who challenged another to pistols at 30 paces would become the object of ridicule. Likewise, for the vast majority of people, the idea of owning slaves had become unthinkable, not just because it was illegal but because the very idea of slavery had become reprehensible. War, in contrast, even to the most civilized nations of the mid twentieth century, remained a "necessary evil."

Yet, over time, the idea of war has become less and less acceptable. In part, this is due to its ever-increasing physical and psychological costs. Already by World War I, the technologies of the Industrial Revolution had brought destruction and killing to a scale and pace that no one could have anticipated. With the development of nuclear weapons and other "weapons of mass destruction," Clausewitz's dictum about war being merely "the continuation of policy" was fast becoming obsolete. What policy objectives, many began to ask, could justify the costs that twenty-first-century warfare would exact on both winners and losers alike?

Of course, the idea of war is not becoming discredited spontaneously. It is, instead, facilitated by the work of **norm entrepreneurs**—the multiple individuals, nongovernmental organizations, and transnational advocacy networks that

norm cascade
The stage at which a previously emergent norm reaches a tipping point of broad acceptance and consensus among a critical mass of states.

norm entrepreneurs
The mix of individuals and organizations who work to define and promote the establishment of a new norm.

have challenged the idea of war as an acceptable policy instrument. Dismissed originally as naive and unsophisticated about how the world works, their views gradually have become more widely embraced. The "norm" of peace that they have promoted is spreading.

The success of these efforts is manifested concretely in the "long peace" that has characterized relations among the great powers beginning in 1945 and that has been maintained for what is now almost three-quarters of a century. Despite unresolved differences among states, and in a world where international institutions remain weak and state sovereignty persists, great power war has been avoided due to the global consensus that it is no longer a realistic option. While smaller wars have persisted well into the twenty-first century and cannot be ruled out even today, so many states have joined the consensus against war that, even if wars do break out, they will likely remain geographically well contained.

In short, the addition of the idea of war to that of slavery, dueling, and other long and universally discredited practices, and the unprecedented "long peace" that has resulted, affirm the insight of constructivist theorists that subjective ideas more than objective structural factors ultimately shape human behavior. To paraphrase constructivist thinker Alexander Wendt, world politics is what human beings make of it.

The Critique: For most realist and liberal scholars, the argument that war could become unthinkable, that it can no longer be viewed as an "instrument of policy by other means," especially without prior change in the basic structure of the international system or the character of individual states, remains unpersuasive. First, even in a world where the vast majority of people and governments find war unacceptable, it only takes a single state and its leadership to violate the norm against war and disrupt the peace. Without effective global institutions of order and collective security to punish aggression, what is to stop a future Hitler from operating against, and perhaps taking advantage of, the prevailing consensus for peace?

Second, the argument that war has become unthinkable rests on an assumption of rationality. It assumes that states will see that the cost–benefit calculation clearly balances against the use of the military and that leaders will behave accordingly. Yet the history of warfare and international relations suggests that states do not always behave rationally; they often miscalculate, misperceive, and blunder their way into circumstances that they, in retrospect, wish they had avoided. If this were not the case, then no country that ever started a war would end up on the losing side. The very nature of modern warfare, and the speed with which its destruction can occur, may actually increase the likelihood of global devastation by accident or miscalculation. Unlike a traditional army sent into battle, a missile launched from a silo cannot be called back at the last minute. Thus, there is less chance to correct a potentially devastating military miscalculation. Moreover, since potential adversaries are aware of this, and since they cannot be 100 percent sure of other states' intentions, they feel pressure in times of crisis to attack first.

Finally, and perhaps most fundamentally, the assumption that human beings are coming to a universal consensus against war because of its psychological and physical costs is belied by recent evidence. States continue to spend enormous amounts of scarce resources on the weapons of warfare. Moreover, we live in a world where individuals will take their own and countless innocent lives by flying planes into buildings or by exploding bombs strapped to their waists. When such actions are attached to extremist religious beliefs about rewards in the afterlife, the assumption that no rational human being can find the cost–benefit calculation to favor war, even a nuclear war, has to be reassessed.

While some parts of the world—most notably, the Western European security community—may have concluded that war is no longer acceptable, this antiwar consensus has not spread on a global scale. To the extent that Mueller and others base their argument about the norm against war largely on the experience of Western, and, especially, European nations, the argument might be based on a flawed Eurocentrism. Looking at recent trends and tensions in Asia, between Japan and China or in the South China Sea, one could reasonably argue that the future of Asia will more likely replicate Europe's bloody past than its pacifist present.

Future V: An Engendered Peace

9-5 **Identify the key assumptions of the "engendered peace" vision of the global future, and evaluate the plausibility of that vision.**

The Vision: Humans have repeatedly experimented with ways to make the world of international relations more peaceful. Arms control, international law, collective security, and democracy promotion represent just a few of the many attempts to change the way the world works. All those efforts have met with, at best, only limited success, as every outbreak of hostilities trumped each great hope that the problem of war had been solved.

The root cause of those failures, feminist scholars argue, is that both our understanding of how the world works and, thus, the manner in which the actual practice of international relations has been conducted, are rooted in a gendered perspective. In particular, realist assumptions of the need of states to acquire and balance power and to relegate considerations of ethics and justice in international relations to, at best, a secondary role are good examples of this gendered perspective. However, those assumptions, and the behaviors they spawn, can be challenged by the empowerment of women and the inclusion of a critical mass of female leaders in the conduct of world politics.

During the twentieth century, women made considerable progress in many areas of life. Especially in the most developed nations, women emerged as leaders in business and society. Where they had not made much progress was in government, and foreign policy-making in particular. A 2007 study noted that, worldwide, women occupied only 17 percent of parliamentary seats and 14 percent of ministerial positions, with most of the latter limited to "women's concerns" such as family, education, and health.[16] By 2015, evidence of progress, as we saw in Chapter 1, was slight with women occupying 17 percent of ministerial positions and with only 10 women serving as heads of state and 15 as heads of government. In the few cases where women have reached the pinnacle of foreign policy-making authority—British Prime Minister Margaret Thatcher in the 1980s, US Secretaries of State Condoleezza Rice and Hillary Clinton in the early years of the twenty-first century, German Chancellor Angela Merkel as of 2005—they had to operate within a man's world, where women were the exception rather than the rule.

The relative lack of women involved at the highest decision-making levels in areas related to war and peace may, at least partly, reflect the fact that the conduct of war has been largely male terrain from the ground floor up. As Joshua Goldstein notes in his book on gender and war, at the beginning of the twenty-first century 97 percent of soldiers in uniform across the world were men, and in only six states did women make up more than five percent, with most women in uniform having noncombat roles.[17] War, he concludes, is both historically and universally the most gendered of all human activities.[18] While explanations of this phenomenon are multiple and complex, with scholars disagreeing, for example, about the relative impact of biology and socialization, it certainly provides a basis to anticipate differences in approach to international relations by men and women.

Thus, if over the course of the twenty-first century a critical mass of women were to gain positions of government authority at the highest levels, the impact would be significant. In fact, there is research that has demonstrated the benefits that come with the political empowerment of women.[19] According to some of this research, women leaders are less prone to corruption and more inclined to peaceful, negotiated solutions than their male counterparts. Their presence in positions of power correlates with an increase in trust in government that pays dividends both domestically and internationally. Indeed, one might argue that the key to democratic peace theory is related, at least in part, to the greater ability of women to participate in the political process in democratic regimes.[20]

A world characterized by more significant empowerment of women will still, of course, face its share of problems and challenges. However, the feminization of politics has the potential to make the world a more peaceful place, improving the odds that differences of interest among states will be resolved with words rather than with guns. In so doing, it will make clear that once-dominant perspectives such as "realism" were gendered perspectives and a reflection of the fact that the world of international relations—both in government and academia—has been overwhelmingly male.

The Critique: Critics of the feminist approach agree with feminists that women are underrepresented in government and foreign policy-making, and that, as a simple matter of equal opportunity, an enlarged role for women in this area is desirable. However, these critics dispute the assumption that gender makes a difference in the conduct of world affairs. The critique is based on both the empirical record of women in power and differing assessments of the sources of foreign policy behavior.

As many have noted, when women have risen to positions where they can directly shape foreign policy, they have often demonstrated, for better or worse, a willingness to rely on military power as readily as any man. It was, after all, the "Iron Lady" Margaret Thatcher who led the British to war with Argentina over control of the Falkland Islands in 1982, and who in 1990 prevailed on a wavering President George H. W. Bush not to let Saddam Hussein get away with invading Kuwait. Indian Prime Minister Indira Gandhi presided over the early development of India's nuclear weapons program and led the country in its 1971 war with Pakistan. More recently, Condoleezza Rice, the first female US national security advisor and later the second woman to hold the position of US secretary of state, provided steadfast support of the 2003 US war in Iraq. Likewise, Secretary of State Hillary Clinton was a stalwart supporter of Obama's war efforts in Afghanistan. In such examples, we see little evidence of the impact of gender on foreign policy.

Many would argue that those women rose to positions of power within a male-dominated world, where men, overall, had established the rules. However, as some observers have noted, archeological evidence indicates that ancient societies dominated by women were no more war-averse than those in which men prevailed, and that women often played a direct role in combat.[21] Katha Pollitt suggests that women's involvement in the pacifist movement (a movement that includes many men as well) is relatively recent, and she argues against the notion that women have anything inherent in their outlook that makes them less warlike than men.[22]

Those who critique the feminist perspective argue that the international system and the roles of leaders are the factors that define leaders' behavior, not their gender. That Margaret Thatcher behaved "like a man" is, from this perspective, less because she is an atypical woman than because she is a typical prime minister—a leader who is responsible, as a good realist would argue, for the country's safety and security in an international system characterized by anarchy and insecurity. When Secretary of State Condoleezza Rice combined unwavering support for the Iraq War with an approach to foreign policy that often emphasized diplomacy and negotiation, her actions were less about trying to fit into a man's world than they were about a secretary of state trying to please her boss, the president, while also fulfilling her role as America's chief diplomat.

Future VI: A Clash of Civilizations

9-6 Identify the key assumptions of the "clash of civilizations" vision of the global future, and evaluate the plausibility of that vision.

The Vision: When Samuel Huntington first published his clash-of-civilizations thesis in 1993, it caused quite a stir.[23] Huntington, a former realist, struck a pessimistic chord that was at odds with the prevailing optimism generated by the decline of Soviet Communism, the end of the Cold War, the diffusion of democratic government, and the prosperity associated with globalization. In his original article, and in the 1998 book that followed, Huntington advanced and developed three basic arguments.

First, Huntington argued that the world was divided along civilizational lines. While the standard realist map of the world stresses the political boundaries of sovereign states, for Huntington the most important lines of demarcation on the world map are the cultural boundaries between the great world civilizations. His multipolar map of the late twentieth-century world (see Figure 9.1) included nine great civilizations (Western, Islamic, Chinese [Sinic], Orthodox, Hindu, Latin American, Japanese, Buddhist, and African). Religion figured prominently in his analysis of the grand cultural differences distinguishing civilizations from one another and is reflected in the fact that four of his civilizations are named after major religions. Huntington saw this growth of cultural and civilizational identity as a backlash against the challenge to local cultures and traditions posed by economic globalization.

Second, Huntington argued that these civilizations would clash. Contrary both to the "one-worlders," who thought that globalization would render

---

Figure 9.1 Huntington's Map of Civilizations

SOURCE: Based on map by Simon & Schuster, Inc., from *The Clash of Civilizations and the Remaking of the World Order* by Samuel P. Huntington. Copyright © by Samuel P. Huntington. Base map: Copyright © Hammond World Atlas Corp.

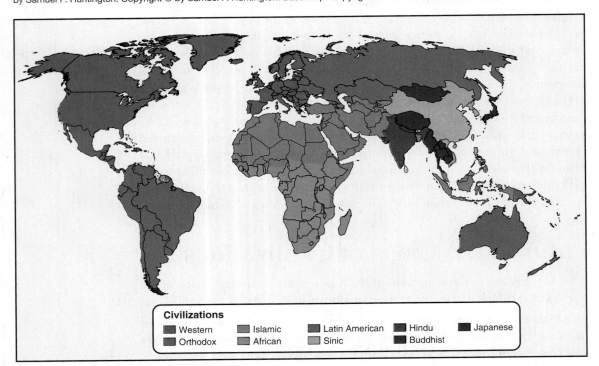

Civilizations

- Western
- Orthodox
- Islamic
- African
- Latin American
- Sinic
- Hindu
- Buddhist
- Japanese

military conflict obsolete, and to the democratic peace theorists who envisioned a peaceful end of history, Huntington anticipated a bloody twenty-first century, with most conflicts occurring along civilizational fault lines. Among the most active of those fault lines, Huntington argued, were those where Islamic civilization bordered other civilizations including Western, Orthodox, and Hindu civilizations. Much of this conflict would carry strongly religious overtones, given the centrality of religion to civilizational identity and the related rise of religious fundamentalism worldwide that was reversing the secularizing trends of the previous century.

Third, Huntington anticipated the relative decline of Western civilization in the twenty-first century. The combination of growing strength and confidence in some civilizations (e.g., Chinese) and growing resentment against the West in others (e.g., Islamic) was leading to a world where much future conflict would pit "the West against the rest." Huntington was not confident that the West remained in a position where it would prevail.

In 1993, the predominant view of Huntington's clash-of-civilizations thesis was that it was provocative but wrong. At a time when optimism about globalization and democratization was peaking and at the moment of the West's triumph in Cold War, an argument that stressed cultural fragmentation instead of integration, conflict instead of peace, and Western decline instead of Western ascendency struck all the wrong notes. But fast forward a quarter century and Huntington arguably looks like a man ahead of his time. The September 11, 2001 terrorist attacks on the United States, the US wars in Iraq and Afghanistan, the rise of ISIS, and the deadly January 2015 attack on the Paris office of the satirical magazine *Charlie Hebdo* all seem to fit into Huntington's clash-of-civilizations narrative and, in particular, his emphasis on a clash between Islam and the West (see Theory in Practice 9.2). Indeed, both al-Qaeda and ISIS leaders have themselves defined their struggles in precisely such terms.

In addition to the tension between Islamic and Western civilizations, the twenty-first century does, more generally, resemble a clash between the West and the rest, and, as Huntington anticipated, there are signs of the West's relative decline. With the United States overstretched by it asymmetrical war with Islamic terrorists including two major wars in the Middle East, and with the crisis of confidence in Western Europe brought on by the post-2008 Eurozone crisis, declining birthrates, and the stalling of the idea of European political integration, other civilizations have emerged as challengers to Western political, economic, and cultural dominance. China, the core state of Chinese or Sinic civilization in Huntington's scheme, has, on the basis of its remarkable economic growth, been increasing its military power and becoming more assertive globally.

In short, after a brief flirtation with the idea of a universal, global culture, the twenty-first century has, arguably, been characterized by a backlash, and people around the world have sought a return to their separate cultural and religious roots. In this world, wars fought or alliances formed may have less to do with ideology or political beliefs than with a new, globalized politics of identity.

Theory in Practice 9.2

The Cartoon Crisis and the *Charlie Hebdo* Massacre: A Clash of Civilizations?

On September 30, 2005, a Danish newspaper published a series of 12 editorial cartoons depicting the Islamic prophet Mohammed. Many Muslims claimed the cartoons were an insult to Islam. Some argued that any depiction of Mohammed was unacceptable, but especially offensive were cartoons that appeared to link Mohammed to violence and terrorism. One depicted him holding a sword; another had him wearing a bomb in his turban; a third showed him on a cloud saying, "Stop, we have run out of virgins" to suicide bombers trying to enter heaven.

Over the days that followed, tension built. Ambassadors from Islamic countries demanded meetings with the Danish prime minister, Muslim clerics called for an apology and for punishment of the Danish newspaper, thousands took to the streets in protest across the Islamic world, and a Pakistani cleric put a bounty on the heads of the offending cartoonists. Many in the West defended the right of the newspaper to publish the cartoons, based on the principles of a free press and free expression. However, many news outlets in Europe and the United States refused to reproduce the depictions, partly to avoid further offending Muslims but also, in some cases, out of fear of violent retribution.

One publication that did reproduce the cartoons, along with some of its own, was the French satirical magazine, *Charlie Hebdo*. In 2011 the publication's headquarters were firebombed, but it continued to produce and publish additional caricatures of Mohammed in the ensuing years. In January 2015 two men, claiming to represent an Islamic terror group, forced their way into the *Charlie Hebdo* offices, shooting and killing 12 people in retaliation. Demonstrations in support of those killed followed, in Paris and around the world, as people proclaimed *Je suis Charlie* (I am Charlie).

In the eyes of some, the cartoon crisis and the *Charlie Hebdo* terror attack were another indication of a clash of civilizations as predicted by Huntington. Like realism, Huntington's thesis clearly rejects the liberal view of a more peaceful, cooperative future. Yet, as the cartoon crisis suggests, future conflict may have as much to do with differences over cultural values as with realist concerns with the balance of military power.

- If you were the author or publisher of this textbook, would you have included a sample of the cartoons in question? Why or why not?

- Huntington suggests that cultural clashes are harder to resolve than clashes over national interests. Is he right? Explain.

- Huntington says clashes over cultural differences are the wave of the future. Others suggest that globalization is creating a common global culture. Who is right? Why?

The Critique: Huntington's clash-of-civilizations thesis has spawned much debate. While its defenders suggest that it is the best template for understanding the twenty-first-century world, the critics suggest that it is not only wrong, but also dangerous.

The central weakness of the thesis, according to critics, is that it treats civilizations as monolithic and internally homogeneous. For example, critics of Huntington argue that no single Islamic civilization exists. Instead, there are many Islams divided by sect (Sunni versus Shiite), politics (theocrats versus secularists), geography (Middle East versus Southeast Asia), and culture (Arab versus Persian). Indeed, much of the conflict and bloodshed involving Islam in the world today seems less like a clash of civilizations than a clash *within* Islamic civilization. In places such as Iraq and Syria, this intra-Islamic conflict has been violent and bloody, pitting the fundamentalist Sunni ISIS movement against Shiites. Indeed, that Sunni–Shiite rift is also manifested in the deep animosity between Sunni (and Arab) Saudi Arabia and other Persian Gulf states, on the one hand, and Shiite (and Persian) Iran, on the other.

It is perhaps no accident that Huntington's theoretical background is within the realist tradition, for his clash-of-civilizations thesis incorporates many assumptions and, arguably, deficiencies of traditional realist thought. His assumption of the inevitability of war and conflict and the view of key actors as unitary, rational actors fit squarely within the realist tradition. That the key actors, for Huntington, are civilizations rather than individual states is less a challenge to realism than it might first appear. As realist scholar John Mearsheimer has noted, "Realism merely requires anarchy; it does not matter what kinds of political units make up the system."[24]

Huntington's thesis, critics fear, is not only wrong but also potentially dangerous, as it could become a self-fulfilling prophecy. To the extent, for example, that

Two women walk down a street in Marseille, France. In July 2010 the lower house of the French parliament voted 335-1 to ban wearing of the burqa in public. In your judgment, is Huntington's clash of civilizations idea a useful way to understand the world of the early twenty-first century?

Western politicians come to see the "war on terror" and the struggle with al-Qaeda and ISIS as part of Huntington's clash between Islam and the West, they play into the hands of the Islamic extremists they are fighting by defining the struggle in their enemy's terms. Likewise, if politicians lay the clash-of-civilizations template atop the rise of Chinese economic power, they respond in a very different way than they would if they viewed Chinese economic modernization and integration into the global economy as a path to global peace. In short, the critics fear, preparing for a clash of civilizations is the best way to ensure that such a clash will occur.

Future VII: Great Power War

9-7 Identify the key assumptions of the "great power war" vision of the global future, and evaluate the plausibility of that vision.

The Vision: Like Huntington, twenty-first-century realists reject as utopian expectations that war is becoming obsolete. For realists, neither democracy, globalization, institutions, changing norms, nor gender have, individually or collectively, eliminated the possibility that states will resort to war as needed. Where they part company with the clash-of-civilization thesis is that realists see war not as a violent culture clash between civilizations, but as an instrument of the pursuit of national interests by sovereign states. Most significantly, and despite the "long peace" that has prevailed since 1945, realists continue to assume that great power war remains not only possible, but, perhaps, even probable in the twenty-first century. No serious scholar would pretend to be able to predict exactly when, where, how, and why a future great power war would break out, yet there are those who are worried that the unthinkable could happen.

The more immediate source of that worry is war between the United States and Russia. In an April 2015 article, Graham Allison and Dimitri Simes challenged the complacent view that such a war is inconceivable and that cool heads will ultimately prevail. Without suggesting that such a war is inevitable or even likely, they "are more concerned … than at any point since the end of the Cold War."[25] The source of the concern, of course, is Ukraine where the combination of competing strategic visions of the region coupled with tactical miscalculation could prove disastrous. Strategically, Russia sees Ukraine and Eastern Europe as its historically rightful and essential sphere of influence—temporarily lost in the 1990s at a moment of Russian weakness. In contrast, the United States sees the post–Cold War realignment in the region as the new status quo that needs to be defended, not least because it suits US interests. Tactically, the concern is that Russia might overplay its hand there and underestimate a US and NATO response or that the United States might push Russia too hard with political isolation and sanctions and thereby cause Putin to escalate militarily, an area in which he holds more regional cards.

If a Russia–US war is the greater short-term worry, it is the possibility of war between the United States and China that is the longer term concern. Whether the specific catalyst to such a war is control of the South China Sea, the status of Taiwan, or Chinese–Japanese tension over the tiny Senkaku Islands in the East China Sea (called the Diaoyu Islands in China), the more general concern is the dynamic of the rise of a new power in China and the US response. As discussed in Chapter 1, defensive realists argue that to feel secure, states will attempt to balance the power of others, while offensive realists take it a step further and suggest that security requires, at a minimum, not balance but regional hegemony. Either way, the expectation is that China will have to challenge the dominance of the Pacific region that the United States has maintained since World War II and that the United States will have to resist. As offensive realist John Mearsheimer has argued, China will seek to dominate Asia in much the same way that the United States has dominated the Western Hemisphere. He contends that the United States, together with other regional actors, will resist, leading to "intense security competition with considerable potential for war."[26]

The US National Intelligence Council (NIC), which supports The Director of National Intelligence with long-term strategic analysis, provides support to the view that interstate war is potentially poised for a comeback. In its *Global Trends 2030* report, it argued that the post–Cold War decline in interstate war might be coming to an end as changes in the international system are increasing the chances for war.[27] As for China, the report issues the following cautionary note:

> Heated debates are occurring among China's elites, for example, regarding whether China should move away from its traditional policies—not having overseas bases or major military alliances and not interfering in the internal affairs of other countries—as its overseas interests expand. The outcome of these debates will be critical indicators of whether China intends to become a global superpower, which in turn will have major implications for the prospect of future great power competition. Historical parallels with other great power rises suggest that Chinese assertiveness might increase as its economic growth slows and there is political need at home to demonstrate China's standing in the world.[28]

In fact, developments since the publication of that report provide further support for such concerns; China, under Xi Jinping, has become more assertive since 2012. Despite or, as the NIC report suggests, because of concerns about slowing economic growth, the rapid modernization of China's military has continued and a more determined approach to promotion of Chinese interests in places like the East China and South China Seas has been in evidence. In 2015 a particular cause of concern was the Chinese transformation of small reefs in the South China Sea into man-made islands, some with military capable airstrips, which would both bolster claims of Chinese sovereignty over the entire South China Sea and provide bases to help defend those claims. In response, the Obama administration leaked plans for an increased US naval presence to counter and challenge those Chinese claims. It is not hard to imagine such tensions, whether by design or miscalculation, escalating into a US–Chinese war.

The Critique: This vision of a global future characterized by a rise in interstate and, potentially, even great power war reflects the unrepentant realist view that the more things appear to change, the more they remain the same. While key actors rise (China) and fall (the Soviet Union), and although the action in world politics may shift from one theater (Europe) to another (Asia), anarchy, the basic fact of international life, remains. From the realist perspective, the arguments predicting peace in the twenty-first century share an excessively Eurocentric perspective, as they project the current peace found in Western Europe to the world as a whole. In so doing, those arguments not only ignore Europe's bloody past but fail to appreciate that Europe's past may be Asia's future.

Critics of realism, however, do not accept this "back to the future" perspective.[29] Consider, for example, the realist concern about a possible war between the United States and China. First, that scenario fails to consider changes in internal politics. For realists, China may or may not make a transition to democracy, but it does not matter because in the realist view the external security considerations of states rather than the internal qualities of their governments determine their foreign behavior. For critics of realism, that assumption seems quite unrealistic. Chinese democracy may or may not be in the cards, but many doubt the realist argument that it would have no impact on Chinese policy or on perceptions of China by the United States and other Western democracies. That is like saying that an authoritarian coup in Germany would have no impact on French–German relations, or that the peaceful, unprotected border between the United States and Canada would survive the emergence of an authoritarian government on one or both sides of that border.

Second, the scenario dismisses the liberal commercialist argument regarding the pacifying impact of economic interdependence. Yet in a real shooting war between the United States and China, each side would destroy some of their own assets. The city of Shanghai, for example, is not only the economic capital of China but also America's workshop, where products destined for American consumers are made by subsidiaries of US multinational corporations and packaged for shipping to Walmarts and other stores throughout the United States. Likewise, the billions of US dollars held by the Chinese central bank, which constitute a significant store of Chinese wealth, would be potentially worthless in a postwar world with a devastated US economy. Economic interdependence did not prevent the outbreak of World War I, and it may not prevent a future US war with China. At the same time, one cannot automatically assume that such economic considerations will fail to deter war. Such a war, one might argue, is only one possible outcome of the evolving US–Chinese relationship; it is not preordained.

Third, the scenario glosses over the impact of nuclear weapons. Neither China nor the United States could take the prospect of a nuclear war lightly, though some still fear they could engage in a conventional war precisely because they feel that it could never escalate to the nuclear level (a good example of what we termed, in Chapter 4, the stability/instability paradox). However, whether and how escalation to the nuclear level could be stopped in the midst of a full-scale conventional conflict remains unclear. That very threat of uncontrollable nuclear escalation may be enough to ensure that neither the United States nor

China contemplates war as an instrument of their policy with one another in the twenty-first century.

Finally, the realist scenario for US–Chinese war could become a self-fulfilling prophecy. The more we assume that war is inevitable, the more both sides act on that belief and transform it into a reality. Constructivist critics of realism, in particular, would emphasize that how we think about the US–Chinese relationship will itself define that relationship. To paraphrase Wendt, US–Chinese relations will be what the two states make of them. As human beings, we have the ability to control our own destiny.

Making a Better World

Each major paradigm of world politics discussed in this text, and extended to its logical conclusions in the seven visions of the global future sketched above, has both a descriptive and a prescriptive dimension. In judging and evaluating the perspectives, we must ask how well each describes the way world politics works. At the same time, for most scholars, and certainly for those of you reading this text, the point of understanding the world is to provide a foundation on which to formulate policy and behavior. As should be quite clear to anyone who has read this far, the prescription you embrace for peace and security in the world will depend on which paradigm you judge to be most accurate.

A liberal internationalist persuaded by the logic and record of the democratic peace, for example, would clearly embrace a foreign policy that aims at promoting democracy. For a liberal commercialist, the promotion of free markets, international trade, and global investments are the path to a better world. For liberal institutionalists, the foreign policy priority should be to develop and strengthen international institutions. For a feminist, the path to global peace and security is the empowerment of women. For a constructivist, it is all about establishing new norms of behavior by changing the discourse about world politics.

Despite these differing prescriptions, they share the sense that one can, assuming the embrace of the correct foreign policy prescription, fundamentally change the way the game of world politics is played. Optimism along these lines reached a peak in the 1990s. As Robert Kagan describes it:

> When the Cold War ended, it was possible to imagine that the world had been utterly changed: the end of international competition, the end of geopolitics, the end of history. When in the first decade after the Cold War people began describing the new era of "globalization," the common expectation was that the phenomenon of instantaneous global communications, the free flow of goods and services, the rapid transmission of ideas and information, and the intermingling and blending of cultures would further knit together a world that had already just patched up the great ideological and geopolitical tears of the previous century. "Globalization" was to the late twentieth century what "sweet commerce" was to the late eighteenth—an anticipated balm for a war-weary world.[30]

From this optimistic perspective, realist notions of how the world works were obsolete, and foreign policy prescriptions emanating from realist thinking were an obstacle to progress. For realists, in contrast, the game remains the same. Citing Hans Morgenthau, Kagan notes:

> After the Second World War, another moment in history when hopes for a new kind of international order were rampant, Hans Morgenthau warned idealists against imagining that at some point "the final curtain would fall and the game of power politics would no longer be played." But the world struggle continued then, and it continues today.[31]

Thus, for realists, old and time-tested prescriptions to accumulate one's own power, to balance the power of one's rivals, to focus on the national interest, and to avoid being distracted by ethical crusades remain the guiding principles.

The fundamental divide between realists and their critics is over the question of whether we can do better than the world that realists describe. In the realist view, the best is the enemy of the good. In seeking to transform the world, to render war obsolete, or to prioritize justice over power in international relations, we are not only doomed to fail, but we also leave ourselves unprepared to deal with other states that have less sentimental and more "realistic" views of the world. Thus for realists, the better and, arguably, the ethically superior policy, is not to focus on utopian dreams of ending all war but, instead, to accumulate the power necessary to avoid a particular war. For critics of that view, however, realism in the twenty-first century provides a recipe for Armageddon. Given the state of military technology, the next great power war might well be the last.

Some of you who have read this book might be stimulated to go on to graduate school, where you can become a scholar who will further contribute to our understanding of world politics and international relations. Most of you, however, have read this book and taken this course in order to become more informed citizens. In ways big and small, over the course of your life, you may participate in the world of politics as a means of making a better world for yourself and future generations. Knowing something about how the world works is a first step in preparing you to make a difference.

Review Questions

- To which paradigm or paradigms of world politics discussed in Chapter 1 are each of the global futures discussed in this chapter most closely related?
- In your view, which global future described in this chapter is best supported by current trends in world politics? How so?

- Hypothetical futures I–V are optimistic about the prospects for fundamental change in world politics. Do they share any other commonalities? What are the points of agreement and disagreement between the two most pessimistic visions, futures VI and VII?

Key Terms

modernization theory

new medievalism

global governance

democratic deficit

norm cascade

norm entrepreneur

Endnotes

1. Stanley Michalak, *A Primer in Power Politics* (Scholarly Resources, 2001), 173.
2. John Mearsheimer, "Back to the Future: Instability in Europe After the Cold War," *International Security* 15:1 (1990): 5–56.
3. Francis Fukuyama, "The End of History?" *National Interest*, Summer 1989, 3–18.
4. Francis Fukuyama, *The End of History and the Last Man* (Free Press, 1992), 245.
5. Robert Kagan, "The End of the End of History," *The New Republic*, April 23, 2008, http://www.newrepublic.com/article/ environment-energy/the-end-the-end -history.
6. Edward D. Mansfield and Jack Snyder, "Democratization and War," *Foreign Affairs*, May/June 1995, 79–97.
7. Azar Gat, "The Return of Authoritarian Great Powers," *Foreign Affairs*, July/August 2007, 59–69.
8. Thomas Friedman, *The Lexus and the Olive Tree,* (Farrar, Strauss, and Giroux, 1999), xviii.
9. Norman Angell, *The Great Illusion: A Study of the Relation of Military Power in Nations to Their Economic and Social Advantage* (Putnam, 1910).
10. Thomas Friedman, *The World Is Flat,* (Farrar, Strauss, and Giroux, 2005), 419–425.
11. Jessica Mathews, "Power Shift," *Foreign Affairs*, January/February 1997, 50–66.
12. Alexander Wendt, "Why a World State Is Inevitable: Teleology and the Logic of Anarchy," *European Journal of International Relations* 9:4 (2003): 491–542.
13. Ramesh Thakur and Thomas Weiss, "The UN and Global Governance: An Idea and Its Prospects," http://www.unhistory.org.
14. Martha Finnemore and Kathryn Sikkink, "International Norm Dynamics and Political Change," *International Organization* 52:4, Autumn 1998, 895.
15. John Mueller, *Retreat from Doomsday: The Obsolescence of Major War* (Basic Books, 1989).
16. Swanee Hunt, "Let Women Rule," *Foreign Affairs*, May/June 2007, 109–120.
17. Joshua S. Goldstein, *War and Gender: How Gender Shapes the War System and Vice Versa* (Cambridge University Press, 2001), from Chapter 1, online at http://www .warandgender.com/wgch1.htm.
18. Joshua S. Goldstein, "War and Gender," *Encyclopedia of Sex and Gender* (Springer Science and Business Media, 2003), 107.
19. Hunt, "Let Women Rule."
20. Francis Fukuyama, "Women and the Evolution of World Politics," *Foreign Affairs*, September/October 1998, 24–40.
21. Barbara Ehrenreich, "Men Hate War Too," *Foreign Affairs*, January/February 1999, 118–122.
22. Katha Pollitt, "Father Knows Best," *Foreign Affairs*, January/February 1999, 122–125.
23. Samuel P. Huntington, "The Clash of Civilizations?" *Foreign Affairs*, Summer 1993, 22–50. Also see Samuel P. Huntington, *The Clash of Civilizations and the Remaking of World Order* (Simon & Schuster, 1998).
24. John Mearsheimer, *The Tragedy of Great Power Politics* (Norton, 2001), 365.
25. Graham Allison and Dimitri K. Simes, "Russia and America: Stumbling to War," *The National Interest*, May–June 2015, digital edition, http://nationalinterest.org/ feature/russia-america-stumbling-war- 12662?page=2.

26. See the revised concluding chapter of John Mearsheimer, *The Tragedy of Great Power Politics*, (Norton, 2014), available online at *The National Interest*, October 25, 2014, http://nationalinterest.org/commentary/can-china-rise-peacefully-10204.

27. National Intelligence Council, *Global Trends 2030: Alternative Worlds*, December, 2012, p. 64, https://globaltrends2030.files.wordpress.com/2012/11/global-trends-2030-november2012.pdf.

28. National Intelligence Council, p. 65.

29. Mearsheimer, "Back to the Future."

30. Robert Kagan, "End of Dreams, Return of History," *Policy Review* 144 (August/September 2007): 17–44, http://www.hoover.org.

31. Kagan, "End of Dreams, Return of History."

Credits

Index